Communications
in Computer and Information Science 59

Dominik Ślęzak Tai-hoon Kim
Akingbehin Kiumi Tao Jiang
June Verner Silvia Abrahão (Eds.)

Advances in Software Engineering

International Conference on Advanced Software Engineering and Its Applications, ASEA 2009
Held as Part of the Future Generation Information Technology Conference, FGIT 2009
Jeju Island, Korea, December 10-12, 2009
Proceedings

Volume Editors

Dominik Ślęzak
University of Warsaw & Infobright Inc., Warsaw, Poland
E-mail: slezak@infobright.com

Tai-hoon Kim
Hannam University, Daejeon, South Korea
E-mail: taihoonn@hnu.kr

Akingbehin Kiumi
University of Michigan, Dearborn, MI, USA
E-mail: kiumi@umich.edu

Tao Jiang
University of California, Riverside, CA, USA
E-mail: jiang@cs.ucr.edu

June Verner
Drexel University, Philadelphia, PA, USA
E-mail: june.verner@cis.drexel.edu

Silvia Abrahão
Valencia University of Technology, Valencia, Spain
E-mail: sabrahao@dsic.upv.es

Library of Congress Control Number: 2009939508

CR Subject Classification (1998): D.2, K.6.3, D.2.5, C.4, H.4, I.7, K.6

ISSN 1865-0929
ISBN-10 3-642-10618-8 Springer Berlin Heidelberg New York
ISBN-13 978-3-642-10618-7 Springer Berlin Heidelberg New York

springer.com

Printed in Germany

Typesetting: Camera-ready by author, data conversion by Scientific Publishing Services, Chennai, India
Printed on acid-free paper SPIN: 12805846 06/3180 5 4 3 2 1 0

Foreword

As future generation information technology (FGIT) becomes specialized and fragmented, it is easy to lose sight that many topics in FGIT have common threads and, because of this, advances in one discipline may be transmitted to others. Presentation of recent results obtained in different disciplines encourages this interchange for the advancement of FGIT as a whole. Of particular interest are hybrid solutions that combine ideas taken from multiple disciplines in order to achieve something more significant than the sum of the individual parts. Through such hybrid philosophy, a new principle can be discovered, which has the propensity to propagate throughout multifaceted disciplines.

FGIT 2009 was the first mega-conference that attempted to follow the above idea of hybridization in FGIT in a form of multiple events related to particular disciplines of IT, conducted by separate scientific committees, but coordinated in order to expose the most important contributions. It included the following international conferences: Advanced Software Engineering and Its Applications (ASEA), Bio-Science and Bio-Technology (BSBT), Control and Automation (CA), Database Theory and Application (DTA), Disaster Recovery and Business Continuity (DRBC; published independently), Future Generation Communication and Networking (FGCN) that was combined with Advanced Communication and Networking (ACN), Grid and Distributed Computing (GDC), Multimedia, Computer Graphics and Broadcasting (MulGraB), Security Technology (SecTech), Signal Processing, Image Processing and Pattern Recognition (SIP), and u- and e-Service, Science and Technology (UNESST).

We acknowledge the great effort of all the Chairs and the members of advisory boards and Program Committees of the above-listed events, who selected 28% of over 1,050 submissions, following a rigorous peer-review process. Special thanks go to the following organizations supporting FGIT 2009: ECSIS, Korean Institute of Information Technology, Australian Computer Society, SERSC, Springer LNCS/CCIS, COEIA, ICC Jeju, ISEP/IPP, GECAD, PoDIT, Business Community Partnership, Brno University of Technology, KISA, K-NBTC and National Taipei University of Education.

We are very grateful to the following speakers who accepted our invitation and helped to meet the objectives of FGIT 2009: Ruay-Shiung Chang (National Dong Hwa University, Taiwan), Jack Dongarra (University of Tennessee, USA), Xiaohua (Tony) Hu (Drexel University, USA), Irwin King (Chinese University of Hong Kong, Hong Kong), Carlos Ramos (Polytechnic of Porto, Portugal), Timothy K. Shih (Asia University, Taiwan), Peter M.A. Sloot (University of Amsterdam, The Netherlands), Kyu-Young Whang (KAIST, South Korea), and Stephen S. Yau (Arizona State University, USA).

We would also like to thank Rosslin John Robles, Maricel O. Balitanas, Farkhod Alisherov Alisherovish, and Feruza Sattarova Yusfovna – graduate students of Hannam University who helped in editing the FGIT 2009 material with a great passion.

October 2009

Young-hoon Lee
Tai-hoon Kim
Wai-chi Fang
Dominik Ślęzak

Preface

We would like to welcome you to the proceedings of the 2009 International Conference on Advanced Software Engineering & Its Applications (ASEA 2009), which was organized as part of the 2009 International Mega-Conference on Future Generation Information Technology (FGIT 2009), held during December 10–12, 2009, at the International Convention Center Jeju, Jeju Island, South Korea.

ASEA 2009 focused on various aspects of advances in software engineering and its applications with computational sciences, mathematics and information technology. It provided a chance for academic and industry professionals to discuss recent progress in the related areas. We expect that the conference and its publications will be a trigger for further related research and technology improvements in this important subject.

We would like to acknowledge the great effort of all the Chairs and members of the Program Committee. Out of around 150 submissions to ASEA 2009, we accepted 46 papers to be included in the proceedings and presented during the conference. This gives an acceptance ratio firmly below 30%. Five of the papers accepted for ASEA 2009 were published in the special FGIT 2009 volume, LNCS 5899, by Springer. The remaining 41 accepted papers can be found in this CCIS volume.

We would like to express our gratitude to all of the authors of submitted papers and to all of the attendees, for their contributions and participation. We believe in the need for continuing this undertaking in the future.

Once more, we would like to thank all the organizations and individuals who supported FGIT 2009 as a whole and, in particular, helped in the success of ASEA 2009.

October 2009

Dominik Ślęzak
Tai-hoon Kim
Akingbehin Kiumi
Tao Jiang
June Verner
Silvia Abrahao

Organization

Organizing Committee

General Chair — Haeng-kon Kim (Catholic University of Daegu, Korea)

Advisory Board — Tien N. Nguyen (Iowa State University, USA)
Jose Luis Arciniegas Herrera (University of Cauca, Colombia)
Byeong-Ho Kang (University of Tasmania, Australia)

Publication Chair — Yong-ik Yoon (Sookmyung Women's University, Korea)

Program Chairs — Tai-hoon Kim (Hannam University, Korea)
Akingbehin Kiumi (University of Michigan-Dearborn, USA)

Publicity Chairs — Tao Jiang (Huazhong University of Sci. and Tech., China)
June Verner (University of New South Wales, Australia)
Silvia Abrahao (Camino de Vera, Spain)

Program Committee

Chia-Chu Chiang
A. Hamou-Lhadj
Ami Marowka
Andrea De Lucia
Chima Adiele
Doo-Hwan Bae
Emilia Mendes
Gongzhu Hu
Harvey Siy
Hironori Washizaki
Houari Sahraoui
Hyeon Soo Kim
Jennifer Pérez Benedí
Jiro Tanaka
Jonathan Lee
Jongmoon Baik
Jose L. Arciniegas
Joseph Balikuddembe
Karel Richta
Kendra Cooper
Kin Fun Li
Kurt Wallnau
Laurence Duchien
Luigi Buglione
Maria Bielikova
Maria Tortorella
Morshed Chowdhury
Olga Ormandjieva
Praveen R. Srivastava
Rattikorn Hewett
Ricardo Campos
Robert Glass
Rudolf Ferenc
Shawkat Ali
Silvia Abrahao
Tokuro Matsuo
Wuwei Shen
Yijun Yu

Table of Contents

A Systematic Literature Review of Software Process Improvement in Small and Medium Web Companies

Muhammad Sulayman and Emilia Mendes

Department of Computer Science, Private Bag 92019, The University of Auckland, New Zealand
msul028@aucklanduni.ac.nz, emilia@cs.auckland.ac.nz

Abstract. The objective of this paper is to identify existing Software Process Improvement (SPI) models and techniques used by small and medium Web companies. We performed a systematic review of studies that applied SPI models and techniques to Web companies. Four papers applied SPI techniques or models to Web companies, and our results showed that none suggested any customized model or technique to measure the SPI of Web companies. The SLR also revealed the characteristics of some small and medium companies and suggested that they have tight budget constraints, tight deadlines and a short term strategy. Finally, our SLR showed that the measures of success for small and medium Web companies included development team and client satisfaction, increase in productivity, compliance with standards and overall operational excellence. The results of this review showed that very few studies have specifically focused on SPI for Web companies, despite the large number of existing Web companies worldwide, and the even larger number of Web applications being currently developed. This clearly indicates a research gap in this area, with numerous avenues for future work.

Keywords: Software Process Improvement, Systematic Literature Review, Small and medium Web companies.

1 Introduction

Software processes play an important role by helping project teams in software development organizations and motivating the use of similar and sound practices [10]. Formal processes emphasize the explicit command-and-control side of the organization due to their concrete nature, while informal team practices emphasize the mutual adjustment and explorations needed to accomplish a software project and associated process tasks successfully [13].

Almost all modern software organizations operate in a competitive market, under tight time and cost constraints [4]. As an answer to their needs, organizations have started to undertake software process improvement (SPI) initiatives (see [24] for an overview of different approaches) aimed at increasing the maturity and quality of their software processes [6] [25]. Investment in process improvement has had various business benefits i.e. improved product quality, reduced time to market, better productivity [25], increased organizational flexibility and customer satisfaction [54].

D. Ślęzak et al. (Eds.): ASEA 2009, CCIS 59, pp. 1–8, 2009.

SPI for small and medium organizations has emerged as a separate research area given that large SPI models are not suitable for small and medium companies due to their complex nature and expensive costs [1]. As a consequence, a number of studies have proposed their own SPI frameworks for small and medium software organizations [22], and corporate SPI giants like ISO and CMMI have also formulated focus groups for small and medium software companies [14][15].

Web development differs from the traditional software development due to numerous factors [9], such as its strong focus on hypermedia context and a continuous evolutionary approach [5]. Some examples of Web development methods are OOHDM [23], SWM [27], UWE [11] and WebML [9]. Web requirements Engineering is moving from task orientation towards goal orientation [2] based on NDT (Navigational Development Techniques) [7]. Researchers are also focusing on devising special project management initiatives like WIPSE (Web Integrated Project Support Environment), Action minutes and PAWS (Project administration Web Site) for Web development companies [12]. Testing of Web applications can also differ from traditional software testing, revolving around different quality dimensions motivated by rapid evolution and cross-platform operability [18]. Finally, Rich Internet Applications (RIA) is using the above specified Web Engineering practices [21].

The fact that the engineering of Web applications differs from the engineering of software applications motivated this work. As previously illustrated, many development methodologies and techniques were proposed specifically to tackle issues associated with Web applications' development and project management. Therefore, SPI for small and medium Web companies also seemed a relevant research topic worth investigating. This is the objective of this Systematic Literature Review (SLR), and also the objective of this research. We focus explicitly on small and medium Web companies, which are characterized by companies that only provide Web-related services such as Web application development, Web hosting and Web data management. It is also observed that such companies can develop small to very large Web applications, independently of the company's process maturity.

2 Systematic Literature Review (SLR)

2.1 Overview

A SLR is defined by Kitchenham [16] as,

"A systematic literature review (often referred to as a systematic review) is a means of identifying, evaluating and interpreting all available research relevant to a particular research question, or topic area, or phenomenon of interest".

Systematic reviews are used to gain effective insight into a problem and understand existing approaches. Conducting systematic review is a rigorous process.

A SLR is a detailed process comprising of the steps listed below [16]:

- Formulation of Research Questions
- Development of a Study Protocol
- Identification of Relevant Literature
- Determining Inclusion & Exclusion Criteria
- Selection of Studies

- Study Quality Assessment
- Data Extraction from Selected Studies
- Data Synthesis and Summarization of Results
- Interpretation of Results
- Report Write Up

2.2 Formulation of Research Questions

Identifying valid research questions is an important component of any SLR [16]. For the formulation of the research questions in this SLR, we have used the PICOC (Population, Intervention, Comparison, Outcome, and Context) criteria defined by Petticrew and Roberts [19].

The research questions investigated were the following:

Research Question 1: Which software process improvement models/techniques are applied by small and medium Web development organizations?

Research Question 2: Which software process improvement models/techniques were successful to small and medium Web development organizations and how success is being measured?

Research Question 3: Are there any software process improvement models that have been specifically made to measure for small and medium Web companies?

Research Question 4: What are the important characteristics of small and medium Web organizations that pursue software process improvement activities and practices?

Research Question 5: What constitutes a small or medium Web organization for the studies investigated?

2.3 Identification of Relevant Literature

The identification of relevant literature required exhaustive, rigorous and thorough searching of the relevant material. The data sources used by this study included online databases, research journals; conferences and some grey literature.

Formulation of search string. Constructing search terms is a key step for the identification of relevant literature. We derived our search terms based on PICOC, synonyms from thesaurus and key terms from the relevant literature. Boolean OR was used to concatenate the relevant terms followed by the use of Boolean AND to restrict the search results to the ones most relevant to our SLR.

Inclusion and Exclusion Criteria. The Inclusion criteria was defined to select only those studies that focused on software process improvement activities in the small and medium Web companies. The studies that did not explicitly focus on small or medium Web companies, or did not investigate the use of SPI models or techniques were excluded.

Search Results. Initially, the comprehensive search string did not yield any results; therefore the Computer Science subject librarian was consulted. She suggested the use of a simpler search string, practice also supported by Kitchenham [16]. The search string used in our primary search phase was therefore replaced by:

("(software process improvement)" AND ("(small)" OR "(medium)")).

The term 'Web Company' was removed from the search as otherwise no results would be found. However, to comply with our inclusion criteria, we then manually searched for that term in the papers that were found.

As part of the search process, both authors applied the inclusion and exclusion criteria to all the titles and abstracts of the papers that had been retrieved by applying the abovementioned search string, and agreed upon those that should be selected as primary studies. Whenever there were doubts as to whether a study should be included, its full text was also taken into account.

Whenever studies did not make clear whether their focus was Web companies, their authors were contacted for clarification. Authors of 61 studies were contacted, of which 39 replied, leading to the inclusion of another three studies in our SLR. Studies for which no clarification was received were removed from the SLR. Very surprisingly, of the 88 studies initially shortlisted only 4 studies met the inclusion criteria. Author of only one study from ACM confirmed that his study was applied on Web companies along with software companies but he was unable to provide any separate data for Web companies which made us not to select his study. Table 1 summarizes the complete search results and sources on which the searches were run.

Selected Studies. After careful investigation, the study selection process shortlisted the following 4 studies:

- S1 → Scott L., Jeffery R., Carvalho L., D'Ambra J. and Rutherford P. (2001), Practical software process improvement - the IMPACT project, Proceedings of Australian Software Engineering Conference, Australia.
- S2 → El Sheikh A. and Tarawneh H. (2007) A survey of web engineering practice in small Jordanian web development firms, Proceedings of the the 6th joint meeting of the European software engineering conference and the ACM SIGSOFT symposium on The foundations of software engineering, Croatia.
- S3 → Allen P., Ramachandran M. and Abushama H. (2003) PRISMS: an approach to software process improvement for small to medium enterprises, Proceedings of Third International Conference on Quality Software, USA.
- S4 → Naidu R., Software Process Improvement of Small & Medium Organizations (2003) MSc thesis, Department of Computer Science, University of Auckland, New Zealand.

2.4 Study Quality Assessment

Two quality assessment checklists were developed in order to assess the quality of the evidence provided by the selected studies and, if necessary, to further refine the study selection process. The purpose of establishing two checklists was to enable the detailed assessment of the quality of quantitative and qualitative studies separately, based on the criteria proposed in [16] [19] [3] [8].

The compliance of a study with each checklist item was measured using a score based on a three-point scale: 0 for no compliance; 0.5 for partial compliance, and 1 for full compliance. Therefore, based on the quality assessment checklists, the maximum score a quantitative and qualitative study could obtain were 18 and 9, respectively.

From the four studies selected, three were quantitative (S2 to S4) and one was qualitative (S1). The summarized scores of each study, and shows that studies S1 and S4 presented the highest quality based on our quality assessment criteria, followed by studies S2 and S3.

2.5 Data Extraction

The purpose of the data extraction phase is to extract the relevant data from the selected studies, to be used to prepare summary tables and quality scores; these are later used to answer the SLR's research questions.

The first author read all the related studies and filled out all the data extraction forms. The quality of the data extraction was validated by the second author, who also read and extracted data for two of the selected studies. Results were compared and points of conflict were also discussed. The purpose of this activity was to remove possible problems related to the understanding of the studies.

Table 1. Summary of Search Results

Serial No.	Database Name	Number of Publications Found	Relevant	Irrelevant
1	IEEE Explore	15	2	13
2	INSPEC	23	1	22
3	Scopus	13	0	13
4	ISI Web of Science	0	0	0
5	Pro Quest	3	0	3
6	Computer Database	1	0	1
7	ACM	17/255 (Initially 255 found)	0	17
8	Springer	5/187 (Initially 187 found)	0	5
9	Google Scholar	No new results	0	0
10	Grey literature (Limited)	1	1	0
	Total:	**88**	**4**	**84**

3 Data Synthesis and Results of Systematic Literature Review

In the data synthesis phase the results from all the findings were tabulated, summarized and each question was assessed individually against the findings. This section will elaborate on the synthesis process for each research question.

In the case of research question 1, synthesized data from all four studies show that some studies proposed an applicable model of software process improvement for small and medium Web companies while others just relied on a set of techniques/practices believed to be useful for the cause. Within the context of this SLR, models are understood as established paradigms to perform certain tasks with an implied order of execution [62]. Techniques exist in isolation to perform a certain activity that can be best practice and can be implemented inside a model [62].

All the four studies included in this SLR proposed either a SPI model or a SPI technique for small and medium Web development companies. Study S1 has also been included in another SLR [20], which considers SPI of small and medium companies. Our explicit focus is on the SPI of small and medium Web companies and therefore our population is a subset of the set of all small and medium companies. S1 satisfies the inclusion criteria of both reviews (ours and S1's). Note that the research questions addressed in S1 differed from ours; therefore it would not be applicable to assume that out SLR presents a subset of the findings presented in S1.

Post project analysis and process management & measurement were the techniques that have been used in all four studies; followed by project tracking and feedback analysis, change management/configuration management and the mapping of business goals with SPI.

All the suggested SPI models used an iterative approach influenced by CMM/CMMI, and showed a strong tendency to use of the IDEAL model [17]. Similarly, all these studies suggested a measurement and management program for processes that govern the use of Web metrics.

For research question 2 the five studies demonstrate certain measures of success and also exhibit certain common factors that are present in different studies. Increase in productivity, reduced time for development, client and development team satisfaction, operational excellence and feedback from discussion are considered as the most important measures of success by four of the five studies included in SR.

For research question 3, none of the five studies considered are specific to the software process improvement of small and medium Web development companies. The previous studies applied conventional software SPI frameworks to Web companies without adaption to the Web context. All of them treated Web companies as a subset of small and medium software companies.

In research question 4, we wanted to investigate Web projects' type, company's age, turnover, target market, average number of employees, average project cost and process model used for the companies considered in the selected studies. However, none of the selected studies provided data relevant to answer this question, and therefore this question remains unanswered in this SLR.

For research question 5, synthesized data from the four studies suggested certain commonalities like: small and medium Web companies operate under tight budget constraints and with short deadlines; their strategies do not tend to be risk-based; they always demand quick results, using a "quick-to-market" approach.

4 Discussion and Conclusions

The number of studies that met our inclusion criteria was small, which indicates the scarcity of research in this area suggesting the need to future research in this field. However, our results highlighted some common and important patterns, one of which being the lack of models and techniques specifically made to measure for Web companies.

Therefore, the investigation of SPI within the context of Web companies formulates an interesting research case. Studies S1, S3 & S4 indicate the application of existing software SPI models to Web Companies; however the way in which these models were applied was not fully documented and there was no indication as to how existing SPI models should be tailored to existing Web standards and procedures.

The systematic review did not identify any SPI model or technique specifically customized for Web companies. This is also evident from the small number of studies that has met the inclusion criteria of our SLR in which we were specifically looking at the SPI for small and medium Web companies rather than the SPI for conventional software companies. However, this should not be understood as indicating that there is no need for specific Web SPI models and techniques. We argue that in terms of SPI it may also be the case that research on result oriented, cheaper and lesser time consuming SPI strategies for small and medium Web companies need to be conducted, which is the focus of our future work. The different context and nature of Web projects makes an interesting case to investigate as to how SPI should be tailored to their needs and what factors may be influential for its success. This review, as mentioned earlier, helped us understand the current state of research in Web SPI, and also in identifying research gaps and directions. One of the research gaps lies in proposing a specific SPI model for Web companies, which keeps in view their characteristics and aims to help them measure their success and improve continuously. This can be achieved by either enhancing some existing SPI model or by proposing one from scratch. This is the line of our future work.

Our detailed documentation for the conducted SLR may be browsed at the following Web link:
http://www.cs.auckland.ac.nz/~mria007/Sulayman/

References

1. Alexandre, S., et al.: OWPL: A Gradual Approach for Software Process Improvement In SMEs. In: Proceedings of 32nd EUROMICRO Conference on Software Engineering and Advanced Applications, Dubrovnik, Croatia, 29 August - 1 September, pp. 328–335 (2006)
2. Bolchini, D., Mylopoulos, J.: From task-oriented to goal-oriented Web requirements analysis, Engineering. In: Proceedings of the Fourth International Conference on Web Information Systems, WISE 2003, pp. 166–175 (2003)
3. Crombie, I.: The Pocket Guide to Appraisal. BMJ Publishing Group Inc., UK (1996)
4. Cugola, G., Ghezzi, C.: Software Processes: A Retrospective and a Path to the Future. Software Process Improvement and Practice J 4, 101–123 (1998)
5. Deshpande, Y., Hansen, S.: Web engineering: creating a discipline among disciplines Multimedia J. IEEE 8(2), 82–87 (2001)
6. Dybå, T.: An Empirical Investigation of the Key Factors for Success in Software Process Improvement. IEEE Trans. of Software Eng. 31(5), 410–424 (2005)
7. Escalona, J., Gustavo, A.: NDT. A Model-Driven Approach for Web Requirements. IEEE Transactions on Software Engineering 34(3), 377–390 (2008)
8. Fink, A.: Conducting Research Literature Reviews. In: From the Internet to Paper. Sage Publication s Inc., CA (2005)
9. Fraternali, P., Paolini, P.: Model-driven development of Web applications: the AutoWeb system. ACM Transactions on Information Systems (TOIS) 18(4), 1–35 (2000)
10. Glass, R.L.: Software Creativity. Prentice-Hall, Englewood Cliffs (1995)
11. Gomez, J., Cachero, C.: OO-H method: extending UML to model web Interfaces. In: Information modeling for internet applications. Idea Group Publishing, Hershey (2003)
12. Griffiths, G.: CASE in the third generation. Software Engineering J. (1994)
13. Harjuma, L., et al.: Improving Software Inspection Process with Patterns. In: Proceedings of Fourth International Conference on Quality Software, Germany (2004)

14. IPSS Project, Improving processes in small settings (IPSS project). SEI, Carnegie Mellon, USA (2006), http://www.sei.cmu.edu/iprc/ipssbackground.html
15. ISO/IEC, ISO/IEC JTC1/SC7 Working Group 24. Software Life Cycle Profiles and Guidelines for use in Very Small Enterprises (VSE) (2007), http://www.iso-iec-sc7wg24.gelog.etsmtl.ca/Webpage/iso-iec-sc7wg24_english.html
16. Kitchenham, B.: 2007 Guidelines for Performing Systematic Literature Review in Software Engineering, Version 2.3. EBSE Technical Report. Software Engineering Group, School of Computer Science and Mathematics, Keele University, UK and Department of Computer Science, University of Durham, UK (2007)
17. McFeeley, B.: 1996 IDEALSM: A User's Guide for Software Process Improvement. In: Handbook CMU/SEI-96-HB-001. Software Engineering Institute, Carnegie Mellon University, Pittsburgh, PE, USA (1996)
18. Nguyen, H.: Web application testing beyond tactics. In: Proceedings of Sixth IEEE International Workshop on Web Site Evolution, Chicago, USA, p. 83 (2004)
19. Petticrew, M., Roberts, H.: Systematic Reviews in the Social Sciences: A Practical Guide. Wiley-Blackwell, UK (2005)
20. Pino, F.J., García, F., Piattini, M.: Software process improvement in small and medium software enterprises: a systematic review. Software Quality Control J 16(2), 237–261 (2008)
21. Preciado, J., Linaje, M., Comai, S.: Designing Rich Internet Applications with Web Engineering Methodologies. In: 9th IEEE International Workshop on Web Site Evolution China, pp. 23–30 (2007)
22. Santos, G., et al.: Implementing Software Process Improvement Initiatives in Small and Medium-Size Enterprises in Brazil. In: Proceedings of 6th Int'l Conference on Quality of Information and Communications Technology, QUATIC, Lisbon, Portugal, September 12-14 (2007), pp. 187–198 (2007)
23. Schwabe, D., Rossi, G.: An Object Oriented Approach to Web-Based Application Design. Wiley and Sons, New York (1998); ISSN 1074-3224,Theory and Practice of Object Systems J, 4(4) (1998)
24. Thompson, H., Mayhew, P.: Approaches to Software Process Improvement. Software Process Improvement and Practice J 3(1), 3–17 (1997)
25. Zahran, S.: Software process improvement: practical guidelines for business success. Addison-Wesley Publication Company, Reading (1998)

An XCP Based Distributed Calibration System

Yang He and Xiaomin Sun

State Key Laboratory of Intelligent Technology and Systems, Tsinghua National Laboratory for Information Science and Technology, Department of Computer Science and Technology, Tsinghua University, Beijing 100084, P.R. China
heyang07@mails.tsinghua.edu.cn, sxm123@tsinghua.edu.cn

Abstract. Electronic Control Unit (ECU) calibration is a procedure to optimize control parameters to meet some specified requirements such as performance, fuel consumption and emissions. It is more important to calibrate several ECUs simultaneously than calibrating only one ECU at a time. We developed a distributed calibration system based on the Universal Measurement and Calibration Protocol (XCP) which is the newest communication protocol beyond the Controller Area Network (CAN) Calibration Protocol (CCP). Some new features of XCP are implemented in our system, which successfully achieves these goals: minimal slave resource consumption, efficient communication and program scalability.

Keywords: Electronic Control Unit (ECU), Universal Measurement and Calibration Protocol (XCP), distributed calibration system.

1 Introduction

ECU (Electronic Control Unit) calibration is a procedure to optimize control parameters to meet some specified requirements such as performance, fuel consumption and emissions. With the development of vehicle industry, the number and complexity of these parameters are increasing dramatically, thus, how to reduce costs and save time becomes a great challenge for automotive manufacturers [1,2,3].

In the future, ECU's functions will be distributed across several ECUs [1,4,5], so it will be more important to calibrate several ECUs simultaneously than calibrating only one ECU at a time. Meanwhile the relations among ECU control parameters make calibrating one ECU at a time impossible in some special scenarios. Therefore, it is highly needed to design a distributed calibration system.

The universal measurement and calibration protocol (XCP) is defined by the Association for Standardization of Automation and Measuring Systems (ASAM) organization [6,7,8,9]. XCP can be used as a communication protocol between ECU and PC. It is the newest communication protocol beyond the CAN (Controller Area Network) Calibration Protocol (CCP) which can only use CAN as transport media [10]. In order to support various transport media such as CAN, TCP/IP, USB, FlexRay, XCP is designed to be independent of them. The universal interfaces defined in protocol layer isolate function implementation from specified transport media. What is more important, XCP has several new developed features based on the experiences from CCP.

D. Ślęzak et al. (Eds.): ASEA 2009, CCIS 59, pp. 9–15, 2009.

A multi-node calibration system, proposed by [4,5], was first based on CCP and then on XCP. In their system, the configuration of CAN message identifier and message filter are adopted to support the name identification of multi-node system, so calibration data can be sent to their destinations correctly. XCP is thought as a normal communication protocol in their system. However, XCP has defined some advanced functions obtained from experiences of using CCP, and the distribution nature of XCP has optimized both the utilization cost and performance of the distributed calibration system.

We developed a distributed calibration system which implements new features of XCP mainly including synchronous data transfer, flash programming, power-up data transfer, block transfer. Design goals of our distributed calibration system are: minimal slave resource consumption, efficient communication and program scalability.

This paper is organized as follows: section 2 describes the system architecture including hardware components and software architecture; section 3 describes some details of implementation; section 4 shows an experiment to compare the performance of CCP and XCP; and section 5 concludes.

2 System Architecture

The distributed system consists of three components: the master PC node, the slave ECU nodes and physical connection media. MPC555 is used as the slave ECU [11]. The transport media between ECU and PC is CAN bus. TouCAN module is CAN controller integrated in MPC555, and it is connected to the CAN bus through CAN transceiver PCA82C250. The master PC is connected to CAN bus with Kvaser LAPcan which is a two-channel CAN interface for the PC card (PCMCIA) bus with dual Philips SJA1000 CAN controllers [12]. In order to expand ECU's memory, we used 4 IS61LV5128 static RAM (2M bytes memory in total) and 2 Am29LV160D flash (4M bytes memory in total).

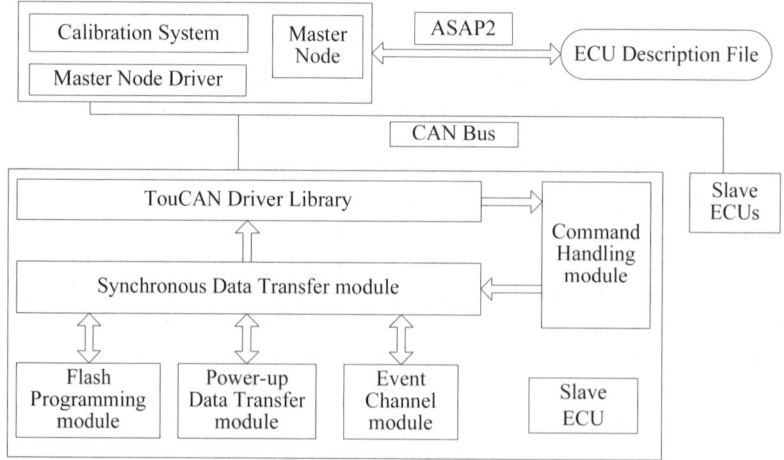

Fig. 1. System architecture

Figure 1 shows the basic architecture of the system. Several slaves are connected to one master through different transport media permitted by XCP. CAN is used in our system. The master PC controls the behaviors of all distributed slaves. The ECU description file for describing the ECU's internal memory is the knowledge basis for the calibration system. It is part of ASAP2 (Working Party on Standardization of Applications), defined by ASAM [13]. When new slave ECU is added into the calibration system, new ECU description file is created according to its internal data. This method is cost-effective due to avoiding any application modifications. When the slave node receives messages from CAN bus, the program in ECU will complete some tasks using resources of ECU in term of contents of messages. A state machine is maintained in each ECU.

3 Implementation

The design goals of our distributed calibration system are: minimal slave resource consumption, efficient communication and program scalability. In order to achieve these goals, we make the best use of new features of XCP.

The XCP driver in slave is the core of the whole calibration system as figure 1 showed. It is divided into four levels. The lowest level is TouCAN driver library which is used to handle message transfer between PC and ECU. Its functions are encapsulated into APIs called by upper level. The second level is command handling module. This module parses the commands transferred from calibration system and calls functions of synchronous data transfer module. Synchronous data transfer module is the third level which implements synchronous data transfer semantics. The top level implements new features of XCP which includes flash programming module, power-up data transfer module, event channel module. More modules will be added into this level with the development of our calibration system.

3.1 TouCAN Driver Library

The ECU is connected to CAN bus by PCA82C250 as the CAN transceiver and TouCAN as the CAN controller [11]. Message communication functions are packaged into a library, thus the upper level can use the interface easily without considering the underlying details.

The TouCAN module contains 16 message buffers which are used for transmitting and receiving messages. The extended identifier message format was used to specify the identifier. It also contains message filter adopted to qualify the received message identifier. In order to ensure simultaneous real-time communication, the interruption mechanism is used. The interrupt configuration register determines which interrupt signal is driven onto the bus when an interrupt is requested. Each of the 16 message buffers could be an interrupt source, if its corresponding IMASK bit is set. Each of the buffers is assigned one bit in the IFLAG register, and an IFLAG bit is set when the corresponding buffer completes a successful transmission or reception.

With the TouCAN interface, we can set slave node address, communication speed, priority mechanism and so on. If transport media is changed, we just need to change this library without affecting the upper level program.

3.2 Command Handling Module

Command handling module is used to parse commands received from calibration system. For a specified command, it calls functions of upper module to transfer data to calibration system.

3.3 Synchronous Data Transfer

Data elements in the slave's memory are transmitted in data transfer objects DAQ from slave to master and STIM from master to slave [7]. The object description table (ODT) describes the mapping between the synchronous data transfer objects and slave's memory as figure 2 showed. The synchronous data transmission object is

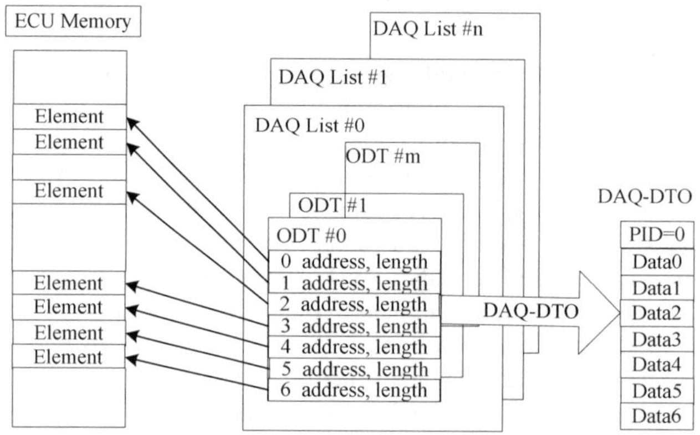

Fig. 2. ODT List Organization

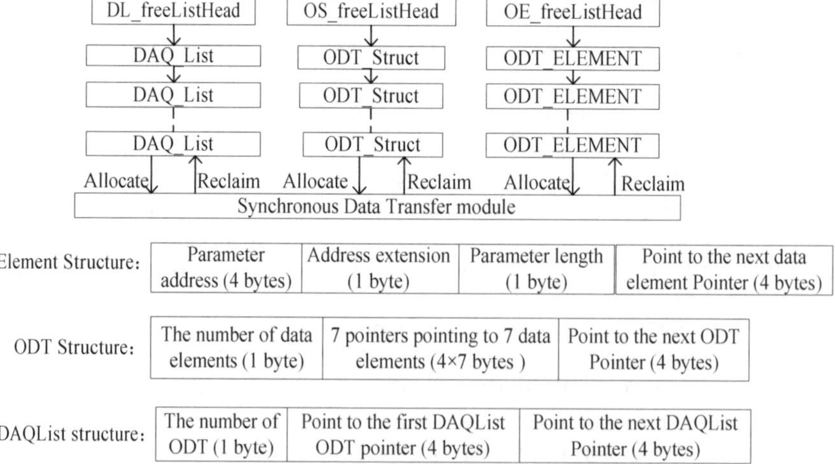

Fig. 3. Implementation of ODT and DAQ-list

transmitted with a packet identifier (PID) that associates an ODT. An entry in an ODT references a data element by its address and length. ODT entries are grouped into ODTs, and several ODTs can be grouped into a DAQ-list. Compared to CCP, XCP allows for dynamic configuration of the number of DAQ lists.

Based on the logical organization of ODT and DAQ list, a data structure is proposed to organize lists. Three linked lists are used to manage three kinds of data structures [14], and the number of linked lists can be configured dynamically as needed. Some interfaces are implemented to manage these linked lists. The element can be deleted, added, modified dynamically. Element memory can be released when it is not used and can be reallocated when it is insufficient. Figure 3 shows the details of implementation.

3.4 Event Channel Module

XCP allows for several DAQ-lists, which may be simultaneously active. The sampling and transfer of each DAQ-list are triggered by individual events in the slave node. An event channel builds the generic signal source that determines the data transfer timing effectively.

MPC555 supports a plenty of clock counting device such as PIT, DEC, TB, RTC and so on [11]. In our design, DEC is used to trigger the transfer of DAQ-list. The decrementer register (DEC) is 32-bits decrement counter which provides an exception after a programmable delay. The initial value of DEC is set by specified XCP command, and then triggers an interrupt to transfer DAQ-lists when the value of DEC is 0.

3.5 Power-Up Data Transfer

Power-up data transfer is a new feature of XCP compared to CCP. The purpose of the power-up data transfer mode is to enable automatic data transfer on power-up instead of waiting for setup instructions from the master which reduces redundant communications and is more efficient.

Power-up data transfer mode satisfies the requirements of distributed calibration. When a new ECU is added, the DAQ configuration information is loaded into ECU's flash memory and the flag of power-up data transfer mode is set. After power-up the slave will check this flag and read DAQ configuration from fixed address of ECU's flash memory if power-up data transfer mode is supported.

3.6 Flash Programming

Flash programming is also a new feature of XCP. It provides a mechanism to directly access data in flash memory for calibration system.

In standard communication model, each request packet can be responded by a corresponding response packet or an error packet. The master device may not send a new request until the response to the previous request is received. To speed up memory uploads, downloads and flash programming, the block transfer mode is introduced as a new feature. It allows that there are several requests before a response or a request followed by several responses. The slave device may have limitations of the maximum block size and the minimum separation time. The block transfer model will increase throughput of data uploading, downloading and flash programming.

4 Experiments

From the above analysis, the performance of XCP has been significantly improved compared to CCP. Efficiency and throughput have been increased by low message overhead, block transfer model and power-up transfer model.

For downloading, most 5 bytes of data can be transferred per command of CCP and most 6 bytes of data can be transferred per command of XCP in block transfer mode. For uploading, most 5 bytes of data can be transferred per command of CCP and most 7 bytes of data can be transferred per command of XCP in block transfer mode.

We implemented a complete distributed calibration system based on XCP and did an experiment to compare the performance between XCP and CCP. In the experiment, there are 1 master node and 2 slave nodes. The master controls calibration task. To show the effect of the power-up data transfer, we cut off the connections between PC and ECUs two seconds after start, then, we re-connect them after one second. Thus we can compare the communication throughput between XCP and CCP.

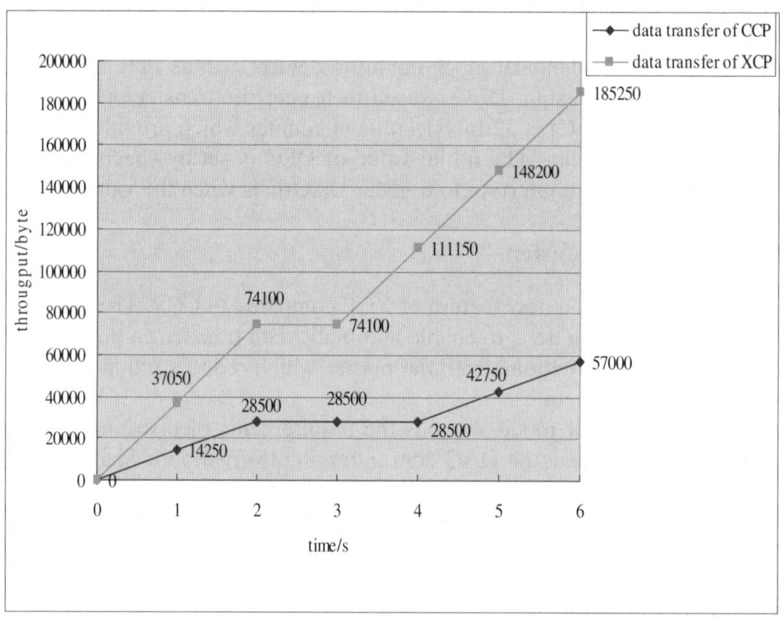

Fig. 4. Data transfer of XCP and CCP

Results show that 5700 messages can be transferred due to the restriction of physical connection media. As the block transfer mode and power-up data transfer module are used in XCP, the throughput increases significantly.

5 Conclusions

A distributed calibration system based on XCP is discussed including the system architecture and the implementation details. Both theoretical analysis and experiment results prove that XCP is more efficient than CCP, and our distributed calibration system successfully achieves the design goals: minimal slave resource consumption, efficient communication and high scalability.

References

1. Andre, R., Jobst, R., Robert, L.: A new calibration system for ECU development. SAE 03-03-2003 (2003)
2. Bohn, C., Stober, P., Magnor, O.: An Optimization-Based Approach for the Calibration of Lookup Tables in Electronic Engine Control. In: Conference on Computer Aided Control Systems Design, pp. 2315–2320. IEEE, Los Alamitos (2006)
3. Helmuth, H., Wolfgang, K., Manfred, S.: Fully automatic determination and optimization of engine control characteristics. SAE 02-24-1992 (1992)
4. Yang, S.W., Yang, L., Zhuo, B.: Developing a multi-node calibration system for can bus based vehicle. In: The International Conference on Vehicular Electronics and Safety, pp. 199–203. IEEE, Los Alamitos (2006)
5. Yang, S.W., Zhu, K.Q., Xu, Q.K., Zhou, B.: Multiple electronic control units calibration system based on explicit calibration protocol and J1939 protocol. Chinese Journal of Mechanical Engineering 21(1), 42–47 (2008)
6. Information about ASAM, `http://www.asam.net`
7. Roel, S., Hans-Georg, K., et al.: XCP Version1.1 Part 1 - Overview, `http://www.asam.net` (2008)
8. Roel, S., Hans-Georg, K., et al.: XCP Version1.1 Part 2 - Protocol Layer Specification (2008), `http://www.asam.net`
9. Roel, S., Hans-Georg, K., et al.: XCP Version1.1 Part 3 - XCP on CAN - Transport Layer Specification (2008), `http://www.asam.net`
10. Kleinknecht, H., et al.: Can Calibration Protocol Version 2.1 (1999), `http://www.asam.net`
11. MOTOROLA. MPC555/MPC556 User's Manual (2000), `http://www.freescale.com/files/microcontrollers/doc/user_guide/MPC555UM.pdf`
12. Information about Kvaser LAPcan, `http://www.kvaser.com/prod/hardware/lapcan_i.htm`
13. Brian, P., William, D., et al.: ASAP Interface Specification Interface 2 Version 1.51 (2003), `http://www.asam.net`
14. Qu, Z.Q.: Component-based Design and Implementation of the Tsinghua Tool Suite for Vehicles. Master's thesis, Department of Computer Science and Technology, Tsinghua University (2007)

Structural and Behavioral Detection of Design Patterns

Nadia Bouassida[1,2] and Hanene Ben-Abdallah[1,3]

[1] Mir@cl Laboratory
[2] Institut Supérieur d'Informatique et de Multimédia,
Sfax University, Sfax, Tunisia
[3] Laboratory, Faculté des Sciences Economiques et de Gestion,
Sfax University, Sfax, Tunisia
Nadia.Bouassida@isimsf.rnu.tn, Hanene.BenAbdallah@fsegs.rnu.tn

Abstract. We propose a technique that recognizes occurrences of a pattern in a design using both static and dynamic information. To tolerate pattern instantiations with certain degree of variability, we adapt an XML document retrieval technique. Our technique has the advantage of basing the design pattern identification not only on static, structural information of a pattern but also on the methods of the pattern which represent the dynamic aspect.

Keywords: design pattern identification, design pattern instantiation, XML document retrieval.

1 Introduction

A major problem behind benefiting from design patterns [7] is the difficulties inherent to first understanding and then applying them to a particular application. On the other hand, one way to benefit from design patterns is to assist an inexperienced designer to improve his/her design by finding design patterns that could better structure his/her design. To offer such assistance, several approaches propose to determine the potential similarities of the structure, the class names and/or method calls between the design and a given pattern. These approaches differ mainly in the pattern concepts they consider (*i.e.*, only the structure, the structure and the methods) and the degree of structural discordance they tolerate: exact match [3] or partial match [4], [11].

Evidently, pattern identification should tolerate a certain degree of structural discordance between the design and a pattern. However, while some elements can be deleted in a design approximating a pattern, others representing the essence of the pattern should not; otherwise the pattern would be lost. Hence, all the pattern elements should not be treated equally. However, all pattern identification approaches that tolerate structural discordance treat them equally. Furthermore, most of the existing approaches for pattern identification focused on identifying the pattern structure and neglected the pattern dynamic aspects and the methods. However, relying only on the structural information to detect design patterns can produce imprecise results for patterns with a similar structure. On the other hand, the few works that treated the methods dealt with method calls [11] [4]; nevertheless, this represents only partially the dynamic aspect of a pattern: the method invocation order is often very important, essentially, in behavioral and creational design patterns.

D. Ślęzak et al. (Eds.): ASEA 2009, CCIS 59, pp. 16–24, 2009.

In this paper, we present a new pattern identification technique that: 1) can be used to identify the structure, class names and methods of the pattern, 2) accounts for dynamic method invocation of the pattern, and 3) tolerates variability in a pattern instantiation (statically and dynamically).. Our identification technique reuses an XML document retrieval approach where the pattern is seen as the XML query and the design as the XML document in which the query is searched.

The remainder of this paper is organized as follows. Section 2, first, overviews currently proposed approaches for pattern identification, and then it presents the basic concepts of XML document retrieval in general. Sections 3 and 4 present our approach for pattern identification in terms of its structure and method invocations, respectively. In Section 5, the approach is illustrated through the observer design pattern and a fragment of the JHotDraw framework for graphical drawing editors [12]. Section 6 summarizes the paper and outlines our future work.

2 Related Works

2.1 Current Pattern Identification Approaches

For reverse engineering purposes, several proposals looked in automating the identification of design patterns in source code, *cf.*, [2], [9], [5]. For instance, Lee and al. [9] combine static and dynamic analyses of source code: The static analysis collects the structural aspect of the software while the dynamic analysis elucidates dynamic aspects of the program during its execution like message passing between objects. The analysis results are represented as XMI documents parsed to look for matching design pattern descriptions. This technique allows only an exact match of patterns, which assists in better understanding parts of the program.

For both reengineering and code improvement purposes, Albin-Amiot et al. [1] use a constraint satisfaction technique to detect patterns within a given source code. Their technique takes into account refractoring aspects and identifies distorted versions of the pattern in the source code. In this work, the dynamic aspect is limited to method calls between pairs of related classes, independently of the overall temporal behavior.

Besides the source code level, other works extract design patterns from a design, *cf.*, [2], [4], [5], [6], [11]. For example, Tsantalis [11] proposes a design pattern detection methodology based on similarity scoring between graphs coded as matrices. Besides the structural aspect of patterns, this work examines methods through a graph representation; two methods are considered similar either when they have the same signature, or when explicitly stating the base class method (*e.g.*, via the super identifier in Java). This type of method invocation is one particular aspect of behavioral information in design patterns; another aspect, important for behavioral and creational patterns, is the temporal information about method invocation. In addition, the main drawback of similarity scoring-based approaches is their convergence time which depends on the graph size of the design.

A second purpose of pattern identification within a design is to improve the quality of the design. Within this context, Bergenti and Poggi [2] propose a tool, called IDEA, to improve UML designs (class and collaboration diagrams) using automatic pattern detection. Their method relies on a knowledge-base where each pattern is described by a structure template and a collaboration template (described internally using Prolog rules). This method allows only an exact match with the pattern. When IDEA finds a pattern instance, a set of design rules are verified to test if the design could be improved.

On the other hand, recognizing the importance of behavioral information in a pattern, Ka-Yee *et al.* [8] use dynamic analysis and constraint programming to identify behavioral and creational patterns in source code. Using dynamic analyses, they reverse engineer the UML sequence diagrams from Java source code. Then they transform design pattern identification into a constraint propagation problem in terms of variables, constraints among them and their domains. This approach focuses only on the behavioral aspect of the pattern, while neglecting the structural aspect. Moreover, an important challenge using dynamic analysis to trace the behavior of a system is the large amount of data involved and thus the execution time to solve the huge CSP.

In summary, none of the proposed approaches combines the structural and dynamic aspects in their pattern identification. Except for Ka-Yee [8], none of the few works treating the dynamic aspect describes the behavior in terms of scenarios of ordered method invocations and tolerates behavioral variability.

2.2 XML Document Retrieval

In their comprehensive description of XML document retrieval techniques, Manning *et al.*, [10] adapt the vector space formalism for XML retrieval by considering an XML document as an ordered, labeled tree. The tree is analyzed as a set of paths starting from the root to a leaf. In addition, each query is examined as an *extended* query – that is, there can be an arbitrary number of intermediate nodes in the document for any parent-child node pair in the query. Documents that match the query structure closely by inserting fewer additional nodes are given more preference.

A simple measure of the similarity of a path c_q in a query Q and a path c_d in a document D is the following *context resemblance* function [10]:

$$C_R(c_q, c_d) = \begin{cases} \dfrac{1+|c_q|}{1+|c_d|} & \text{if } c_q \text{ matches } c_d \\ 0 & \text{if } c_q \text{ does not match } c_d \end{cases}$$

where:

- $|c_q|$ and $|c_d|$ are the number of nodes in the query path and document path, respectively, and
- c_q *matches* c_d if and only if we can transform c_q into c_d by inserting additional nodes.

Note that the value of $C_R(c_q, c_d)$ is 1 if the paths c_q and c_d are identical. On the other hand, the more nodes separate the paths of Q and D, the less similar they are considered, *i.e.*, the smaller their context resemblance value will be.

3 A New Pattern Detection Approach

To detect patterns within a design, we consider that a given pattern may be represented in various forms that differ from the basic structure without loosing the essence of the pattern. Our pattern identification approach operates in three steps:

1. Identification of the structural features of the class diagram of the pattern: the classes, generalizations, aggregations, compositions, *etc.* For this, we will transform the pattern and the design into XML documents.
2. Identification of the method declarations: This step validates the class correspondence determined during the first step. It relies on method name comparison.
3. Identification of the dynamic aspect of the pattern: This relies on validated correspondence results. It also adapts an XML document retrieval approach to examine the conformity of the design behavior to that of the pattern. It supposes that the behavior is specified in terms of sequence diagrams.

3.1 Resemblance Determination: Structural Information

In XML document retrieval in general, the context resemblance function (C_R) is calculated based on an exact match between the names of the nodes in the query and the document paths. However, for pattern detection, the nodes representing the classes are often different in the pattern from those in the design. Thus, we first need to calculate the resemblance values for the various matches between the class nodes in the query (pattern) and those in the design. Secondly, we need to take into account: 1) the number of times a given match between two class nodes is used to calculate C_R; and 2) the importance of each relation in the pattern.

The structural resemblance between a pattern and a design starts by calculating the resemblance between each path of the pattern and all the paths in the design. In this calculation, we assume that the structural variability should be limited between the pattern and its potential instantiation in the design. That is, we assume that a design path may differ from a pattern path by adding at most N nodes compared to the longest path of the pattern. The larger the N, the more scattered the pattern instantiation would be in the design, which might loose the pattern essence. The tolerated maximal intermediate nodes N can be fixed by the designer.

Note that each tree in the XML document representing a class diagram is composed of class nodes interconnected by relation nodes (generalization, association, *etc*). In addition, each path in a tree contains relation nodes from the same type. Thus, in our resemblance calculation, we examine one type of relation among classes at a time.

Furthermore, the match between the pattern path and the design path may not necessarily start at the root node; hence, we need to consider all possible sub-paths of the design, that start at different class nodes in the design path. Note that since the structural difference between the pattern path and the design path is limited, then each sub-path can cover at most $L+N$ class nodes (L being the length of the longest path); thus the number of sub-paths to be considered is reduced. This in turn limits the temporal complexity of our algorithm.

While comparing the paths, we collect the resemblance scores between the classes of the design and the classes of the pattern in a matrix: This matrix sums up the values of the context resemblance scores for each class in the design with respect to a class in the pattern. This sum is weighted to account for the importance of the relations in the pattern; for instance, in the Composite pattern, the aggregation relation is more important than the inheritance relation.

Finally, these scores are normalized with respect to the total number of classes in the design; the final matching results are collected in a matrix (*NormalizedCRMatrix*) whose columns are the classes in the pattern and whose rows are the classes of the design. Now given this matrix, we can decide upon which correspondence better represents the pattern instantiation: For each pattern class, its corresponding design class is the one with the maximum resemblance score in the *NormalizedCRMatrix*.

On the other hand, given two design fragments $D_1$and D_2, to decide upon which design better instantiates a pattern *P*, we first compute their normalized resemblance matrices. Secondly, we compute the sum of the normalized resemblance scores for all the matched pattern classes in $D_1$and D_2; the design with the maximum sum is the one that better instantiates the pattern. Note that in a worst case instantiation, each pattern class must be matched to at least one class in the design; thus, on average, the sum of the normalized resemblance scores of the matched classes should not be less than the number of classes in the pattern divided by the number of classes in the design.

3.2 Resemblance Determination: Method Definition Information

Once the static classes and relations of the pattern have been identified within the design, the pattern identification continues with the identification of pattern methods within the design. This identification should examine both the method name and signature. However, it is not possible to compare the method signatures since, in the design, the methods are adapted to the application or domain; thus their parameters are different from those of the pattern.

For method names, the resemblance is based on a linguistic/semantic similarity determined through either a dictionary or a domain ontology when available. A method *m* is said to *resemble* another method *m'*, if the name of *m* is either a synonym or homonym of the name of *m'*.

To determine the correspondences among the design and pattern methods, we use a normalized matrix (called *NormMethodDecMatrix*) that for each design class (row), it gives the percentage of resembling methods it has with each pattern class (column).

3.3 Static Design Pattern Identification

To identify statically a pattern within a design, we combine the above two normalized matrices. The combination can be either a simple addition of the two normalized matrices, or a weighted sum to reflect the importance of the two types of collected information: classes and their relations *vs.* classes and their method declarations. The combined information reinforces the quality of the identification results.

4 Behavioral Resemblance Determination

To determine the behavioral resemblance between a design *D* and a pattern *P*, we rely on their sequence diagrams. In addition, to compare two sequence diagrams, we will compare the ordered message exchanges for each pair of objects that were already identified as similar during the static identification phase.

For each object O in a sequence diagram, its ordered message exchanges are represented through an XML path. Each node of these paths represents the type of the message (sent/received) along with the message being exchanged; this information allows us to derive a path where the edges have the same meaning: temporal precedence.

To compute the resemblance function scores between message paths, we slightly modify the C_R function defined in Section 2.2 to tolerate (as oppose to penalize) the additional, intermediate nodes. In fact, for message exchanges (represented as nodes), the important factor is the presence of pattern messages in a given order; that is, additional message exchanges to those of the pattern will not affect the behavior of the pattern instantiation. Thus, the new C_{RM} function to compare message paths is as follows:

$$C_{RM}(c_q, c_d) = \begin{cases} 1 & \text{if } c_q \text{ matches } c_d \\ 0 & \text{if } c_q \text{ does not match } c_d \end{cases}$$

Let *Op* be an instance of a class *Cp* in the pattern *P; Od* be an instance of a class *Cd* in a given design; and suppose that *Cd* was identified as resembling *Cp*. Then, *Op* and *Od* have *resembling behavior* if and only if the sum of the C_{RM} of the sub-paths in the XML message paths of *Op* and *Od* is at least equal to the number of sub-paths in the XML message paths of *Op*. When this constraint is not satisfied, then *Od* either lacks messages exchanged by *Op*, or it does not respect the order of message exchanges.

5 Example: The JHotDraw Framewok and the Observer Pattern

To illustrate the steps of our approach, let us consider a fragment of the JHotDraw framework for graphical drawing editors [12] and let's identify the observer design pattern. Due to space limitation, we next illustrate only the behavioral resemblance identification through this example. Figure 1 shows the JHotDraw design fragment we will analyze. Note that, for an easier comprehension of the patterns involved in the design, this class diagram indicates in ellipses the roles played by each class. Figure 2 illustrates one of JHotDraw's sequence diagrams. Figures 3 shows the sequence diagram for the Observer pattern which we will identify in the JHotDraw fragment.

The structural identification matched the class Figure with the Subject class and the class StandardDrawing with ConcreteObserver. However, it produced two matches for the class AbstractFigure: the Observer and the ConcreteSubject classes. To decide upon the best match, we continued with the identification of the method declarations.

After summing up the normalized method matrix and the normalized context resemblance matrix, we obtain a matrix where the match score of *AbstractFigure* to *Observer* is equal to the match score of *FigureChangeListener* to *Observer* (0.66); however, since *AbstractFigure* has been identified as *ConcreteSubject* with a greater matching score (0.83), then *FigureChangeListener* is identified as *Observer.*

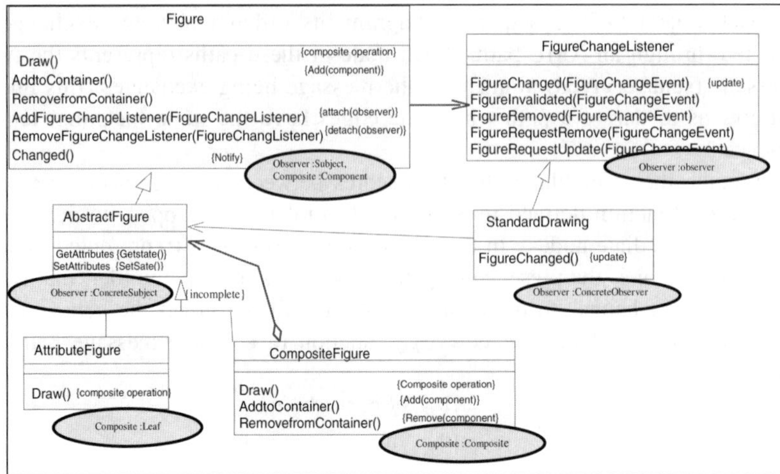

Fig. 1. A design fragment from the Jhotdraw framework

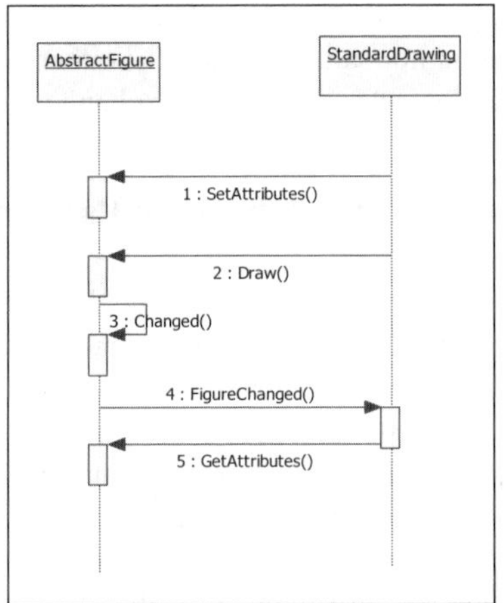

Fig. 2. A sequence diagram for a scenario of Jhotdraw

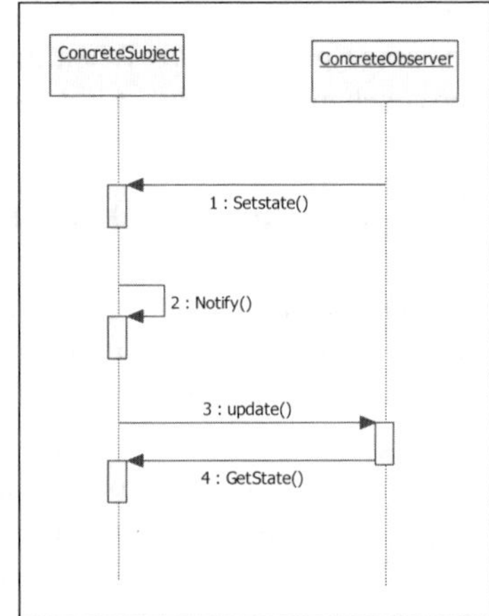

Fig. 3. A sequence diagram for the Observer pattern

Note that, in Table 1, in order to optimize the resemblance score calculation, we treated the pattern XML path by considering two messages at a time; this covers the total order of message exchanges for each object. However, for the design, we need to consider XML paths with lengths 2 and longer; this allows us to tolerate additional, intermediate message exchanges.

For a design to cover *all* the message exchanges of the pattern, we need to find, in *each column*, at least one entry in this table that has the value of 1. Otherwise, the column that is missing a one indicates that the corresponding message exchange is missing in the design. On the other hand, our method tolerates additional, intermediate

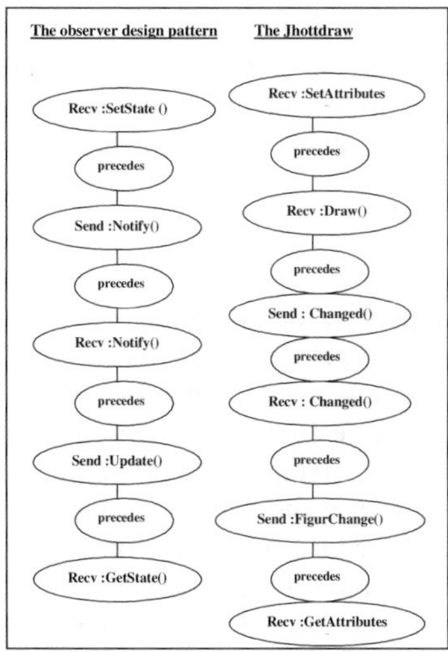

Fig. 4. XML path for the sequence diagrams of the Observer pattern and JHotDraw

Table 1. Context resemblance scores

	Recv:SetState() preceds ⟶ *Send:Notify*	*Send:Notify* preceds ⟶ *Recv:Notify*	*Recv:Notify* preceds ⟶ *Send:Update*	*Send:Update* preceds ⟶ *Recv:GetState*
Recv:SetAttribut preceds ⟶ *Recv :Draw*	$C_{RM}(c_q, c_d)$ =0	$C_{RM}(c_q, c_d)$ =0	$C_{RM}(c_q, c_d)$ =0	$C_{RM}(c_q, c_d)$ =0
Recv:SetAttribut preceds ⟶ *Recv :Draw* preceds ⟶ *send:changed*	$C_{RM}(c_q, c_d)$ =1	$C_{RM}(c_q, c_d)$ =0	$C_{RM}(c_q, c_d)$ =0	$C_{RM}(c_q, c_d)$ =0
Recv:Draw preceds ⟶ *send : changed*	$C_{RM}(c_q, c_d)$ =0	$C_{RM}(c_q, c_d)$ =0	$C_{RM}(c_q, c_d)$ =0	$C_{RM}(c_q, c_d)$ =0
Recv:Draw preceds ⟶ *send :changed* preceds ⟶ *Recv:Changed*	$C_{RM}(c_q, c_d)$ =0	$C_{RM}(c_q, c_d)$ =0	$C_{RM}(c_q, c_d)$ =0	$C_{RM}(c_q, c_d)$ =0
Changed preceds ⟶ *Changed*	$C_{RM}(c_q, c_d)$ =0	$C_{RM}(c_q, c_d)$ =1	$C_{RM}(c_q, c_d)$ =0	$C_{RM}(c_q, c_d)$ =0
Changed preceds ⟶ *FigureChanged*	$C_{RM}(c_q, c_d)$ =0	$C_{RM}(c_q, c_d)$ =0	$C_{RM}(c_q, c_d)$ =1	$C_{RM}(c_q, c_d)$ =0
FigureChanged preceds ⟶ *GetAttribute*	$C_{RM}(c_q, c_d)$ =0	$C_{RM}(c_q, c_d)$ =0	$C_{RM}(c_q, c_d)$ =0	$C_{RM}(c_q, c_d)$ =1

message exchanges in the design. In our example, we tolerated at most one additional message; it is represented through the node representing the message *Draw*.

At the end of this dynamic aspect identification step, the designer has more confidence in the results of the structural and method identification steps.

6 Conclusion

The proposed approach for pattern identification reuses an XML document retrieval technique. It considers a design pattern as an XML query to be found in an XML document representing a design. It uses an adapted context similarity function [10] to determine the most probable correspondences between the classes of the design and those in the pattern. It has the advantage of tolerating certain structural differences in the design compared to the pattern; the designer can fix a threshold below which the differences are un-tolerated. A second advantage of our approach is that it can be applied for both structural and behavioral correspondences.

We are currently examining how to add more intelligence in our assistance for the recognition of pattern problems inside a design. This will be conducted by alleviating the search task by adding priorities in the computation of resemblance scores.

References

1. Albin Amiot, H., Cointe, P., Guéhéneuc, Y.G.: Un meta-modele pour coupler application et detection des design patterns. L'objet 8, 1–18 (2002)
2. Bergenti, F., Poggi, A.: Improving UML design pattern detection. In: Proceedings of the 12th international conference on software engineering and knowledge engineering, SEKE (2000)
3. Brown, K.: Design reverse-engineering and automated design pattern detection in Smalltalk. Technical Report TR-96-07, University of Illinois at Urbana-Champaign (1996)
4. Dong, J., Sun, Y., Zhao, Y.: Design pattern detection by template matching. In: SAC 2008, Ceara, Brazil (2008)
5. El Boussaidi, G., Mili, H.: Detecting patterns of poor design solutions by using constraint propagation. In: Czarnecki, K., Ober, I., Bruel, J.-M., Uhl, A., Völter, M. (eds.) MODELS 2008. LNCS, vol. 5301, pp. 189–203. Springer, Heidelberg (2008)
6. Florijin, G., Meijers, M., Van Winsen, P.: Tool support for object oriented patterns. In: Aksit, M., Matsuoka, S. (eds.) ECOOP 1997. LNCS, vol. 1241, pp. 472–495. Springer, Heidelberg (1997)
7. Gamma, E., Helm, R., Johnson, R., Vlissides, J.: Design patterns: Elements of reusable Object Oriented Software. Addisson-Wesley, Reading (1995)
8. Ka-Yee, J., Ng, G.Y.G.: Identification of behavioural and creational design patterns through dynamic analysis. In: Proceedings of the 3rd International Workshop on Program Comprehension through Dynamic Analysis (PCODA), October 2007, pp. 34–42 (2007)
9. Lee, H., Youn, H., Lee, E.: A design pattern detection technique that aids reverse engineering. The International Journal of security and applications 2(1) (January 2008)
10. Manning, C.D., Raghavan, P., Schütze, H.: An introduction to information retrieval. Cambridge University Press, England (2008)
11. Tsantalis, N., Chatzigeorgiou, A., Stephanides, G., Halkidis, S.T.: Design pattern detection using similarity scoring. IEEE transactions on software engineering 32(11) (2006)
12. Gamma, E., Eggenschwiler, T. (2005), `http://www.jhotdraw.org`

Test Case Minimization and Prioritization Using CMIMX Technique*

Praveen Ranjan Srivastava[1], Mahesh Ray[1], Julian Dermoudy[2], Byeong-Ho Kang[2], and Tai-hoon Kim[3]

[1] Computer Science & Information System Group, BITS PILANI – 333031 (India)
{praveenrsrivastava,maheshray123}@gmail.com
[2] School of Computing and Information Systems, University of Tasmania, Australia
{Julian.Dermoudy,bhkang}@utas.edu.au
[3] Dept. of Multimedia Engineering, Hannam University, Korea
taihoonn@hnu.kr

Abstract. Test case prioritization techniques schedule test cases for execution in an order that attempts to increase their effectiveness at meeting some performance goal. Various goals are possible; one involves rate of fault detection i.e. the measure of how quickly faults are detected within the testing process. To improve the performance of regression testing two objectives to be achieved. I.e. test case minimization and test case prioritization. In this paper both the processes are considered along with special care has given to the data dependencies within the source code. So, path coverage is taken, which proves better option than the previous methods adopted.

Keywords: Regression Testing, Path Testing, Test Case Prioritization, Test Case Minimization.

1 Introduction

Regression testing is an expensive testing process used to validate new features and detect regression faults, which occurs continuously during the software development lifecycle. Software engineers often save test suites so that they can reuse them later during regression testing. However, due to time and resource constraints, it may not be possible to execute all the test cases on every testing iteration [1,2]. Therefore, testers may want to order the test cases such that those with the higher priorities, according to some criterion, are run earlier than those with lower priorities.

Typically, empirical evaluations of prioritization techniques have focused on assessing a prioritized test suite's rate of detection of regression faults: faults created in a system version as a result of code modifications and enhancements. For experimentation, such faults can be obtained in two ways: by locating naturally occurring faults, or by seeding faults. Naturally occurring faults, however, are costly to locate and typically cannot be found in numbers sufficient to support controlled experimentation.

* The registration fee was supported by the Security Engineering Research Center, granted by the Korea Ministry of Knowledge Economy.

D. Ślęzak et al. (Eds.): ASEA 2009, CCIS 59, pp. 25–33, 2009.

In contrast, seeded faults, which are typically produced through hand-seeding or program mutation, can be provided in large numbers, allowing more data to be gathered than otherwise possible. Test case prioritization techniques schedule test cases in an order that increases their effectiveness at meeting some performance goals, such as code coverage, rate of fault detection. In other words, a prioritization technique is used to increase the likelihood that the prioritized test suite can better meet the goal than would a random order of test cases. Numerous prioritization techniques have been presented in the research literature [3-22]. The first dimension along which these techniques can be distinguished is in terms of the type of code elements they consider. For example, statements, basic blocks, or functions. The second dimension involves the use of "feedback". For example, additional function coverage prioritization adjusts the coverage information for remaining test cases using the feedback information. The third dimension is the use of other sources of information. For example, test cost, fault severity or fault propagation probability [5]. To measure the performance of prioritized test suite, some metrics are provided, such as total statement coverage, additional function coverage, rate of fault detection and so on.

Rothermel et al. [23] distinguish two types of test case prioritization: general and version-specific. In general test case prioritization, given program P and test suite T, test cases in T are prioritized with the goal of finding a test case order that will be useful over a sequence of subsequent modified versions of P. Thus, general test case prioritization can be performed following the release of some version of the program during off-peak hours and the cost of performing the prioritization is amortized over the sub-sequent releases. The expectation is that the resulting prioritized suite will be more successful than the original suite at meeting the goal of the prioritization, on average over those subsequent releases.

In contrast, in version-specific test case prioritization, given program P and test suite T, test cases in T are prioritized with the intent of finding an ordering that will be useful on a specific version P' of P. Version-specific prioritization is performed after a set of changes have been made to P and prior to regression testing P'. Because this prioritization is performed after P' is available, care must be taken to prevent the cost of prioritizing from excessively delaying the very regression testing activities it is supposed to facilitate. The prioritized test suite may be more effective at meeting the goal of the prioritization for P' in particular than would a test suite resulting from general test case prioritization, but may be less effective on average over a succession of subsequent releases. In this paper a version specific test case prioritization method is described.

Many previous papers adopts the methods like statement coverage, function coverage etc. But in the existing methodology after prioritizing test cases, it is found that the dependencies between the elements (variables, constants) in the source code is neglected, which may cause failure of the product after delivery to client. So, in this paper path coverage is considered. As a result if any statement within a particular path is changed in the modified version of the product then the test case executing that particular path is to be again executed.

2 Test Case Prioritization

Test Case Prioritization is the process of scheduling test cases in an order to meet some performance goal. Test case Prioritization as defined in [23].

Given: T, a test suite; PT, the set of permutations of T; f, a function from PT to the real numbers.

Problem: Find $T' \in PT$ such that $(\forall T'')\ (T'' \in PT)\ (T'' \neq T')\ [f(T') \geq f(T'')]$

Here, PT represents the set of all possible prioritizations (orderings) of T, and f is a function that, applied to any such ordering, yields an award value for that ordering. The definition assumes that higher award values are preferred over the lower ones. There can be number of possible goals of test case prioritization e.g., testers may wish to increase the rate of fault detection, or testers may wish to find the critical faults at the earliest or may wish to cover the maximum code during testing at the earliest. But all these goals lead to one major goal / prime goal that testers want to increase their confidence in the reliability of the system at a faster rate. So, testers are interested in finding maximum number of faults as well as the most critical faults at the earliest [24].

Test Case prioritization problem is found in Regression Testing Technique. Regression testing is performed on modified software to provide confidence that the software behaves correctly and that the modifications have not adversely impacted the software quality. Software engineers often save the test suites they develop for their software so that they can reuse those test suites later as the software evolves. There are two varieties of test case prioritization viz. general test case prioritization and version specific test case prioritization. In general test case prioritization, for a given program P and test suite T, we prioritize the test cases in T that will be useful over a succession of subsequent modified version of P without any knowledge of modified version. In version specific test case prioritization, we prioritize the test cases in T, when P is modified to P′, with the knowledge of the changes that have been made in P. Various researchers have given different prioritization techniques. Studies have shown that some of these techniques can significantly increase the rate of fault detection of test suite in comparison to unordered or randomly ordered test suite. Most of these prioritization techniques are general prioritization techniques. In this work, we concentrate on version-specific test case prioritization. In this paper a modified Test Case Prioritization Technique is proposed which tests the source code at the fastest rate possible.

3 Problem Statement

Let P be a procedure or program

P′ be a modified version of P

T be a set of code coverage based tests (a test Suite) created to test P.

When P is modified to P′, we have to find T′, which is subset of T that achieves maximum code coverage at the earliest and should be given highest priority during Regression Testing. For this purpose, we want to identify tests that

- Execute code that has been deleted so that test cases that have gone redundant can be deleted from T.
- Execute modified code at least once at the earliest.

4 Algorithm

Steps of Algorithm:

1. Prioritize the Test Cases on the basis of their Importance. So, Go for Path Coverage Testing.
   1.1 Draw the CFG of the given Source Code.
   1.2 Find the possible Paths of execution.
   1.3Find the Statements changed after project enhancement.
   1.4 Check whether the statements changed are affecting the whole path or not? (Which was not possible in statement coverage method?).
   1.5 If it affects any line within the path then simply re execute the Test Case.

2. Optimize the number of test cases by using CMIMX procedure [25].
   2.1 Set minCov = Φ, YetToCover = m. Unmark each of the n tests and m entities. An unmarked test case is still under consideration whereas; a marked test is already added to minCov.
   2.2 Repeat the steps when YetToCover > 0.
   Among unmarked entities find the ones having less number of 1s. And LC be the set of indices having all such columns.
   Among all the unmarked tests that also cover entities in LC, find those that have the maximum number of non-zero entities. Let S be one of these rows.
   Mark Test S and add it to minCov. Mark all entities covered by test s. reduce YetToCover by the number of entities covered by S.

5 Application

The above proposed algorithm is implemented in the source code of Binary Search algorithm. As the algorithm is proposed in two steps in the first phase the CFG of the given source code is drawn. Then possible paths of execution are taken and the statements changed within the path in the enhanced project are considered. Priority level is given to the test cases executing the definite paths on the basis of the number of statements have changed. In the next phase of the algorithm, from the existing set of test cases normalized test cases are chosen by n-way testing technique, so that the modified test suite must be efficient enough to cover all the possible sets of combinations formed from the previous one.

Source Code:

```
Void binary_search (elem key, elem*T, int size, boolean &found, int &L)
        int bott, top, mid;
        top=size-1;
        L= (top+bott)/2;
        if (T [L] ==key) found=true;
        else
                Found=false;
        while (bott<=top &&! found)
```

```
        {
                Mid= (mid+bott)/2;
                If (T[mid] ==key)
                {
                found=true;
                L=mid;
        }
    else if (T[mid] <key)
                {
                bott=mid+1;
        else top=mid-1;
        }
```

CFG of the above source code is given in the Figure 1.

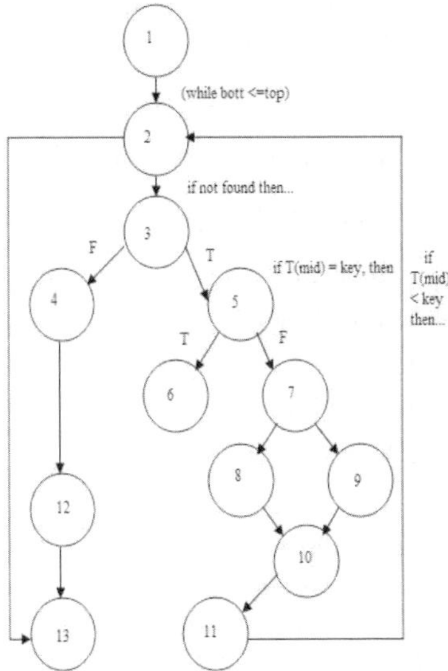

Fig. 1.

From the Figure 1, the possible paths of execution of the source code obtained are,

1. 1-2-12-13
2. 1-2-3-4-12-13
3. 1-2-3-5-6-11-2-12-13
4. 1-2-3-5-7-8-10-11-2-12-13
5. 1-2-3-5-7-9-10-11-2-12-13

Suppose Test Cases T1 to T5 are executed for the individual paths of the source code. Hence the statements covered by the Individual Test Cases are given in the below table 1.

Table 1. Paths executed

Test Case_id	Paths Executed
T1	1-2-12-13
T2	1-2-3-4-12-13
T3	1-2-3-5-6-11-2-12-13
T4	1-2-3-5-7-8-10-11-2-12-13
T5	1-2-3-5-7-9-10-11-2-12-13

Suppose, after enhancement of the project statement numbered 10 and 11 in the source code have modified. Hence, the paths covering the above statements have affected after the modification in the source code. As a result test cases executing the paths have to be executed again in the regression testing. But, due to time constraint instead of executing all the test case a subset of test cases are to be executed. Hence a priority level is required, to decide which test cases are to be executed and which are not to be. To assign the priority level of test cases, the extent of each test case is to be calculated. At first number of statements changed associated with each rest case is calculated and given in Table 2.

Table 2. Statements changed

Test Case_id	Paths Executed	No_of_Stat Changed
T1	1-2-12-13	0
T2	1-2-3-4-12-13	0
T3	1-2-3-5-6-11-2-12-13	1
T4	1-2-3-5-7-8-10-11-2-12-13	2
T5	1-2-3-5-7-9-10-11-2-12-13	2

The weight associated with each test case is calculated by number of statements changed associated with each test case and given in the table 3. It can be observed that T4, T5 are having highest priority level should be executed first and accordingly Test Cases T3 and then, T1 and T2.

Table 3. Priority vector

Test Case_id	Priority Level
T4	2
T5	2
T3	1
T1	0
T2	0

After Completion of First Step of the algorithm, the next part is to be executed. In the Second Step procedure CMIMX [25] is applied. Hence, it helps to calculate Minimum Coverage of entities and the Test cases can be optimized.

Suppose, the above source code has 3 input variables: X = {bott, mid, top}, where D (bott) = {i, j}, D (mid) = {k, l}, and D (top) = {m, n}. Hence 6 entities are there and 5 test cases to be executed. So, a 5*6 matrix is found as shown in Table 4.

Table 4. Input matrix in CMIMX

Test Case_id	i	j	k	l	m	n
T1	1	1	1	0	0	0
T2	1	0	0	1	0	0
T3	0	1	0	0	1	0
T4	0	0	1	0	0	1
T5	0	0	0	0	1	0

Applying the Step 2 of the algorithm, the result found is step wise given.

Step 1

MinCov = Φ, YetToCover = 6

Among unmarked entities l and n, each contain a single 1 and hence qualifies as the highest priority entities. Thus LC = {l, n}. Among the unmarked tests, T2 covers entities i and l, and T4 covers entities k and n. Both test cases have identical benefits of 2 each in terms of the number of entities they cover. So, arbitrarily considering T2. Thus s = 2.

minCover = {2}. Test case T2 is marked. Entities i and l covered by Testcase T2 are also marked. YetTo Cover = 6-2 =4.

Step 2

Again continue with the second loop. Here T6 has the least cost. Hence LC = {n}. Only T4 covers entity n and hence S=4.

minCov = {j, l}. Testcase T4 and entities k and l are marked. YetToCover =4-2 =2.

Step 3

Again continue with the third loop. Here j and m have the least cost. Hence LC = {j, m}. T1, T3, T5 covers entities j and m. T3 has the maximum benefit of 2. Hence S =3.

minCov = {j, k, l}. Testcase T3 and entities j and m are marked. YetToCover = 2-2 =0.

Hence, the loop terminates with minCov = {j, k, l}.

6 Conclusion and Future Work

This paper, describes the shortcomings in the previous techniques of prioritizing test cases for regression testing and empirically examined their relative abilities to improve how quickly faults can be detected during regression testing. The suggested techniques can improve the rate of fault detection and can also optimize the set of test cases.

In previous approaches statement coverage or function coverage has been considered, which cannot produce fully tested product because data dependency arises there. As a result change in the source code may affect some other portion. To overcome this problem path coverage criterion has been introduced here, which tests the whole path again if any statement within the path has been modified.

Secondly, CMIMX procedure is applied, which optimizes the pre-existing test cases to a greater extent. All the possible combinations are tested but with executing less number of test cases. By increasing the value of n the test cases size must be minimized again. Hence combination of both the techniques i.e. minimization and prioritization gives an effective method of regression testing.

Similarly, other factors could be optimized parallel, i.e. time or numbers of test cases to be minimize and the result of performance must be achieved to be maximized. This multi factors can be optimize simultaneously by using Multi-objective optimization technique. Several Multi-disciplinary design optimization algorithms are there like pareto-optimization etc.

References

1. Leung, H., White, L.: Insights into regression testing. In: Proceedings of the International Conference on Software Maintenance, Miami, Florida, U.S.A, pp. 60–69 (October 1989)
2. Onoma, K., Tsai, W.-T., Poonawala, M., Suganuma, H.: Regression testing in an industrial environment. Communications of the ACM 41(5), 81–86 (1998)
3. Elbaum, S., Malishevsky, A.G., Rothermel, G.: Prioritizing Test Cases for Regression Testing. In: Proceedings of the International Symposium on Software Testing and Analysis, pp. 102–112 (August 2000)
4. Elbaum, S., Malishevsky, A.G., Rothermel, G.: Incorporating varying test costs and fault severities into test case prioritization. In: Proceedings of the 23rd International Conference on Software Engineering, pp. 329–338 (May 2001)
5. Elbaum, S., Malishvesky, A.G., Rothermel, G.: Test case prioritization: A family of empirical studies. IEEE Transactions on Software Engineering 28(2), 159–182 (2002)
6. Elbaum, S., Rothermel, G., Kanduri, S., Malishevsky, A.G.: Selecting a Cost-Effective Test Case Prioritization Technique. Software Quality Journal 12(3), 185–210 (2004)
7. Harrold, M.J.: Testing: A Roadmap. In: Proceedings of the International Conference on Software Engineering, Limerick, Ireland, pp. 61–72 (2000)
8. Jeffrey, D., Gupta, N.: Test Case Prioritization Using Relevant Slices. In: Proceedings of the 30th Annual International Computer Software and Applications Conference, pp. 411–420 (2006)
9. Kim, J.M., Porter, A.: A History-Based Test Prioritization Technique for Regression Testing in Resource Constrained Environments. In: Proceedings of the 24th International Conference on Software Engineering, pp. 119–129 (May 2002)
10. Leung, H., White, L.: Insights into regression testing. In: Proceedings of the International Conference on Software Maintenance, Miami, Florida, U.S.A., pp. 60–69 (October 1989)
11. Li, Z., Harman, M., Hierons, R.M.: Search Algorithms for Regression Test Case Prioritization. IEEE Transactions on Software Engineering 33(4), 225–237 (2007)
12. Malishevsky, A.G., Ruthruff, J., Rothermel, G., Elbaum, S.: Cost-cognizant Test Case Prioritization, Technical Report TR-UNL-CSE-2006-0004, Department of Computer Science and Engineering, University of Nebraska - Lincoln (March 2006)

13. Onoma, K., Tsai, W.-T., Poonawala, M., Suganuma, H.: Regression testing in an industrial environment. Communications of the ACM 41(5), 81–86 (1998)
14. Rothermel, G., Untch, R.H., Chu, C., Harrold, M.J.: Test Case Prioritization: An Empirical Study. In: Proceedings of the International Conference on Software Maintenance (September 1999)
15. Rothermel, G., Untch, R.H., Chu, C., Harrold, M.J.: Prioritizing test cases for regression testing. IEEE Transactions of Software Engineering 27(10), 929–948 (2001)
16. Srikanth, H.: Requirements-Based Test Case Prioritization. In: Student Research Forum in 12th ACM SIGSOFT International Symposium on the Foundations of Software Engineering (2004)
17. Srikanth, H., Williams, L.: On the economics of requirements-based test case prioritization. In: Proceedings of the 7th international workshop on Economics-driven software engineering research, pp. 1–3 (May 2005)
18. Srivastava, A., Thiagarajan, J.: Effectively prioritizing tests in development environment. In: Proceedings of the International Symposium on Software Testing and Analysis, pp. 97–106 (July 2002)
19. Walcott, K.R., Soffa, M.L., Kapfhammer, G.M., Roos, R.S.: Time-Aware Test Suite Prioritization. In: Proceedings of the International Symposium on Software testing and Analysis, pp. 1–12 (July 2006)
20. Wong, W.E., Horgan, J.R., London, S., Agrawal, H.: A Study of Effective Regression Testing in Practice. In: Proceedings of the 8th IEEE International Symposium on Software Reliability Engineering, pp. 264–274 (November 1997)
21. Zhang, X., Xu, B., Nie, C., Shi, L.: An Approach for Optimizing Test Suite Based on Testing Requirement Reduction. Journal of Software (in Chinese) 18(4), 821–831 (2007)
22. Zhang, X., Xu, B., Nie, C., Shi, L.: Test Suite Optimization Based on Testing Requirements Reduction. International Journal of Electronics & Computer Science 7(1), 9–15 (2005)
23. Rothermel, G., Untch, R.H., Chu, C., Harrold, M.J.: Prioritizing Test Cases for Regression Testing. IEEE Trans. Software Eng. 27(10), 929–948 (2001)
24. Aggarwal, K.K., Singh, Y.: Software Engineering, Programs Documentation Operating Procedures. New Age International Publishers (2001)
25. Mathur, A.P.: Foundations of Software Testing, Pearson Education, 1st edn. (2008)

Embedded Control Software Design with Aspect Patterns

Takahiro Soeda, Yuta Yanagidate*, and Takanori Yokoyama

Tokyo City University,
1-28-1, Tamazutsumi, Setagaya-ku, Tokyo 158-8557 Japan
g0981517@tcu.ac.jp, y-yanagidate@ak.jp.nec.com, yokoyama@cs.tcu.ac.jp

Abstract. The paper presents an aspect-oriented design for embedded control software such as automotive control. In the control logic design phase, we build a control model with a CAD/CAE tool such as MATLAB/Simulink, in which "zero-time execution" is assumed. In the software design phase, we design timing issues such as task structures and mechanisms for data integrity to execute the control software in the preemptive multi-task environment. We represent mechanisms for timing design as reusable aspect patterns. We define aspect patterns of triggering methods, synchronizations and inter-task communications. We also provide a model weaver to weave the aspect patterns into the base model incrementally. In the timing design, we only have to select the aspect patterns and weave them into the functional model with the model weaver.

Keywords: embedded control system, real-time system, aspect-oriented modeling, design pattern, model weaver.

1 Introduction

The embedded control software development process consists of the control logic design phase and the software design phase. In the control logic design phase, model-based design with CAD/CAE tools such as MATLAB/Simulink [1] has become popular. A control model is designed and verified by simulation in an ideal environment in which "zero-time execution" is assumed.

In the software design phase, we design control software to implement the control model, taking account of not only functional properties but also non-functional properties such as real-time constraints. We design tasks and mechanisms for the preemptive multi-task environment.

Aspect-oriented programming has been applied to separate non-functional properties from functional properties [2][3]. Model level aspects are required for language-independent design. Some model level aspects of non-functional properties have been presented [4] and some model weavers have been developed to weave aspects into base models [5][6]. However, aspect-oriented modeling for the timing design of embedded control software has not been presented.

* Presently with NEC Corporation.

D. Ślęzak et al. (Eds.): ASEA 2009, CCIS 59, pp. 34–41, 2009.

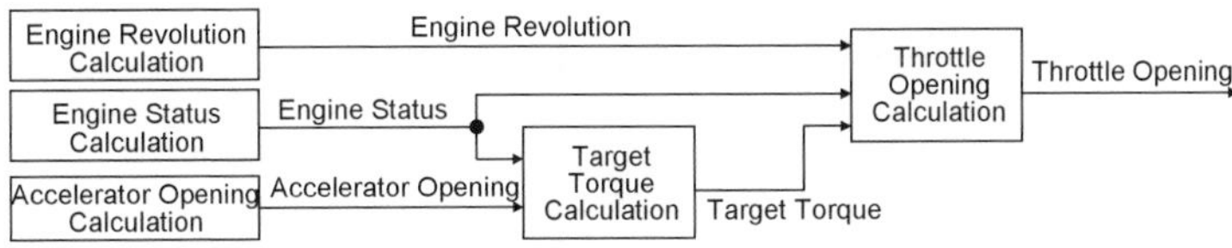

Fig. 1. Example block diagram

The paper presents an aspect-oriented design method for the timing design of embedded control software. Our main target application is automotive control, the logic of which is designed with a block diagram based tool such as Simulink. We represent mechanisms used in the timing design as aspect patterns in UML. We also present a model weaver to weave aspect patterns into a functional model. We can design the software for the preemptive multi-task environment only by selecting the aspect patterns and weaving them into the functional model.

The rest of the paper is organized as follows. Section 2 presents a design method with aspect patterns. Section 3 describes the aspect description and the model weaver. Section 4 describes aspect patterns for timing design. Section 5 compares our work with related work and Section 6 concludes the paper.

2 Embedded Control Software Design

2.1 Functional Design

Control engineers build a control model with a block diagram based tool such as Simulink. Fig. 1 shows a part of an example block diagram that consists of the blocks periodically calculating *EngineRevolution*, *EngineStatus*, *AcceleratorOpening*, *Target Torque* and *ThrottleOpening* in the control periods.

We translate the block diagram into a UML model according to the translation method presented in [7]. We call the UML model the functional model because the model represents functional properties. Fig. 2 shows the functional model corresponding to Fig. 1. Each class has attribute *value*, method *update* to calculate its own *value*, and method *get* to read *value*. The association named *cons* means that the following object consumes the value of the preceding object. For example, method *update* of *TargetTorque* gets the values of *EngineStatus* and *AcceleratorOpening*, and calculates and stores the value. The *update* methods are periodically called in the control periods.

2.2 Timing Design

In the timing design, we design the task structure, scheduling policy, task priorities, triggering methods (time-triggered or event-triggered[8]), and then design synchronizations, mutual exclusions and inter-task communications.

The timing design is done incrementally, because timing design issues depend on each other. The necessity of a mechanism for data integrity depends on the task structure, task priorities and the scheduling policy. For example, if all the

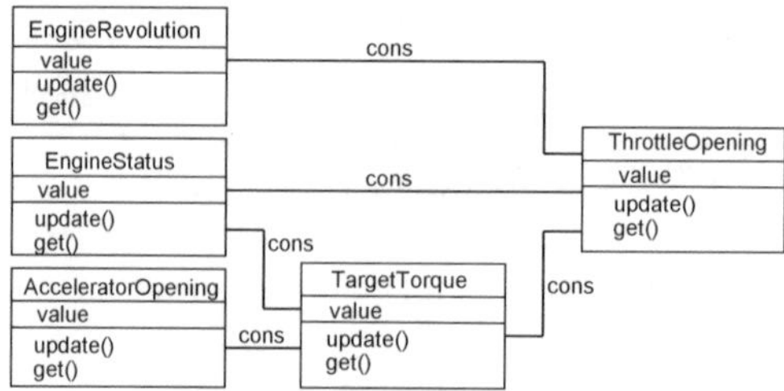

Fig. 2. Class diagram of functional model

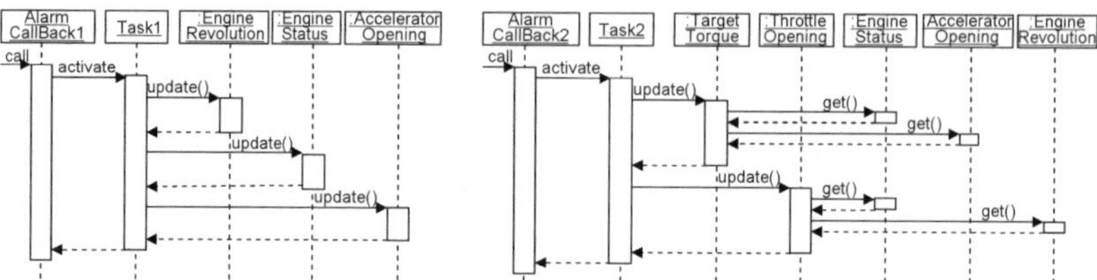

Fig. 3. Sequence diagrams of functional model

objects of Fig. 2 are executed by one task, no mechanism is required. However, if we use multiple tasks, mechanisms for data integrity are required. Fig. 3 shows sequence diagrams in the case of using two periodic tasks of OSEK OS[9]. A periodic task is activated by an alarm-callback routine in OSEK OS. *Task1* is activated by *AlarmCallBack1* and *Task2* is activated by *AlarmCallBack2*. We assume the priority of *Task1* is higher than the priority of *Task2*. If *Task2* is preempted by *Task1* after *TargetTorque* gets the value of *EngineStatus* and before *ThrottleOpening* gets the value of *EngineStatus*, the data integrity is violated.

We define design patterns for the timing design and represent them as aspects. We call them aspect patterns. To add a mechanism for data integrity, we select an appropriate aspect pattern and weave it into the functional model.

3 Aspect Description and Model Weaver

3.1 Aspect Description

We have defined the syntax of aspect description referring to Theme/UML[10]. Theme/UML represents crosscutting elements by template parameters. Composition (weaving) is done by binding the template parameters with the elements of the base model. The binding, however, can not be represented by the standard UML. To design a control software model with an existing UML editor, we present a method to represent the binding using the standard UML. We also present a method to weave structural elements into a class diagram. A buffer class has to be woven into an association between two classes for buffer-based inter-task communication as shown in Section 4.3.

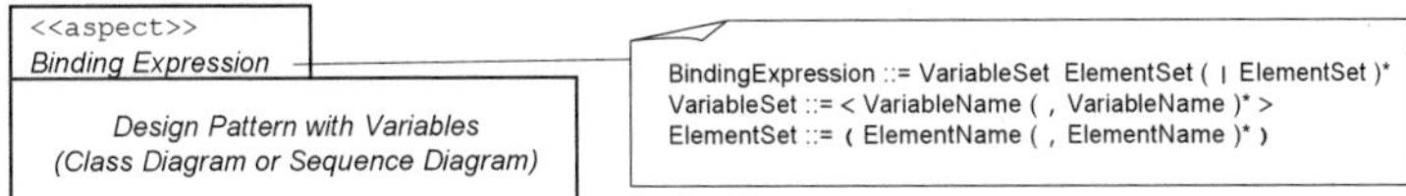

Fig. 4. Aspect description

Fig. 4 shows our aspect description method. We use a package with stereotype <<aspect>> to represent an aspect. The design pattern to be woven is represented as a class diagram or as a sequence diagram enclosed by the package. We represent crosscutting elements as variables, and bind them with actual elements of the base model. The binding expression is written under <<aspect>>. To deal with crosscutting concerns, we can bind a set of variables to multiple sets of elements concatenated with "|". We can also use wild card characters.

3.2 Model Weaver

We have developed a model weaver to weave aspect patterns into a base model. Both the format of input files and the format of output files are XMI[11]. A woven model, which is generated by weaving an aspect pattern into a functional model, can be dealt with as a base model into which another aspect pattern is woven. So aspect patterns can be incrementally woven into the functional model.

The model weaver inputs XMI files of a functional model and aspect patterns, analyzes them, and identifies variables and element names to be bound. The model weaver then searches for the elements to be bound, and weaves the design patterns of the aspects into the model by binding the variable elements with the actual elements of the model. Finally, the model weaver outputs XMI files of the woven model. We have developed the model weaver in Java.

4 Aspect Patterns

4.1 Aspect Patterns for Timing Design

We have identified aspect patterns by analyzing automotive control software. Table 1 shows the aspect patterns for timing design. We have defined three aspect patterns for triggering methods: the time-triggered pattern, the event-triggered pattern and the demand-triggered pattern. We have got those by translating source code level aspects[2] into sequence diagrams, so we do not describe the details in this paper. We get the sequence diagrams shown in Fig. 3 by weaving the time-triggered aspect pattern for *update* method calls into the tasks.

We have also defined two aspect patterns for synchronization: the event control pattern and the mutual exclusion pattern. Those are represented by sequence diagrams to weave OSEK OS system service calls. We mention the mutual exclusion aspect pattern in this paper.

We have defined two aspect patterns for inter-task communications: the simple buffering pattern and the double buffering pattern. Those are represented

Table 1. Aspect patterns

Category	Aspect Pattern	UML Diagram
Triggering Method	Time-triggered	Sequence Diagram
	Event-triggered	Sequence Diagram
	Demand-triggered	Sequence Diagram
Synchronization	Event Control	Sequence Diagram
	Mutual Exclusion	Sequence Diagram
Inter-Task Communication	Simple Buffering	Class Diagram, Sequence Diagram
	Double Buffering	Class Diagram, Sequence Diagram

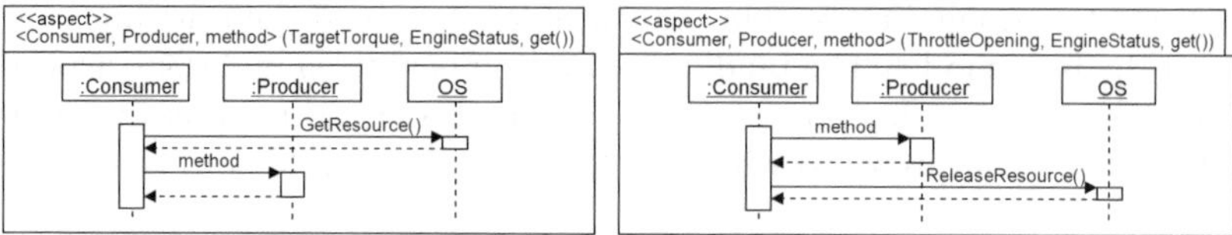

Fig. 5. Mutual exclusion aspect pattern

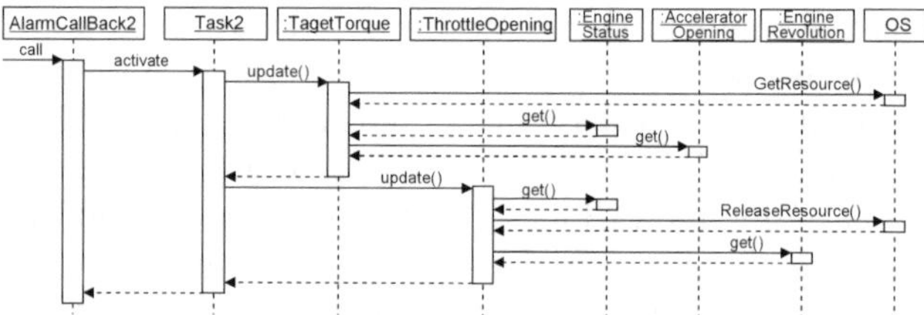

Fig. 6. Sequence diagram with mutual exclusion

by both class diagrams and sequence diagrams. The simple buffering temporally holds the value to prevent the violation of data integrity described in Section 2.2. However, it does not perfectly preserve the semantics of the control model designed with Simulink. The double buffering algorithm has been presented to preserve the semantics[12]. We mention the double buffering aspect pattern.

4.2 Mutual Exclusion

Fig. 5 shows the mutual exclusion aspect pattern. The left-hand side sequence diagram means that *Consumer* calls *GetResource* before calling *method* of *Producer*. The binding expression declares the variables *Consumer*, *Producer* and *method* and specifies to bind them with *TargetTorque*, *EngineStatus* and *get*. This means to weave the *GetResource* call into the join point before calling *get* of *EngineStatus*. The right-hand side package of Fig. 5 means to weave the *ReleaseResource* call into the join point after calling *get* of *EngineStatus*.

We put the right-hand side sequence diagram of Fig. 3 and the aspect patterns shown in Fig. 5 into the input of the model weaver, and we get the sequence diagram shown in Fig. 6.

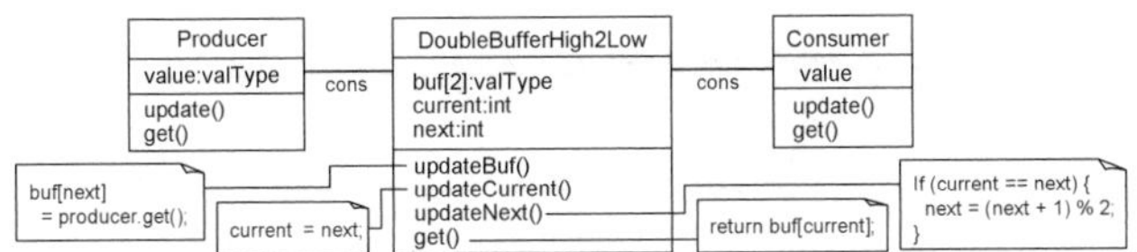

Fig. 7. Double buffering design pattern

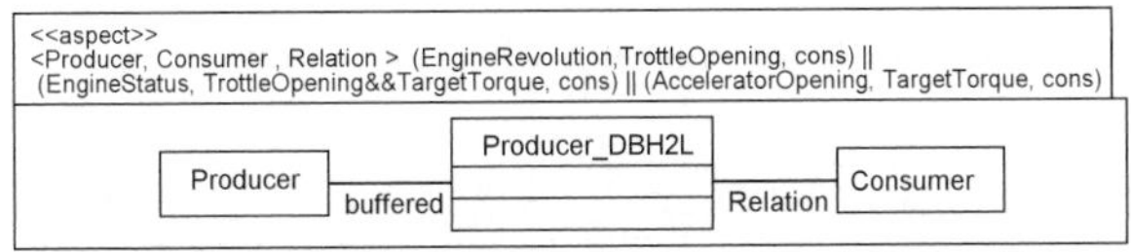

Fig. 8. Class diagram of double buffering aspect pattern

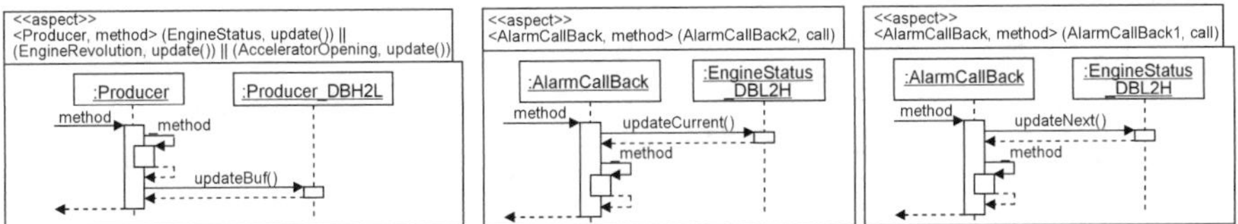

Fig. 9. Sequence diagrams of double buffering aspect pattern

4.3 Double Buffering

We have defined the double buffering design pattern referring to [12]. Fig. 7 shows the design pattern in the case that the priority of the task executing *Producer* is higher than the priority of the task executing *Consumer*. *DoubleBufferHigh2Low* is a class for double buffering.

Fig. 8 shows the structural aspect pattern of the double buffering to store the values of *EngineRevolution*, *EngineStatus* and *AcceleratorOpening*. Fig. 9 shows the behavioral aspect patterns to call *updateBuf* of the double buffers, to call *updateCurrent* of *EngineStatusDBH2L*, and to call *updateNext* of *EngineStatus-DBH2L*. Behavioral patterns for the *updateNext* calls and *updateCurrent* calls of *AcceleratorOpening* and *EngineRevolution* are similar to them. The *updateCurrent* calls and the *updateNext* calls are woven into alarm-callback routines.

We put the functional model shown in Fig. 2 and Fig. 3, the aspect patterns shown in Fig. 8 and Fig. 9, and the similar behavioral patterns described above into the input of the model weaver, and we get the class diagram shown in Fig. 10 and the sequence diagram shown in Fig. 11. *EngineRevolutionDBH2L*, *EngineStatusDBH2L* and *AcceleratorOpeningDBH2L* are subclasses of *Double-BufferHigh2Low*.

5 Related Work

Wehrmeister et al. have discussed model level aspects for non-functional requirements of distributed embedded real-time systems[4]. However, few concrete

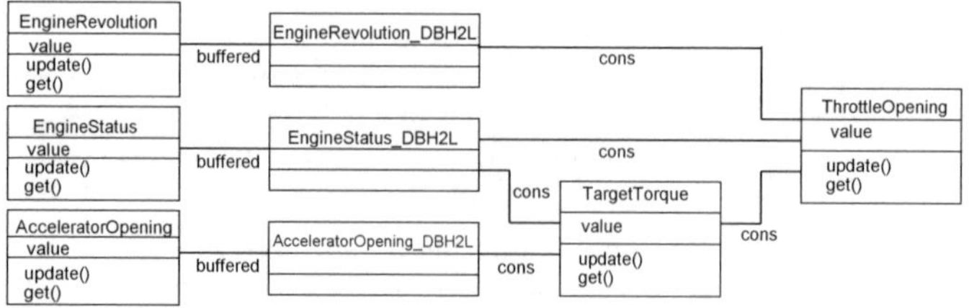

Fig. 10. Class diagram with double buffering

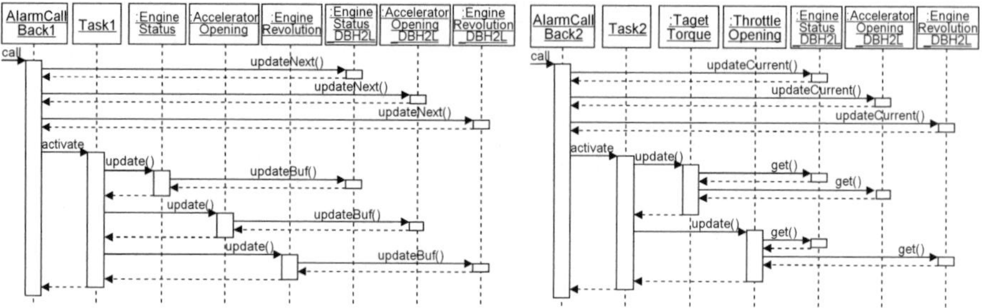

Fig. 11. Sequence diagrams with double buffering

model level aspect patterns for embedded control software have been presented. In this paper, we have presented aspect patterns for the timing design of embedded control software.

Ho et al. have presented a UML based tool for model level weaving[6]. Gray et al have presented a model weaver using domain specific modeling language[13]. De Niz et al. have presented a model weaver for embedded real-time systems[14]. Their goals are automatic code generation and their model weavers output not UML models but source code, so we cannot verify woven models nor incrementally weave aspects. Our model weaver generates woven UML models and supports incremental weaving. Groher et al. have presented a model weaver supporting incremental weaving[15]. The model weaver deals with only the class diagram. Cotteiner et al. have presented a practical model weaver[5]. The model weaver does not support structural aspects. Our model weaver supports structural aspects required for buffer-based inter-task communications.

6 Conclusions

We have presented an aspect-oriented design for embedded control software. We represent the mechanisms used for the preemptive multi-task environment as reusable aspect patterns. We have also developed a model weaver to weave aspect patterns into a functional model incrementally. We only have to select appropriate aspect patterns and weave them with the model weaver. This makes timing design more efficient. We are going to define aspect patterns for reliability and distribution and extend the model weaver to deal with other UML diagrams.

Acknowledgments

This work is partially supported by KAKENHI (20500037).

References

1. The Mathworks Inc., http://www.mathworks.com/
2. Yokoyama, T.: An Aspect-Oriented Development Method for Embedded Control Systems with Time-Triggered and Event-Triggered Processing. In: Proc. of the 11th IEEE Real-Time and Embedded Technology and Application Symposium, pp. 302–311 (2005)
3. Cunha, C.A., Sobral, J.L., Monteiro, M.P.: Reusable Aspect-Oriented Implementations of Concurrency Patterns and Mechanisms. In: Proc. of 5th International Conference on Aspect-Oriented Software Development, pp. 15–26 (2006)
4. Wehrmeister, M.A., Freitas, E., Pereira, C.E., Wagner, F.R.: An Aspect-Oriented Approach for Dealing with Non-Functional Requirements in a Model-Driven Development of Distributed Embedded Real-Time Systems. In: Proc. of 10th IEEE International Symposium on Object and Component-Oriented Real-Time Distributed Computing, pp. 428–432 (2007)
5. Cotteiner, T., van den Berg, A., Elrad, T.: The Motorola WEAVER: Model Weaving in a Large Industrial Context. In: Proc. of 6th International Conference on Aspect-Oriented Software Development, Industry Track (2006)
6. Ho, W.-M., Jézéquel, J.-M., Pennaneac'h, F., Plouzeau, N.: A Toolkit for Weaving Aspect Oriented UML Designs. In: Proc. of 1st International Conference on Aspect-Oriented Software Development, pp. 99–105 (2002)
7. Yokoyama, T., Naya, H., Narisawa, F., Kuragaki, S., Nagaura, W., Imai, T., Suzuki, S.: A Development Method of Time-Triggered Object-Oriented Software for Embedded Control Systems. Systems and Computers in Japan 34(2), 338–349 (2003)
8. Kopetz, H.: Should Responsive Systems be Event-Triggered or Time-Triggered? IEICE Transaction on Information & Systems E76-D(11), 1325–1332 (1993)
9. OSEK/VDX: Operating System, Version 2.2.3 (2005)
10. Clarke, S., Baniassad, E.: Aspect-Oriented Analysis and Design: The Theme Approach. Addison-Wesley, Upper Saddle River (2005)
11. Object Management Group: XML Metadata Interchange Specification, Version 2.0.1 (2005)
12. Scaife, N., Caspi, P.: Integrating model-based design and preemptive scheduling in mixed time- and event-triggered systems. In: Proc. of 16th Euromicro Conference on Real-Time Systems, pp. 119–126 (2004)
13. Gray, J., Bapty, T., Neema, S., Schmidt, D.C., Gokhale, A., Natarajan, B.: An Approach for Supporting Aspect-Oriented Domain Modeling. In: Proc. of 2nd International Conference on Generative Programming and Component Engineering, pp. 151–168 (2003)
14. de Niz, D., Bhaitia, G., Rajkumar, R.: Model-Based Development of Embedded Systems: The SysWeaver Approach. In: Proc. of 12th IEEE Real-Time and Embedded Technology and of Applications Symposium, pp. 231–242 (2006)
15. Groher, I., Voelter, M.: XWeave: Models and Aspects in Concert. In: Proc. of 10th International Workshop on Aspect-Oriented Modeling, pp. 35–40 (2007)

Towards a Consistent Semantics for Unsafe Time Petri Nets

Abdelkrim Abdelli

LSI Laboratory- Computer science Department- USTHB University
Bp 32 El Alia Babezzouar Algiers Algeria
Abdelli@Lsi-usthb.dz

Abstract. We discuss in this paper the consistency of time Petri net semantics when assuming a monoserver hypothesis. This hypothesis assumes that for a given marking of the net, only one instance of an enabled transition should be considered. We show that for unsafe nets, the standard semantics is not sound and may induce false behaviors in presence of conflicting transitions. To fix this problem, we propose a new semantics that removes these incoherences by managing accurately after each firing the status of enabled transitions. We prove that our semantics is sound when assuming a monoserver hypothesis.

1 Introduction

Real time systems are systems which behavior must satisfy strict temporal constraints. They are more and more used in daily live and are often apart of critical applications. They are generally characterized by complex interactions with their environment whose time constraint's violation could cause serious consequences; so, safety is an important property to hold. The conception of such systems needs to develop methods and tools making it possible to describe accurately their behaviors (specification), in order to prove their correctness (analysis).

Among real time specifications, we can quote Time Petri nets [4]. This model is very popular in the discrete event systems and industrial communities as it allows to model real-time systems in a simple and elegant way. A TPN (*Timed Petri Net*) [4] is a Petri net wherein a time interval $[tmin, tmax]$ is associated with each transition, expressing thus the interval within which a transition has to fire once enabled. The simulation and the analysis of general and quantitative properties of a system modeled by a TPN requires the construction of its reachability graph. However, if the semantics is well defined for *safe* time Petri nets[1], it remains that the standard semantics for *unsafe* time Petri nets is enforced under two different hypotheses : A *monoserver* hypothesis where is it is assumed that a transition can be enabled only once for a given marking even though the latter allows many instances to be enabled [1]; and a *multisever* hypothesis where it is assumed that a transition can be enabled many times by a given marking [2]. Since the last

[1] In a safe Petri net is, the marking does not provide enough tokens to enable a transition more than once.

D. Ślęzak et al. (Eds.): ASEA 2009, CCIS 59, pp. 42–49, 2009.

hypothesis is very complex to work out (as it may yield an infinity of clocks, thus impeding seriously the analysis of the model), already defined methods and tools have mainly considered a monoserver semantics [5][8][7][6][1][3]. Although the monoserver semantics is proved to be sound for *Safe* time Petri net, we show in this paper that for unsafe time Petri nets this semantics can lead to inconsistent behaviors when dealing with conflicting transitions. Hence, we propose a new semantics making it possible to manage consistently these situations and to remove the false behaviors that stand in the standard semantics. Moreover, we prove that our semantics is sound when assuming a monoserver hypothesis.

The remainder of this paper is organized as follows: *Section* 2 lays down the syntax and the formal semantics of a TPN. In the *Section* 3, we discuss, through appropriate examples, where stand the inconsistencies in the standard semantics. In the last section, we present our new semantics and we prove its soundness.

2 Time Petri Net

Time Petri Nets [4] have been widely used to model critical systems and protocols, and many approaches and tools have been dedicated to their analyzes [5][8][7][6][1][3]. A TPN is a standard Petri net where a time interval $[tmin, tmax]$ is associated with each transition. A transition t is said to be enabled if the number of tokens in each input place of t satisfies the precondition of the arc linking this place to the transition t. Hence, if t is enabled at time τ, then it can be fired first only after $tmin + \tau$ and no later than after $tmax + \tau$, provided that t remains continuously enabled. More formally, a TPN is defined as given next:

Definition 1. *A TPN (*Time Petri Net*) is defined as a tuple $R = (P, T, M_0, B, F)$, where P and T are two nonempty sets of places and transitions respectively; M_0 is a function called initial marking which associates with each place of the net a number of tokens: $M_0 : P \longrightarrow \mathbb{N}$; B and F are two functions called respectively, backward and forward functions, such that: $B : P \times T \longrightarrow \mathbb{N}$ and $F : P \times T \longrightarrow \mathbb{N}$; FI is a delay interval mapping function which associates with each transition $t \in T$ an interval defined on $\mathbb{Q}^+ \times (\mathbb{Q}^+ \cup \{\infty\})$. Thus, FI gives the time interval within which a transition t can fire: $FI(t) = [EFT(t), LFT(t)]$ with $EFT(t) \leq LFT(t)$. The interval is delimited by an earliest firing time $EFT(t)$, and a latest firing time $LFT(t)$, taking their values on the set of positive rational numbers.*

2.1 Formal Semantics of TPN

Let R be a TPN:

- We call a marking M the mapping that associates with each place of R a number of tokens: $M : P \rightharpoonup \mathbb{N}$.
- A transition $t \in T$ is said to be *enabled* for the marking M, iff the number of tokens in each input place of t is greater or equal to the valuation of the arc linking this place to t, $\forall p \in P, B(p,t) \leq M(p)$; we denote hereafter by $Te(M)$ the set of transitions enabled for M.

– Let M be a marking; two transitions t_i and t_j enabled for M are said to be in conflict for M, if $\exists p \in P, \quad B(p, t_i) + B(p, t_j) > M(p)$.
– We note hereafter by $Conf(M)$ the relation built on $Te(M)^2$ such that $(t_1, t_2) \in Conf(M)$, iff t_1 and t_2 are in conflict for the marking M.

In the standard semantics [1], if a place p contains additional tokens that can be used to enable one or more transitions in the future, only the number of tokens reported in the arc connected to p is considered. The remaining tokens will be used for firing next transitions. This hypothesis is called a *monoserver semantics*. Hence only one instance of an enabled transition is considered for each marking and therefore only one clock is associated with each enabled transition. The selection of the instance follows next policy:

– The oldest instance of the transition among those enabled is considered.
– If different instances have the same age, then the instance that is not in conflict with an other transition is promoted.

The semantics can be extended so that all the enabled instances of a same transition are considered for a same marking [2]. In this case a multiserver hypothesis is considered and the number of clocks become potentially infinite.

The formal semantics of a *TPN* that assumes a monoserver hypothesis is given next:

Definition 2. *The semantics of a TPN is defined by the transition system* $ST = (\Sigma, e_0, \rightarrow)$, *such that :*

– Σ *is the set of accessible states; each state* $e \in \Sigma$ *is a tuple* (M, V), *where* M *is a marking, and* V *is the function that associates with each enabled transition* t *its dynamic firing constraints* $V(t) = [x(t), y(t)]$.
– $e_0 = (M_0, V_0)$ *is the initial state, where* $V_0(t) = [EFT(t), LFT(t)]$.
– $\rightarrow \in \Sigma \times (T \times \mathbb{Q}^+) \times \Sigma$ *is the transition relation between states, such that:*
$((M, V), (\delta, t_f), (M^\uparrow, V^\uparrow)) \in \rightarrow$, *iff*
(1) $t_f \in Te(M)$.
(2) $\exists \delta \in \mathbb{Q}^+, \; x(t_f) \leq \delta \leq \underset{\forall t \in Te(M)}{MIN} \; y(t)$
such that:
– - $\forall p \in P, \; M^\uparrow(p) := M(p) - B(p, t_f) + F(p, t_f)$.
- *if* t *is newly enabled* $t \in New(M^\uparrow) \qquad V^\uparrow(t) := [EFT(t), \; LFT(t)]$
- *if* t *is persistent* $t \notin New(M^\uparrow) \qquad V^\uparrow(t) := [MAX(0, \; x(t) - \delta), \; y(t) - \delta]$

Where $New(M^\uparrow)$ *denotes the set of transitions newly enabled for* $M^\uparrow$. *A newly enabled transition is* t_f *if it is enabled for* $M^\uparrow$, *or that which is enabled for* $M^\uparrow$ *but not for* M, *or that which is different from* t_f *and enabled for* $M^\uparrow$ *and* M *and is in conflict with* t_f *for the marking* M, *namely* $(t, t_f) \in Conf(M)$. *Otherwise, an enabled transition which does not belong to* $New(M^\uparrow)$ *is said to be persistent.*

A transition t_f can be fired at the relative date δ from the state $e = (M, V)$ if t_f is *enabled* for the marking M; if the time can progress with δ, such that the lower bound $x(t_f)$ is reached without overtaking any upper bound of another enabled transition. After firing t_f the new state $e^\uparrow = (M^\uparrow, V^\uparrow)$ is obtained by :

- consuming a number of tokens in each t_f-input place p (given by $B(p, t_f)$), and then by producing a number of tokens in each t_f-output place p (given by $F(p, t_f)$);
- assigning to each persistent enabled transition its last firing interval shifted with the firing time of t_f. However, a newly enabled transition is assigned its static firing interval.

3 Discussion

Let us discuss through some examples the semantics presented in $Definition$ 2. In the *safe* net of *Fig 1.a*, we have $M_0 : \{p \rightarrow 1\}$ and hence $Te(M_0) = \{t_1, t_2\}$. We notice that t_1 and t_2 are in conflict for M_0, which means that firing one of them will disable the other. However, only t_1 can fire since the time can not progress to reach the lower bound of t_2. After firing t_1, the token in p will be consumed (thus disabling both transitions), and a new one will be produced, thus enabling again t_1 and t_2. Hence the transitions t_1 and t_2 are newly enabled after firing t_1.

In the *unsafe* net of *Fig 1.b*, the transitions t_1 and t_2 are enabled but not in conflict for the initial marking $M_0 : \{p \rightarrow 2\}$. Actually, as we have two tokens in the place p, t_1 and t_2 are twice enabled each. However the monoserver semantics considers only one instance for each enabled transition; that which avoids, if possible, conflicts with other enabled transitions. In this case, firing t_1 to reach the marking $M' : \{p \rightarrow 2\}$ will disable only t_1 because it is the fired transition; the transition t_1 becomes then newly enabled for M'. Regarding the transition t_2, two instances are enabled: the oldest one enabled by the first token created in p; and the instance newly enabled by the new token created after firing t_1. Therefore, the oldest instance is considered and hence t_2 is persistent. Furthermore, t_1 and t_2 are not in conflict for M' since their elected instances have not been enabled by the same token.

However, this semantics, as defined in [1], may lead to incorrect behaviors in some cases. To evidence this statement, let us consider the net of *Fig.2.a*.

Initially, we notice that t_1, t_2 and t_3 are enabled for the marking $M_0 : \{p_0 \rightarrow 1, p_1 \rightarrow 1\}$ and t_2 and t_3 are in conflict for M_0. So after firing the transition t_1 the token in the place p_0 is consumed and a new one is produced in the place p_1 to reach the marking $M' : \{p_0 \rightarrow 0, p_1 \rightarrow 2\}$. According to the standard semantics t_2 and t_3 are enabled for the marking $M\prime$ and are persistent

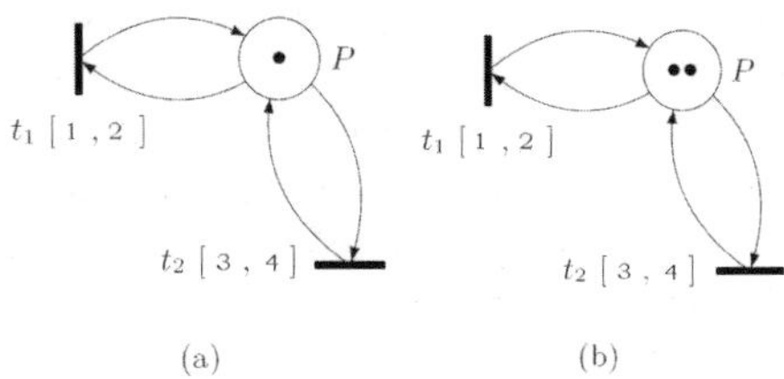

Fig. 1. $TPN's$ with conflicted transitions

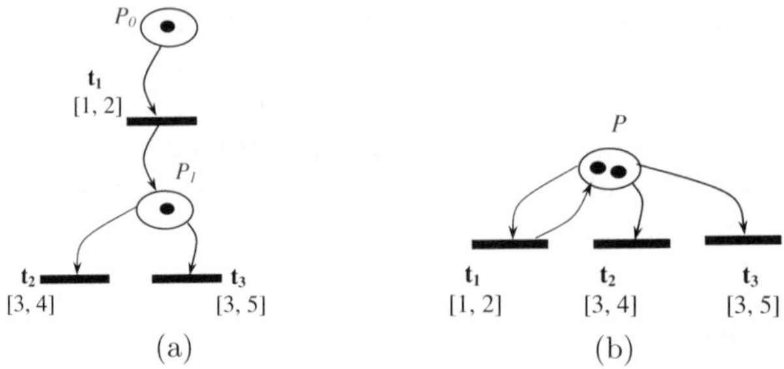

Fig. 2. $TPN's$ with inconsistent standard semantics

since both are not in conflict with t_1 for M_0. However, they are considered as not in conflict for $M\prime$ whereas they are for M_0. There stands the incoherence of the standard semantics, if it admits that t_2 and t_3 are not in conflict for $M\prime$, then normally one of the two transitions has to be newly enabled since the additional token in p_1 is created when reaching M'. Actually, t_2 and t_3 must be in conflict in $M\prime$ because this semantics considers the oldest enabled instance of both transitions, namely those enabled for M_0. These instances are persistent in $M\prime$ and still remain in conflict for the first token created in p_1 that has enabled them.

Hence, if we apply the standard semantics, as given in $Definition.2$, the firing of t_2 from $M\prime$, for instance, keeps t_3 enabled and persistent for the new marking $M" : \{p_0 \to 0, p_1 \to 1\}$ while t_2 is considered as newly enabled. This leads to a false behavior because the firing of t_2 must disable t_3; hence both transitions should stand as newly enabled in $M"$.

An other example of a false behavior induced by this semantics is depicted by the net of $Fig.2.b$. We have the transitions t_1, t_2 and t_3 which are enabled initially for $M_0 : \{p \to 2\}$. If we consider the transitions two by two, we find out that they are not in conflict for M_0, but if we consider all three transitions together we admit that at least two of them must be in conflict for a same token. At this stage, it is not false to consider two transitions as not in conflict because the additional token in p can be used to enable the other transition; thus removing the conflict. However the semantics becomes inconsistent after firing t_1: there we reach the marking $M' : \{p \to 2\}$ where t_1 is considered as newly enabled while t_2 and t_3 as persistent. One of the two tokens located in p has been consumed and a new one is produced; the latter is that which newly enables t_1 whereas the oldest token is that which keeps t_2 and t_3 persistent. Hence all three transitions are considered mistakenly as not in conflict for M', since it is obvious that the persistent instances of t_2 and t_3 are in conflict[2] for $M\prime$, whereas they should not be in conflict with the newly enabled instance of the transition t_1. Therefore, firing t_2 should disable t_3 to reach the marking $M" : \{p \to 1\}$ where t_2 and t_3 become newly enabled, whereas t_1 stands as persistent.

[2] The instances that are not in conflict for M_0 have been disabled by firing t_1. Only those which are in conflict for M_0 are persistent in M_1.

As we can imagine the construction of the graph basing on $Definition.2$ may lead to incorrect behaviors in presence of conflicted transitions. This is due to the fact that the definition of a TPN state, as given in [1], can not preserve the status of conflicted transitions as long as the firing process is going head. To fix the problem, we have to extend the definition of a state to the relation $Conf$ and to set up thoroughly when transitions become conflicting. For this effect, the next section lays down a new semantics for a TPN that we prove to be sound when dealing with conflicting transitions.

4 A Sound Time Petri Net Semantics

The next definition puts forward a new semantics for TPN when assuming a monoserver hypothesis.

Definition 3. *The new semantics of a TPN is defined by the transition system $ST = (\Sigma, e_0, \rightarrow)$, such that:*

- *Σ is the set of accessible states; each state $e \in \Sigma$ is a tuple $(M, V, Conf)$,*
- *$e_0 = (M_0, V_0, Conf_0)$ is the initial state, such that M_0 and V_0 are defined as in Definition 2. and $Conf_0$ is a relation built on $Te(M_0)^2$ as follows:*
  $\forall(t,t') \in Te(M_0)^2$, $(t,t') \in Conf_0$, iff $\exists p \in P, \quad B(p,t) + B(p,t') > M_0(p)$
- *$\rightarrow \in \Sigma \times (T \times \mathbb{Q}^+) \times \Sigma$ is the transition relation between states, such that:*
  $((M,V,Conf),(\delta,t_f),(M^\uparrow,V^\uparrow,Conf^\uparrow)) \in \rightarrow$, iff $\exists \delta \in \mathbb{Q}^+$,
  (1) $t_f \in Te(M)$.
  (2) $x(t_f) \leq \delta \leq \underset{\forall t \in Te(M)}{MIN} \; y(t)$

  such that:
- *$M^\uparrow$ and $V^\uparrow$ are computed as defined in $Definition.2$.*
- *$Conf^\uparrow$ is computed as follows:*
  $\forall(t,t') \in Te(M^\uparrow)^2$, $(t,t') \in Conf^\uparrow$, iff

$$\begin{cases} t \in New(M^\uparrow) \wedge \exists p \in P, \quad B(p,t) + B(p,t') > M^\uparrow(p) & or \\ \left((t,t') \notin New(M^\uparrow)^2\right) \wedge ((t,t') \in Conf) & or \\ \left((t,t') \notin New(M^\uparrow)^2\right) \wedge ((t,t') \notin Conf) \wedge \exists p \in P, B(p,t_f) + B(p,t) + B(p,t') > M(p) \end{cases}$$

The last definition allows to fix TPN semantics to handle conflicted transitions. Therefore, if at least one transition is newly enabled for the new marking we should check whether the available number of tokens needed to enable both transitions is not coming short regarding the current marking. Further, if two conflicted transitions still remain enabled after firing t_f, then they stand in conflict in the accessible states as long as they will not have been disabled in the run. However, if two transitions are not in conflict before firing t_f, but are in conflict when removing the tokens needed by t_f to fire, then they will become in conflict after firing t_f, providing that they remain persistent. However, we should prove now that our semantics remain sound for any state of the graph, namely that the monoserver hypothesis is satisfied for any state.

Theorem 1. *The TPN semantics defined in Definition.3 is sound when assuming a monoserver hypothesis.*

Proof. Let $ST = (\Sigma, e_0, \rightarrow)$ be a transition system obtained as defined in *Definition.3*. It is obvious that the initial state e_0 is sound. We should prove therefore that for any state $e = (M, V, Conf)$ of Σ, if e is sound then firing t_f from $e = (M, V, Conf)$ yields a state $e^{\uparrow} = (M^{\uparrow}, V^{\uparrow}, Conf^{\uparrow})$ which is also sound, namely we have to prove that:

1. For any persistent transition t enabled for $M^{\uparrow}$, the oldest instance among those possible is promoted.
2. For any transition t enabled for $M^{\uparrow}$, if they are different instances of t having the same age, the one which avoids conflict with other transitions is promoted.

Let us prove these clauses:

1. If e is sound, then t satisfies the clause 1. If t is persistent in $e^{\uparrow}$ then the oldest instance in e is considered in $e^{\uparrow}$. Hence, $e^{\uparrow}$ satisfies (1).
2. We have to prove that the working out the parameter $Conf$, as given in the $Definition$.3, is sound
   (a) Let us assume that the instances of the two enabled transitions t_1 and t_2 are in conflict for M. Note that as e is sound, there is no possibility to elect other instances of the same age that are not in conflict for M. Hence if these instances are persistent in $M^{\uparrow}$ (namely no token for which they are in conflict has been consumed by the firing of t_f), then they remain in conflict for $M^{\uparrow}$. All other instances newly enabled by the new tokens created in $M^{\uparrow}$, even those which are not in conflict for $M^{\uparrow}$, are ignored since they are not as old.
   (b) Let us assume that t_1 is newly enabled for $M^{\uparrow}$, namely all the oldest instances of t_1 have been disabled by the firing of t_f. Therefore, the instance of t_1 which should be considered for $M^{\uparrow}$ is that which is not in conflict with any other enabled transition for $M^{\uparrow}$.
   (c) Let us assume that the instances of the two enabled transitions t_1 and t_2 are not in conflict for M. If two by two, both transitions are not in conflict with t_f, then firing t_f keeps their instances persistent in $M^{\uparrow}$. These instances switch in conflict for $M^{\uparrow}$, if the three transitions taken all together are in conflict for M. Put in other words, firing t_f removes the tokens that have promoted the non conflicting instances of t_1 and t_2 in M; these instances are disabled by the firing of t_f. Therefore, only instances that are in conflict in M are persistent in $M^{\uparrow}$.

Assuming the semantics given in $Definition$.3, the behavior of a TPN can be defined by a timed firing sequence given as a succession of pairs (t_f^i, δ^i). The timed sequence $S^t = ((t_f^1, \delta^1), (t_f^2, \delta^2), .., (t_f^n, \delta^n))$ denotes that t_f^1 is fired after δ^1 time units, then t_f^2 is fired after δ^2 time units and so on, such that t_f^n is fired after an absolute time $\sum_{i=1}^{n} \delta^i$. Because the time is dense, the graph ST is infinite.

Therefore, so that one can analyze the model, we need to compute an abstraction of it that preserves the most important properties. The *symbolig graph* that preserves only the untimed sequences of ST may yield a finite abstraction. However, this contraction may be infinite too when the number of accessible markings is unbounded. As the last property is undecidable for TPN, there is no guarantee to compute a finite graph. However, we deem that the construction of an abstraction of the graph ST can be achieved by applying the state class method as it is has been successfully done when assuming the standard semantics [1].

5 Conclusion

We discussed in this paper the consistency of time Petri net semantics when assuming a monoserver hypothesis. We showed that for unsafe nets, the standard semantics may yield false behaviors in presence of conflicting transitions. To tackle this issue, we have proposed a new semantics that removes these incoherences by managing accurately the status of enabled transitions. We proved that our semantics is sound when assuming a monoserver hypothesis. Further work will lead us to propose an algorithm to compute efficiently the state class graph of a TPN basing on our semantics.

References

1. Berthomieu, B., Diaz, M.: Modeling and verification of time dependant systems using Time Petri Nets. IEEE Transactions on Software Engineering 17(3), 259–273 (1991)
2. Berthomieu, B.: La méthode des classes d'états pour l'analyse des réseaux temporels. In: Modélisation des Systèmes Réactifs (MSR 2001), Toulouse, France (October 2001), pp. 275–290 (2001) Hermes
3. Boucheneb, H., Rakkay, H.: A More Efficient Time Petri Net State Space Abstraction Useful to Model Checking Timed Linear Properties. Fundam. Inform. 88(4), 469–495 (2008)
4. Merlin, P.: A study of the recoverability of computer system. PHD Thesis Dep. Computer. Science, Univ. California, Irvine (1974)
5. Bérard, B., Cassez, F., Haddad, S., Lime, D., Roux, O.H.: When are Timed Automata weakly timed bisimilar to Time Petri Nets? Theor. Comput. Sci. 403(2-3), 202–220 (2008)
6. Vicario, E.: Static Analysis and Dynamic Steering of Time-Dependent Systems. IEEE Trans. Software Eng. 27(8), 728–748 (2001)
7. TINA Tool, `http://www.laas.fr/tina/`
8. ROMEO TOOL, `http://romeo.rts-software.org`

A Multiple Viewed Interrelated Ontology Model for Holistic Component Specification and Retrieval

Chengpu Li, Xiaodong Liu, and Jessie Kennedy

School of Computing, Edinburgh Napier University, Edinburgh, UK
{c.li,x.liu,j.kennedy}@napier.ac.uk

Abstract. Despite the success that Component-Based Development has achieved so far, component mismatch remains as a major hurdle for wider and smoother component reuse due to the lack of effective and automated approaches to component specification and retrieval. This paper presents a novel ontology-based approach to solve the above problem via holistic, semantic-based and adaptation-aware component specification and retrieval. The Multiple-Viewed and Interrelated Component Specification ontology model (MVICS) provides an ontology based architecture to specify components in a spectrum of perspectives. A semantic-based component retrieval method is then developed and the result of retrieval is presented to CBD engineers in a comprehensive component matching profile. Uniquely, the effect of possible component adaptation is included in the MVICS model and associated component specification and retrieval, which enables a more systematic and holistic view in component specification and selection.

Keywords: component repository, component retrieval, ontology-based component specification, component reuse, adaptation assets, result profile.

1 Introduction

Component-Based Development (CBD) is an approach to developing a software system by assembling and composing already built software components. Numerous advantages of CBD have been identified [3][7][12]. However, at present CBD still fails to reach its full potential due to a few unsolved major hurdles, one of which is the lack of effective and automated methods for holistically and semantically specifying and retrieving components that precisely match users' requirements [8].

The above problem is basically caused by the lack of competent semantic-based component specification/repository and retrieval technologies. Existing approaches failed to specify components at a systematic and complete spectrum of perspectives and utilize such specification in retrieval. Although a few approaches started to use domain model and ontology in component retrieval process, to date it is clear that the ontology in these approaches has too simple and monolithic structure and few relationships to deal with the specification and retrieval of modern components [14]15][16]. Moreover and as part of the consequence, these approaches also failed to rank the found components with accurate relevance rating and clear unsatisfied discrepancy to reuse requirements, all of which provide critical guidelines for user's

D. Ślęzak et al. (Eds.): ASEA 2009, CCIS 59, pp. 50–60, 2009.

decision on component selection and the subsequent component adaptation and integration.

In this paper, a novel ontology-based approach is proposed to achieve holistic and semantic-based component specification and then automatic and precise component retrieval. As a foundation of the approach, a Multiple-Viewed and Interrelated Component Specification ontology model (MVICS) for component specification and repository is first developed. The MVICS model provides an ontology based architecture to specify components in a spectrum of perspectives, it accommodates domain knowledge of CBSE and application domains, and supports ontology evolution to reflect the continuous developments in CBD and components. A semantic-based component retrieval method is then developed based on MVICS model. The results of retrieval include not only the matching components but also accurate relevance rating and unsatisfied discrepancy, which are presented to CBD engineers in a comprehensive component matching profile. Another unique feature of the proposed approach is that the effect of possible component adaptation is included in the MVICS model and associated component specification and retrieval, which enables a more systematic and holistic view in component specification and selection. A prototype tool with an example component repository is built to verify and automate the approach. Extensive user feedbacks have been received based on case studies, which show the approach and tool is effective for the problem.

The reminder of the paper is organized as follows: Section 2 discusses related work with critical analysis. Section 3 introduces the Multiple-Viewed and Interrelated Component Specification ontology model. Section 4 describes the MVICS based holistic component retrieval. Section 5 describes the resultant prototype tool and a case study. Section 6 discusses the results of an initial evaluation of the system from practical use. Finally, section 7 presents the conclusion and future work.

2 Related Work

Existing component description and retrieval approaches can be classified into two types: traditional and ontology-based. The traditional approaches include keyword searching [8], faceted classification [10][13], signature matching [17] and behavioral matching [5][18]. Traditional approaches are not efficient, and suffer from lower recall and precision. Recall is a measure of the completeness of components matching, which can be defined as the proportion of the number of relevant found components to the number of all relevant components in the repository. Precision is a measure of the accuracy of component matching, which can be defined as the ratio of the number of retrieved relevant components to the number of the all retrieved components [13]. The traditional approaches are rather limited in accommodating semantics of user queries and domain knowledge. To solve this problem, ontology is thus introduced to help understand the semantics of components. The typical work include Pahl [11], Sugumaran [14], Liu [8], Yao [15], Yen [4][15].

To summarize, although ontology-based technologies have been used in component specification and retrieval, existing approaches have the following limitations: i) ontology in existing approaches has too simple and/or monolithic architecture and few relationships and consequently incapable for a holistic specification of components, in particular large and complex ones; ii) the gauge of relevance in component retrieval is too simple, inaccurate and only based on incomplete factors; iii) the evolution of the component specification ontology is not considered; iv) the impact of component adaptation is not included as an integral part of component specification and retrieval.

3 Multiple-Viewed Interrelated Component Specification Ontology Model (MVICS)

A holistic ontology model of component specification will provide the foundation for effective semantic reasoning in the component retrieval and improve substantially the precision of component retrieval. The MVICS ontology model has a pyramid architecture, which contains four facets: *function model, intrinsic model, context model* and *meta-relationship model,* as shown in Figure 1. Each of the four models specifies one perspective of a component and as a whole they construct a complete spectrum of semantic-based component specification. All the four models are ontology-based, and are extracted from the analysis of CBSE knowledge and have extension slots for specific application domains.

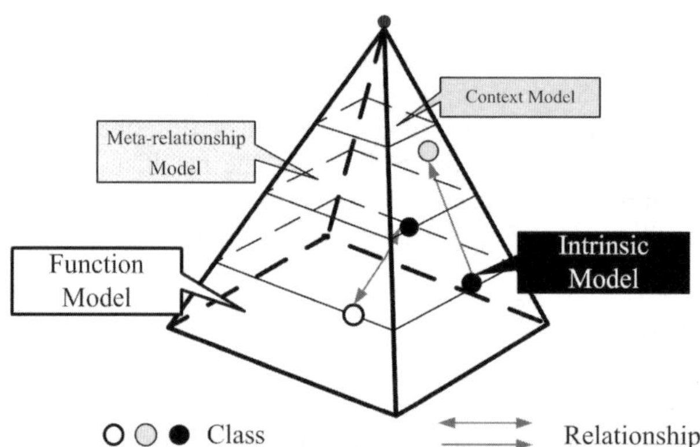

Fig. 1. Multiple-Viewed and Interrelated Component Specification Ontology Model

3.1 Intrinsic Model

The intrinsic model specifies the information of a component which is essential but irrelevant with functionality and quality features of the component, e.g. its name, type, and applicable software engineering phases. In the proposed approach, such information is defined as "intrinsic information" of the component. A taxonomy of the intrinsic information is developed, which includes attributes such as *component name, component vender, component price, component version, component type.* These attributes are then further modeled in levels of sub-attributes. The intrinsic attributes are finally modeled as classes in the intrinsic ontology model. Among these classes, two types of relationships are used to show the links between the classes in different layers. *isA* relationship is used to describe super- and sub-class links between component types. *isAttributeof* defines the value set of an attribute of a class in the ontology model, e.g., *component vender* class is linked with a set of venders under the "*isVenderof*" relationship.

3.2 Function Model

The function model specifies the functionality and quality of service of components. Functions are performed by components which represent fundamental characteristics of software, and a component provides specific functionality or carries out a specific task in a particular business domain. As an ontological model, the top level classes include *function type*, *component domain* and *QoS*. Due to the classes overlap between different domains, the subclasses of the function type are defined in detail and are classified without any overlap, such as *data conversion*, *data entry, data validation* and so forth. The way to link the classes is the same as intrinsic model. *isAttributeof* is used to connect classes which are used to describe a sort of component attribute such as *component function* and *component domain*. Some of these classes link to instances directly, but some of them have large tree type architecture of subclass, sub subclass and so forth. In this sub model, *isA* is used to link the classes and its subclass.

3.3 Context Model

The context model is used to represent the reuse context information of the components, including but not limited to the application environment, hardware and software platform, required resources and possible dependency with other components. The top level classes consist of *operating system, component container, hardware requirement* and *software requirement*. The context model is built in the same way as above two models, i.e., using *isA* to build ontology hierarchies of class *operating system* and class *component container,* and using *isAttributeof* to specify the value set of the attributes of the classes of *hardware requirement* and *software requirement*.

3.4 Meta-relationship Model

Meta-relationship model provides a semantic description of the relationships among the classes in different facets (sub-models) of MVICS. Four types of relationships are identified, namely *Matching Propagation Relationship*, *Conditional Matching Propagation Relationship, Matching Negation Relationship* and *Supersedure Relationship*. Let's define a relationship as $A \rightarrow B$, where A and B are classes in different facets of the MVCIS model. The above four relationships are then defined as follows:

Matching Propagation Relationship

$A \xrightarrow{Pro} B$, which reads as the matching propagates from A to B. It means that if A satisfies the requirement of a component search then B and all its subclasses will satisfy the requirement as well. In component retrieval, such a relationship will enable all the components under class B and its subclasses to be part of the result components for a user query that is matched by class A. The impact on the search path of this relationship is given in part a) of Figure 2. When the search engine identifies class A as a match with the user search keyword K_1, it will continue to search for result components in the subclasses of A, and at the same time also identify class B as a match. It

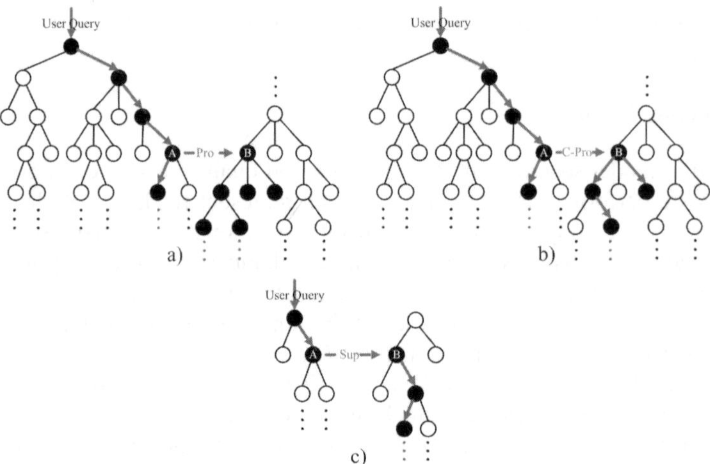

Fig. 2. The impact on search path: a) Matching Propagation Relationship; b) Conditional Matching Propagation Relationship; and c) Supersedure Relationship

would not continue the search in subclasses of *B*, because all the subclasses of *B* are deemed as matching.

Conditional Matching Propagation Relationship
$A \xrightarrow{C\text{-}Pro} B$ (*attri*=*V*), which reads as the matching propagates from *A* to *B* on the condition that value of attribute *attri* is *V*. In MVICS, $A \xrightarrow{C\text{-}Pro} B$ (*attri*=*V*) means that if *A* satisfies the requirement of a component search then *B* and its subclasses may satisfy the requirement if their attribute *attri* has value *V*. In component retrieval, the relationship enables that the components under class *B* are part of the result components for a user query that is matched by class *A,* if their *attri* has value *V*. This relationship will impact on the search path as follows: when the search engine identifies class *A* as a match with a user search keyword K_1, it will continue to search for result components in the subclasses of *A*, and at the same time search *B* and its subclasses on the condition of *attri*=*V*, as shown in b) of Figure 2.

Matching Negation Relationship
$A \xrightarrow{Neg} B$, which reads as the matching with *A* implies not matching with B. In MVICS, this relationship means that if a result component (C_1) is obtained by a keyword matching with class *A*, then C_1 is not the result component obtained by another keyword matching with class *B*. This relationship deals with problems caused by the incompatible requirements in a user query. When user input several keywords, class *A* and class *B*, which are matched with two different keywords respectively, may have Matching Negation Relationship, i.e., a result component can not belong to both classes simultaneously. To tackle this problem, the user query can be treated as two groups of keywords. One group consists of the keyword matched with class *A*, the other group consists of the keyword matched with class *B*.

Supersedure Relationship
$A \xrightarrow{Sup} B$ reads as the matching of A is superseded by that of B. In MVICS, Supersedure Relationship means that if the content of class B has higher priority to the content of class A, then the result components obtained by matching A will be replaced by the result components obtained by matching B. This relationship provides the following impact on the search path, as shown in c) of Figure 2: when the search engine identifies A as a match with a user search keyword K_1, it will stop searching in the subclasses of A, but turn to search from B and its subclasses.

All the above four sub component specification ontology models are defined in OWL. These OWL documents can be seen as the paths that connect user queries and result components.

4 Holistic and Precise Component Retrieval

4.1 Class Weight Calculation Method

Weight of Class (*Wc*) is defined as the foundation for calculating the precision of result components. In each sub-model of MVICS, every class is given a weight to calculate the relevance of each search result. The rules of weight assignment are: i) In one facet, the lower a layer is, the heavier weight its classes have; ii) In different facets, classes at the same depth in the function model are heavier than those in the intrinsic model and the context model. The weight assignment rules are formally defined as follows:

$$Wc = (1+x)^n \tag{1}$$

where n is the level of the layer in which the class locates, $x = 0.5$ if the class belongs to the function model, $x = 0.3$ if the class belongs to the intrinsic model, $x = 0.2$ if the class belongs to the context model. The weight of a search path (*Wp*) is the sum of the weight of the classes included in it.

4.2 Retrieval Algorithm

Based on MVICS, a search algorithm was developed. This algorithm accepts composite search conditions with multiple keywords linked with logic connectors. It recognizes the keywords with ‘and’ as a group of requirements, which are then searched together. Those keywords linked with ‘or’ are considered as two different search requirements, which are then searched one after the other. To correspond with the MVICS model in which component specifications are classified into three aspects, the keywords of a user query are also divided into three groups: Function Keywords (*FK*), Intrinsic Keywords (*IK*), and Context Keywords (*CK*).

The search engine will then search the three groups of keywords in the MVICS OWL documents one by one, even though the value of keywords in any group may be ‘Null’. Meanwhile, it will record the search path of every keyword from the result class to top class and then calculate the path weight by summing up every class weight in this path. The search engine will record the components that link to the result class.

4.3 Precision Calculation Method

After retrieval, a set of records is obtained for each keyword, which includes the result component name, the search path and its weight. The match precision of a result component (*Pc*) is calculated with the following unified formula:

$$Pc = \frac{\sum_{r=1}^{a} WpFK_r}{\sum_{t=1}^{i} WpFK_t} \times 0.5 + \frac{\sum_{r=1}^{b} WpIK_r}{\sum_{t=1}^{j} WpIK_t} \times 0.3 + \frac{\sum_{r=1}^{d} WpCK_r}{\sum_{t=1}^{n} WpCK_t} \times 0.2 \quad (2)$$

The numerators in the formula represent the path weight of the result components that partially match with the keywords in each facet, and the denominator represents the path weight of those perfectly matched.

4.4 Adaptive Component Matching

Component adaptation is a popular means to alter the functionality and quality features of selected components [1][2]. The proposed approach accommodates the impact of adaptation in the specification and selection of matching components. This unique feature will allow a more systematic and holistic view in component specification and selection. We call those components whose function and QoS may vary via the application of adaptation assets "adaptive components". In MVICS, the adaptive components are linked to a class via an adaptation method or assets if the component becomes relevant to that class after adaptation with that method or asset. These adaptation methods and assets are defined as classes or instances in MVICS. The retrieval path is then recorded as an adaptive path, in contrast to the direct path, i.e. without adaptation.

The specification of adaptive components in MVICS and the retrieval algorithm take into account the adaptation effects, the adaptation methods/assets, and the effort associated with the adaptation.

4.5 Search Result Profile

In contrast to most existing approaches, which present to the user the name and precision of the result component, our approach provides a holistic profile of the result component to help the user make the best decision in component selection.

The profile shows the matching result in each sub ontology model and the corresponding adaptation information. The profile consists of: *i)* the result component name; *ii)* the overall precision of the component match, including the precision with component adaptation, and the precision without adaptation; *iii)* the match results in sub models: function model, intrinsic model, and context model; *iv)* the associated adaptation method or asset and its incurred effort.

5 The Prototype Tool and Case Study

A prototype tool with an example component repository is built to verify and automate the approach. In this tool, the MVICS ontology is implemented in OWL. The function, intrinsic and context sub-models are implemented in three different OWL files. The relationships in the meta-relationship model are implemented as links between classes in the above OWL files.

The tool has a simple user interface (Figure 3 a)), where the user can fill the query into text area, and the keywords of the user query are classified by different facets of MVCIS in background process of the tool. The search engine will search the OWL documents first and then connect to the components. The search result is shown in the component match profile which we mentioned before. Furthermore, this tool also provides SQL database search by filling component names directly or clicking the component names in the match profile.

The tool and approach have been applied to a case study. As an example from the case study, a user wants to search for a component with the following requirements:

Function: *File Transfer and Encryption*
Component Type: *.NET Class, and WPF*
Component Platform: *Window XP and Window Vista*
Component Container: *Microsoft Visual Basic 2008, IBM VisualAge, and Oracle JDeveloper*

The search engine searched the keywords one by one in function, intrinsic and context sub-model of MVICS. In the same time, the relationships between the sub-models add more semantics, e.g., the class *IBM VisualAge* in the Context model has a Matching Propagation Relationship with *Java Class* and *C++ Class*, which are subclasses of *Component Type* in the intrinsic model. This implies that components which run on IBM VisualAge should have a component type of Java or C++. This indicates that the result component obtained while the user query is matched. This indicates that the result component obtained while the user query is matched class *Java class* or *C++ class* are also the result components when the user search keyword is *IBM VisualAge*.

The names of the result components and their precisions are displayed in the right pane of the interface, as shown in a) of Figure 3. When a result component is highlighted, its search result profile will pop up, as shown in b) of Figure 3. The upper part of the profile illustrates the result component name and the overall precision of the component search. The first and the second number indicate the precision after the component adaptation, more than one adaptation path (AP_i) is possible.

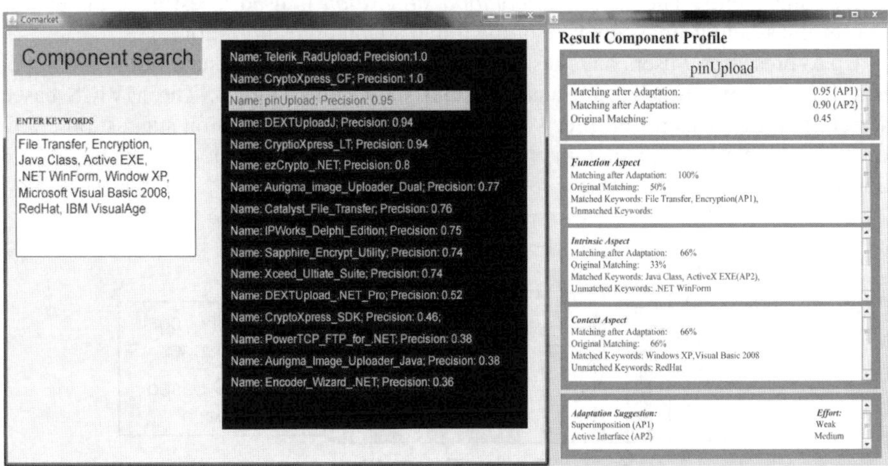

Fig. 3. a) The UI of the MVICS prototype tool b) The Result Component Profile

The third number (0.45) indicates the original match precision. The three output areas in the middle indicate the match results in Function, Intrinsic and Context model. The text area at the bottom of the profile shows the adaptation method(s) or asset(s) used in the component search and their efforts to apply. By clicking the component name in the profile, the complete specification of the component will be presented.

6 Validation

To test the validity of the approach, a project website was built. The prototype tool was transformed to a web application and published on the site. 300 components (acutely component specifications) were selected from several component sale websites, e.g. Componentsources, Componentplanet and Allfreeware with possible adaptation assets developed, and then were populated into a corresponding component repository. Software engineers, researchers and amateurs are able to use the application and comment on it via a questionnaire. The above users followed the following steps to evaluate the MVICS tool against traditional component retrieval approaches:

1) Proposing requirements based on the exiting component specifications and selecting suitable result component (R_1) manually.
2) Using the MVCIS based prototype tool to search the same requirements and receive a set of search results (R_2).
3) Using the SQL database search tool which is supported by traditional approaches to search the requirements again and record another set of results (R_3).
4) Comparing R_2 and R_3 with R_1 respectively, and then fill out a questionnaire regarding how well each search performed according the four criteria: Recall (R), Precision (P), Result Display (RD), and Adaptation Suggestion (AS).

Recall and *precision*, as motioned in section 2, are crucial dimensions to judge the effectiveness of component retrieval. The *result display* is to indicate the degree of user satisfaction with the completeness, clearness and usefulness of the display of the result components. The criteria *adaptation suggestion* is used to estimate the degree of usefulness and user acceptance of the found adaptation suggestion.

Up to present, 69 users have tested the tool in practice. The results of these component retrieval experiments are analyzed and shown in Figure 4. The MVICS based search tool improves recall, precision, result display, and adaptation suggestion effectively at a rather large extend, in particular on the criteria of result display and adaptation suggestion.

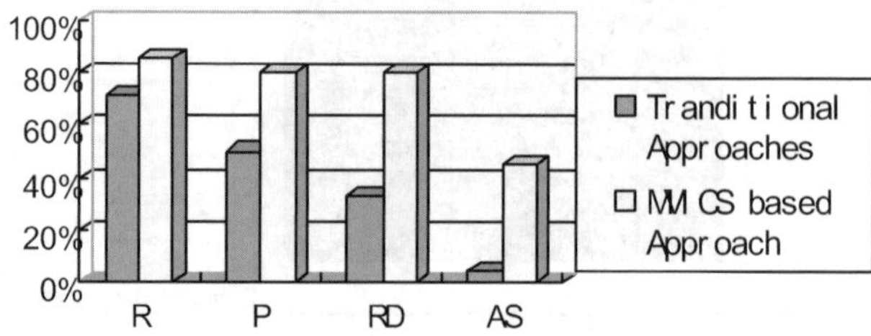

Fig. 4. The level of satisfaction of MVICS prototype tool and traditional search tools

7 Conclusions

The objectives of the research are to develop an ontology-based approach to solving the component mismatch problem via holistic, semantic-based and adaptation-aware component specification and retrieval. Our literature investigation has shown that the proposed approach has novel contributions to the research area and similar work has not been done.

The MVICS ontology model has a novel architecture. It gets rid of the over-complication problem in traditional monolithic ontology, because it has a set of highly coherent and relatively loosely coupled sub-models. The inter-relationships among the classes in different sub-models ensure a holistic view in component specification and selection, and improve the retrieval precision and efficiency. Another contribution is that search result is presented in a profile which consists of a spectrum of elements instead of simply the components and their relevance. Unlike existing approaches, in the MVICS approach component adaptation is considered as an integral part of component specification and selection. Available adaptation assets and methods such as wrappers and aspects are defined in MVICS. During component selection, appropriate adaptation assets/methods will be selected or suggested against the unsatisfied discrepancy.

Our case studies and user feedbacks have shown that the approach and the tool are promising in their ability and capability to solve the identified drawbacks in component specification and selection. In the future, we could improve the MVICS approach by extending MVICS to popular application domains. i.e., add more domain specific attributes to improve its capability, and by developing a mechanism for MVICS model evolution.

References

1. Bosch, J.: Superimposition: A Component Adaptation Technique. Information and Software Technology 41(5) (1999)
2. Bracciali, A., Brogi, A., Canal, C.: A formal approach to component adaptation. Journal of Systems and Software 74(1), 45–54 (2005)
3. Due, R.: The Economics of Component-Based Development. Information Systems Management 17(1) (2000)
4. Gao, T., MA, H., Yen, I.-L., Khan, L., Bastani, F.: A Repository for Component-Based Embedded Software Development. International Journal of Software Engineering and Knowledge Engineering 16(4), 523–552 (2006)
5. Hall, J.: Generalized Behavior-Based Retrieval. In: Proceedings of the Fifteenth International Conference on Software Engineering, pp. 371–380 (1993)
6. Han, J.: A Comprehensive Interface Definition Framework for Software Components. In: Proceedings of Asia-Pacific Software Engineering Conference APSEC 1998, p. 110 (1998)
7. Kim, Y., Stohr, E.A.: Software Reuse: Survey and Research Directions. Journal of Management Information Systems 14(4), 113–147 (1998)
8. Liu, Q., Jin, X., Long, Y.: Research on Ontology-based Representation and Retrieval of Components. In: 8th ACIS International Conference, vol. 1, pp. 494–499 (2007)

9. Mili, A., Mili, R., Mittermeir, R.: Storing and Retrieving Software Components: A Refinement- Based System. IEEE Transactions on Software Engineering 23(7), 445–460 (1997)
10. Ostertag, E., Hendler, J., Prieto-Diaz, R., Braum, C.: Computing Similarity in a Reuse Library System: An AI-based Approach. ACM Transactions on Software Engineering and Methodology 1(3), 205–228 (1992)
11. Pahl, C.: An ontology for software component matching. International J. Software Tools Technology Transfer 9, 169–178 (2006)
12. Patrizio, A.: The new developer portals. Information Week (799) (August 2000)
13. Prieto-Diaz, R., Freeman, P.: Classifying Software for Reuse. IEEE Software 4(1), 6–16 (1987)
14. Sugumaran, V., Storey, V.: A Semantic-Based Approach to Component Retrieval. The Database for Advances in Information Systems, Volna 34(3) (2003)
15. Yao, H., Letha, E.: Towards A Semantic-based Approach for Software Reusable Component Classification and Retrieval. ACMSE 2004 (2004)
16. Yen, I., Goluguri, J., et al.: A Component-based Approach for Embedded Software Development. In: Proceedings of the 5th IEEE International Symposium on Object-Oriented Real-Time Distributed Computing. ISORC, p. 0402 (2002)
17. Zaremski, A.M., Wing, M.: Signature Matching: A Key to Reuse. Software Engineering Notes 18(5), 182–190 (1993)
18. Zaremski, A.M., Wing, J.M.: Specification Matching of Software Components. Software Engineering Notes 20(4), 6–17 (1995)

A Conflict-Based Model for Problem-Oriented Software Engineering and Its Applications Solved by Dimension Change and Use of Intermediary

Jung Suk Hyun[1] and Chan Jung Park[2,*]

[1] Dept. of Management Information Systems, Jeju National University,
1 Ara-dong Jeju-si Jeju-do, 690-756, South Korea
[2] Dept. of Computer Education, Jeju National University,
1 Ara-dong Jeju-si Jeju-do, 690-756, South Korea
{jshyun,cjpark}@jejunu.ac.kr

Abstract. In order to develop desirable software, defining problems is the most important among all software development activities. In this paper, we propose a model, namely Butterfly model, which defines various kinds of problems by means of contradiction relationships. Our Butterfly model is based on TRIZ and is useful for creative problem solving. By using the proposed model, we review 4 problems and then, solve the problems by eliminating the contradictory relationships. All the problems in this paper have the same features in some aspects. All can be defined as a problem having a trade-off between 'volume' and 'efficiency'. In other words, we can find some problem frames. Finally, we apply the dimension change principle and the use of intermediary principle of TRIZ to solve the problems.

Keywords: TRIZ, Problem Frame, Problem-Oriented Software Engineering, Contradiction-based Problem Solving, Creative Problem Solving.

1 Introduction

Traditionally, the software development process is defined as a set of phases such as requirement analysis, design, implementation, testing, and maintenance. Among them, the requirement analysis is critical to a software development. During the requirement analysis phase, software engineers try to define a solution that can be described with functional characteristics or non-functional characteristics. Thus, the traditional methods for software development can be regarded as solution-oriented methods [1].

On the other hand, problem-oriented development (POD) approach is domain-independent [2]. Especially, problem-oriented software engineering (POSE) tries to provide a generic structure that can combine the results of different development processes [3]. If there is a model for describing problems with their requirements, solution domains, and environmental factors formally, we can solve various kinds of problems easily.

* Corresponding Author.

D. Ślęzak et al. (Eds.): ASEA 2009, CCIS 59, pp. 61–69, 2009.

In this paper, we propose a model, namely the Butterfly model, which defines problems with contradictions by a diagram. And then, by using TRIZ tools, we review 4 problems and find their solution principles (or problem frames [4]). The problems belong to various kinds of areas such as marketing, computer hardware, and software. In addition, we already knew about their solutions. However, we redefine the problems with our model and apply the same rule to the problems. We found some interesting things that if problems have a trade-off between *the large volumes of data* vs. *the efficiency of process*, then they can be solved with the same way. The same way means dimension change and the use of intermediary.

The rest of this paper is organized as follows. In Section 2, we introduce the theory of TRIZ. And then, we review a few software engineering problems with TRIZ. In Section 3, we propose a model, namely Butterfly model, which defines a problem as a contradictory relationship. And then, we give an example and its solution to explain our model. In Section 4, we define 3 problems with our model and then, give their solution by applying the same method. Finally, we conclude our paper in Section 5.

2 TRIZ and Software Engineering

2.1 Contradictions

Before we describe TRIZ, we define what contradictions are. A contradiction consists of an incompatibility. It occurs when two or more things have different characteristics which form the inversions of each other [5][6]. A contradiction occurs between A and B because if A is getting better, then B is getting worse and vice versa. Contradictions can be classified into two groups as shown in Figure 1. One occurs between two useful functions and the other occurs between a useful function and a harmful function. For example, if speed increases, then safety decreases and the amount of fuel consumption increase. While the flexibility of a programming language is high, the efficiency of the programming language is low.

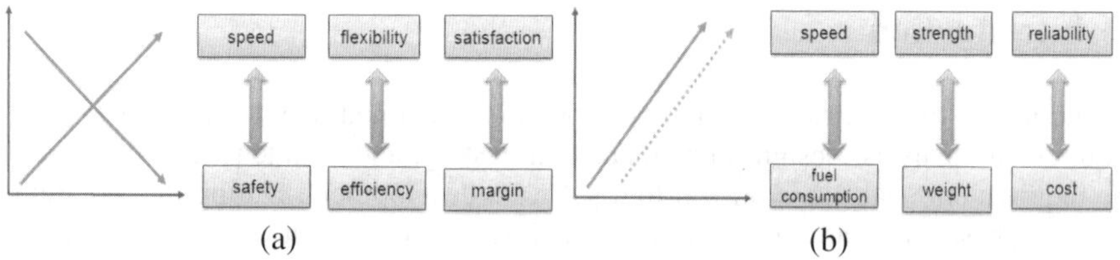

Fig. 1. Two Kinds of Contradictions

In TRIZ, there is another way to divide contradictions. There are two types of contradictions: physical contradictions and technical contradictions. The physical contradictions are the situations where the same component must satisfy mutually exclusive demands to its physical state. For example, the wings of an airplane should be wide and narrow. While flying, the wings of the airplane should be narrow for high speed. While taking off or landing, the wings of the airplane should be wide for safety. Due to the same reason, the wheels of the airplane should exist and not exist. These are physical contradictions. The technical contradictions are the situations when a useful action simultaneously causes a harmful effect. For example, if a highly secure software causes the less performance of a system. And, if a programming language is highly flexible, then it causes low efficiency.

Many engineers think that there is no way to have them both at the same time. Especially, in case of technical contradictions, many people hardly believe that the technical contradictions can be solved. However, in TRIZ, a technical contradiction is redefined as a physical contradiction and is solved by various kinds of TRIZ tools. Contradictions are the same as requirements in software engineering. Thus, if we eliminate (solve) some contradictions, we can satisfy some requirements in software engineering. That's why contradictions are important.

2.2 TRIZ

TRIZ is the acronym for "Theory of Inventive Problem Solving". It was developed by Genrich Altschuller and his colleagues [7]. Comparing with traditional method, TRIZ can reduce the number of trial-and-errors by abstraction and analogical reasoning when engineers solve problems as shown in Figure 2. In other words, given a specific problem to be solved, the problem is transformed into more generalized form. There are many tools in TRIZ to solve problems. Figure 3 shows the basic process of problem solving with TRIZ [9]. In this paper, we use Ideal Final Result (IFR) and 40 principles when solving problems. IFR is an ideal solution of an engineering design problem [5]. And, 40 principles are the principles for inventions such as segmentation, extracting, and so on [9].

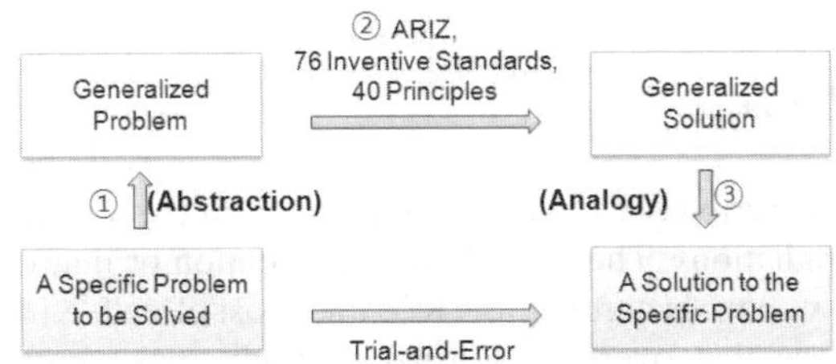

Fig. 2. Basic Process of Problem Solving with TRIZ [6][8]

2.3 Software Engineering Problems with TRIZ

From the beginning of 2000, people have adopted TRIZ to IT problems. Especially, in Japan, several professionals have reviewed software engineering topics with TRIZ [10] [11]. The purposes of the research were to apply TRIZ to software development problems and to extend the application of TRIZ into software engineering [10].

The first attempt was the concept of structured programming [10]. In this research [10], the contradiction between goto and goto-less was redefined, and the structured programming was given as an alternative. The structured programming can be driven by TRIZ Inventive principle 1 (segmentation), principle 7 (nesting), and principle 16 (partial or excessive actions) [10].

The second attempt was the stepwise refinement and the Jackson method [12]. In the Jackson method, a program structure of a problem is driven from its data structures of inputs and outputs [11][12]. In this research [11], the author found out TRIZ-related principles. Among them, the Inventive principles, 35 (parameter change), 40 (composite materials), and 5 (merging) are used for the Jackson method. The parameter change means to change the degree of flexibility and the composite materials means to change a homogeneous component to composite components [11]. The merging means that multiple operations or functions work together in time [11].

From these researches, we found that the principles and knowledge in TRIZ can be applied to software engineering and vice versa. If a similar problem was already solved in software engineering but not in TRIZ, we can apply the same method to TRIZ. In the same manner, we can apply the same method to software engineering when a similar problem was already solved in TRIZ.

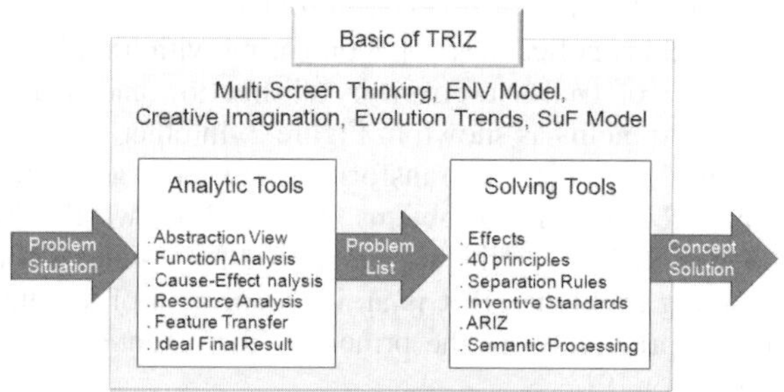

Fig. 3. Basic Process of Problem Solving with TRIZ [9]

3 Butterfly Model

In this Section, we describe our model for defining a problem. Our model is based on diagrams and contradictions. The root of almost invention or innovation is in a solved contradiction of a system. According to TRIZ, the most effective inventive solution of a problem is the one that overcomes some contradictions. A contradiction occurs when we improve one parameter of a system which affects the same or other parameters of the system. A problem solver has to extract a contradiction from the problem and fit into the solution for the problem [5][6]. Usually a problem is not solved if its contradiction is not overcome. Now, we define our model by using an example, namely a cart problem.

Figure 4 shows the structure of our model. The given example is not related to software engineering directly, but gives some hints when we solve the problems in software engineering. In addition, this example is related to the problems described in the next section. In this example, in order to earn money, a retail store wants customers to buy a lot of goods at a time. Thus, the owner tries to prepare bigger shopping baskets to achieve his/her goal. However, if the baskets become bigger, the customers feel heavy. For customers, smaller baskets would be better than heavier baskets. A technical contradiction occurs. The procedure to solve a problem is given as follows:

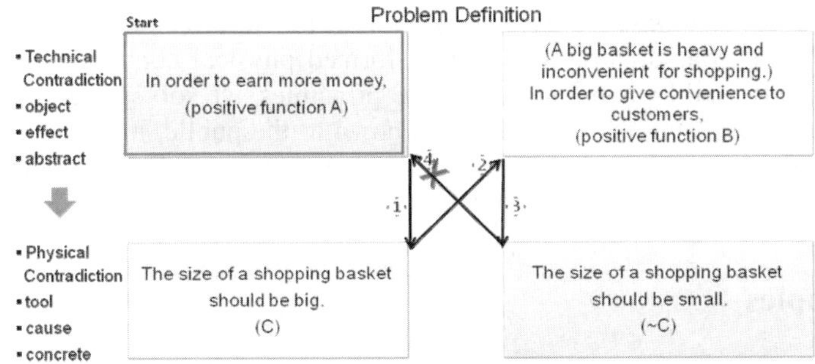

Fig. 4. The Butterfly Model

① We firstly *extract a technical contradiction* between speed and capacity.

② And then, we *transform this contradiction into a physical contradiction* as shown in Figure 4. When we assume that a technical contradiction is an object, its physical contradiction can be a tool.

③ Next, we *find an IFR* as an analytic process. An IFR should satisfy any combination of technical contradictions and physical contradictions at the same time. For simplicity, in our model we make an IFR as combination of one of a technical contradiction and the other side of a physical contradiction. For example, an IFR can be $A \wedge \sim C$ in Figure 4. At this time, you can make the other IFR. The other IFR is $B \wedge C$ in Figure 4.

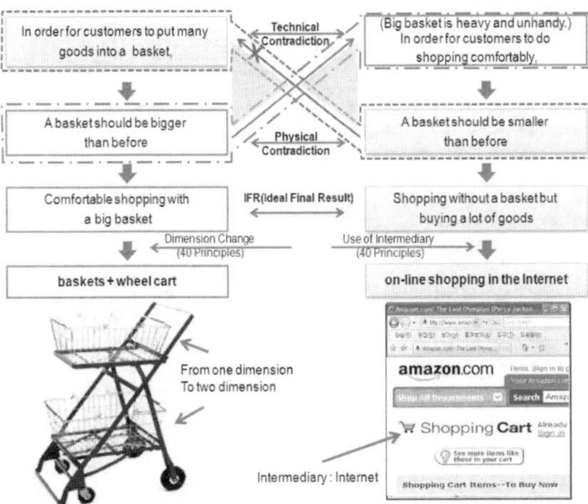

Fig. 5. A shopping cart problem is described by our Butterfly Model and its solution is given. When we find a solution we apply TRIZ tools such as 40 principles, ARIZ, and so on. We can solve this problem by using Invention principle 17 (Dimension change) and 24 (Intermediary). Sylvan Goldman's shopping cart [13] can be a solution (the dimension change). And online shopping like amazon.com can be another solution (the intermediary).

④ Next, we can *find a concept solution* by using 40 principles. Figure 5 shows a technical contradiction and its transformed physical contradiction. We made two IFRs and by using them with 40 principles, we solved the problem. Even though the solutions were already known to the public, it is important to find out the principles 'dimension change' and 'intermediary' worked together when we solve the above problem.

4 Examples

In this section, we describe 3 problems interpreted by our Butterfly Model. All the problems of this paper have a technical contradiction between the large volume of data and the efficiency of process.

The first problem is ***a hard disk problem***. Many hard disk vendors want to make small size hard disks with a huge amount of capacity. In order to increase the capacity of a hard disk, engineers should reduce the size of particle for containing a bit. However, if the size is reduced too small, the disk header cannot read data exactly. Thus, a technical contradiction occurs. In our model, we transform the technical contradiction to the physical contradiction shown in Figure 6. We also made two IFRs and by using them with 40 principles, we found out the solution principles. Like the shopping cart problem, we found out that the principles 'dimension change' and 'intermediary' were also used together in this case.

The second problem is ***QR Code with smart phones***. Recently, since almost everyone has a mobile device such as a cell phone, a smart phone, or a PDA, various kinds

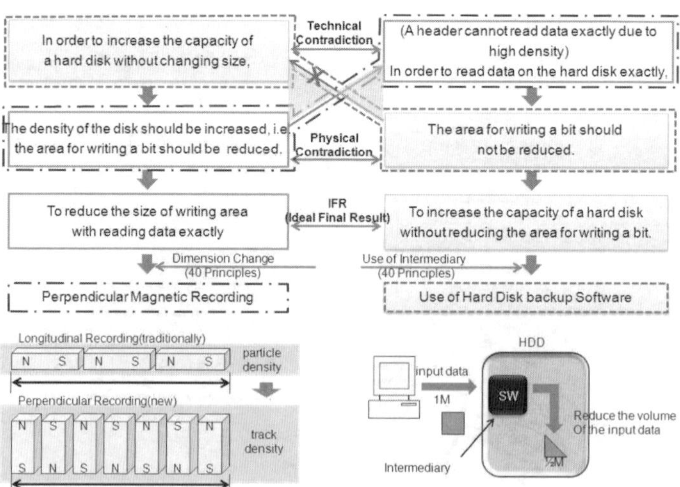

Fig. 6. A hard disk problem. We can also solve this problem by using Invention principle 17 (Dimension change) and 24 (Intermediary). Perpendicular magnetic recording technique can be a solution (the dimension change). And the use of hard disk backup software to reduce the size of original input data can be another solution (the intermediary).

of applications running on the mobile devices have been developed rapidly. In addition, due to the keen competition, in various areas such as education, politics, tourism, and festival as well as industry, the effort for producing fruitful marketing is spread by performing effective publicity[14]. In spite of the diversity of publicity media, the pamphlet, which provides core summarized information, still plays a key role among various media. Recently, the type of pamphlet is changed from off-line to on-line. If off-line and on-line media are combined to provide publicity content, it can influence on successful publicity. QR code is a good intermediary to achieve the above goal. QR code is a two dimensional barcode and it is a quick and efficient *tell me more* mechanism [15][16].

As shown in Figure 7, QR code applications have a technical contradiction: for applications, a large volume of data should be contained in QR code. Thus, the QR code size should be bigger. However, it causes longer decoding time due to the bigger size. In our model, we defined a physical contradiction by using the technical contradiction. And then, we applied the same principles to this problem.

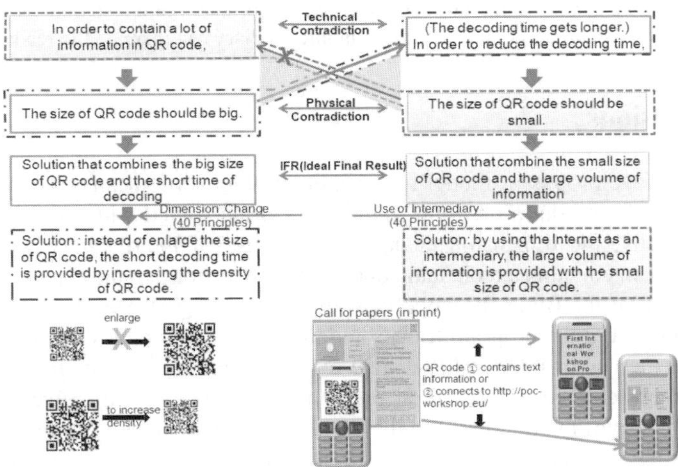

Fig. 7. QR code problem. We can also solve this problem by using Invention principle 17 (Dimension change) and 24 (Intermediary). To increase the density and to use the Internet as an Intermediary are possible solutions.

The last problem is ***the technical contradiction between readability and efficiency of software***. When we develop software, the readability and the efficiency of the software are both important. However, there exists a technical contradiction between them. This problem can be solved with the dimension change principle and the use of intermediary principle in the same manner. For solving this problem, we firstly divide the original software into two things. One is the source code of the software only. The other is the document of the software. Next, we can use functions as the intermediary. The use of functions makes modular programming, and this feature can keep the readability of the software. Figure 8 shows the technical contradiction and its corresponding physical contradictions.

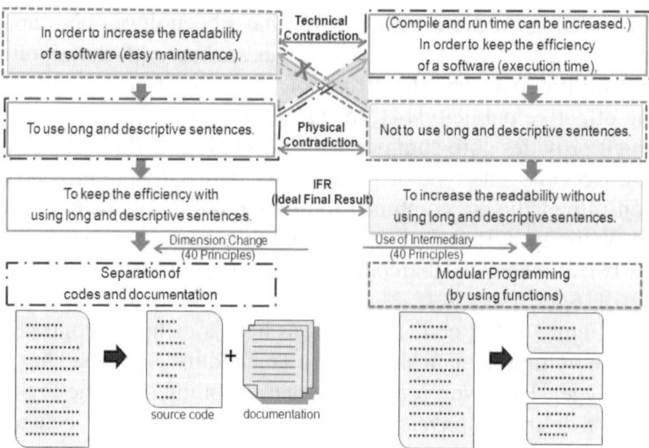

Fig. 8. Readability vs. Efficiency. By using Invention principle 17 (Dimension change) and 24 (Intermediary), we can solve the problem. We divide a problem into a source code + its documentation. Also, the adoption of functions as an intermediary can increase the readability.

5 Conclusions

In this paper, we propose a model for defining problems by means of contradictions. And then, we found out a problem frame that can be solved with TRIZ's 40 principles. Especially, the dimension change and the use of intermediary were adopted when a problem contains a technical contradiction between 'volume' and 'efficiency'. The prototype of the Butterfly model was introduced at [17]. However, there was no consideration about the program frames and the solution principles that the dimension change and the use of intermediary came together. Due to the page limit of a paper, we did not present Steve Job's iPod problem. However, we can solve our solution principle (by use of intermediary) to the problem. Briefly, we can summarize the iPod problem as the contradictions between 'to contain a lot of music in the iPod' vs. 'to reduce the size for comfortable carriage'. Recently, we solve another problem which is similar to the problems of this paper and has no solution yet. We found one solution by using the dimension change. In the near future, we can find another solution that can be solved by the use of intermediary.

References

1. http://poc-workshop.eu/page_1235693775153.html
2. http://www.allconferences.com/conferences/2009/20090311103607/
3. Hall, J., Rapanotti, L., Jackson, M.: Problem Oriented Software Engineering: Solving the Package Router Control Problem. IEEE Transactions on Software Engineering 34(2), 226–241 (2008)
4. Jackson, M.A.: Problem Frames and Software Engineering. Journal of Information and Software Technology 47(14), 903–912 (2005)

5. Fey, V., Rivin, E.: Innovation on Demand: New Product Development Using TRIZ, Cambridge (2005)
6. Savransky, S.D.: Engineering of Creativity: Introduction to TRIZ Methodology of Inventive Problem Solving. CRC Press, Boca Raton (2000)
7. Pala, S., Srikant, A.: TRIZ: A New Framework for Innovation Concepts and Cases, ICFAI Books. The ICFAI University Press (2005)
8. Lee, K.: http://miso.yeskisti.net/C/miso_v.jsp?s_cd=CB&record_no=20899
9. TRIZ center, http://www.trizcenter.co.kr
10. Nakagawa, T.: Software Engineering and TRIZ 1: Structured Programming Reviewed with TRIZ. In: Proceedings of the 7th TRIZCON Conference, Detroit (2005)
11. Nakagawa, T.: Software Engineering and TRIZ 2: Stepwise Refinenemt and the Jackson Method Reviewed with TRIZ. In: Proceedings of the 5th ETRIA Conference, Austria (2005)
12. Jackson, M.A.: http://www.ferg.org/papers/jackson-a_system_development_method.pdf
13. Sylvan Goldman's Shopping Cart, http://realcartu.com/goldman/
14. Park, C., Hyun, J., Kang, J., Kim, M., Park, J., Hong, Y., Oh, J.: U-Pamphlet for Jeju Fire Festival. In: Proceedings of the 1st Asia TRIZ Conference (2009)
15. Mediaseek, http://www.camreader.jp/english/pdf/SymbolDecoder_E.pdf
16. http://www.qrme.co.uk/qr-code-news/qr-code-applications.html
17. Hyun, J., Park, C.: Butterfly Bridge Model as a Simplified ARIZ. In: Proceedings of the 4th Japan TRIZ Conference (2008)

Requirements Engineering Problems and Practices in Software Companies: An Industrial Survey

Badariah Solemon[1], Shamsul Sahibuddin[2], and Abdul Azim Abd Ghani[3]

[1] College of IT, Universiti Tenaga Nasional, Km 7 Jalan Kajang-Puchong, 43009 Kajang, Selangor, Malaysia
badariah@uniten.edu.my
[2] Universiti Teknologi Malaysia, Kuala Lumpur, Malaysia
shamsul@utm.my
[3] Universiti Putra Malaysia, Selangor, Malaysia
azim@fsktm.upm.edu.my

Abstract. This paper presents about a study conducted to investigate the current state of Requirements Engineering (RE) problems and practices amongst the software development companies in Malaysia. The main objective of the study is to determine areas in RE process that should be addressed in future research in order to improve the process. Information required for the study was obtained through a survey, questionnaires distributed to project managers and software developers who are working at various software development companies in the country. Results show that software companies in this study are still facing great challenges in getting their requirements right due to organizational and technical factors. Also, we found out that high-maturity ratings do not generally correlate better performance and do not indicate effective, high-maturity practices especially to the RE practices. The findings imply that we must consider both human and technical problems, with extra care should be given to the technical issues and all the RE practices in our future research which is to re-build a specialized RE process improvement model.

Keywords: Requirements Engineering (RE), RE problems, RE state-of-the-practice.

1 Introduction

System and software development projects have been plagued with problems since the 1960s [1]. Since then, Requirements Engineering (RE) has become one of the central research topics in the field of software engineering. Although progress in RE has been painfully slow with software development projects continue to experienced problems associated with RE [2], research effort in the area continues to be done. These research are mainly motivated by the list of advantages expected to be brought about by the successful implementation of an improved RE process. Review made on recent related literatures discovered at least two research that study the state of RE problems experienced by organizations in different parts of the world. The first research by Sarah Beecham et al. [3],[4] studied the RE problems in twelve software

D. Ślęzak et al. (Eds.): ASEA 2009, CCIS 59, pp. 70–77, 2009.

companies in UK. Their main findings suggest that most of the requirements problems experienced in the companies in their study were organizational. Also, results of the study suggested that the higher the maturity level of the company the less frequent are the requirements problems. The second research performed similar study covering eleven Australian software companies [5]. In this study, however, it concluded that while companies with immature RE process experience technical problems; companies with mature RE process cited more organizational problems. We also uncover several field surveys of RE practices. RE practices, especially those good ones, can "either reduces the cost of the development project or increases the quality of the resulting project when used in specific situation" [6]. Research that study the state of RE practice include those in [7],[8],[9],[10]. However, relationships between company's maturity and RE practices are not shown in the research.

Since most of these existing surveys results, which focus at identifying either the RE problems or practices to improve RE process, may not be appropriate to generalize from such a relatively small samples used, it is obviously useful to conduct similar studies, in other part of the world. The new study, however, must be designed carefully to guaranty its highest representativeness. Furthermore, the situation in Malaysia is not quite known as there are not any research done thus far to study both the current state of the RE problems and RE practices in this country. Motivated mainly by the work done by [3],[5], we performed a similar study in Malaysia. The main objective of the study is to determine areas in RE process that should be addressed in order to improve the process.

In the next three sections, the materials and data collection method, the results on valid responses, and the analyses performed to interpret the results of the study are explained.

2 Data Gathering

We used mailed, self-administered questionnaires as our main approach to investigate those RE problems and practices. Questionnaires entitled "A Survey to Investigate the Current Requirements Engineering (RE) Practices and Problems amongst the Software Companies in Malaysia" were distributed to practitioners working at various software development companies in Malaysia. Practitioners in our study refer to project managers and software developers as suggested in [3]. Self-administered questionnaires are chosen mainly because of their suitability to cater our target population, i.e. practitioners who are working at various software development companies located throughout the country, in line with the recommendation made in [11].

2.1 Questionnaire Design

The questionnaire was organized into four main sections: section A, section B, section C and section D. Section A has two parts: part 1 and part 2. Part 1 contains questions that ask for the company profiles of our respondents whilst part 2 contains question that find out the background information of the respondents. Section B contains a list of project problems, organizational and technical RE related problems. Section C aims to find out the respondents' RE practices in a software development project that they have taken part recently. This section lists 82 RE practices which are grouped into 9 key practices: requirements document, requirement elicitation, requirements analysis and negotiation, describing requirements, requirements modeling, requirements verification and validation, requirements management, and other practices. The practices mainly were gathered from literature such as [1], [2], [3], [5], [12], [13].

2.2 Population Determination

In this study, a software development company is defined, following definition by Sison et al.[14], as "a for-profit organization whose main business is the development of software for customers external to the organization. Excluded in this definition is IT departments that cater primarily to the needs of the organization of which they are part". Our main source of information to estimate the number of software development companies in Malaysia is the Multimedia Super Corridor (MSC) portal [15] where a list of Information and Communication (ICT) related companies awarded the MSC Malaysia status is publicly available. This portal is considered the most reliable source of information in estimating the number of software development companies in Malaysia and referred by a number of research such as [16],[17],[18],[19]. Based on the company information in the portal, the population of our study is 1193 and we randomly selected 500 of the software development companies.

2.3 Data Collection

Prior to posting the questionnaires, pilot studies were conducted to assess respondents' level of understanding, level of difficulty in responding and level of relevance to subject area. We also used the pilot studies to assess the level of time commitment required to complete the questionnaire which was estimated to be 30 minutes. The pilot studies involved five software development companies which were chosen from a convenience sampling. Changes were made to the questionnaires as results of the feedback received.

This survey data was collected through February and March 2008. A total of 113 responses were received, making up 23% response rate. However, only 64 responses are complete and considered valid for analysis. Most are excluded mainly due to incomplete answers. Despite the low valid response rate (13%), we decided to proceed with analyzing the responses. According to Lethbridge et al. [11], a low response rate of about 5% would already be sufficient for an exploratory study of this kind. Furthermore, the 13% response rate is consistent with the exploratory study done in [14] on software practices in five ASEAN countries (Malaysia, Philippines, Singapore, Thailand and Vietnam) reported in 2006.

3 Results

In the following sections, we present the analyses performed on the information gathered from 64 valid responses.

3.1 Demographic of Respondents

The survey participants include 73.4% companies which are "100% locally owned" type of company. Interestingly, about half of these companies (54.7%) employed less than 19 IT staffs only. About 18.8% (12) companies are appraised with various levels of the Software Engineering Institute's Capability Maturity Model Integration (CMMI) and 6 (6.25%) companies in the survey are currently in the process of getting the CMMI-DEV appraisals. About one third of the respondents are project managers (35.9%) and another one third (37.6%) are business analyst, software engineer, and consultant. The remaining 26.5% respondents who chose "Others" range from senior software process engineer to high-level managers. The respondents' experiences in handling RE are mainly between 1 to 5 years (45.3%) and some have had been handling RE between 5 to 10 years (40.6%).

3.2 Size of RE Problems

Following classification by [3], [4], we classify problems experienced related to RE into two: organizational-based and RE process-based. Research conducted by [1], [3] show that 63% of RE problems can be attributed to organizational factors that are external to the RE process where almost all organizational-based RE problems are human-based. Our results show that 60% of RE problems experienced by the companies in our study can be attributed to factors inherent within the RE process rather than to factors external to the RE process. This suggests an opposite pattern in term of RE problems experienced by companies in Malaysia and companies in the study by [3], [4]. Our results also show that organizational issues contributing to the RE problems are quite diverse, similar in data collected by [1], [3]. However, our data suggested a few problems have different pattern of supportive response. Also, the results suggests that about half of the problems can be contributed by lack of customer and user communication problem, lack of developer communication problem, and poor time and resources allocations issues. We also discovered that almost 60% RE process-based problems are related to changing requirements, incomplete requirements, ambiguous requirements and poor user understanding.

3.3 RE Problems Pattern and Company Maturity

A finer grained analysis was done to view the relationship between these problems and the maturity level of the companies. Unlike the study in [3] that performed self-assessment activity to the companies' maturity prior execution of the focus groups, we based our study only on the formal CMMI appraisal. For analysis purpose, we did a two-by-two cross tabulation between the CMMI appraised companies and the RE problems. Then, we performed the Fisher's exact test [20] to see the significant difference between these two types of companies. As shown in Table 1, the resulting p-values, greater than 0.05 for all the RE problems excluding Item 2.12, indicate there is no statistical difference (at the $\propto = 0.05$ level) in the critical and supportive responses between these companies. For Item 2.12, the p value 0.048 indicates there is statistical difference in the critical and supportive responses between the two types of companies. We suspect that this is related to the companies having been formally appraised at various CMMI maturity levels. It is likely that the appraisal process has made everyone very aware of the companies' state of RE processes.

Table 1. The p-values of RE problems

RE problem	Fisher's exact test Exact Sig (2-sided)
Organizational-based:	
2.4 Lack of customer and user communication	1.000
2.5 Lack of developer communication	0.117
2.6 Lack of training	1.000
2.7 Inappropriate skills	0.531
2.8 Lack of defined responsibility	0.537
2.9 Unstable workforce (low staff retention)	0.754
2.10 Poor time and resource allocations	0.750
RE process-based:	
2.11 Complexity of application	0.345
2.12 Undefined RE process	0.048
2.13 the actual requirements	0.514
2.14 Poor user understanding	0.484
2.15 Incomplete requirements	1.000
2.16 Inconsistent (changing) requirements	0.381
2.17 Inadequate requirements traceability	0.308
2.18 Ambiguous requirements	0.715

4 Top-Ten RE Practices

As described in subsection 2.1, section C of the questionnaire aimed at obtaining information on the current RE practices of the practitioners via the list of 82 items. According to Sommerville and Sawyer [12], there are ten basic practices which are so important that they should be implemented on all organisations at any level of RE process maturity. In our study, we do not measure any RE process maturity level of the companies involved. In the following paragraphs we performed analysis limited to these ten practices.

In section C of the questionnaire, the respondents were required to rate each RE practices according to a different 4-point measurement scales (0 = never, 1 = used at discretion of project manager, 2 = normal used, 3 = standardized). The points of the ten practices by each company in the survey were then calculated based on the score of the four types of the REAIMS assessments [12]. From Fig. 1(a), we can see the typical points obtained by the companies in the study is somewhere between 14.73 and 25.7. Furthermore, we can see that half of the companies score 21 points or less, the most common score is 22 and the range is from 8 to 30 points. We performed a detail analysis of the points scored by two types of companies in the study: companies appraised with CMMI and companies without CMMI appraisal as shown in Fig. 1(b). From Fig. 1(b), we can see that these different groups of companies scored quite differently except the maximum score points. Interestingly, even though typical companies appraised with CMMI score higher points (between 21.18 and 29.32, with most common companies of this kind score full points 30) in the ten practices, these

Statistics

Points		
N	Valid	63
	Missing	1
Mean		20.4286
Median		21.0000
Mode		22.00
Std. Deviation		5.70714
Minimum		8.00
Maximum		30.00

(a)

Statistics

		Points: Companies appraised with CMMI	Companies without CMMI appraisal
N	Valid	12	51
	Missing	0	1
Mean		25.2500	20.7059
Median		25.5000	21.0000
Mode		30.00	22.00
Std. Deviation		4.07040	5.54001
Minimum		19.00	9.00
Maximum		30.00	30.00

(b)

Fig. 1. (a) Points scored (b) Points scored for companies with and without CMMI appraisal

companies still experienced almost all the RE problems as described in the subsection 3.3 and other general project problems as discussed in [23].

5 Discussion

Results in our study show that the pattern of RE problems experienced by software development companies in Malaysia is similar to the findings reported in [5]. However, the result is the opposite from the results reported in [3], [4]. Our results suggest that RE problems experienced by the companies in our study can be attributed more to factors inherent within the RE process rather than to factors external to the RE process. This means problems, such as changing requirements, incomplete requirements, ambiguous requirements, and poor user understanding, are still the challenges faced by the software development companies apart from the common human-based organizational problems. One possible explanation for this pattern probably is because of the ability to adapt to increasingly rapid and unpredictable change is still one of the challenges facing 21st-century organizations as mentioned by Boehm in [21]. These findings imply that we must consider both human and technical problems, with extra care should be given to the technical issues, in re-building a specialized RE process improvement model which is discussed in [22].

Our results also suggest that statistically there is no difference in the RE problems faced by companies appraised with the CMMI and companies without the CMMI appraisal. It is not surprising for the companies without the CMMI appraisal. Points scored for the ten practices indicate that the RE practices are not widely followed. However, it is exciting to know that companies which claimed that they widely followed and checked, at least, the ten practices as part of the companies' quality management process, still experience almost all the RE problems as discussed in the subsection 3.3 and other general project problems in [23]. This finding shows another confirm case where high-maturity ratings do not indicate effective, high-maturity practices as in [24]. However, as further explained by Humphrey in [24], "it is not the appraisal process is faulty or that organizations are dishonest, merely that the maturity framework does not look deeply enough into all organizational practices". This provides justification and motivation to the work described in [22].

6 Conclusion

In this paper, the results of a study done on investigating the current state of RE problems and practices amongst Malaysian practitioners are presented. The study was accomplished through mailed, self-administered questionnaires distributed to 500 sampled software development companies throughout the country. Despite the low response rate (13%) for the complete and valid responses, we decided to proceed with the data analysis. Analyses performed to the valid responses received are then compared with findings from similar studies reported in [3], [4], [5]. Although not all the RE problems patterns in this study are the same, they still indicate that software companies are currently facing great challenges in getting their requirements right due to organizational and technical factors. Also, we found out that high-maturity ratings do not generally correlate better performance and do not indicate effective, high-maturity practices especially to the RE practices. These findings provide justification and right direction to work on enhancing and improving a specialized RE process improvement framework called R-CMM [25] as described in [22] by looking more deeply into all the RE practices.

References

1. Kotonya, G., Sommerville, I.: Requirements Engineering. Processes and Techniques. John Wiley & Sons, Chichester (1997)
2. Young, R.R.: Effective Requirements Practices. Addison-Wesley, Boston (2001)
3. Beecham, S., Hall, T., Rainer, A.: Software Process Improvement Problems in Twelve Software Companies: An Empirical Analysis. Empirical Software Engineering 8(1), 7–42 (2003)
4. Hall, T., Beecham, S., Rainer, A.: Requirements Problems in Twelve Software Companies: An Empirical Analysis. IEEE Proceedings of Software 149(5), 153–160 (2002)
5. Niazi, M., Shastry, S.: Role of Requirements Engineering in Software Development Process: An Empirical Study. In: IEEE INMIC 2003, pp. 402–407 (2003)
6. Davis, A.M., Zowghi, D.: Good Requirements Practices are neither Necessary nor Sufficient. In: Requirements Eng., vol. 11(1-3). Springer-Verlag London Ltd., Heidelberg (2006)
7. El Emam, K., Madhavji, N.H.: A Field Study of Requirements Engineering Practices in Information Systems Development. In: 2nd IEEE International Symposium of Requirements Engineering, pp. 68–80. IEEE Press, New York (1995)
8. Nikula, U., Sajaniemi, J., Kalviainen, H.: A State-of-the-Practice Survey on Requirements Engineering in Small- and Medium-Sized Enterprises. Technical Report. Telecom Business Research Center, Lappeenranta University of Technology, Finland (2000)
9. Damian, D., Zowghi, D., Vaidyanathasamy, L., Pal, Y.: An industrial case study of immediate benefits of requirements engineering process improvement at the Australian Center for Unisys Software. Empirical Software Engineering Journal 9(1-2), 45–75

10. Niell, C.J., Laplante, P.A.: Requirements Engineering: The State of the Practice. IEEE Software, 40–45 (2003)
11. Lethbridge, T.C., Sim, S.E., Singer, J.: Studying Software Engineers: Data Collection Techniques for Software Field Studies. In: Empirical Software Engineering, vol. 10, pp. 311–341. Springer Science + Business Media, Inc., The Netherlands (2005)
12. Sommerville, I., Sawyer, P.: Requirements Engineering. A Good Practice Guide. John Wiley & Sons, Chichester (1997)
13. Hofmann, H.F., Lehner, F.: Requirements Engineering as a Success Factor in Software Projects. IEEE Software, 58–66 (2001)
14. Sison, R., Jarzabek, S., Hock, O.S., Rivepiboon, W., Hai, N.N.: Software Practices in Five ASEAN Countries: An Exploratory Study. In: The 28th International Conference in Software Engineering ICSE 2006, pp. 628–631. ACM, China (2006)
15. MSC Malaysia Status for Companies, `http://www.msc.com.my/cs/company/default.asp` (last accessed 3 March 2008)
16. Aris, H.: Exploring the Potential of Components-Oriented Software Development Application. In: UNISCON, pp. 355–366. Springer, Heidelberg (2009)
17. Seta, F., Onishi, T., Kidokoro, T.: Study about Locational Tendency of IT Companies in City Centers and Suburbs – Case Study of Malaysia. In: International Symposium on Urban Planning, pp. 257–266 (2001)
18. Raja Kassim, R.S., Kassim, E.S.: Knowledge Management Practices amongst MSC Status Companies in Malaysia: A Survey. International Journal of Knowledge, Culture and Change Management 5(9), 63–70 (2000)
19. Schreiner, K.: Malaysia's Silicon Valley Moves Forward. IEEE Software, 126–130 (1999)
20. Keith, M., Bower, M.S.: When to Use Fisher's Exact Test. American Society for Quality. Six Sigma Forum Magazine 2(4), 35–37 (2003)
21. Boehm, B.W.: Making a Difference in the Software Century. In: Computer, pp. 32–38. IEEE Computer Society, Los Alamitos (2008)
22. Solemon, B., Sahibuddin, S., Abd Ghani, A.A.: Re-building the RE Process Improvement Model. In: Accepted in the 16th Asia-Pacific Software Engineering Conference (APSEC 2009), Penang, Malaysia (2009)
23. Solemon, B., Sahibuddin, S., Abd Ghani, A.A.: An Exploratory Study of Requirements Engineering Practices in Malaysia. In: 4th Malaysian Software Engineering Conference, Universiti Malaysia Terengganu (UMT), Terengganu (2008)
24. Chrissis, M.B., Konrad, M., Shrum, S.: CMMI. Guidelines for Process Integration and Product Improvement, 2nd edn. Addison Wesley, Upper Saddle River (2007)
25. Beecham, S., Hall, T., Rainer, A.: Defining a Requirements Process Improvement Model. Software Quality Journal 13, 247–279 (2005)

A Formal Methodology for Semantics and Time Consistency Checking of UML Dynamic Diagrams

Youcef Hammal

LSI Laboratory, Department of Computer Science, USTHB University
B.P. 32, El-Alia, 16111, Bab-Ezzouar, Algiers, Algeria
hammal@lsi-usthb.dz

Abstract. The consistency checking of designed UML artifacts for real-time systems is a difficult task because of the imprecise dynamic semantics of UML diagrams and the expressiveness gap between them. In this setting, this paper proposes a formal methodology for semantical and time consistency checking between the behavioral models of StateCharts and scenario-based specifications.

1 Introduction

UML notations for scenarios are called sequence diagrams [8] which show the intended interactions between the system components and their relationships, including the messages that may be dispatched among them. Hence, the sequence diagram of any system can be seen as its specification model depicting expected interactions between its components whereas the related state diagram focuses more on internal behaviors of components and thus can be considered as the implementation model of the system under design. However, the key issue to support the design of reliable software systems is to prove that sequence diagrams are faithfully implemented into StateCharts which correctly realize the intended interactions. In other terms, designers have to check the consistency of UML dynamic models composed of state and sequence diagrams.

In this paper, we aim to formally check wether a real-time design behaves according to a collection of timed sequence diagrams and to test the absence of time deadlocks. That is, time constraints as specified on the interaction diagrams would be fulfilled by the statecharts enhanced with appropriate time information related to implementation platforms. Therefore, we propose to project the problem onto an suitable formalism level which is able to handle real-time constraints. A further restriction is imposed by the fact that practical verification is only feasible if tool support is available. Thus, we selected timed automata as our basic behavioral formalism [1].

Since UML diagrams lack formal semantics we make use of the formalization method defined in [4] to translate sequence diagrams into transition systems which depict all the allowed paths of the system interactions. This paper extends this approach and discusses the suited way to properly extract time and duration observations and constraints and map them into timing constraints on the derived specification graphs.

Similarly, we extend the formalization method defined in [3] which translates state diagrams into an enhanced time Petri nets. We propose as well to translate the time annotations on the arcs of StateCharts into time constraints on the transitions of the reachability graph we have to build from our derived Petri nets.

D. Ślęzak et al. (Eds.): ASEA 2009, CCIS 59, pp. 78–85, 2009.

Hence, our method can be used for consistency checking of dynamic diagrams of the system under design and for testing the absence of time deadlocks in derived graphs. For this purpose, we propose to merge these graphs by means of a synchronization product and then to proceed to prove that all intended interactions of the sequence diagram are realizable by the state diagram especially when considering time constraints.

In contrast to our approach supporting both semantics and time consistency checking, authors of [6] use weak bisimulation to compare untimed π-expressions depicting whole dynamic diagrams. Likewise, in [10] entire class diagrams, sequence diagrams, and StateCharts are transformed into description logic for checking consistency between different versions of these diagrams. Also, the approach of [2] verifies the consistency of sequence and state diagrams using dynamic meta-modeling (DMM) rules and [7] uses an algorithmic approach to achieve this checking. In [5], the authors propose to translate the UML diagrams to its equivalent XMI documents and then to check the consistency of these XMI documents. Unfortunately, a comprehensive mapping of UML diagrams using such formalisms can result in very verbose and cumbersome specifications. Also, the main drawback of such translations is the use of only subsets of UML state machines and exclusion of several suitable concepts for reactive systems.

The remainder of the paper is organized as follows: Section 2 discusses the method to translate timing annotations on sequence diagrams into time constraints on their behavioral graphs. Likewise, section 3 addresses the mapping of timing annotations of StateCharts into suitable time constraints on their state space graphs. Hence, section 4 presents a combination operation over timed graphs and shows how to check their time and semantical consistency. Finally, a conclusion is given in section 5.

2 Sequence Diagrams as an Interactions Specification Language

To define timing constraints in standard UML, time annotations can be attached at the beginning and the end of a message arrow. These labels can be used to specify the minimum and the maximum time gap between two marked points in the diagram or to define the duration of a periodic sequence. For instance, the sequence diagram in figure 1 shows how time and timing notations may be applied to describe time observation and timing constraints. The "Train" sends to the "Barrier Control" a signal "approach" which should be dispatched within d units of time. The "Barrier Control" has either to send back to the "train" the message "stop" within the time interval $\{0..3 * d\}$ or let the train enter the secured area.

Our approach consists in extracting time formulas over logical clocks from the time annotations in sequence diagrams. We then adorn with these timing constraints the related nodes and transitions of derived behavioral graphs in a similar way to timed automata [1]. The clocks are variables provided with valuations expressing time progress and the time constraints over these valuations state the conditions to let the control stays in or leaves a node by taking on some transition as explained below.

Definition 1. *Let χ be a finite set of clocks ranging over $\mathcal{R}^{\geq 0}$. The set $\Psi(\chi)$ of timing constraints on χ is defined by the following syntax: $\phi ::= true \mid x \ll c \mid x - y \ll c \mid not(\phi) \mid \phi \wedge \phi \mid \phi \vee \phi$ where $x, y \in \chi$, $c \in \mathcal{R}^{\geq 0}$ and $\ll \in \{<, \leq\}$.*

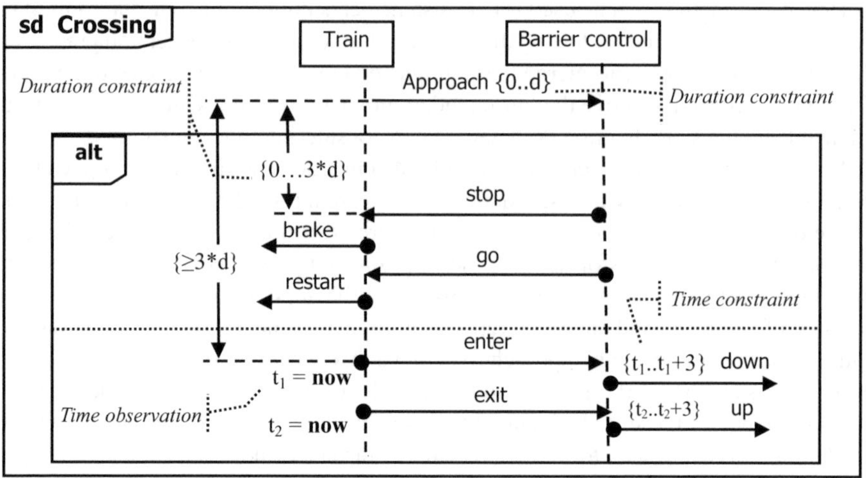

Fig. 1. Sequence Diagram with Timing Annotations

We enhance untimed graphs with timing constrains by adding three mappings I, G and Z as follows: The timed version of an automaton $\mathcal{A} =< Q, \hookrightarrow, \Sigma, q_0 >$ is the graph $\mathcal{A}^{\mathcal{T}} =< \mathcal{A}, \chi, I, G, Z >$ where: χ : is a finite set of clocks. $I : Q \longrightarrow \Psi(\chi)$, $G : T \longrightarrow \Psi(\chi)$,and $Z : T \longrightarrow 2^{\chi}$. The mapping I assigns to each node of the automaton an *activity condition* (i.e., *invariant*), the mapping G assigns to each transition $(e \in \hookrightarrow)$ a *timing guard* which should be true to let the transition fire, and the mapping Z associates with each transition a set of clocks initializations (see fig.3).

The role of invariants is important. Indeed as time progresses, the values of the clocks increase providing the state satisfies the invariant. For states that do not satisfy the invariant, the progress of time is "stopped". This mechanism allows the specification of hard deadlines: when for some action a deadline specified by the invariant is reached, the continuous flow of time is interrupted. Therefore, the action becomes urgent and it is "forced" to occur if it is enabled. A deadlock status will be thus any timed configuration of the automaton which the related active node has a false activity condition and all its outgoing transitions have false timing guards.

Note that time constraints will help us refine more our specification and discard some forbidden transitions away from the behavioral graphs we could derive from our interaction diagrams. For instance, in fig.3, we notice two forbidden transitions depicted by thick arrows. These ones are implied from the sequence diagram even though we did not intend to specify them but thanks to time constraints that we add as guards we can specify when their occurrences become not allowed.

The addressed issue is how to translate faithfully a time annotation into a time constraint on our behavioral graphs. A first solution is to put the constraint on the node source of the arc labeled with the constrained event as illustrated in fig.3(a). However, that can lead to express more time constraints than what one would specify. Indeed, even if only the event e_1 of fig.3(a) is concerned with the activity condition on S_i the time can not progress once the control reaches this node with some valuation of h_1 which makes the condition $false$. This situation makes urgent not only the performance of e_1 but as well of e_2 even if this action is a delayable one. On the other hand, assigning time constraints on the arcs as in fig.3(b) may also lead to some problems: as the activity conditions on nodes are now $true$ the time can progress until making $false$ the guard of the arc labeled with e_1, thereby disabling this transition although it is a real-time one.

A possible solution can be to infer the invariant of the node S_i from the conjunction of the guards of its outgoing arcs. However, this is only suitable for depicting hard timing constrains leading to time deadlock situations when those constraints are not respected. Furthermore, this solution does not allow us depict soft time constraints with timeout or best effort policies where time progress is always possible. For such cases, when guards of timed actions become false either exception actions may happen or the system has only to continue its execution according to a best effort policy.

Consequently, we adopt a trade-off approach which adorns with invariants only nodes having outgoing arcs with hard real-time constraints. However, a timed action guarded with a timeout action does not require putting on its source node any invariant other than $true$. That is, if the timed action fails to occur within its deadline then the timeout action could always happen. For instance, in fig.3(b), the action e_2 plays the role of an exception handling action which could occur if e_1 is not performed within its deadline. Algorithms to derive time constraints can be adapted from those in [4].

In fig.3(c), we present a fragment of the timed graph related to the sequence diagram of fig.1 combined with that of its StateChart of fig.2 (bringing dashed transitions).

3 StateCharts as Implementation Description Language

As the design of time-critical systems requires the observation of quantitative system aspects, a consensus had emerged that UML 1.x is lacking in quantifiable notion of time. Fortunately, UML has all the requisite mechanisms for addressing these issues through its extensibility faculties, namely timing constructs and stereotypes given in the OMG profile of time specification [9]. In the domain model of this time profile, an event is assumed to occur instantaneously. That is, it takes place at a particular time instant and has no duration. An event occurrence can be associated with a time value relative to some clock to identify the time when it occurred. Such an event is called *timed event* though it may be of any kind (e.g., the sending and receiving of signals, the invocation of an operation). When an event occurs, it may cause a number of stimuli to be generated. To allow modeling of stimuli that have an associated timestamp, the time profile introduces the notion of *timed stimulus* which has at least one associated time value. It is also very useful to have a common abstraction for an action that takes time to complete: a *timed action*. This provides a generic facility for modeling behavior that has a definitive start time and a definitive end time.

Our approach consists in extracting time annotations of the StateChart and translating them into time formulas over logical clocks. Then, it assigns these constraints as guards onto related transitions of the marking graph similarly to timed automata [1].

In our approach we have to enhance our implementation graph $\mathcal{A}_{Impl} =< Q, \hookrightarrow, \Sigma, q_0 >$ by adding three partial mappings I, G and Z as follows:
- $I : Q \longrightarrow \{true\}$, - $G : T \longrightarrow \Psi(H)$, - $Z : T \longrightarrow 2^H$.

The first mapping I assigns always to each node a *true invariant* because at the implementation level, we have to ensure that timed actions will occur within their time intervals. Indeed, time progress can not be stopped as at the specification level to express the situation where some hard timed action should be performed. The second mapping G assigns to each arc a guard if it exists otherwise it assigns *true*. The third mapping Z associates with each transition a set of clocks initializations which may be empty.

For example, fig.2 shows two StateCharts related to the train control system components. We then try to check whether the two components always evolve without leading to irregular situations. The part of the behavioral graph presented in fig.2(c) contains dashed arrows which depict potential actions that are not specified within our sequence diagram of fig.1. Anyway, we give later how to discover such irregular paths when comparing timed behavioral graphs related to state and sequence diagrams.

4 Consistency Checking of Dynamic Diagrams

Given some system under design, we would check that StateCharts of its components fulfill their intended interactions of the sequence diagram by comparing their behavioral graphs (called resp. specification and implementation graphs).

4.1 Consistency Checking of Untimed Graphs

We propose to use a verification approach suited to deal with timed graphs. This approach considers the system properties as a process (i.e., the specification graph) which is combined with the system model (i.e., the implementation graph) by means of the merging operator. Then, the resulting graph has to be bisimilar to the implementation graph. This method amounts to assert that all the computations we can derive from a sequence diagram are also available as prefixes of sequences computed from the related StateChart with preservation of its branching structure too.

First, we give below the definition of the comparison criterion which is the equivalence relation of bisimulation denoted by the symbol $\approx$.

Definition 2. *Let* $\mathcal{A}_i = (Q_i, \hookrightarrow_I, \Sigma, q_0^i)\ |_{i=1,2}$ *be two labeled transition systems. A bisimulation is a symmetric relation* $R \subseteq Q_1 \times Q_2$*, such that for every* $(p, q) \in Q_1 \times Q_2$*,* pRq *if and if:* $\forall a \in \Sigma, \forall p' : p \xrightarrow{a} p'$ *then* $\exists q' : q \xrightarrow{a} q'$ *and* $p'Rq'$.

$\mathcal{A}_1$ *and* $\mathcal{A}_2$ *are bisimilar* $(\mathcal{A}_1 \approx \mathcal{A}_2)$ *if their initial nodes are bisimilar.*

Next, we give the definition of our combination operator between graphs. Let $\mathcal{A}_{Impl}$ be the implementation graph $< Q_{Impl}, \hookrightarrow_{Impl}, \Sigma_{Impl}, q_0^{Impl} >$ issued from the translation of the state diagram of the system and let $\mathcal{A}_{Spec}$ be the specification graph $< Q_{Spec}, \hookrightarrow_{Spec}, \Sigma_{Spec}, q_0^{Spec} >$ issued from the translation of its sequence diagram.

Definition 3. *A synchronization product* $\otimes$ *of two graphs* $\mathcal{A}_{Impl}$ *and* $\mathcal{A}_{Spec}$ *yields a new transition system* $\mathcal{A} =< Q, \hookrightarrow, \Sigma, q_0 >$ *such that:* $Q = Q_{Impl} \times Q_{Spec}$ *with* $q_0 = (q_0^{Impl}, q_0^{Spec})$*,* $\Sigma = \Sigma_{Impl}$*,* $\hookrightarrow = \{(p_1, p_2) \xrightarrow{a} (q_1, q_2) \mid a \in (\Sigma_{Impl} \cap \Sigma_{Spec}) \wedge (p_1 \xrightarrow{a} q_1) \in \hookrightarrow_{Impl} \wedge (p_2 \xrightarrow{a} q_2) \in \hookrightarrow_{Spec}\} \cup \{(p_1, p_2) \xrightarrow{a} (q_1, p_2) | a \in \Sigma_{Impl} \wedge \exists q_1 \in Q_{Impl} : (p_1 \xrightarrow{a} q_1) \in \hookrightarrow_{Impl} \wedge \nexists q_2 \in Q_{Spec} : (p_2 \xrightarrow{a} q_2) \in \hookrightarrow_{Spec}\}$.

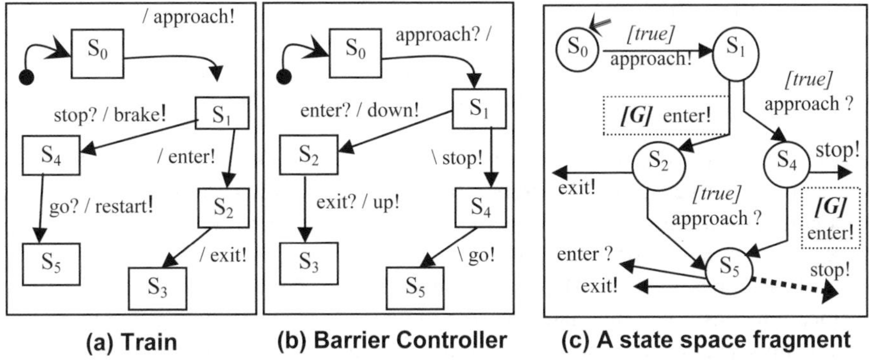

Fig. 2. StateCharts of A Train Control System

Accordingly, if two graphs are able to individually achieve a same action at a point of their evolution, then they have to synchronize its performance in the merged graph. However, when the implementation graph can carry an action which the specification graph does not offer at that point the merged graph is also allowed to perform it because sequence diagram depicts only fragments of possible interactions.

We say that the StateChart of the system Sys *semantically fulfills* the global sequence (or overview interaction) diagram **sd** (denoted $Sys \models$ **sd**) if the synchronization product of their derived graphs is strongly bisimilar to the graph of the system Sys. This means that there is a simulation preorder from the specification graph $\mathcal{A}_{Spec}$ to the implementation graph $\mathcal{A}_{Impl}$. Let the symbol $[\![Sys]\!]$ denote the implementation graph $\mathcal{A}_{Impl}$ of the system and let the symbol $[\![\mathbf{sd}]\!]$ denote its specification graph $\mathcal{A}_{Spec}$.

Definition 4. $Sys \models \textbf{\textit{sd}}$ *iff* $[\![Sys]\!] \otimes [\![\textbf{\textit{sd}}]\!] \approx [\![Sys]\!]$.
Let ***SD*** *be a subset of sequence diagrams.* $Sys \models \textbf{\textit{SD}}$ *iff* $\forall \textbf{\textit{sd}} \in \textbf{\textit{SD}}, Sys \models \textbf{\textit{sd}}$.

Besides this, we can often detect some inconsistencies in the state diagram in comparison with its sequence diagram by extracting and combining their time constraints especially upon the implied transitions presented in fig.3 with thick arrows.

4.2 Consistency Checking of Timed Graphs

When considering time constraints on implementation and specification graphs, the merging operator has to be enhanced to combine these time constraints related both to actions and nodes of these graphs. Indeed, the adopted combination style will have an effect on the ability of each combined constituent to progress in such a way the needed computations are performed within the required deadlines. Obviously, the composition product $\otimes^T$ of two timed graphs $\mathcal{A}^T_{Impl}$ and $\mathcal{A}^T_{Spec}$ yields a new timed graph $\mathcal{A}^T =< \mathcal{A}_{Impl} \otimes \mathcal{A}_{Spec}, I, G, Z >$ where $\otimes$ is the untimed merging operator and I and G are the timing functions defined respectively over nodes and transitions as follows: Let the composite node $(q_1, q_2) \in Q_{Impl} \times Q_{Spec}$ and let e be the combined arc $((q_1, q_2), a, (q'_1, q'_2)) \in \hookrightarrow_{Impl \otimes spec}$. Then,

$I((q_1, q_2)) = I_{Spec}(q_2) \wedge I_{Impl}(q_1) = I_{Spec}(q_2) \wedge true = I_{Spec}(q_2)$.

$$G(e) = \begin{cases} G_{Impl}((q_1, a, q_1')) & \text{if } \exists(q_1, a, q_1') \in \hookrightarrow_{Impl} \wedge \nexists(q_2, a, q_2') \in \hookrightarrow_{Spec} \\ G_{Impl}(e_1) \wedge G_{Spec}(e_2) & \text{if } e_1 = (q_1, a, q_1') \in \hookrightarrow_{Impl} \wedge e_2 = (q_2, a, q_2') \in \hookrightarrow_{Spec} \end{cases}$$

The previous synchronization over time constraints asserts that the specification constraints in the merged graph should be fulfilled. In fact, timing annotations on the implementation graph are almost concerned with execution and transmission durations whereas the timing constraints in the specification graph describe the requirements in terms of deadlines to meet. Hence, the invariant of a composite node is exactly its specification constituent invariant, the role of which is to state whether there is a strict deadline imposed on some outgoing hard timed action. On the other hand, the guard of a synchronized action is the conjunction of the guards of its constituents.

When merging the two graphs, we would verify that they are consistent with each other. That is, the implementation fulfills the specification in a more suited way than what has been stated in the untimed case. In a similar way, we would check that the composition of timed graphs does not raise more incompatibilities. Indeed, the timing constraints have an effect of the reachability of states and deadlines of certain actions may exclude the availability of others.

Definition 5. *Let $e = e_1 \otimes e_2$ be a composite transition outgoing from a composite state $q = (q_1, q_2)$ in the merged graph. We consider that e is timely consistent if $G_{Impl}(e_1) \Rightarrow G_{Spec}(e_2) \Rightarrow I_{Spec}(q_2)$.*

Thus, any time annotation of the StateChart action complies with its timing constraint as specified in the sequence diagram. In a similar way, we apply the same rule to define the time consistency of a simple transition in the merged graph.

Definition 6. *Let the transition e be derived from a simple implementation transition e_1 without synchronization with anyone from the specification graph. e is said timely consistent if $G_{Impl}(e_1) \Rightarrow I_{Spec}(q_2)$.*

In other terms, the invariant brought by the specification to the source node $q = (q_1, q_2)$ would not exclude the performance of the implementation transition e_1.

Definition 7. *We say that the StateChart of the system Sys timely fulfills the global sequence (or overview interaction) diagram* **sd** *if $Sys \models$* **sd** *and all the transitions of the merged graph $\mathcal{A}^T =< \mathcal{A}^T_{Impl} \otimes^T \mathcal{A}^T_{Spec} >$ are timely consistent.*

For instance, fig.3(c) presents a fragment of the graph generated from the combination of specification and implementation graphs of the train control system. We can see that the simple transition outgoing from the node S_2 and labeled with an occurrence of the action "enter!" can be timely consistent if the implementation guard G implies the invariant of its source node S_2. However, the composite transition labeled with an occurrence of the action "enter!" outgoing from the node S_1 is always timely inconsistent because whatever the valuation of the implementation guard G, the specification guard can never imply the invariant of the source node S_1, making it impossible to be enabled.

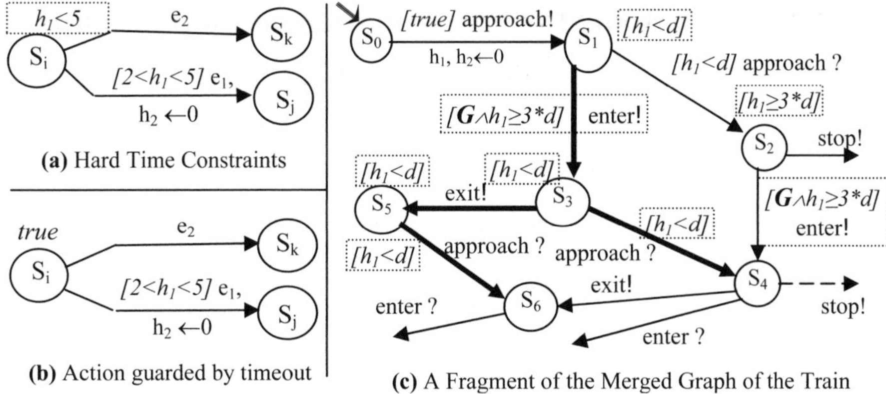

Fig. 3. Timed Graphs

5 Conclusion

We presented herein a methodology for time and semantics consistency checking of UML dynamic diagrams to uncover design flaws and to find out whether timing constraints of sequence diagrams could be fulfilled in respect of time annotations on arcs of StateCharts. For future work, we plan to extend this approach to deal with various time policies and to address the compatibility issue among sequence diagrams. Lastly, modular checking techniques remain a key topic to handle the state explosion problem.

References

1. Alur, R., Dill, D.L.: A theory of timed automata. Theoretical Computer Science 126, 183–235 (1994)
2. Engels, G., Hausmann, J.H., Heckel, R., Sauer, S.: Testing the consistency of dynamic UML diagrams. In: Proc. of Integrated Design and Process Technology (2002)
3. Hammal, Y.: A formal Semantics of UML State Charts by means of Timed Petri nets. In: Wang, F. (ed.) FORTE 2005. LNCS, vol. 3731, pp. 38–52. Springer, Heidelberg (2005)
4. Hammal, Y.: Branching Time Semantics for UML 2.0 Sequence Diagrams. In: Najm, E., Pradat-Peyre, J.-F., Donzeau-Gouge, V.V. (eds.) FORTE 2006. LNCS, vol. 4229, pp. 259–274. Springer, Heidelberg (2006)
5. Kotb, Y., Katayama, T.: Consistency checking of UML model diagrams using the XML semantics approach. In: Proc. of Intl. World Wide Web Conference, Japan, pp. 982–983 (2005)
6. Lam, V.S.W., Padget, J.: Consistency checking of sequence diagrams and statechart diagrams using the π-Calculus. In: Romijn, J.M.T., Smith, G.P., van de Pol, J. (eds.) IFM 2005. LNCS, vol. 3771, pp. 347–365. Springer, Heidelberg (2005)
7. Litvak, B., Tyszberowicz, S., Yehudai, A.: Behavioral Consistency Validation of UML Diagrams. In: Proc. of the 1st Intl. Conference SEFM 2003, p. 118 (2003)
8. Object Management Group, Inc. (OMG): Unified Modeling Language: Superstructure version 2.0, Final Adopted Specification (2004) `http://www.omg.org`
9. Object Management Group, Inc. (OMG): UML Profile for Schedulability, Performance, and Time Specifi-cation (September 2003), Version 1.0, `http://www.omg.org`
10. Van Der Straeten, R., Mens, T., Simmonds, J., Jonckers, V.: Using description logic to maintain consistency between UML models. In: Stevens, P., Whittle, J., Booch, G. (eds.) UML 2003. LNCS, vol. 2863, pp. 326–340. Springer, Heidelberg (2003)

A Process Model for Forensic Analysis of Symbian Smart Phones

Xian Yu, Lie-Hui Jiang, Hui Shu, Qing Yin, and Tie-Ming Liu

National Digital Switching System Engineering & Technology Research Center
Zhengzhou, Henan Province 450002, China
cosineyu@msn.com

Abstract. The smartphone segment has been witnessed the fastest growth in the handset market.Traditional phones will be replaced by smart phones. At the same time, smart phones may be used for fraud, forgery and defamation and other criminal activities.Symbian smartphones forensics is relatively a new field of interest among scientific and law enforcement.There are various mobile phones forensics process models now. But these models may not be able to solve the problems of the Symbian smartphone's adoption.In this paper,we describe a process model for forensic analysis of Symbian smartphones. As a result,this model can overcome some problems of the traditional model of digital investigation on Symbian smartphones.

Keywords: Process Model, Forensic Analysis, Symbian Smart Phones.

1 Introduction

ABI Research recently published a new data;it stated that the smart phones would account for 31% market share among all the cellphoes' market in 2013.Thus,smart phones would become an important tool in our life.Smart phones are embedded with a complete architecture, including: CPU, data bus, ROM, RAM, memory controller, digital signal processor (DSP), radio frequency hardware, a variety of hardware keyboard and interface, LCD etc. Smartphone devices embedded operating system (OS) are stored in ROM. Equipments used in many various types of ROM include the Flash memory[1]and[2]. Figure 1 shows the generic hardware diagram of a modern smart phones device.

Flash memory's non-volatile uniqueness,in terms of being erasable and rewritable makes it easier for developers of smartphones OS upgrade or porting.There are two types of flash memory, NOR and NAND. The names refer to the type of logic gate used in each memory cell.NOR flash is faster, but it is also more expensive and takes longer to erase and write new data. NOR is what so-far has been used mostly in mobile phones. NAND has significantly higher storage capacity than NOR. Some devices could use both NAND and NOR. A smartphone, for instance, can be embedded NOR to boot up the operating system and a removable NAND card for all its other memory or storage requirements.

D. Ślęzak et al. (Eds.): ASEA 2009, CCIS 59, pp. 86–93, 2009.

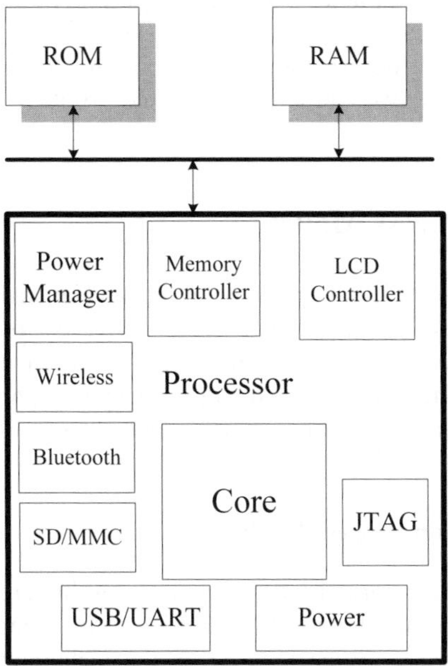

Fig. 1. Smartphones generic hardware diagram

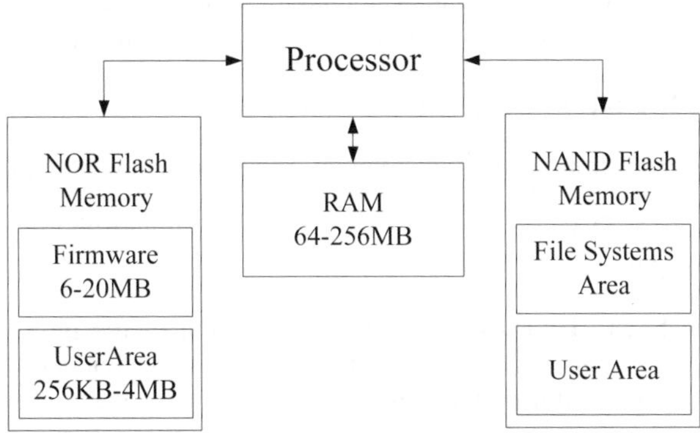

Fig. 2. Flash memory assignments of a modern smartphones

Due to those enriched capabilities, the smartphones can store lots of personal information, even valuable source of analysis in a crime investigation[3].At the time of writing, Symbian is getting greater acceptance among other leading handset vendors which also happens to be a Nokia's major rivals.Symbian's dominance in Europe is unquestionable and it is also doing well in many other key markets.

Obtaining information on Symbian smartphones is often a primary goal as a result of making an forensic analysis.However the security mechanism based on the Trusted Computing introduced by the Symbian OSv9.x.Many smartphones forensics existing process model can not be applied to Symbian smartphones.In this paper, First based on the survey and analysis of some existing models for forensic analysis of normal smartphones. After that,we describe a process model for forensic analysis of Symbian smartphones.By the model,we can overcome some problems of digital investigation on Symbian smartphones.

2 The Existing Process Models

Smart phones are digital devices.In principle,it means that smartphones have the same evidentiary possibilities as in other digital devices,such as hard drives.When smartphones are involved in a crime or other incident, forensic investigators require a process model that better be the most appropriate one.This section details some models so that they can apply to forensic analysis of digital devices including Windows Mobile .

2.1 Digital Investigation Process Models

In the digital investigation practices, there are over hundreds of digital forensics investigation procedures developed all over the world. Each organization tends to develop its own procedures. Some focused on the technology aspects such as data acquisition or data analysis [4]. There are three process models including an incident response model, a law enforcement model, and an abstract model that can apply to the field of digital forensics. Based on the previous process model, Brian Carrier and Eugene Spafford proposed yet anther model that organizes the process into five groups consisting all in all 17 phases[5],which is listed and shown in Figure3.

The Integrated Digital Investigation Model ,IDIP

Readiness Phase: Train investigators,develop procedures,and test equipment.

Deployment Phase: Detect a crime or incident,verify it,and obtain authorization to respond or investigate.

Physical Crime Scene Investigation Phase: The goal of the physical crime scene investigation phases is to collect and analyze the physical evidence and reconstruct the actins that took place during the incident.

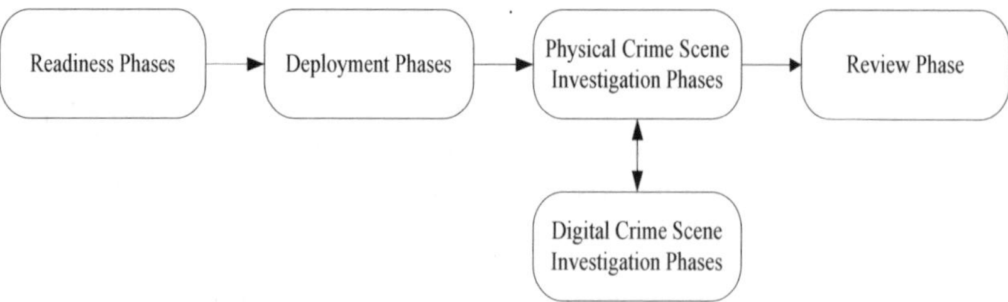

Fig. 3. The integrated digital investigation model, IDIP

Digital Crime Scene Investigation Phase: The goal is to identify the electronic events that occurred on the system and present that to the physical crime scene investigation.

Review Phase: It involves reviewing the investigation to identify areas of improvement.

2.2 Windows Mobile Forensic Process Model

This process model focused on the specific information flow associated with the forensic investigation of Windows mobile devices [6].The model attempted to overcome the major shortcomings of the existing digital forensic models.This proposed model consists of twelve phases,which is shown in Figure 4.

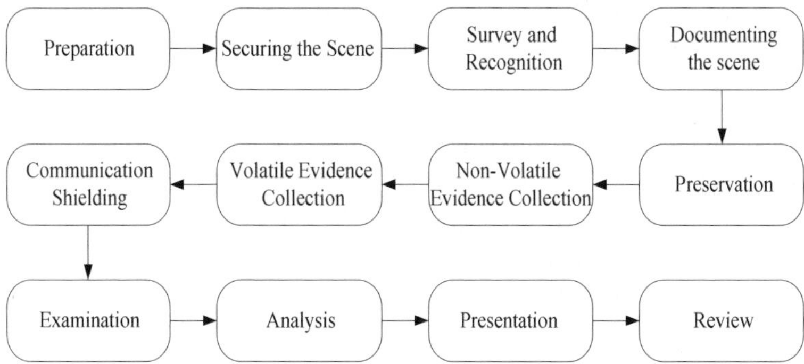

Fig. 4. Phases of the windows mobile device forensic model

3 Process Model for Symbian Smartphones Forensics

Symbian OS is an open source software operating system designed for smartphones [11]. As a descendant of Psion's EPOC and runs exclusively on ARM Processors. Unlike the general purpose devices as PCs,the Symbian Smartphones have some peculiarities,which heavily influence forensic process[7]. This section, first of all, describes the impediments of symbian smartphones forensics.

3.1 The Impediments of Symbian Smartphones Forensics

Symbian smartphones forensics is a new field of digital investigation. Data acquisition on Symbian smartphones is often a primary goal in a forensic analysis. However,Symbian smartphones forensics evidenced there were still many restrictions.

The diversity of Symbian smartphones

Symbian smartphones gain strong support from Nokia,In fact,the Nokia Series 60 UI platform occupies an important position in the market.At this time of writing, there have been several versions: version 1 (eg 7650), 2nd edition (eg 6600), 2nd edition FeaturePack1 (eg 7610), 2nd edition FP2 (eg 6681), 2nd edition FP3 (eg N70), 3rd edition (eg 3250),3rd edition FP1 (eg 6120),3rd edition FP2 (eg 5630MX),5th edition (such as 5800MX),N97.

The unit of trust

Since the introduction of Symbian OS version 9.1, which can also be referred to as Symbian S60 series 3rd edition, Nokia engineers have been introducing comprehensive support for Trusted Computing Base (TCB) concept. TCB is responsible for maintaining the integrity of the device as well as applying the fundamental rules of platform security [8].

The capability model

A capability is an authorization token.It indicates that its owner has been trusted to not abuse resources protected by the token. Symbian smartphone forensics needs to sign an internal forensic tool that requires phone manufacturers' approval of capabilities. The trusted API includes DRM, DiskAccess, NetworkControl and AllFiles capabilities, where the last is referred as the complete access to the filesystem.

The data caging

The data caging relates to file access control. There are two capabilities that signed to control access to the data caged directories includes\sys,\resource,\private[8].

(1) **TCB:**grants write access to executables and shared read-only resources
(2) **AllFiles:**grants read access to the entire file system; grants write access to other processes' private directories.

The access rules are summarized in the following table1:

Table 1. Capabilities and file access

	Capability required to	
	Read	**Write**
\resource	none	TCB
\sys	AllFiles	TCB
\private\<ownSID>	none	none
\private\<other>	AllFiles	AllFiles
\other	none	none

3.2 The Symbian Smartphones Forensic Process Model

In order to solve those problems mentioned above as well as to achieve the purpose of forensics,a forensic process model for Symbian smartphones has been provided.This is an adaptive process model, which is based on different versions of Symbian smartphones.It contains the different stages of forensics and detailed explanations provided in the subsequent sections and shown in Figure 5.

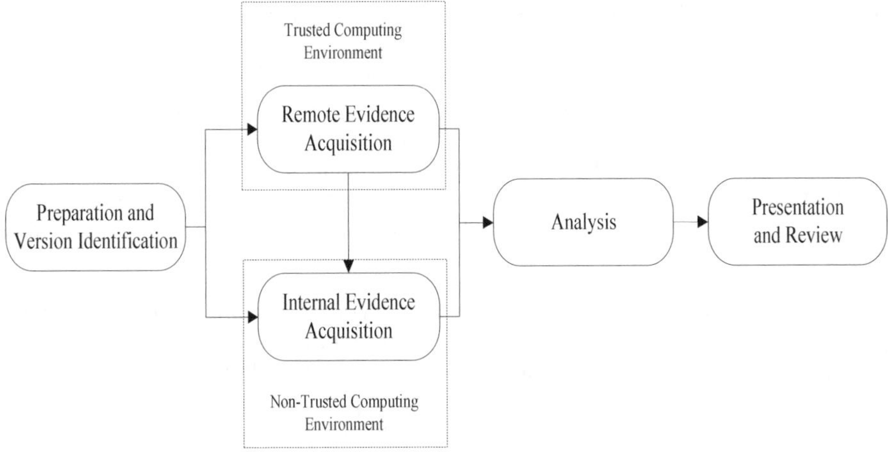

Fig. 5. Stages of the Symbian smartphones forensic process model

Preparation and Version Identification: This stage ,as the first phase of the model is mainly divided into two parts. One is to access its official public information on the target Symbian smartphone version of the identification,.Two is ready to Symbian evidence of tools and accessories of evidence. Then the initial version of the information and tools that are used identify pre-judge the credibility of the smartphone is working in the TCE(Trusted Computing Environment),An example is Symbian OS version 9.1, which can also be referred as Symbian S60 series 3rd edition.

Remote Evidence Acquisition: The introduction of Symbian OS v9.1 platform security (usually is referred to as "PlatSec") is working in the TCE. The stage has two methods in forms of protocol approach and hardware approach so that it can acquire the evidence from the advantage Symbian smartphones based on TCB.Protocol approach is based on command-responseprotocols by connecting to a remote host computer, such as AT Command Set, SyncML, OBEX,Nokia FBUS proprietary protocol[10].Hardware approach permits to acquire a binary image file of the entire flash memory content.JTAG debug port can access the data within the Flash memory[12]and[13]. Above two methods can be affected the least by the security mechanism.Interestingly, the file system restriction policy is fully contained in the file which is known as SWIPOLICY.INI[10].By modifying the file,investigators would get the root certificate of the target Symbian,as a result to jump in to the process of internal evidence acquisition.

Internal Evidence Acquisition: The stage is an adaptive phase.The investigation target is early Symbian smartpnones without TCB.Investigators can access the entire memory through the acquisition tools[7],then copy the files to removable media.As mentioned above, the tool can only be able to perform acquisitions of data from the device. The retrieved data is placed on the same removable media at which the tool resides.The retrieved data can then be acquired and analyzed by using other forensic tools.

Analysis: The platform security is to protect mobile data and the integrity of the foundation.Platform security model works in the software level,as for detecting and preventing application software on hardware, software and system or users data to unauthorized access. It is evidence of the investigating officers could have some impact. Therefore, investigators can extract from the Flash memory of the evidence, disassembled the binary code to deal with further analysis of the code and password in consequence to crack mobile phone or confuse the process. Static code analysis, including pattern matching, lexical analysis, abstract syntax tree analysis and data flow analysis and other methods.

Presentation and Review: The final stage in the model is the presentation and review phase.Almost all existing digital forensic process models have had the same phases and methods.After extracting and analyzing the evidence collected, results may need to be presented.This involves reviewing all the steps in the investigation process and identifying areas of improvement. As a part of the review phase, the results and their subsequent interpretations can be used for the examination and analysis of evidence in future investigations.

4 Conclusion and Future Works

A new forensic process model has been proposed,which it focuses exclusively on Symbian smartphones forensic investigation and standardizing the approach. The proposed set of activities in the model is incomplete;thus there is a need for considerable scope of work in the future.Further works is a must so that the model can be surely against to the anti-forensics such as data erasure, data hiding and data encryption. And the adoption of smart phones may also be evidence of the wireless remote to change the data.

In conclusion,in the view of these circumstances in the future smartphones will be evidences of the following directions;evidences of the standardization of tools; evidence of the automation tools as well as with other theories and technologies. Examples are data mining, dynamic simulation technology, distributed technology.

References

1. Jansen, W.: Guidelines on Cell Phone Forensics. In: National Institute of Standards and Technology Special Publication, pp. 800-101 (2007)
2. Jansen, W.: Guidelines on PDA Forensics. In: National Institute of Standards and Technology Special Publication, pp. 800-72 (2004)
3. Distefano, A., Me, G.: An overall assessment of Mobile Internal Acquisition Tool. Digital Investigation 5(1), 121–127 (2008)
4. Rahayu, S.: Mapping Process of Digital Forensic Investigation Framework. IJCSNS International Journal of Computer Science and Network Security 8(10) (October 2008)
5. Carrier, B.: Getting Physical with the Digital Investigation Process. International Journal of Digital Evidence 2(2) (Fall 2003)
6. Ramabhadran, A.: Forensic Investigation Process Model For Windows Mobile Devices, http://www.forensicfocus.com/downloads/windows-mobile-forensic-process-model.pdf

7. Mokhonoana, P., Olivier, M.: Acquisition of a symbian smart phone's content with an on-phone forensic tool. In: Southern African Telecommunication Networks and Applications Conference (SATNAC 2007) Proceedings (2007)
8. Sales, J.: Symbian OS Internals:Real-time Kernel Programming. John&Wiley Sons, Ltd., West Sussex (2005)
9. Jipping, M.: Smart Phone Operating System Concepts with Symbian OS: A Tutorial Guide. John Wiley & Sons,Ltd., West Sussex (2007)
10. Savoldi, A., Gubian, P.: Issues in Symbian S60 platform forensics. Journal of Communication and Computer 6(3) (Serial No. 52) (March 2009)
11. Morris, B.: The Symbian OS Architecture Sourcebook: Design and Evolution of a Mobile Phone OS. John Wiley&Sons,Ltd., West Sussex (2007)
12. Breeuwsma, M.: Forensics data recovery from flash memory. Small Scale Device Forensics Journal 1(1), 1–17 (2007)
13. Breeuwsma, M.: Forensic imaging of embedded systems using JTAG(boundary-scan). Digital Investigation 3(1), 32–42 (2006)

Reliability Analysis Method for Supporting Traceability Using UML*

Joonhoon Lee, Beoungil Cho, Hyunsang Youn, and Eunseok Lee

Sungkyunkwan University, Suwon, Korea
{trsprs,mes1an,wizehack,eslee}@ece.skku.ac.kr

Abstract. Non-Functional Requirements (NFRs) are very important in software system. Reliability is one of NFRs and should be satisfied for providing high quality service. Many reliability analysis approaches are proposed but they have some limitations such as modeling limitation or analysis limitation. In this paper, we propose reliability analysis method with supporting traceability using UML. This approach can provide reliability analysis result and find non-reliable part of UML.

Keywords: Reliability, UML, Traceability, Petri Nets, Markov Chain.

1 Introduction

Software must satisfy Non-Functional Requirements (NFRs). Reliability is one of these NFRs. In software engineering, software reliability is a probability of failure-free operation of a software system for a specified period of time in a computer environment [1]. Many researchers proposed the reliability analysis method. These are based on the Markov Chain or Petri Nets or other methods. But these approaches have some limitations [2]. One of these limitations is that current reliability analysis methods do not support traceability. Traceability is a trace ability to find out the part of the model which makes problem [3].

UML based reliability analysis method is one of these reliability analysis approach. UML is widely used in software modeling. UML can be modeled with reliability analysis [4]. Software can be tested after development phase. Many UML based approach can provide analysis capability in design phase. In this paper, we use UML model and support the reliability and traceability of software models. This can provide more powerful analysis in early phase of software development.

The rest of this paper is organized as following. Section 2 describes related work and the current shortcomings. Section 3 proposes reliability prediction method and traceability support method using UML. These methods are evaluated in section 4. Finally, we conclude this paper in section 5.

* This work was supported by the Korea Science and Engineering Foundation(KOSEF) grant funded by the Korea government(MEST) (No. 2009-0077453).

D. Ślęzak et al. (Eds.): ASEA 2009, CCIS 59, pp. 94–101, 2009.

2 Related Work

Reussner [5] proposes the reliability prediction approach for component-based software architecture. This is based on Markov and UML and can predict software reliability but is like a black-box approach. This method can analyze external reliability between components while being not able to analyze reliability inside the component.

Cheung [6] predicts the software reliability based on the Hidden Markov Chain (HMC). This approach uses five sources from system experts and so on. This approach can predict reliability of each component using the reliability analysis method based on HMC. But component reliability does not satisfy system reliability.

Trung [7] proposes the reliability prediction model based on UML. The assumption of sequential component execution was valid in the software which is developed with procedural programming paradigm. In object-oriented paradigm, the assumption does not hold. This approach also provides software reliability analysis method but does not provide traceability method.

3 Proposed Approach

In this paper, we propose a reliability prediction model with the traceability based on UML. This approach is to build software reliability prediction model. This model can be transformed to Software Reliability Prediction Model (SRPM). SRPM can analyze software reliability and support traceability of the reliability.

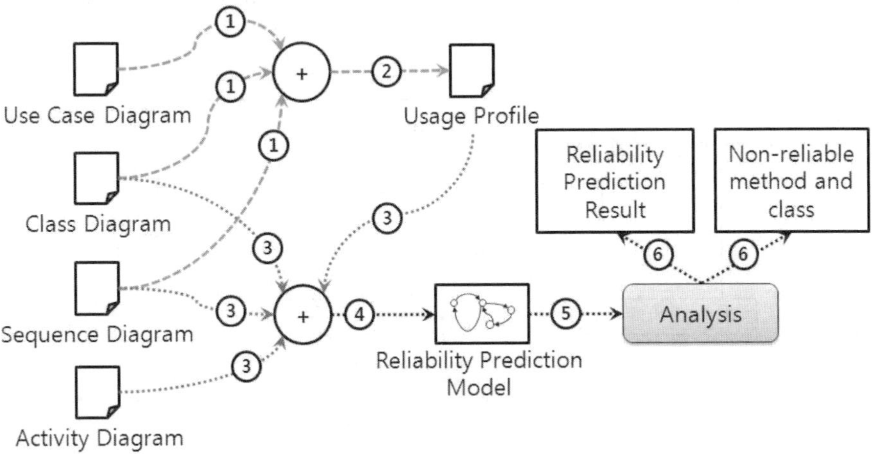

Fig. 1. Reliability prediction & trace process

Figure 1 shows the process for predicting software reliability and tracing the part of the problem. This approach uses 4 diagrams: Use Case diagram, Class diagram, Sequence diagram and Activity diagram. Theses diagrams can build usage profiles and reliability prediction model. Detailed model is described in 3.1. This model can provide reliability prediction result and find non-reliable part of UML.

3.1 Software Reliability Model

Software Reliability Model is based on UML such as Use Case diagram, Sequence diagram, Activity diagram, and Class diagram. Use Case diagram can represent usages of the software. It can represent how many each scenario is used. Sequence diagram can represent scenarios for each use case. This diagram has the number of method call in each sequence and method name and an order of method call. Class diagram can represent classes, methods and attributes. In this diagram, reliability related attributes such as MTTR or MTTF can be described with some annotations. Activity diagram can represent operations for each method. It contains flows of each method.

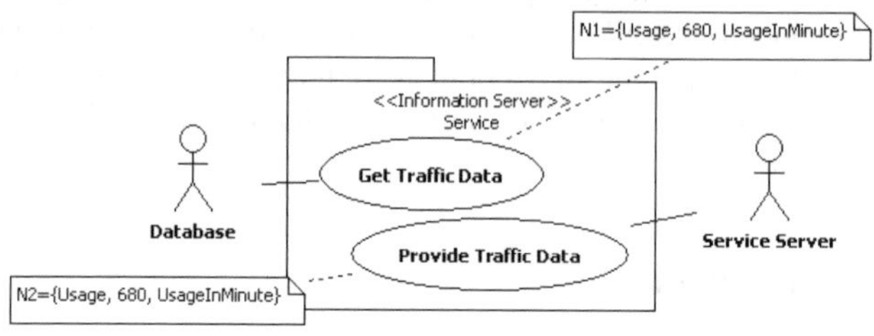

Fig. 2. Use Case diagram with usage profile

Figure 2 shows an example of Use Case diagram with usage profile. N1 and N2 mean the usage count in a minute. In this example, the usage value is 680. This value can be retrieved from system developer's experience or the log of similar system [6].

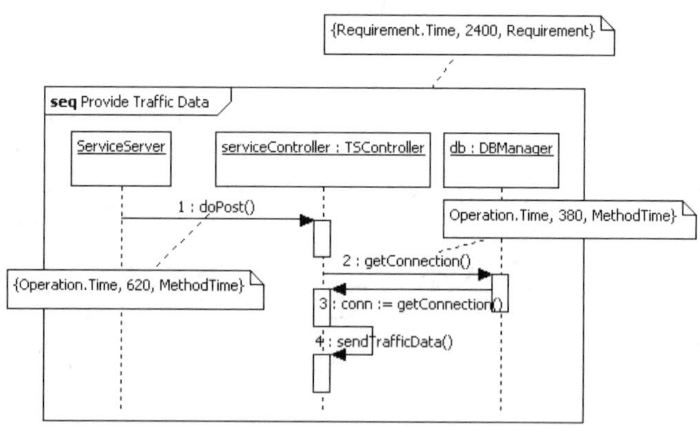

Fig. 3. Sequence diagram with reliability annotations

Figure 3 shows an example of Sequence diagram with reliability annotations. In this diagram, we represent time related value such as operational time requirement. These values are related to the software reliability [1]. Each method on Sequence diagram is represented in Class diagram. Class diagram also represent time related values such as MTTF or MTTR. These values are used for calculating total operational time in section 3.2.

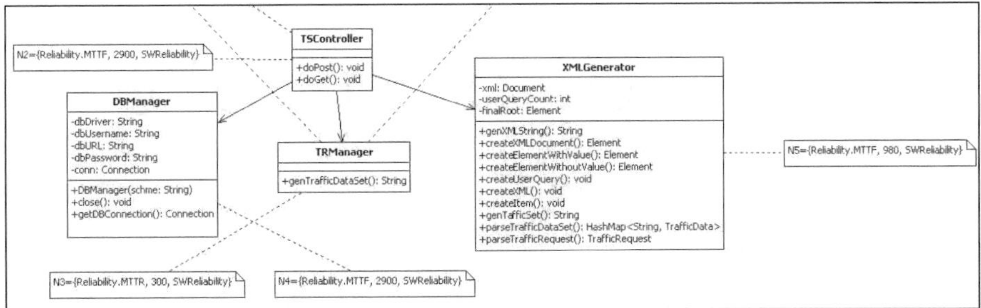

Fig. 4. Class diagram with reliability annotations

3.2 Reliability Prediction Method

We use the reliability prediction model built in 3.1. This model contains many information related the reliability. Reliability Prediction Model consists of some notations. Figure 5 shows one of the notations. This means call-return relationship. If a method is called, the relation goes to next operation. If the method is returned, the relation goes to previous operation.

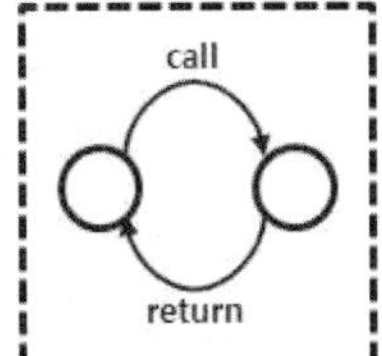

Fig. 5. Reliability model notation

Figure 6 shows the part of reliability prediction model. This contains many reliability model notations. This model has some notation such as *{doPost: 0.9875, 1200}*. This notation follows equation x. mN_n means method name of each sequence diagram. This sequence diagram has n method calls. cR_n means the call rate of the method. This is similar to the transition rate of the Markov Chain. oT_n means the operation time of each method. The sequence can be completed in time based on annotated values by means of reliability definition [1]. Methods have return values or call other methods. In this model, the state should be returned to caller method or final callee method. If this policy does not be satisfied, the model does not be satisfied the software reliability.

$$\{mN_n : cR_n, oT_n\} \tag{1}$$

Figure 7 shows internal analysis model using Petri Nets. We use transform Activity diagram to Petri Nets approach [8]. Activity diagram has activity notation and transition event for going next activity. This can be transformed to place and transition on Petri Nets. This model calculates the probability of the reliability of each method using absorbing states [9]. The predicted reliability can be calculated from this Petri Nets. We use these results to internal reliability on external model.

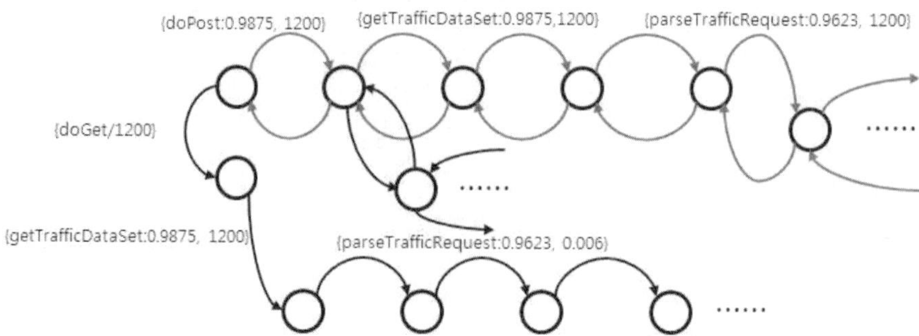

Fig. 6. External reliability analysis model

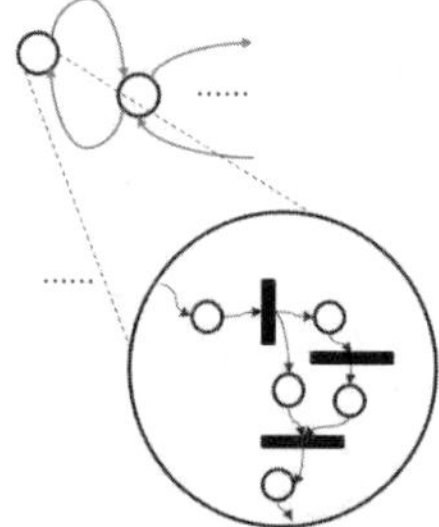

Fig. 7. Internal analysis model using Petri Nets

Table 1. Reliability Prediction Result

Service Name	Required Time (Avg.)	Predicted Time (Avg.)	Over portion (%)
Information Providing Service	2400	2362	9.2

Table 1 described the reliability prediction result. Based on UML annotation, the required time is 2400 time unit, but predicted time is 2362. This service is reliable with the probability 9.2%. This is simple reliability prediction of the software.

3.3 Traceability

Using the result from 3.2, we find out the software reliability. Using this information, this can be tracing the problem part of UML. This means the part may not satisfy the reliability requirements or non-reliable states such as 9.2% on Table 1. If the state goes to next state in the reliability prediction model, the predicted time is increased because of time consuming. In Use Case diagram, the usage of the software is 680 times in a minute. This means about 60 times does not be satisfied the required time. Following the states, we can find overtime state. Finding state has method name because of equation 1. This method may have abnormal activity or something wrong. Frequent activity has connection problem. Architect or designer can check this method part. If the part does not have any problem, the previous state may have some problems following the call relation. From this way, architect or designer can check UML model.

Information Providing Service has some non-reliable state. Many non-reliable case is occurred on *getConnectionDB()* method. This method does not have any connection pool so each process waits for getting DB connection.

4 Evaluation

Reliability means the probability of fault-free operations in specific time. We measured the reliability of the real software and compared this result to predicted result. The target software was web-based traffic service component. This component has a role to get requests for the traffic information and gives the responses with the traffic information related the position including the request. The main objective of the component is to provide the traffic information.

4.1 Reliability Evaluation

This is the result compared measured reliability and predicted reliability. We used JMeter for measuring the reliability [10]. This can generate many requests and check how many requests receive the correct response. The reliability can be calculated equation 2.

$$reliability_{JMeter} = \frac{Y}{X} \times 100 \tag{2}$$

Table 2. Comparison between predicted and measured values

Service	Predicted Reliability	Measured Reliability	Difference (%)	Error (%)
Information Providing Service	0.918	0.7523	81.9499	18.0501

Table 2 describes the result. The predicted reliability is 0.918 but measured reliability using JMeter is 0.7523. The difference is 81.9499%. Error rate is 18.05015. This does not have high accuracy of the reliability prediction but find some non-reliable state on UML.

4.2 Traceability Evaluation

In the real software, the problem part is DB connection. DB can have 10 connection in a second but the over connection has occurred. DB does not response the request. Target component has this problem and the prediction result can find out this part.

Table 3 is the comparison between our approach and other approaches. Not only our approach but also other approaches can predict the software reliability. But other approaches do not support the traceability for reliability. Reusser's approach can predict software reliability but the target group is software integrators. This does not support the internal reliability of the software. Yacoub's approach can support this part but it does not support traceability. Our approach can predict the software reliability and partially support for traceability. This can help software architect and also software designer because of supporting method-level analysis.

Table 3. Comparison summary of reliability analysis methods

	Reusser et al [5]	**Yacoub et al [11]**	**Our approach**
Reliability Prediction	Predict	Predict	Predict
Traceability Support	Not supported	Not supported	Partially supported
Language	RADL	UML	UML
Variability	Not supported	Not supported	Not supported
Target group	Software integrators	Software Architects	Software Architects/Designer

5 Conclusion

This paper is our first step of reliability analysis using UML. We propose the architecture-based reliability prediction with the traceability using UML. The main objective of this approach is to predict the software reliability and trace the non-reliable part and find out the not-reliable-satisfied part. The accuracy is relatively lower than other approach but we can find non-reliable part on UML.

UML is widely used in software engineering. Our approach is based on UML and can be used not only for software architects but also software designer or developers. The advantage of this approach is not to be familiar with specific model representation. This also provides traceability and finds non-reliable part on UML.

In future work, we will extend the UML for more precious reliability analysis. We also find out the non-reliable part with more accuracy. The proposed model cannot be built automatically. Automatic model generation will be proposed. Tool support is also needed. Finally, a method for retrieving the configuration is also needed.

References

1. Eusgeld, I., et al.: Software Reliability. In: Eusgeld, I., Freiling, F.C., Reussner, R. (eds.) Dependability Metrics. LNCS, vol. 4909, pp. 104–125. Springer, Heidelberg (2008)
2. Gokhale, S.S.: Architecture-Based Software Reliability Analysis: Overview and Limitations. IEEE Trans. on Dependable and Secure Computing 4, 32–40 (2007)
3. Immonen, A., Niemela, E.: Survey of reliability and availability prediction methods from the viewpoint of software architecture. J. Software System Model 7, 49–65 (2008)

4. Cukic, B.: The virtues of assessing software reliability early. IEEE Software 22, 50–52 (2005)
5. Reussner, R.H., Schmidt, H.W., Poernomo, I.H.: Reliability prediction for component-based software architectures. J. Software System Model 66, 241–252 (2003)
6. Cheung, L., Roshandel, R., Medvidovic, N., Golubchik, L.: Early Prediction of Software Component Reliability. In: 30th International Conference on Software Engineering, pp. 111–120. IEEE Press, Germany (2008)
7. Trung, P.T., Thang, H.Q.: Building the Reliability Prediction Model of Component-Based Software Architecture. J. Information Technology 5, 17–24 (2009)
8. Bordbar, B., Giacomini, L., Holding, D.J.: Uml and Petro Nets for Design and Analysis of Distributed System. In: The 2000 IEEE International Conference on Control Applications, pp. 610–615. IEEE Press, USA (2000)
9. Goseva-Popstojanova, K., Trivedi, K.S.: Stochastic modeling formalisms for dependability, performance and performability. In: Reiser, M., Haring, G., Lindemann, C. (eds.) Dagstuhl Seminar 1997. LNCS, vol. 1769, pp. 403–422. Springer, Heidelberg (2000)
10. JMeter, `http://jakarta.apache.org/jmeter/`
11. Yacoub, S., Cukic, B., Ammar, H.: Scenario-based reliability analysis of component-based software. In: 10th International Symposium on Software Reliability Engineering, pp. 22–32. IEEE Computer Society, USA (1999)

Applying Agility Framework in Small and Medium Enterprises

Suphak Suwanya[1] and Werasak Kurutach[2]

[1] Department of Computer Engineering
[2] Department of Information Science and Technology
Mahanakorn University of Technology
51 Cheum-Sampan Rd., Nong Chok, Bangkok Thailand
a.suphak@gmail.com, werasak@mut.ac.th

Abstract. In order to achieve the sustainable growth of the development of software industry, it must begin with the Software Process Improvement at personal level. In this paper, we present a new method for software process improvement that focuses on three areas of concern to the process improvement in personal level, the process improvement in project level and the process improvement in organization level. This method is called Agility Software Process Improvement for Small and Medium Enterprises: ASPISME. This method is integrates the strong synergies and techniques of CMMI, PSP, XP and SCRUM appropriately and suitably so that it can be used as an alternative for software enterprises in Thailand.

Keywords: Software Process Improvement, SPI in Thailand, CMMI, PSP, Agile Methodology, ASPISME.

1 Introduction

In past decades, organizations in software engineering industry have taken more interest in Software Process Improvement or SPI because the software that was produced through the software process improvement achieved a high reliability and quality [1]. In present, there are various software development methods which can be divided into 2 categories, i.e. Heavyweight and Lightweight. The examples of Heavyweight method are the quality standard manage system ISO 9000 (International Organization for Standardization 9000: ISO) and the Capability Maturity Model Integration (CMMI). The example of Lightweight method is Agile Methodology.

Most software development process is Top-Down Approach which the processes of system improvement come from the policy or the chief executive's requirements without considering the system or efficiency of the existing personnel in the organization. Moreover, the government supports the large sized software enterprises, though 70% of the software development enterprises in Thailand are small sized enterprises [2] which there are 1-25 staffs and have no software development process that is suitable for such small sized organization. In fact, the productivity aim of most software enterprises can be mentioned by the similar principle that is the need of increasing the quality of the produced software while decreasing the development cost and time to

D. Ślęzak et al. (Eds.): ASEA 2009, CCIS 59, pp. 102–110, 2009.

the minimum. However, the problem from the fault of the software development called "Bug" tends to increase. The program codes that contain these faults have implicated to the unreliability of the domestic software industry. The value of time lost is up to 45% when the computer system is impractical and the production cost which more than 100 thousand million US$ is lost for lack of production capability and maintenance [3].

Hence, in this paper proposed the new method for the software process improvement of which the working operation is proficient and flexible to be an alternative for the small and medium sized software enterprises in Thailand in order to improve the software process to a high level of quality. This method focuses on three areas of concern to the process improvement in personal level, the process improvement in project level and the process improvement in organization level .

The organization of this paper is as follows. Section 2, we presents relevance research work. In section 3, we introduce a new method for the software process improvement. Finally, we conclude and future work in section 4.

2 Relevance Research Work

Software Process Improvement: SPI has diverse procedures/standards .Therefore each organization must study in detail of each method for most suitability to the organization.

2.1 Analysis of the Process Area and Generic Practices in CMMI

CMMI have been favorable and received an acceptance because it is the guideline that is suitable for the software development work. It helps increase the operation capability of the organization and leads to a higher quality software development. CMMI assesses overall organization as the operating process of the organization whereas the agile method is the framework which is only a part the software development process therefore, in conceptual view; they cannot be compared since their aims are different. However they are related because CMMI is the software management method whereas Agile is the software development method. Both methods can be practiced together while supporting each other as well.

To determine of which process area in CMMI that corresponds with PSP and Agile Methods or which process area opposes the agile method, every process areas and specific targets of the process area must be analyzed. The specific practices are simply the expected model components of which the implementation might be varied and different in each organization. Therefore, the determination is considered from the main target while the practices are only considered as a guideline for imagination and other alternative might be used to achieve the target.

The analysis of the process areas in the level of maturity only compares among the second level of maturity because the fourth and fifth level of maturity oppose the principle of Agile Methods. For the general target, two topics which were GG2: Institutionalize a managed process and GG3: Institutionalize a defined process and related generic practices were analyzed. In this case, the process area-specific analysis was not conducted because the Agile Methods could not give the information that was specific to the operation for institutionalization. This topic is considered in the organization level while the Agile Methods relates solely to the project level. The analysis of the coverage of generic practices by level evaluation was applied as follows [15].

1. Conflicting (-) – indicate that the CMMI target cannot be achieved if the Agile Method is still used. There is no extension that can solve the contradiction to the Agile principle.
2. Not addressed (0) – not completely cover but it does not indicate that the target could not be achieved. In order to differentiate this level from the first level, the possible extension of agile method is needed to be examined; therefore the CMMI could be achieved without opposing the agile principle.
3. Partially supported (+) – the coverage has limitation.
4. Supported (++) – the coverage has less limitation.
5. Largely supported (+++) – If the practices of Agile Method are applied, it will corresponds with the components in the important part in the model.

Table 1. Process area coverage of CMMI by PSP, XP and SCRUM

CMMI	PSP	XP	SCRUM
Process Area			
2.1 Requirements Management	0	+++	+++
2.2 Project Planning	++	+++	+++
2.3 Project Monitoring and Control	0	+++	+++
2.4 Supplier Agreement Management	0	0	0
2.5 Measurement and Analysis	+++	+	+++
2.6 Process and Product Quality Assurance	++	+	0
2.7 Configuration Management	0	+++	0

Table 2. Generic practice coverage of CMMI by PSP, XP and SCRUM

CMMI	PSP	XP	SCRUM
Generic Practice			
2.1 Establish an Organizational Policy	0	0	0
2.2 Plan the Process	+++	0	0
2.3 Provide Resources	0	+	+++
2.4 Assign Responsibility	0	+++	+++
2.5 Train People	+++	+++	+++
2.6 Manage Configurations	0	++	0
2.7 Identify and Involve Relevant Stakeholders	0	+++	+++
2.8 Monitor and Control the Process	++	++	++
2.9 Objectively Evaluate Adherence	+++	+	0
2.10 Review Status with Higher Level Management	+++	++	+++

From the comparison of the process area coverage in the second level of maturity, 7 process areas, there were no process areas that contradiction the method. For the comparison of the generic practice coverage, there is no contradiction with CMMI but the additional extension of the practices was required in order to comply with the process areas and generic practices as showed in Table 1: Process area coverage of

CMMI by PSP, XP and SCRUM and Table 2: Generic practice coverage of CMMI by PSP, XP and SCRUM.

2.2 Comparison of the Software Development Methodology

The software development processes of each methodology are different, for example, PSP is waterfall development process whereas XP and SCRUM are iteration development process. Each method has different strong synergies and drawbacks. In this paper, the coverage of software development procedures of each method was analyzed and as showed in Table 3.

Table 3. Comparison of the Coverage of Software Development Processes of each method

Software Development Processes	PSP	XP	SCRUM
Project Planning	0	++	+++
System Architecture Design	0	0	+++
Risk management	0	+++	+++
Requirement Management)	0	++	+++
System development planning	+++	+++	+++
System Analysis and Design	+++	+++	+++
Design Review	+++	+++	+++
Test Driven Design	0	+++	++
Program Code	+++	+++	++
Program Compile	+++	0	0
Code Review	+++	++	0
Program Testing	+++	+++	+++
Daily Building	0	+++	++
Code Refactoring	0	+++	0
Version Control	0	0	+++
Sprint Review	0	0	+++
Daily Meeting	0	+++	+++
Delivery	0	0	+++
System maintenance	0	+	+

The strong synergies and drawbacks of each method were concluded as showed in Table 3. It could be seen that the three methods were similar and had no contradiction. However, there is more discipline in some procedures of PSP development than in XP and SCRUM. For example, in the PSP program design, the program design and design editing are completely performed before coding whereas, in XP, the design is performed earlier in order to understand the program and then the program structure is edited while coding. XP estimates the program developing time from the comparison and prediction from experience but PSP uses Linear Regression method for more precise estimation.

Moreover, there are some important parts in the program development, i.e., project planning, requirement specification and analysis of user requirement, risk management, test driven design, development procedure review, version control and work delivery, which are not mentioned in PSP. But during the software development, the developers must prepare more documents than in XP and SCRUM.

CMMI is suitable for large sized organization that has large size projects and high expense cost for applying the model to the organization. Besides, Agile Method is just the project-level software development method. Agile Methods does not clearly mention the development process in the organization level.

3 The Proposed Method

In this section, we introduce a new method for the software process improvement which can be an alternative for the small and medium sized software enterprises in Thailand.

3.1 Agility Software Process Improvement for Small and Medium Enterprises: ASPISME

ASPISME is the software process improvement method that focuses the skill and discipline improvement of the software developers and production of the high quality software. This process supports the measurement of the project estimations, the measurement of project size, the measurement of defects, etc., for the data analysis and improvement of the development process in the next cycle and the information can be further used as a baseline of the organization. This method integrates the strong synergies and techniques of CMMI, PSP, XP and SCRUM appropriately and suitably. ASPISME consists of five components as showed Figure 2. The main components were:

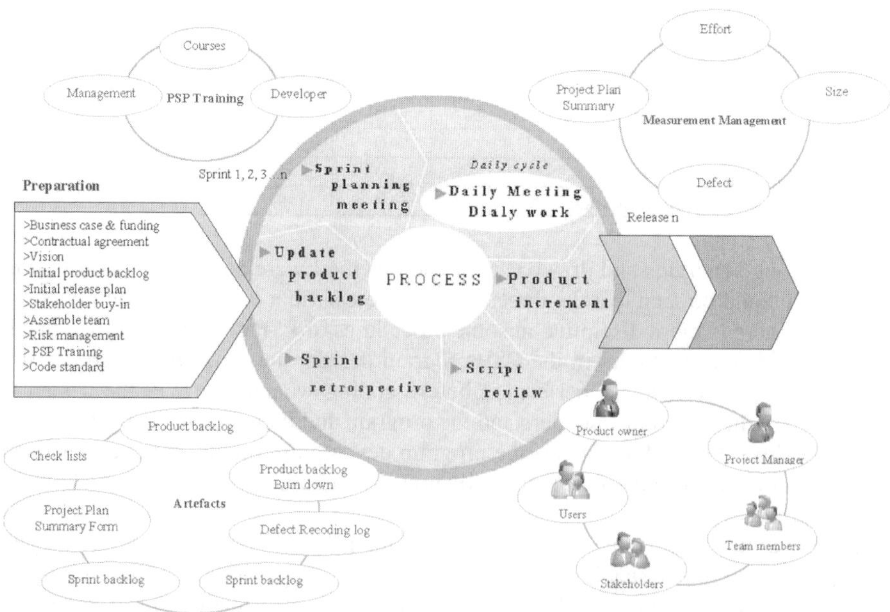

Fig. 1. ASPISME Method Content

3.1.1. The personal discipline development process (PSP Training) – Personal staffs must participate the training course so that they understand the software development process and the work discipline. The course consisted of training course for the project managers and the training course for the software developers.

3.1.2. The software development process – The development is divided into cycles (Sprint). Each cycle takes approximately 2 weeks and after the work cycle ended, the review meeting must be held (Sprint Review) then the work in the last cycle could be adjusted before the next cycle is operated.

3.1.3. The specification of role and responsibility (Role) – for any personal staffs in the project which are Product Owner, User, Project Manager, Team Member and Project Stakeholders.

3.1.4. Measurement process (Measurement Analysis) – consists of the indicators in the personal and project level, e.g., developing time measurement (Effort), program size measurement (Size), the defect recording (Defects) and the measurement of overall project performance (Project Performance).

3.1.5. Artifacts and work product (Artifacts/Work Product) – in each process, there must be the necessary documents that used as the information for the analysis and improvement of every working process in the next cycle. These documents called "Artifacts". If any artifact is delivered to customers, it is called "Work Product".

3.2 ASPISME Process

Besides the emphasis on the process improvement in personal level, the ASPISME software process improvement method also emphasized on the process improvement in the project and organization level. It was found from several researches that, in computer field, the Test-Driven Design was widely used. It proved that the design method which emphasized on the test before operating was proactive working strategy [16]. It means the possible results were considered before an actual action was taken which can make the software achieved the high quality. Hence, this technique was used as ASPISME method for the software development. The software development process was detailed below:

3.2.1. Project Planning – the planning of working operation for entire project, including risk management and customer requirement management.

3.2.2. High Level Architecture Design (Height Level) – is the design of entire information system, e.g. hardware, software, network system, and data processing in order to see the overall view of the system.

3.2.3. Software development cycle (Sprint) – is divided into two weeks per cycle. One cycle consists of system analysis and design, test design, program coding, minor test and daily program building

3.2.4. Sprint Review (Sprint Review) – After working cycle ended, the operation must be reviewed. This review consists of software review, comparison of working Backlog and estimation, backlog editing, addition of new backlog in sprint, responsibility assignment and operation planning of the next sprint.

3.2.5. Change management in the project – e.g. time and customer requirement which must be able to control.

Table 4. Participating Companies

Company	Business area	Industry Experience	Number of Software Developers
Company A	Software Development and System Integrator	Government Agency	15
Company B	Software Development	General Industry	8

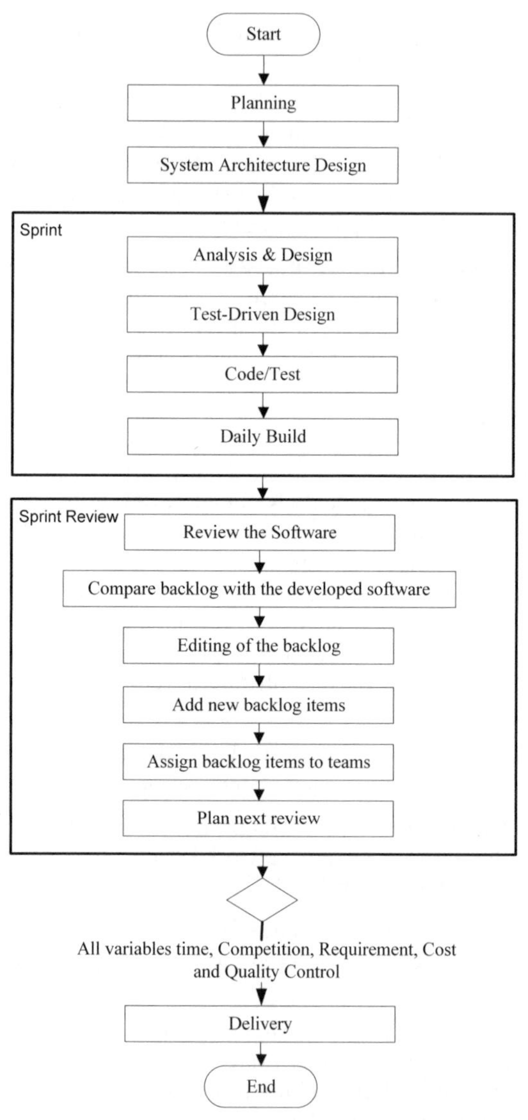

Fig. 2. ASPISME Process

3.2.6. Work delivery – all works that are going to deliver to customers require validation, resource planning for delivery, and also the personnel evaluation in the team and project.

Besides, other important procedures and activities support the successful of the software development process such as version control, tool usage for the work assisting, data collection and software maintenance after the work delivery as depicted in figure 2.

3.3 The ASPISME Project

ASPISME project is an action research project associated with 2 companies. As can be seen from table 4 they cover a wide range of sizes and business areas. We will train to project manager, team member and stakeholders before using method. After we start ASPISME Project, we will be handled how to use formal data collection consist of records of project performance, defect recording, evaluation form, structured interviews and other related techniques for data collection to improve further method.

4 Conclusion and Future Work

ASPISME was created to be used as an alternative for the small and medium sized software enterprises in Thailand. It also emphasized the personal development as same as Agile methods while the project quality evaluation and control were conducted in order that the data could be future used for the process improvement of the organization in the future.

Recently, there are enterprises that demonstrate this method. The suitable projects were selected to participate in this research. Then the results were compared to the project that practice normal procedures of the organization. After the project ended, we will conclude the result so that it can be used to improve and demonstrate the next project to ensure that this method can provide the software enterprises improve the software process effectively.

References

1. McGuire, E.G.: Initial Effects of Software Process Improvement on an Experienced Software Development Team. IEEE, Los Alamitos (1996)
2. Suwanya, S., Kurutach, W.: An Analysis of Software Process Improvement For Sustainable Development in Thailand. In: Proceedings of IEEE 8th International Conference on Computer and Information Technology (CIT2008), Sydney, Australia, July 8-11, pp. 724–729 (2008)
3. Ricadel, A.: The state of software: Quality InformationWeek, 838, 43 (2001)
4. CMMI Team, Capability Maturity Model Integration foe Systems Engineering, Software Engineering, Integrated Product and Process Development, and Supplier Sourcing (CMMI-SE/SW/IPPD/SS), Version 1.1, Continuous Representation, Software Engineering Institute, Carnegie-Mellon University, Pittsburgh (December 2001)
5. Hayes, W., Over, J.W.: The Personal Software Processsm (PSPsm): An Empirical Study of the Impact of PSP on Individual Engineers, Technical Report CMU/SEI-97-TR-001 ESC-TR-97-001 (1997)

6. Beck, K., Andres, C.: Extreme Programming Explained: Embrace Change, 2nd edn. Addison-Wesley, Reading (2004)
7. Cockburn, A., Highsmith, J.: Agile Software Development: The People Factor. IEEE Computer 34(11), 131–133 (2001)
8. Cohen, D., Lindvall, M., Costa, P.: Agile Software Development: A DACS State0of-the-art Report. Technical report (2003)
9. Highsmith, J.: Extreme Programming: Agile Project Management Advisory Service White Paper, http://www.cutter.com/freestuff/ead0003.pdf (accessed in 2005)
10. Schwaber, K., Beedle, M.: Agile Software Development with Scrum. Prentice-Hall, Upper Saddle River (2001)
11. Beck, K., Beedle, M., van Bennekum, A., Cockburn, A., Cunningbam, W., Fowler, M., Fren-ning, J., Highsmith, J., Hunt, A., Jeffries, R., Kern, J., Marick, B., Martin, R.C., Mellor, S., Schwaber, K., Sutherland, J., Thomas, D.: Manifesto for Agile Software Development, http://AgileManifesto.org/ (accessed in 2006)
12. Cockburn, A.: Agile Software Development. Addison-Wesley, Reading (2002)
13. Dogs, C., Klimmer, T.: Agile Software-Entwicklung kompakt. Mitp-Verlag (2005)
14. Wiki.: The Three Extremos, Portland Pattern Repository, June 8 (2001), http://c2.com/cgi/wiki?TheThreeExtremos
15. Fritzsche, M., Keil, P.: Agile Methods and CMMI: Compatibility or Conflict. Proceedings of e-Informatica Software Engineering Journal 1(1) (2007)
16. Kaufmann, R., Janzen, D.: Implications of Test-Driven Development: A Pilot Study, Anaheim, California, USA, pp. 289–299 (2003)

Using Area-Team to Evaluate the Software Architecture for an Online Banking System: A Case Study

Muhammad Sulayman, Mehwish Riaz, Husnain Naqvi, and Muhammad Amir Aman

Department of Computer Science, International Islamic University Islamabad, Pakistan
sulayman@iiu.edu.pk, mehwish.riaz@gmail.com, naqvi39@yahoo.com, m_amir_aman@hotmail.com

Abstract. Software Architecture plays major role in s successful software. It is one of the key artifacts of modern software development. This paper demonstrates the use of Architecture Requirements Engineering Error and Accuracy ¬ The Analysis Method (AREA¬TEAM) to evaluate an online banking system. This research paper presents the detailed case study of the system and the overall evaluation process that has employed AREA-TEAM. Eventually this paper discusses the results and elaborates the key benefits of the employed method.

Keywords: Software Architecture, Evaluation, Requirements Engineering, AREA-TEAM.

1 Introduction

Software architecture is significant to the quality of any software system. For any company concerned in development of software, the capability to evaluate software architectures before the bugs and errors are identified in the systems can largely shrink the risk that the developed software will not cater their requirements and excellence objectives.

The Software Engineering Group at IIUI has devised the Architecture Requirements Engineering Error and Accuracy - The Analysis Method (AREA-TEAM) [1]. This method allows the evaluation of the software architecture and its agreement with the requirement specifications. The method "Architecture Requirements Engineering Accuracy and Error - The Analysis Method (AREA-TEAM)", provides sound footings to perform architecture evaluation. The method helps in identifying the error factors present in the software architecture. The major advantage of AREA-TEAM is identification of the error made by the architect and the stakeholder, normally the customer or client [1]. This devised method has been applied on multiple industrial and educational applications and one case-study has already been published [2].

This paper narrates the application of AREA- TEAM method to evaluate the software architecture for a data warehouse (DWH) for an online banking system.

D. Ślęzak et al. (Eds.): ASEA 2009, CCIS 59, pp. 111–118, 2009.

2 AREA-TEAM and Software Architecture Evaluation

The software architecture of a program or computing system is the structure or structures of the system, which comprise software elements, the externally visible properties of those elements, and the relationships among them [3] [4] [5].

The AREA-TEAM [1] focuses on the requirements and error factor calculation during the architecture analysis process. The requirement engineering provides the appropriate mechanism for what customer wants, analyzing need, assessing feasibility, negotiating a reasonable solution, specifying requirement and their validation [6] [8][9]. There is always some percentage of error involved on the part of both the development team and the customers. A plus point in the AREA-TEAM [1] is that it calculates both Ea (Architect's error) and Es (Stakeholder's error) separately, which helps identifying the competency of the architect and the maturity of the customer. The details of AREA-TEAM can found in our base paper [1].

Other methods of architecture analysis with respect to requirements are unable to differentiate between the architect and the customer errors and have no proper measurement mechanism. The initial methods were unable to provide proper mapping from requirements to architecture because many architectural patterns were very complex and provided no provisions of mapping, for example, call and return architecture [10]. For that purpose structured design evolved which stressed modularity [11], top-down design [12] and structured program [13]. Myers and Stevens proposed dataflow oriented design translation from the architectural patterns but they were not able to measure neither the performance of dataflow diagrams nor the architectural competency and error responsible authority.

Another method design space quantization [7], a spread sheet model based on realization mechanisms and contribution analysis in the software architecture and the architectural decisions are prioritized. The drawback is that the requirements weights are neglected and no error finding mechanism is present for architecture measurement.

The ATAM [4] is another method which focuses on quality attribute requirements. It evaluates the quality attributes by considering each quality attribute in isolation and identifies sensitivity of quality attributes by various architectural attributes, which may result in evaluating the architecture w.r.t the quality scenarios [13] but there are no proper metrics for architecture correctness percentage and error propagation authority.

3 Case Study of an Online Banking System

This paper is a demonstration of AREA-TEAM on the case study of an online banking system. The system requires efficient mechanism for online transaction processing. A major requirement is synchronization of data from various sources and stores them into the data warehouse. The bank management needs trend analysis for strategic analysis and formulation of intelligent decisions. In order to have the cutting edge advantage bank is also interested in having an additional Apple I-phone application.

This paper is written in cooperation with a software house which was contracted for the banking system. The name of bank and software house is not shown due to the confidentiality reasons.

4 Architecture Evaluations through AREA-TEAM

There are two phases of AREA-TEAM which are similar to [1] and [2] which are contributed by same authors as of this paper. The phase 1 is called as Rehearsal.

In this phase the AREA-TEAM analysis team prepares itself for the analysis session. The stepwise solution for phase 1 is given below:

Step 1: Identify Stakeholders
All the concerned stakeholders of the project were identified which represented the bank, clients, users, software engineers, IT manager etc.

Step 2: Prepare Core Requirements
Software Project Manager and the Software Architect identified the core requirements which were used to prepare the architecture and these were the result of the requirements engineering phase.

Step 3: Architecture Briefing
The Software Architect prepared a briefing that explained all the components and connectors as well as the hierarchy and granularity of the architecture.

Step 4: Architecture Approaches
A list of architectural approaches was prepared that focused on understanding the architecture and will be analyzed further.

Step 5: Prepare Materials
Copies of presentations, core requirements and feedback forms were produced for distribution to the stakeholders during the next phase. The schedule of the meeting was decided and the stakeholders were invited.

Now we enter the phase 2 of the AREA-TEAM. The phase 2 is called "Architecture Requirement Engineering Analysis. 12 stakeholders were present in the evaluation, which included VP of the Bank, 2 members of Board of Directors, 2 clients, 2 users, 2 project managers and 1 software architect, 1 IT manager and 1 quality assurance inspector.

In this phase the AREA-TEAM analysis team prepares itself for the analysis session. The stepwise solution for phase 1 is given below:

Step 6: Present AREA-TEAM
A brief introduction to AREA-TEAM was given to explain the steps of the process to the stakeholders so that the maximum participation of the stakeholders was assured.

Step 7: Present Software Architecture and Core Requirements
The core requirements were distributed among the stakeholders and the software architecture was presented in a session of about one hour. During this session some new requirements were also identified.

Step 8: Requirements Prioritization Factor
Requirement Prioritization Factor (PF) was calculated. The votes for each requirement were counted by show of hand method.

Step 9: Requirement Significance Factor
The requirement significance factor was then gathered with the help of the feedback forms. The data from the feedback forms is recorded in the requirements significance

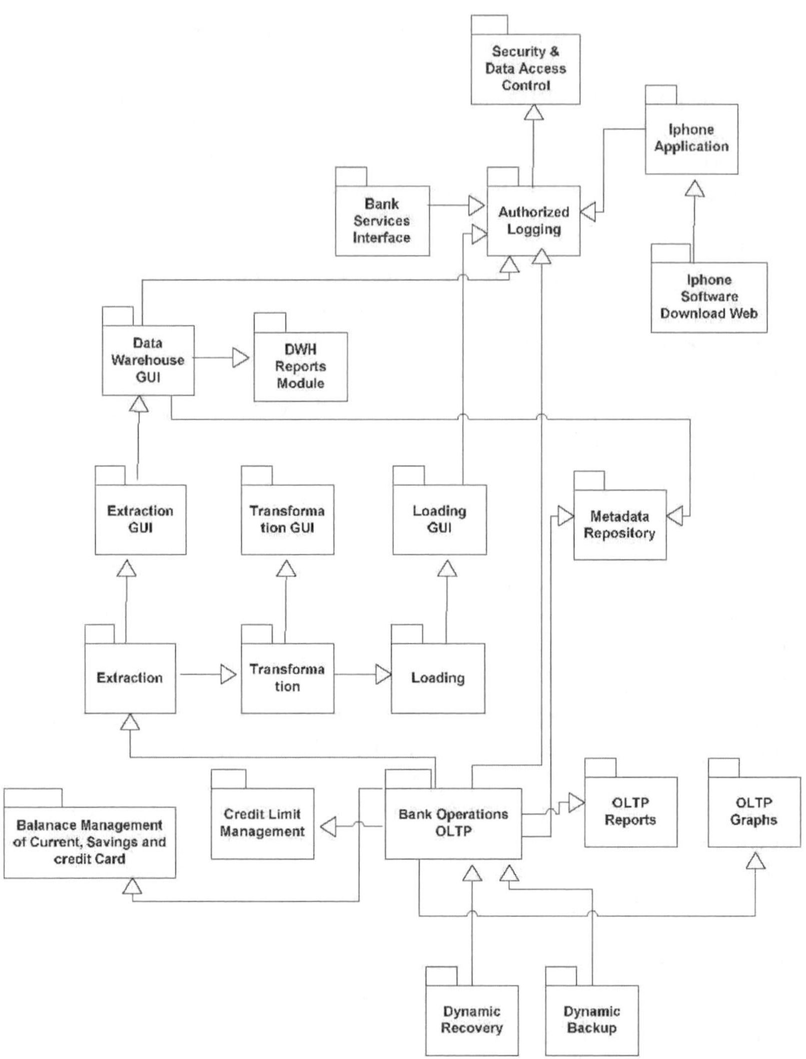

Fig. 1. Software architecture of the system

metric. Then Architecture Significance Factor (ASF) is calculated. The New Requirements are also processed in the same way and nASF is calculated for each new requirement.

Step 10: Requirement Criticality Analysis
The requirement criticality was calculated by finding the mean of prioritization factors and average significance factors for each requirement. The results are recorded in requirements criticality metric. The Total Requirement Criticality (TRC) is then formulated. The same process is applied on the novel requirements and the results are shown in new requirements criticality metric.

Table 1. Core Requirements, Votes & Priority Factor, ACF, RC & AAC

Requirements Prioritization Metric						
	Total Stakeholders	**12**			**TRC**	**16.29**
Req ID	**Requirement**	**(Votes)**	**PF**	**ACF**	**RC**	**AAC%**
REQDWBS1	When and which user tried to access which data.	7	0.7	0	0.74	4.54
REQDWBS2	2D and 3D cross tabbed reports from Data Warehouse	4	0.4	1	0.49	3.00
REQDWBS3	3D graph trend analyzers from Data Warehouse	6	0.6	0	0.6	3.68
REQDWBS4	Authorized logging	10	1	1	0.86	5.27
REQDWBS5	Balance management for different account types i.e. Current, savings, Credit Card	8	0.8	1	0.5	3.06
REQDWBS6	Credit limits should be maintained	10	1	1	0.64	3.92
REQDWBS7	Customers & Banking Staff must be facilitated to access the accounts status through Iphone and online.	10	1	1	0.54	3.31
REQDWBS8	Data mapping objects of sources to data warehouse objects.	9	0.9	0	0.62	3.80
REQDWBS9	Dynamic management of customer data	3	0.3	1	0.56	3.43
REQDWBS10	Efficient transactions processing in OLTP	4	0.4	1	0.58	3.56
REQDWBS11	Efficient trend analysis mechanism for customers & Banking Staff.	7	0.7	1	0.65	3.99
REQDWBS12	Generation of daily transactions reports	10	1	1	0.76	4.66
REQDWBS13	GUI based administration of Data Warehouse	7	0.7	1	0.42	2.57
REQDWBS14	GUI based dynamic backups and recovery	9	0.9	1	0.64	3.92
REQDWBS15	GUI for extraction should be there.	6	0.6	1	0.53	3.29
REQDWBS16	GUI for transformation should be there	10	1	1	0.66	4.05
REQDWBS17	Multipurpose website for Iphone software downloading,	3	0.3	1	0.62	3.80
REQDWBS18	New Customers registration	3	0.3	0	0.42	2.57
REQDWBS19	Online Transaction Processing System	8	0.8	1	0.8	4.91
REQDWBS20	Synchronization between Windows and Iphone OS	9	0.9	0	0.66	4.04
		AAF	**75%**	**AEF**	**25%**	

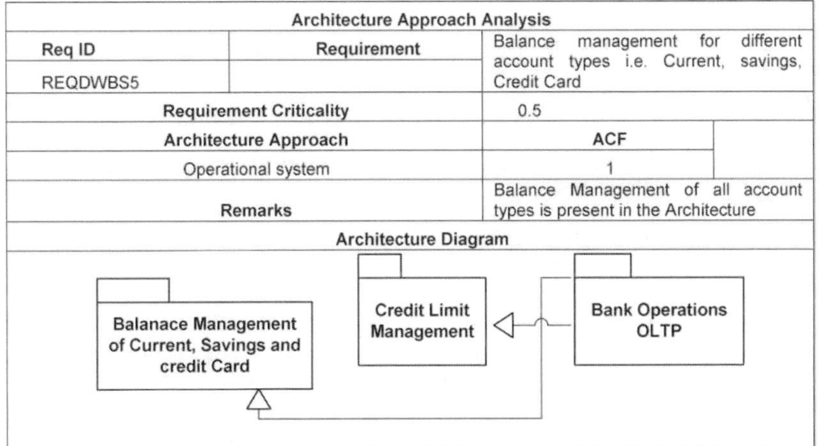

Architecture Approach Analysis		
Req ID	**Requirement**	Balance management for different account types i.e. Current, savings, Credit Card
REQDWBS5		
Requirement Criticality		0.5
Architecture Approach		**ACF**
Operational system		1
Remarks		Balance Management of all account types is present in the Architecture
Architecture Diagram		

Fig. 2. Architecture Approach Analysis Example for REQWBS 5

Architecture Approach Analysis			
Req ID	Requirement	3D graph trend analyzers from Data Warehouse	
REQDWBS3			
Requirement Criticality		0.6	
Architecture Approach		ACF	
Datawarehouse Schema		0	
Remarks		Not handled in the architecture.	
Architecture Diagram			

Fig. 3. Architecture Approach Analysis Example for REQWBS 3

Step 11: Novel Requirements Prioritization Factor, Average Significance Factor and Criticality Analysis

The Novel Requirements Prioritization Factor (nPF), Average Significance Factor (nASF) and the Requirements Criticality (nRC) are

Step 12: Analyze Architectural Approaches

Then each requirement was analyzed and the analysis team queried the architect that how he handled the requirements in the software architecture. The analysis is performed in Architecture Approach Analysis Metric. We are only showing one example from each possible category of the requirements. The first requirement is analyzed. This requirement is not handled in the architecture and the score 0 is given to the architecture contribution factor (ACF). This requirement is handled in the architecture by the architect and score 1 is given to the architecture contribution factor (ACF). In this way the other requirements are also analyzed.

Step 13: Architecture Accuracy Factor and Architecture Error Factor

In the last step for moving towards the final results calculations, the architecture approach contribution percentage (AAC%) is calculated for each requirement. Then the Architecture Accuracy Factor (AAF) and the Architecture Error Factor (AEF) is also calculated.

Table 2. New Requirements, Votes & Priority Factor, ACF, RC & AAC

New Requirements Prioritization Metric						
	Total Stakeholders	Votes (V)	TRC+nTRC		19.29	
New Req ID	New Requirement	10	nPF	nACF	nRC	nAAC%
NREQDWBS1	Instant update from ATM machines should logged	12	1	0	0.76	3.93
NREQDWBS2	Control Panel should be there to manage data entry errors	11	0.92	0	0.6	3.11
NREQDWBS3	Loading logs should be maintained.	6	0.5	1	0.43	2.22
NREQDWBS4	Forecasting of the bank's profits and number of customers	7	0.58	0	0.65	3.36
NREQDWBS5	Different branches data should be synchronized instantly	8	0.67	0	0.56	2.90
			nAAF	60%	nAEF	40%

Architecture Accuracy Factor (AAF) shows the correctness of the architecture in percentage and the Architecture Error Factor (AEF) shows the percentage of error present in the architecture, and this is the error of the architect. To calculate the error propagated due to the stakeholder (normally the customer) we included the new requirements captured in step 7 in our analysis. First of all we calculated the New Total Requirement Contribution (nTRC) for each new requirement captured. Then the Architecture Approach Contribution percentage (nAAC%) is calculated and the results are recorded in Architecture Accuracy Metric with new Requirements. The New Architecture Accuracy Factor (nAAF) and the New Architecture Error Factor (nAEF) is also calculated over here. The New Architecture Error Factor reflects the ratio by which the architecture has not addressed the requirements including the new requirements. The stakeholder error factor (SEF) is calculated. The total error factor in the architecture was 40% including all the new requirements, and without them it was 25%.

5 Conclusions

This case study evaluated the software architecture of an online banking system and identified the error factors of both stakeholder and architect. The early identification of errors helped in the better design decisions and lesser bugs in the later stages of system development. Overall results show significant error and exception handling in the architecture either it was introduced by the stakeholder or it was architect's error. The result is saving a lot of time and revenue. Similarly, with this method important requirements of system were analyzed at the early stages of development which included both functional and quality requirements.

References

1. Aman, M.A., Sulayman, M., et al.: Architecture Requirements Engineering Accuracy & Error – The Analysis Method. In: Accepted and Published in the first International Conference on Quality of service architectures in Net. Object Days, Erfurt Germany (2005)
2. Aman, M.A., Sulayman, M., et al.: Architecture Requirements Engineering Accuracy & Error – The Analysis Method, Islamabad Stock Exchange Case Study. In: Accepted and Published in IASTEAD, SE 2007, Austria (2007)
3. Bass, L., Clements, P., Kazman, R.: Software Architecture in Practice, 2nd edn. Addison-Wesley, Boston (2003)
4. IEEE Computer Society, Software Engineering Standards Committee, Institute of Electrical and Electronics Engineers, IEEESA Standards Board, and IEEE Xplore. IEEE Recommended Practice for Architectural Description of Software Intensive Systems. Institute of Electrical and Electronic Engineers, New York (2000)
5. Clements, P., Bachmann, F., Bass, L., Garlan, D., Ivers, J., Little, R., Nord, R., Stafford, J.: Documenting Software Architectures: Views and Beyond. Addison Wesley, Boston (2003)
6. Pressman, R.: Software Engineering A Practitioner's Approach, 5th edn., Mc Grawhill, International Edition, pp. 256–266 (2004)
7. Asada, T., et al.: The Quantified Design Space. In: Shaw, M., Garlan, D. (eds.) Software Architecture, pp. 116–127. Prentice Hall, Englewood Cliffs (1996)

8. Thayer, R.H., Dorfman, M.: Software Requirements Engineering, 2nd edn. IEEE Computer Society Press, Los Alamitos (1997)
9. Sommerville, I., Sawyer, P.: Requirements Engineering, Wiley, 1997 [10]. In: Bass, L., Clements, P., Kazman, R. (eds.) What is Software Architecture? in Software Architecture in Practice, p. 125. Pearson Education, London (2003)
10. Dennis, J.B.: Modularity. In: Bauer, F.L. (ed.) Software Engineering. LNCS, vol. 30, pp. 128–182. Springer, Heidelberg (1975)
11. Wirth, N.: Program Development by Stepwise Refinement. CACM 14(4), 221–227 (1971)
12. Dijkstra, D.O.E., Hoare, C.: Structured Programming. Academic Press, London (1972)
13. Bass, L., Klein, M., Moreno, G.: Applicability of General Scenarios to the Architecture Trade off Analysis Method, TECHNICAL REPORT, CMU/SEI2001TR014, ESETR2001-014

Architectural Decay during Continuous Software Evolution and Impact of 'Design for Change' on Software Architecture

Mehwish Riaz, Muhammad Sulayman, and Husnain Naqvi

Department of Computer Science, International Islamic University, Islamabad, Pakistan
mehwish.riaz@gmail.com, sulayman@iiu.edu.pk, naqvi39@yahoo.com

Abstract. Software architecture is the blue print of software and guides the development and evolution of the software. A good design produces quality software and careful evolution of software leads to a longer life of the software whereas a bad design and careless evolution leads to decay of the software. This paper discusses the phenomenon of architectural decay and gives an account of the practices suggested in the literature for identification, resolution and prevention of architectural decay. The observations from a controlled experiment to study the impact of the prevention practice 'design for change' are also discussed. The results from the studied metrics suggest that software created without following a proper design has a greater tendency to decay.

Keywords: Software Architecture, Architectural Decay, Software Evolution.

1 Introduction

Software architecture [17] is concerned with both functional and non-functional software requirements. Software evolution [15] encompasses all such activities carried out to maintain, enhance and further develop the software such as in evolutionary development [14] and is an intrinsic property of software [11].

Continuous software evolution is implemented by successive modifications in which change upon change upon change is introduced [11]. Continuous evolution preserves most of the aspects of a system [1] whereas in *discontinuous software evolution* an outdated system is entirely replaced by a new system [11].

Evolution in software also involves evolution in the software architecture due to architecturally significant [10] changes. Changes introduced in an uncontrolled manner start the process of decay also degenerating software architecture [17]. When no more changes can be accommodated, the result is reengineering or an early retirement of the software. This suggests that there is a strong need to mitigate the phenomenon of decay in software architecture.

In this research we consider following research questions:

D. Ślęzak et al. (Eds.): ASEA 2009, CCIS 59, pp. 119–126, 2009.

RQ1: What is architectural decay and what are the common factors that contribute to it during continuous software evolution?

RQ2: What is the relationship of architectural decay with software evolution and code decay?

RQ3: What are the possible proactive measures to mitigate architectural decay?

RQ4: What is the possible impact of different preventive measures on software architectural decay?

The answers to RQ1, RQ2, and RQ3 have been synthesized from the literature. For RQ4, the impact of only one preventive i.e., 'design for change' is observed.

The remainder of this paper is organized as follows: Section 2 presents a definition of architectural decay; section 3 presents a discussion on the relationship of architectural decay with software evolution and code decay; section 4 gives a classification of the factors that contribute to architectural decay; section 5 presents a list of symptoms of architectural decay, the practices that may be used to identify, resolves and prevent architectural decay, and the evaluation of the practices suggested in the literature; section 6 presents the controlled experiment and the observations made from the experiment followed by conclusions and future work in section 7.

2 Architectural Decay

Architectural decay is due to violation of architecture caused by the process of evolution [13]. Architectural decay has been defined as non-compliance between conceptual and concrete architecture [18]; deviation from original design [7]; increased resistance to change [13]; and cumulative, negative effect of changes on the quality of a software system [20], etc.

We believe that non-compliance of actual with planned architecture may not necessarily have a negative impact on the quality of software architecture. Architecture is driven by a set of key quality attributes and unless the software fails to satisfy them, any enhancive or preventive changes cannot decay the software architecture. So we assume that decay occurs when the key quality attributes are violated. Therefore, we propose a definition of architectural decay as below.

"Architectural decay is the phenomenon when concrete (as-built) architecture of a software system deviates from its conceptual (as-planned) architecture where it no longer satisfies the key quality attributes that led to its construction OR when architecture of a software system allows no more changes to it due to changes introduced in the system over time and renders it un-maintainable".

3 Architectural Decay, Software Evolution, and Code Decay

Architecture decay is essentially the result of software evolution. The process of evolution increases brittleness in the system increasing its resistance to change [13]. The design of a system becomes less and less suitable with every new version of software to incorporate new features [19]. The process of maintenance worsens the situation leading to architectural decay [3]. Therefore, we can conclude that the more the system is evolved, the more it moves closer to architectural decay.

The changes to well-engineered modularized code are local [6]. This connotes that if changes remain no more local; they scatter across various modules, suggesting problems with the software architecture and indicate decay that is at a higher level of abstraction. Similarly when the interfaces to a software unit are several, structural changes may be observed as changes propagate in other sections of the code [6]. Code decay is a result of problems with components and interactions of components which requires repair in multiple components and is a sign of decay in the software architecture [16]. Therefore, repeated changes found in the code that span multiple software units is essentially architectural decay.

4 Factors Contributing to Architectural Decay

According to Van Gurp et. al., the solution to the problem of architectural decay lies in addressing its causes [19]. Therefore, a classification of various factors presented in the literature that contribute to architectural decay is presented in Fig. 1.

5 Symptoms and Practices for Identification, Resolution and Prevention of Architectural Decay

This section presents the symptoms of architectural decay and summarizes the practices suggested in the literature for its identification, resolution, and prevention.

5.1 Symptoms of Architectural Decay

To identify decay in software systems, it is first important to observe the symptoms of erosion [20]. Some common symptoms of decay in software architecture include *Poor code quality* [6] [20], *Un-localized changes and regressions* [6], *High defect rates* [20] [9], *Deviation of actual or concrete architecture from planned or conceptual architecture* [8], *Inability to keep up with the market* [12], *Reduced performance* [12], *Uncertainty about the software* [20], and *Deployment problems* [20], etc.

5.2 Practices for the Identification, Resolution and Prevention of Architectural Decay

After the decay has been identified, something must be done to repair the system and prevent further damage. The best practice, however, is to prevent architectural decay by addressing causes of decay [19]. This section presents practices suggested in the literature for the identification, resolution and prevention of architectural decay and evaluation of these practices using evaluation criteria given in tables 1 and 2. Table 3 gives the evaluation of practices based on the presented criteria.

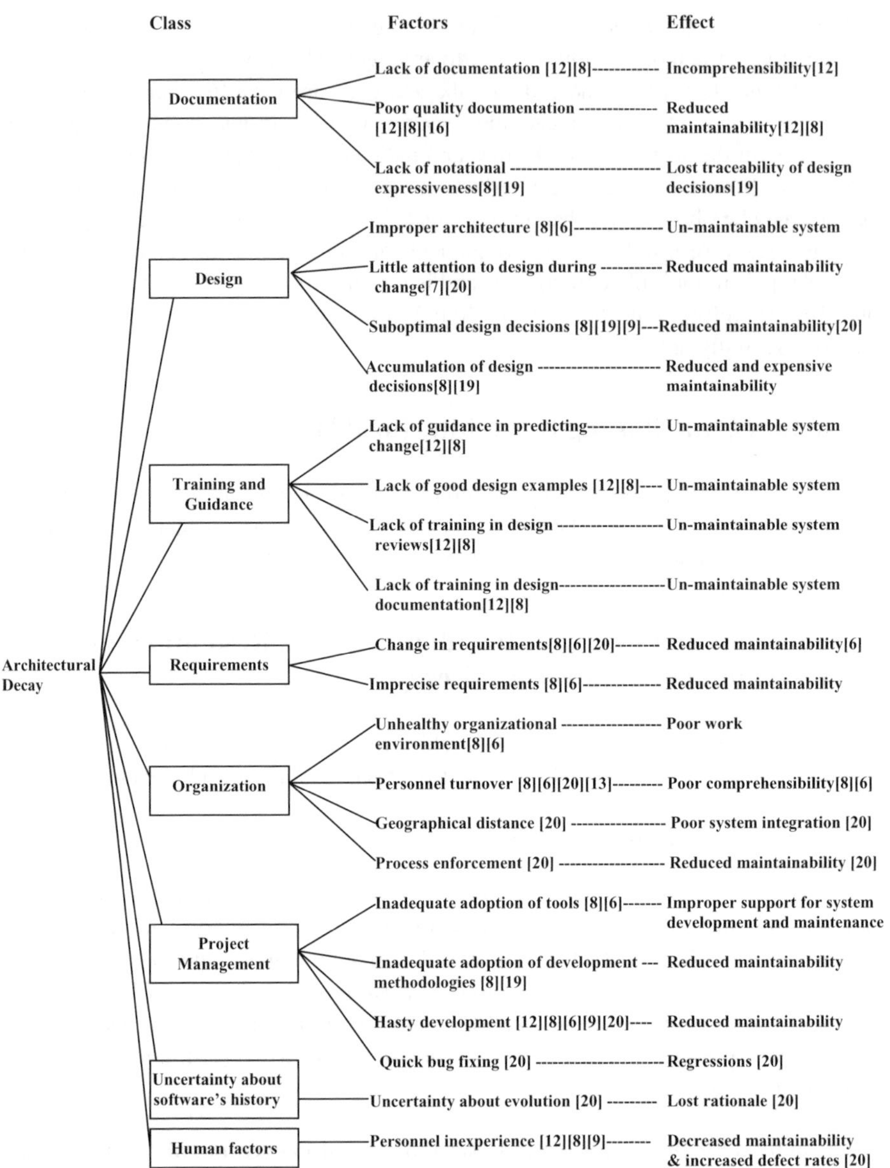

Fig. 1. Factors contributing to architectural decay

Table 1. Evaluation criteria for the maturity of practices suggested in the literature

Value	Criterion for Maturity
A	Suggested practice is given without justification but with obvious benefit of its use
B	Suggested practice is given with a sound logical argument
C	Suggested practice is given in the form of method/tool support
D	Suggested practice is based on an empirical proof of its effectiveness through application on an industrial case study

Table 2. Evaluation criteria for the coverage of practices suggested in the literature

Value	Criterion for Coverage
α	Suggested practice only identifies decay
Φ	Suggested practice only resolves architectural decay
∂	Suggested practice only prevents architectural decay
μ	Suggested practice resolves and prevents architectural decay but in isolation
Σ	Suggested practice prevents, identifies and resolves architectural decay in an integrated fashion

Table 3. Evaluation of practices suggested in the literature

Sr. No.	Suggested Practice	Maturity	Coverage
	IDENTIFICATION		
1	Checking compliance of actual with planned architecture [8]	C	α
2	Tracking defect densities [20]	D	α
3	Internal evaluations [20]	D	α
4	Increased difficulty to incorporate additional requirements [20]	D	α
5	Change of staff [20]	D	α
	RESOLUTION		
6	Use of design principles [12] [20]	D	μ
7	Creation and review of new documentation [12] [20]	B	μ
8	Replacement of decayed parts [12] [20]	D	Φ
9	Restructuring [12] [20]	D	Φ
10	Refactoring [8]	D	Φ
	PREVENTION		
11	Design for change [12] [20]	B	μ
12	Documentation [12] [20]	D	μ
13	Reviews [12]	B	∂
14	Imposition of standards [12]	A	∂
15	Software architecture analysis methods [5][8]	C	∂
16	Documented design patterns and architecture styles [5]	A	∂
17	Design-level modeling languages and architecture description languages [5]	C	∂
18	Inspection methods [5]	C	∂
19	Requirements frameworks [5]	C	∂
20	Implanting design decisions in source code [5]	C	∂
21	Automated regression testing [20]	D	∂
22	Aligning maintenance activities with product release [20]	D	∂
23	Process Enforcement [20]	D	∂
24	Experienced team [20]	D	∂

From the overall analysis of the practices (see table 3) we observe the following:

- The impact of using or not using only one preventive practice on the overall software architecture has not been addressed or evaluated.
- Most, if not all, practices lack empirical evidence of their effectiveness.
- There practices have been reported separately and without providing a concrete link among them. These have been discussed in isolation, and lack coverage with respect to addressing all the aspects of architectural decay.
- The results *after* the practices were applied (especially for preventive techniques) have not been discussed in the literature.

6 Controlled Experiment to Observe the Impact of *Design for Change* on Architectural Decay

To observe the effectiveness of different individual prevention practices on architectural decay, we intend to run a series of controlled experiments. The first such experiment was planned to observe the effect of *design for change*.

6.1 Experimental Design and Software under Study

The experiment was designed to observe the impact preventive practice of design for change on software architecture. A small domain of an Online Book Store (OBS) was considered and only a subset of modules capturing the functionalities of managing customers and items including books, CDs, and Software; shopping; and order processing, was implemented. Two versions of OBS were developed, referred in this paper as OBS1 and OBS2. The experiment was performed in collaboration with one of the leading software companies which provided the requirements and the architecture to be used for OBS1. Therefore, the implementation of OBS1 followed a proper design whereas OBS2 did not follow a proper design.

The implementation of OBS1 and OBS2 was performed by six fourth year Bachelor students, three each for OBS1 and OBS2, all of which had previously studied the course on software architecture.

In the first phase of the experiment, the students were explained the requirements. In the second phase, the students were given the task of implementing the system. The third phase consisted of implementing four change requests (CRs) with varied levels of complexity.

6.2 Experimental Results

For analysis, the measures considered were Number of Classes, Coupling between Objects (CBO) [4], Data Abstraction Coupling (DAC) [2], and Message Passing Coupling (MPC) [2]. Number of classes was considered to observe the growth trend in the size of the application. CBO, DAC and MPC were used to observe changes in the coupling values. Table 4 presents a comparative analysis of OBS1 and OBS2.

Table 4. Comparison of OBS1 and OBS2 for *Design for Change*

	OBS1	OBS2
After Implementation:		
Number of classes	11	16
CBO	6 (0.54 per class)	12 (0.75 per class)
DAC	3 (0.27 per class)	7 (0.44 per class)
MPC	8 (0.72 per class)	14 (0.88 per class)
CR1:		
Effort in hours	2	4
Number of classes	11	16
CBO	6 (0.54 per class)	12 (0.75 per class)
DAC	3 (0.27 per class)	7 (0.44 per class)
MPC	8 (0.72 per class)	14 (0.88 per class)
CR2:		
Effort in hours	8	18
Number of classes	13	20
CBO	8 (0.62 per class)	16 (0.8 per class)
DAC	4 (0.31 per class)	10 (0.5 per class)
MPC	9 (0.69 per class)	17 (0.85 per class)
CR3:		
Effort in hours	3	5.5
Number of classes	13	21
CBO	8 (0.62 per class)	17 (0.81 per class)
DAC	4 (0.31 per class)	11 (0.52 per class)
MPC	9 (0.69 per class)	18 (0.86 per class)
CR4:		
Effort in hours	16	30
Number of classes	14	27
CBO	9 (0.64 per class)	24 (0.9 per class)
DAC	5 (0.36 per class)	19 (0.7 per class)
MPC	11 (0.79 per class)	26 (0.96 per class)

A careful analysis of the values of measures used show a greater increase in the values for OBS2 in comparison to OBS1. Number of classes almost doubled for OBS2 The Effort values for the CRs indicate that almost double the effort spent on OBS1 was spent on OBS2. The values of CBO, DAC, and MPC also show a greater deviation for OBS2 than OBS1 between first implementation and after CR4.

From the experiment results, we can safely deduce that when software does not follow a proper design, it is harder to maintain and introducing changes involves more effort. In addition to reduced maintainability, software also starts showing decay signs. This can be observed by an increase in the values of coupling measures. Although some increase in the values can be attributed to the increase in software size, the trends in the change pattern for OBS2 indicate deterioration in the software.

7 Conclusions and Future Work

It is well known that software architecture plays a very important role in the creation of software systems. Therefore, it is imperative to get the architecture right and follow the rules behind its creation throughout software development and maintenance. In this paper, a definition of architectural decay has been proposed in addition to providing the state-of-art on architectural decay and a controlled experiment to observe the impact of 'design for change' on software architecture.

The results of the controlled experiment suggest that software when not created by following proper design has a greater tendency to deteriorate than properly designed software.

For future work, in addition to addressing the issues presented in section 5.5, we propose that a subset of best practices for identification, resolution and prevention of architectural decay be studied and suggested for practitioners to follow.

References

1. Aoyama, M.: Continuous and Discontinuous Software Evolution: Aspects of Software Evolution across Multiple Product Lines. In: IWPSE 2001 (2001)
2. Henderson-sellers, B.: Object-Oriented Metrics, Measures of Complexity. Prentice-Hall, Englewood Cliffs (1996)
3. Carriere, S.J., et al.: The Perils of Reconstructing Architectures. In: ISAW 1998 (1998)
4. Chidamber, S.R., Kamerer, C.F.: A metrics Suite for Object-Oriented Design. IEEE Trans. Soft. Eng. SE-20(6), 476–493 (1994)
5. Dobrica, L., Niemela, E.: A Survey on Software Architecture Analysis Methods. IEEE Trans. Soft. Eng. 28(7), 638–653 (2002)
6. Eick, S.G., et al.: Does Code Decay? Assessing the Evidence from Change Management Data. IEEE Trans. on Soft. Eng. 27(1), 1–12 (2001)
7. Williams, B.J., Carver, J.C.: Characterizing Software Architecture Changes: An Initial Study. In: ESEM 2007, pp. 410–419 (2007)
8. Hochstein, L., Lindvall, M.: Combating Architectural Degeneration: A survey. Information and Software Technology 47(10), 693–707 (2005)
9. Kraft, J.: Software Aging and Code Decay Phenomenon. TR, Mälardalen University (2007)
10. Yang, Y., et al.: Scenarios for Mining the Software Architecture Evolution. In: MSR 2006 (2006)
11. Lehman, M.M., Belady, L.A.: Program Evolution – Processes of Software Change. Academic Press, London (1985)
12. Parnas, D.L.: Software Aging. In: ICSE 1994, pp. 279–287 (1994)
13. Perry, D.E., Wolf, A.L.: Foundations for the Study of Software Architecture. ACM SIGSOFT Software Engineering Notes 17(4), 40–52 (1992)
14. Pressman, R.S.: Software Engineering – A Practitioner's Approach. Sixth Edition. McGraw-Hill, New York (2005)
15. Ramil, J.F.: Algorithmic Cost Estimation for Software Evolution. In: ICSE 2000 (2000)
16. Stringfellow, C., et al.: Comparison of Software Architecture Reverse Engineering Methods. Information and Software Technology 48, 484–497 (2005)
17. Taylor, R.N., van der Hoek, A.: Software Design and Architecture – The Once and Future Focus of Software Engineering. In: FOSE 2007 (2007)
18. Tran, J.B., et al.: Forward and Reverse Repair of Architecture. In: CASCON 1999 (1999)
19. Van Gurp, J., Bosch, J.: Design Erosion: Problems and Causes. Journal of Systems and Software 61(2) (2002)
20. Van Gurp, J., et al.: Design Preservation Over Subsequent Releases of a Software Product: A Case Study of Baan ERP. Journal of Soft. Maint. & Evol: Research and Practice 17, 277–306 (2005)

Software Fault Localization Using Elastic Net: A New Statistical Approach

Saeed Parsa, Mojtaba Vahidi-Asl, Somaye Arabi, and Behrouz Minaei-Bidgoli

Department of Computer Engineering, Iran University of Science and Technology, Tehran, Iran
parsa@iust.ac.ir, {mojtaba_vahidi,atarabi}@comp.iust.ac.ir, minaeibi@cse.msu.edu

Abstract. Fault localization is an important task in software testing process. The aim is to find latent semantic faults which do not violate program syntactic rules. Statistical debugging techniques are amongst best methods for identifying faults in the program source code. However, they have some drawbacks. They require a large number of executions to identify faults. Furthermore, they do not consider the simultaneous effect of predicates on program termination status. To resolve the problems, in this paper a new approach based on elastic net has been proposed. The proposed approach finds the smallest effective subset of program predicates known as bug predictors. Detecting most effective bug predictors considering fewer amounts of executions as much as possible is highly desirable. The elastic net is advantageous when the number of executions is much smaller than the number of predicates. After selecting bug predictors, the main causes of faults are detected by using existing program slicing technique. The experimental results on two well-known test suites reveal the effectiveness and accuracy of the proposed approach.

Keywords: Software Testing, Statistical debugging, Elastic Net, Program Slicing, Bug Predictors.

1 Introduction

Limitations on available time, money and people to improve software on one hand and increases in complexity and size of software on the other hand, make manual correction of programmatic errors impractical [2]. Therefore, it is necessary to develop automated software-debugging techniques with minimum need for human intervention. One well-known debugging technique is dynamic approach which determines a program behavior by analyzing the value of decision making statements, appearing in the program code, in several executions of the program [3].

One recently developed dynamic technique is statistical debugging which has attracted many researchers over the past few years and has reached significant and promising development [2-6]. In fault localization process, the statistical debuggers measure the value of program predicates such as branches, loops and function return values in different executions of program and try to explain which predicates relate to the faults of the program [4]; To achieve this, statistical methods usually extract

D. Ślęzak et al. (Eds.): ASEA 2009, CCIS 59, pp. 127–134, 2009.

program behavioral model [2]. The extracted models are further applied to detect the program misbehaviors leading to the identification of different types of faults which may appear in the program.

The existing statistical techniques have three major limitations. First, a huge number of both failing and passing executions are required in order to perform the statistical analysis. Providing the passing executions is practical, using regression testing before the deployment phase of software. But, since the software companies remove most critical bugs before the software release, there might be a few number of failing test cases to build a model for the fault localization purpose [7]. Constructing statistical model with few number of failing executions may result in poor support of the model. Thus, we require an approach that could be applicable when the number of predicates of a program is much greater than the number of passing and failing executions. The second main problem is the simultaneous effect of predicates on each other result in failing or passing execution of the program. However, because of high correlation among the predicates, the proposed method has to consider the problem which is known as multicollinearity [9]. The third important problem is the huge number of predicates which is common in large scale programs. In each run of a program, many of the predicates are logically redundant having no predictive power [2].

To cope with the mentioned problems, in this paper we have proposed an algorithm based on elastic net [1], a well-known shrinkage method to select most effective bug predictors. We further applied backward slicing technique, to identify the main causes of failure [7]. The privilege of shrinkage methods is their ability to penalize coefficients in order to minimize the residual sum of squares [10]. The elastic net method provides a stable estimation method that may be used to advantage when there is high multicollinearity among predictor variables [9]. The elastic net estimators are stable in the sense that they are not affected by slight variations in the estimation data [1]. Elastic net method has grouping effect which means that it could select the high collinear features and put them into a group. This characteristic is very useful in fault localization techniques, since it could select fault relevant predicates and put them into groups which we call bug predictor group. This is also advantageous when program has several faults. Elastic net could also produce interpretable models and tends to assign high coefficients to most relevant predicates [1]. In other words, it ignores redundant and irrelevant predicates. The most important advantage of elastic net is in cases that the number of features is much more than the number of observations.

After using elastic net to find the groups of bug predictors, we apply a backward slicing technique based on the extracted bug predictors to determine the main causes of failure.

The remaining parts of the paper are organized as follows. In section two, the previous works which have been done in this context are presented. In section three, we describe our proposed approach. The empirical results on two test cases are shown in section four. Finally, concluding remarks are described in section five.

2 Related Work

One important field in automated fault localization techniques is Statistical debugging. To select a set of predicates that best predict the outcome of every run of a program, Liblit et al. [6] proposed a method based on regularized logistic regression.

The state of art technique has promising results for small programs containing a single fault. But for large programs containing multiple faults, it suffers from some serious scalability problems result in misclassification errors.

In an approach presented in [4], predicates are ranked in the order of their effects on the program failure. It uses a technique based on probabilistic correlations of predicates value and program termination status. However, due to ignoring the *false* value of predicates, the ranks are not determined appropriately. In other words, it considers only whether a predicate was ever observed *true* during an execution.

To resolve the difficulty, both the *true* and *false* values of the predicates observed in correct and incorrect executions of the program are applied to construct the ranking model. The technique called SOBER is based on hypothesis testing which aims to solve single fault problems, incapacitate to detect multiple faults in the program [3].

Liblit et. al. in an approach presented in [5] analyze the combinational effect of predicates on program failures by combining all the statically dependent predicates. However, there may be statically independent predicates, simultaneously, effecting the program failure.

3 The Proposed Approach

In the approach proposed in this section, in order to localize faults in a program, three major steps are followed. In the first step, the program is instrumented in order to collect data from its runtime behavior. In the second step, a recursive algorithm based on elastic net is proposed to select most effective bug predictors. Finally, in the third step, backward slicing technique is employed to detect the likely causes for faults manifested by each of the bug predictors.

3.1 Instrumentation

In order to build statistical model, describing a program behavior, the program has to be executed several times. Execution data, for each run of the program, can be collected by adding extra code to store the value of each program predicate. A predicate is a Boolean expression determining the execution path of the program [5]. This technique of inserting extra code for collecting the value of predicates, at run time, is called instrumentation [2]. Since, in some programming constructs such as *if*, the *else part* is optional, two different predicates are considered. One predicate controls the execution of the *then* part and the other controls the *else* part. Thereby, only the true value of each predicate is considered. After each trial execution of the instrumented program, a file is accessed to count the number of times each predicate has been evaluated as *true*.

3.2 Bug Predictor Selection

To automate the process of bug predictor selection, a recursive elastic net method has been applied in this paper. A brief description of the proposed algorithm for bug predictor selection is shown in Figure 1.

As shown in Figure 1, the algorithm iteratively applies the elastic net method to build a linear classifier which best fits the program predicates. In each iteration, the method extracts most relevant predicates with the program *failing* or *passing* state. The relevance of a predicate with program termination status is determined by its coefficient (i.e. weight) in elastic net linear equation. The parameters *m and t* are completely dependent to the test suite programs and should be tuned in order to achieve the best result. To find the best values for *m and t*, we have applied cross validation technique. In each iteration, some redundant features with the least weights in the equation are removed and the model is reproduced with remaining predicates in next iteration. Since the number of available program runs could be less than the number of predicates, the iteration stops when we have got at most *t* predicates or there is no execution left. At the last part of the algorithm, the remaining predicates are grouped based on their coefficient in the elastic net model. Each group could represent a specific fault in the program.

ELASTIC NET ALGORITHM

*1. Let p_1, p_2, ..., p_n be the **n** program predicates, and let **y** be the binary response variable based on the program termination status and consider there are m trial executions.*

2. While ($n \geq t$)and (m>0)

Begin {while loop}
a. Apply elastic net method to fit a linear classifier, train the classifier and get predicates weights $\mathbf{w}_i$
*b. Delete **k** predicates with the smallest weight in absolute value and set $n \leftarrow n - k$.*
(the values of k, t and elastic net tuning parameters depend on the application)
c. $m \leftarrow m - 1$.
{the value of t could be variable in each iteration based on the application}
End {while loop}

3. Group the remaining predicates, based on their weights (all predicates in each group have the same weight)

Fig. 1. The elastic net algorithm in recursive manner for bug predictor selection

Analysis of the proposed algorithm. In order to understand the role of elastic net method in the proposed fault localization technique, we first describe the problem.

In order to find a relationship between program predicates and the failing or passing state of the program, a linear regression model could be constructed. Let $P_i=(p_{i1},p_{i2},..,p_{in})$ be the vector of predicates' values and y_i be the corresponding program termination status for the *i*th execution. The relationship between P_1, P_2, P_3,..., P_m (*m* is the number of program executions) and the program termination status Y is formulated as

$$Y = \beta_0 + \beta_1 P_1 + P_2 X_1 + \cdots + \beta_n P_n + \varepsilon \tag{1}$$

The term β_0 in equation (1) is the intercept, also known as the bias in machine learning. β_i's are constants known as regression coefficients (weights) and ε is the error of model.

The elastic net is a shrinkage method which could be effective when the number of features is more than the number of observations. It also has grouping effect which gives groups of high correlated features. These privileges make the elastic net a very good method for selecting bug predictors in the program. The β parameters in elastic net method are estimated as

$$\hat{\beta}^{elastic.net} = arg\min_{\beta} \sum_{i=1}^{m} (y_i - \beta_0 - \sum_{j=1}^{n} p_{ij}\beta_j)^2$$
$$subject\ to\ \lambda \sum_{j=1}^{n} \beta_j^2 + (1-\lambda) \sum_{j=1}^{n} \beta_j \leq r \qquad (2)$$

Where $\hat{\beta}$ is the estimated vector of coefficients. r is a tuning parameter which depends on the dataset features. As shown in equation (2), elastic net, imposes two penalties on the coefficients. The parameter λ in penalty function is in [0,1) in most applications. If λ=0, the equation (2) becomes the lasso equation [11] and if λ=1, it would be the ridge regression [10]. Thus, by choosing an appropriate value of λ between zero and one, the equations may have the characteristics of both lasso and ridge regression methods [1]. There are different well-known methods to select such tuning parameters [10]. In the case we have only training data, cross-validation method is an appropriate one to estimate the prediction error and compare different models. For the two tuning parameters in the elastic net and two others in the proposed algorithm, described earlier, we applied two different cross-validation on a two-dimensional surface. For choosing r, we examine different values of λ, such as 0,0.001,0.05,0.1,…,0.95 and for each one we tried 5 and 10 fold cross validation dependent on the training data. The tuning parameter, r, is the one giving the smallest miss-classification error.

An important characteristic of elastic net is its grouping power which finds group of highly correlated features. Consider a program has multiple faults and each fault is manifested in one or more predicates. In other words, each fault is related to its corresponding group of bug predictors. In order to localize faults, all the bug predictors in each group should be reported to the debugger to seek for the main cause of the bug with the help of program slicing technique which has been described in section 3.3. To achieve this, the selected features are grouped based on the values of their coefficients. In other words, the coefficient values of features in each group are identical or close to identical.

3.3 Backward Slicing Technique

A program dependency graph can be extracted from a program source code, by analyzing data and control dependencies in between the program statements. Starting with a bug predictor, the dependency graph is traversed in the opposite directions to find all the instructions on which the values applied in the predicate are calculated [7]. For each bug predictor detected in section 3.2, the backward slicing technique is applied to find the potential causes of faults, inspecting less amount of code.

4 Experimental Results

In this section, the results of applying the proposed approach are presented. The evaluation of the proposed method has been done on Siemens and EXIF test suites.

4.1 Experiments on EXIF

EXIF is image processing software. There exist three known semantic faults in this software which make it to crash. These faults are mentioned in [2]. The approach that is presented in this paper finds the faults by detecting the most relevant bug predictors. We have found one bug predictor which was previously unknown in addition to the three known bug predictors.

Table 1 shows four bug predictors in EXIF which are ranked based on their relevancy to the software faults. These four predicates are compared with Liblit method [2][7] in Figure 2. Here, only the four highest ranked predicates are reported. As shown in the Figure 2, the elastic net method gives higher scores to the predicates which are mentioned in Table 1; in the next stage, using backward slicing technique on these predicates, all statements affecting the bug predictors have been reported to the user.

4.2 Experiments on Siemens

Another test suite we have used to evaluate our approach is Siemens test suite [3]. Siemens contains seven programs. Each program has several test cases and some faulty versions where the faults have been inserted manually.

In order to analyze the proposed approach, an appropriate criterion is to study the amount of localized faults in this test suite. However, it is not adequate when we aim to compare different debugging approaches. In fact it is required to study not only the amount of revealed bugs, but also the proportion of code that has been traced manually after using the corresponding automated debugging approach in order to find the main causes of faults.

The proposed approach in this paper could manifest 92 out of 132 faults (i.e. 71%) by manual inspecting nearly 10% of code; whereas the method introduced in [3] has detected 68 faults (i.e. %52.31).

The experiments show effectiveness of backward slicing technique in detecting the main causes of failure in 75% of cases which helps the user to inspect less amount of code.

In Figure 3, the proposed approach has been compared with two well-known debugging techniques: Liblit [5] and Sober [3].

Table 1. The four bug predictors with highest scores in EXIF software

Predicate #	Bug relevant predicate	Function
P_1	*o + s > buf_size is TRUE*	exif-mnote-data-canon()
P_2	*i<0*	Jpeg_data_set_exif_data()
P_3	*maxlen > 1900*	exif_entry_get_value()
P_4	*strlen (val)==NULL*	exif_entry_get_value()

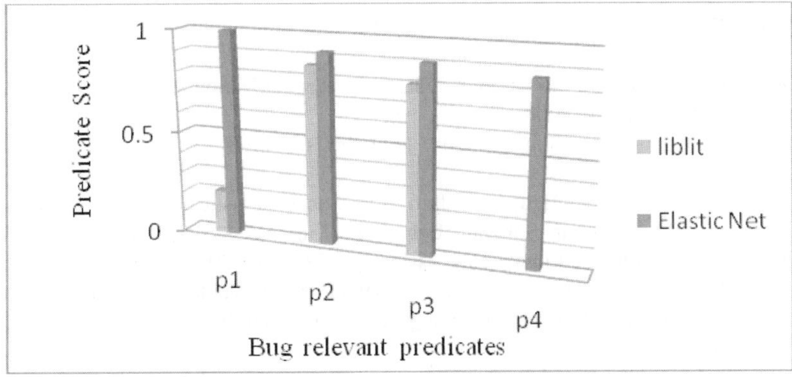

Fig. 2. The scores given to high bug predictors in Elastic Net and Liblit methods

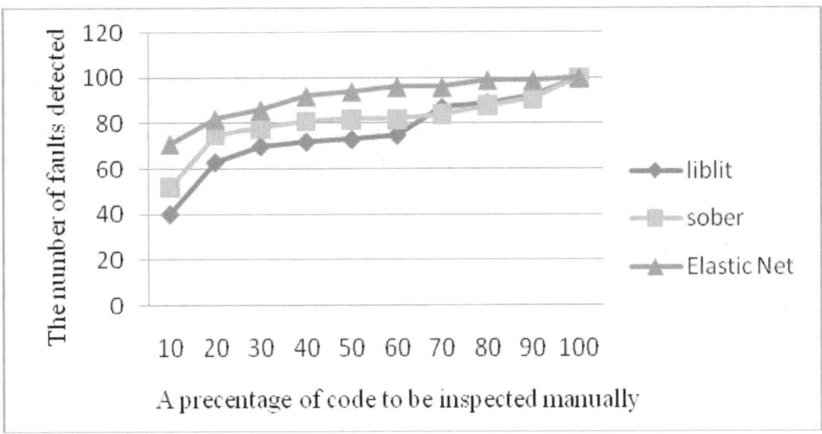

Fig. 3. The proposed approach compared with known statistical approaches on Siemens test suite

5 Concluding Remarks

In this paper, we have presented a novel statistical debugging approach for fault localization. It has two main stages: Identifying accurate bug predictors using elastic net method and finding the potential causes of failure based on detected bug predictors by applying backward slicing technique. Although backward slicing has been applied in various debugging techniques, but it has not been examined in statistical debugging approaches working with bug predictors. The Experimental results show that our approach is able to localize more faults compared to previous techniques with less amount of code inspection by the user.

References

1. Del Mol, C., De Vito, E., Rosasco, L.: Elastic-Net regularization in Learning Theory, technical report, MIT press (2008)
2. Liblit, B.: Cooperative Bug Isolation. PhD thesis, University of California, Berkeley (2004)
3. Liu, C., Yan, X., Fei, L., Han, J., Midkiff, S.P.: Sober: Statistical model-based bug localization. In: 10th European Software Eng. Conf./13th ACM SIGSOFT Int'l Symposium Foundations of Software Engineering, Lisbon, pp. 286–295 (2005)
4. Liblit, B., Naik, M., Zheng, A., Aiken, A., Jordan, M.: Scalable Statistical Bug Isolation. In: Int'l Conference Programming Language Design and Implementation, Chicago, pp. 15–26 (2005)
5. Arumuga Nainar, P., Chen, T., Rosin, J., Liblit, B.: Statistical debugging using compound Boolean predicates. In: International Symposium on Software Testing and Analysis, pp. 5–15. ACM Press, London (2007)
6. Liblit, B., Aiken, A., Zheng, X., Jordan, M.I.: Bug isolation via remote program sampling. In: Proceedings of the ACM SIGPLAN 2003 Conference on Programming Language Design and Implementation, pp. 141–154. ACM Press, San Diego (2003)
7. Zeller, A.: Why Programs Fail: A Guide to Systematic Debugging. Morgan Kaufmann, San Francisco (2006)
8. Fei, L., Lee, K., Li, F., Midkiff, S.P.: Argus: Online statistical bug detection. In: Baresi, L., Heckel, R. (eds.) FASE 2006. LNCS, vol. 3922, pp. 308–323. Springer, Heidelberg (2006)
9. Chatterjee, S., Hadi, A., Price, B.: Regression Analysis by Example, 4th edn. Wiley Series in Probability and Statistics, New York (2006)
10. Hastie, T.J., Tibshirani, R.J., Friedman, J.: The Elements of Statistical Learning: Data Mining Inference and Prediction. Springer, New York (2001)
11. Tibshirani, R.: Optimal Reinsertion: Regression shrinkage and selection via the lasso. J.R.Statist. Soc. 58, 267–288 (1996)

Applying Formal Methods to Process Innovation

Antonella Santone and Maria Tortorella

Dipartimento di Ingegneria, University of Sannio, Benevento, Italy
{tortorella,santone}@unisannio.it

Abstract. Continuous improvement of the software processes, including both production and maintenance, is a necessary condition to ensure fundamental software quality. An improvement opportunity comes from the availability of innovative process components to be integrated in a working software process. Formal methods are more and more used for modeling and verifying software systems. In this paper formal methods are instead used for modeling an innovative process component and understanding its integrability degree in an operative software process.

Keywords: Formal methods, CCS, process innovation, process improvement, process modelling.

1 Introduction

Continuous improvement of the software processes, including both production and maintenance, is a necessary condition to ensure fundamental software quality [2,11]. Software quality problems are widely acknowledged to affect the development cost and time. To mitigate these problems, much attention has to be paid to developing approaches, models and standards for Software Process Improvement (SPI). However, the number of organisations that have systematically adopted strategies to process improvement is only a part of the entire population of the software organisations [13]. This is partly due to the complexity and length of the timeframe needed for reaching a certain recognised level with reference to the chosen models, for example CMMI or Spice. Therefore, an SPI approach is often considered an expensive undertaking. In addition, political pressures often focus more on obtaining a specific level than creating actual improvements. All this creates demotivations in facing software process improvement tasks [10]. Nevertheless, improving software processes is an important task to be performed within a software organisation for avoiding that innovative initiatives are individually undertaken from the software engineer without recognising and codifying them in the official software process.

The aim of this paper is to propose an approach to improvement through the integration of innovative process components within the software process to be improved. This integration has to guarantee the operativeness of the software process. In this paper, the term process component is used in a very generic manner and it can indicate: a guideline; a technique; a method; or a simpler process.

D. Ślęzak et al. (Eds.): ASEA 2009, CCIS 59, pp. 135–142, 2009.

This paper faces the problem of exploiting process components already defined and proposed in literature. In particular, an approach is proposed for modelling and characterising a process component with the aim of using it in an operative context. The idea follows the work presented in [15] where a process characterisation framework, divided in specification and evaluation sections, was defined. The technique proposed in this paper is based on formal methods is proposed. Once the process component to be innovated is identified, the aim is to provide a support for: simulating the behaviour of the old process; checking the integrability of innovative process components; and verifying that properties and behaviour of the innovated process are held.

Using formal description techniques for process innovation permits having an unambiguous description of the analysed software processes. First, a methodology to specify software components is introduced based on the Calculus of Communicating Systems (CCS) [8]. Afterwards, equivalence notions are used for establishing whether a process component can be replaced by an innovative one and a temporal logic [14] is used for describing properties representing the innovation.

The paper is organised as follows: Section 2 discusses concepts regarding process improvement and formal methods; Section 3 shows the core of the approach; while Section 4 presents an application of the methodology through a simple example. Finally, considerations and conclusions are given in Section 5.

2 Preliminaries

The improvement of a software process may concerns: the extension of an existing process by introducing one or more innovative process components; the replacement of one or more components of the process by semantically equivalent innovative ones; or the modification of one or more software process components.

The above modalities also include building a new software process, where the constituting process components will be integrated by extending each other.

Four tasks can be considered for improving a software process:

1. identification of the improvement goals and innovative characteristics of the process component to be integrated in the process [2,6];
2. identification of the process components to be substituted or added for attaining the preset improvement goals;
3. definition and/or identification of the process components to be integrated;
4. quantitative assessment of the quality and integrability of the process components identified, and of the risks their adoption may entail.

This paper is mainly focussed on task 3 and faces the problem of exploiting process components already proposed in literature. In fact, the richest sources of innovative process components is the specialist literature in the Software Engineering field, reports of research projects, tools and documentation provided by software houses, information available on the Internet, etc. It is needed to choose the most suitable process component for integration in the software process and fully understand it. This paper follows an approach proposed in [15], and introduces formal method techniques for formally defining the approach and favouring its deterministic application.

Formal methods have a sound mathematical foundation and support reasoning about properties of systems. There is a large diversity of formal methods for system, software and hardware development. This section focuses on model checking [4], an automated technique for exhaustively verifying finite state concurrent systems. In the model checking framework, systems are modelled as transition systems and requirements are expressed as formulae in temporal logic. A model checker accepts two inputs, a transition system and a temporal formula, and returns "true" if the system satisfies the formula and "false" otherwise; in this case the model checker reports the error via an execution trace called a counterexample, showing where the violation occurred. For applying model checking, we need: (i) a precise notation for defining systems; (ii) a precise notation for defining properties.

To cope with the first need, specification languages were developed such as CCS [8]. The second need can be solved by using a temporal logic such as the mu-calculus logic [14]. Many environments for formal verification were developed, one of the most popular is the Concurrency Workbench of New Century (CWB-NC) [5], which includes several different specification languages, among which CCS. The specifications can be checked for different equivalences, and different logics can be used to express properties. Fore brevity, CCS [8] and mu-calculus temporal logic [14] are not treated here. The reader can refer to the literature.

3 The Method

The proposed CCS-based technique will be used for both modelling a process component and undestanding its integrability in a working software process for innovating it. In this context, modelling activities are important as the literature is populated of process components described in a redundant and ambiguous manner making difficult their direct analysis, evaluation and exploitation.

The CCS language is used for expressing some of the most relevant aspects of a software process and its components. This information is also evaluated for understanding if an innovative process component can be integrated into the software process, in place of an already used one, by keeping the elaboration goals. A process component is modelled in terms of structural and qualitative aspects. Structural aspects are related to: input to the process component; output it produces; its goal; applied techniques; used tools; and so on. The qualitative aspects regard the quality of the analysed process component and its results.

This paper regards mainly structural aspects of the software component to be analysed: goal, input, output and technique. In the following, it will be explained how the CCS specification will be used for formalising a process component. From now on we use well-terminating processes: *A CCS process is well-terminating if it performs an action* $\overline{\delta}$ *if and only if it terminates right after that.* The typical

Table 1. Operators for well-terminating processes

$$p\|q = (p[\delta_1/\delta] \mid q[\delta_2/\delta] \mid (\delta_1.\delta_2.DONE + \delta_2.\delta_1.DONE))\backslash\{\delta_1, \delta_2\}$$
$$p; q = (p[\delta_3/\delta] \mid \delta_3.q)\backslash\{\delta_3\}$$
$$DONE \stackrel{\text{def}}{=} \overline{\delta}.nil$$

use of δ can be found in the definition of the operators $\|$ and ";" (see Table 1). The two operators (defined as in Milner [8]) correspond to the sequentialization and parallel execution of two well-terminating processes. The processes resulting from their applications are well-terminating too.

The constant $DONE$ corresponds to a process whose task is to terminate without further moves. The ";" operator will be suitably used to express the sequentiality of two processes p and q: p must terminate before q can start its execution. The process "$p\|q$" represents the parallel execution of p and q and terminates only if both processes terminate. Formally the CCS specification of a process component is so defined:

$$M_i \stackrel{\text{def}}{=} goal_{M_i}.(input_{M_i}\|technique_{M_i}\|output_{M_i})\backslash L_{M_i}$$

where:

- $goal_{M_i}$ indicates the goal of the specified process component;
- $input_{M_i}$ is the CCS process specifying the inputs that the process component has to receive;
- $technique_{M_i}$ is the process CCS representing only the operations used to reach the specified goal. Further refinements can be easily added;
- $output_{M_i}$ is the CCS process specifying the outputs that the process component has to return;
- L_{M_i} is a set of the communication actions of the three CCS processes: $input_{M_i}$, $technique_{M_i}$, $output_{M_i}$.

Once defined each process component, a working process can be modelled as the following CCS process: $All \stackrel{\text{def}}{=} (M_1 \| \cdots \| M_n)\backslash L$ where each M_i, $i \in [1..n]$, represents a process component, and L is a set of messages sent from one component and accepted by another one, representing, thus, synchronisation points.

Improving a working process means that a process component, M_i, (or more than one) can be replaced by an innovative one, X, but some properties must be guaranteed: (i) the innovative process must simulate the behaviour of the old process; (ii) the innovative process can be integrated with the other old components; (iii) new properties, representing the innovation, must hold.

Formally, if we substitute M_i, $i \in [1..n]$, with X, for guaranteeing the above properties, some conditions must be checked using notion of behavioural equivalence and temporal logic. We define the ρ-simulation meaning that q simulates p, over ρ, when q's behaviour patterns are at least as rich as those of p over ρ.

Definition 1. *Let p, q be two CCS processes and ρ a set of actions.*

- *A ρ-simulation, $\mathcal{S}$, is a binary relation on $\mathcal{P} \times \mathcal{P}$ such that $p\mathcal{S}q$ implies: $p \xrightarrow{\alpha}_\rho r'$ implies $q \xrightarrow{\alpha}_\rho q'$ with $p'\mathcal{S}q'$;*
- *q ρ-simulates p ($p \prec_\rho q$) iff there exists a ρ-simulation $\mathcal{S}$ containing the pair (p, q).*

The conditions to be checked are formally defined as follows:

1. $M_i \prec_S X$ for $i \in [1..n]$; where $S = goal_{M_i} \cup sort(input_{M_i}) \cup sort(output_{M_i})$;
2. $M_i \approx_L X$ for $i \in [1..n]$;
3. $(M_1 \parallel \cdots \parallel M_{i-1} \parallel X \parallel M_{i+1} \parallel \cdots \parallel M_n)\backslash L \models \varphi$.

The first condition states that the innovative process component X S-simulates M_i, that is X can match all the moves of M_i, considering only the actions in S. This means that X simulates M_i on the goal, inputs and outputs. X can have more moves than M_i. The second condition states that X and M_i behave in the same way with respects to L. Since M_i communicates using a set of actions L, we can observe the behaviour of M_i through L. Thus, M_i can be replaced by an equivalent process X which is indistinguishable from M_i with respect to L.

The third condition states that the new software process obtained by substituting M_i with X satisfies the property φ. The property can be expressed using a temporal logic as for example mu-calculus [14]. To guarantee that this condition holds an attempt can be to use directly the CWB-NC.

4 An Example

In this section a simple example of application of our approach is shown. A simple problem is considered: given two inputs n and m, calculate the greatest common divisor of the factorial of n and the square of m. The process solving the problem is composed of three process components representing the computation of the factorial, square and greatest common divisor.

The following CCS process M_1, representing the process component to calculate the factorial of a number is represented as:

$$M_1 \stackrel{\text{def}}{=} fatt.(I_1 \parallel T_1 \parallel O_1)\backslash\{in, out\} \qquad I_1 \stackrel{\text{def}}{=} input.\overline{in}.DONE$$

$$T_1 \stackrel{\text{def}}{=} in.prod.\overline{out}.DONE \qquad O_1 \stackrel{\text{def}}{=} out.\overline{output}.DONE$$

The goal is defined as $fatt$, and the CCS process T_1 is referred to the applied technique in terms of the used operations; in particular T_1 uses only products (action *prod*). The CCS process I_1 receives only a value as input (through channel *input*) that forwards (channel *in*) to T_1. T_1, after completing its computation, sends (through channel *out*) the result that the CCS process O_1 captures and returns externally, through the channel *output*.

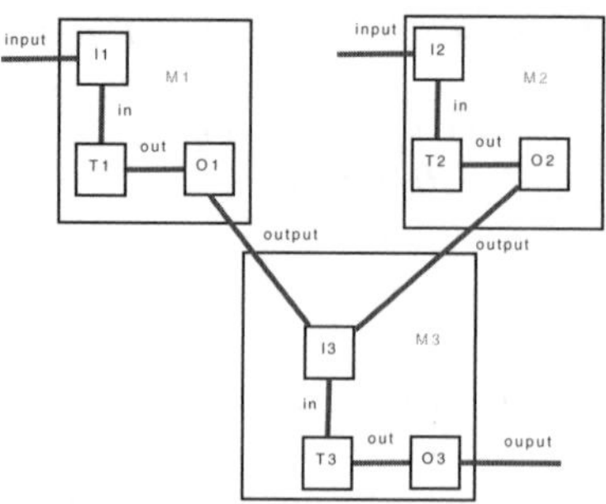

Fig. 1. A graphical view

Similarly, the CCS process M_2 represents the process component to calculate the square of a number and it specified as follows:

$$M_2 \stackrel{\text{def}}{=} square.(I_2 \parallel T_2 \parallel O_2)\backslash\{in, out\} \quad I_2 \stackrel{\text{def}}{=} input.\overline{in}.DONE$$
$$T_2 \stackrel{\text{def}}{=} in.prod.\overline{out}.DONE \qquad O_2 \stackrel{\text{def}}{=} out.\overline{output}.DONE$$

The goal is defined as *square*, and the technique represented by the CCS process T_2 uses only the product operations (action *prod*). The CCS process I_2 waits for the input (through channel *input*) that forwards (channel *in*) to T_2. Finally, the CCS process O_2 returns, through the channel *output*, the result. The action *out* is the communication channel between T_2 and O_2. Finally, the CCS process M_3 represents the process component to calculate the greatest common divisor (gcd) of two numbers. It is defined as:

$$M_3 \stackrel{\text{def}}{=} gcd.(I_3 \parallel T_3 \parallel O_3)\backslash\{in, out\}$$
$$I_3 \stackrel{\text{def}}{=} input.\overline{in}.DONE \parallel input.\overline{in}.DONE$$
$$T_3 \stackrel{\text{def}}{=} (in.DONE \parallel in.DONE); div.\overline{out}.DONE \quad O_3 \stackrel{\text{def}}{=} out.\overline{output}.DONE$$

The goal is defined as *gcd*, and the technique represented by the CCS process T_3 shows only the used operations; more precisely, T_3 computes the gcd by determining the prime factorizations of the two numbers. Therefore the basic operations are divisions (action *div*). The CCS process I_3 waits for both the two inputs (through channel *input*) that forwards (channel *in*) to T_3. Finally, the CCS process O_3 returns, through the channel *output*, the result. The action *out* is the communication channel between T_3 and O_3. The complete CCS process *All* is the following:

$$All \stackrel{\text{def}}{=} (M_1[f_1] \parallel M_2[f_1] \parallel M_3[f_2])\backslash\{c\}$$
$$where\ f_1 = output/c\ f_2 = input/c, input/c$$

Note that, through the two relabelling functions f_1 and f_2, the outputs of the processes M_1 and M_2 are the inputs of the process M_3.

Figure 1 shows a graphical view of the CCS specification of the complete system. Suppose that we want to innovate the process component M_3 using the Euclidean algorithm which uses only subtractions (action sub) and that the innovative process X is formally defined as:

$$X \stackrel{\text{def}}{=} gcd.(I \parallel T \parallel O)\backslash\{in, out\}$$

$$I \stackrel{\text{def}}{=} input.\overline{in}.DONE \parallel input.\overline{in}.DONE$$

$$T \stackrel{\text{def}}{=} (in.DONE \parallel in.DONE); sub.\overline{out}.DONE \qquad O \stackrel{\text{def}}{=} out.\overline{output}.DONE$$

Using formal verification environments it can be proved that:

- $M_3 \prec_S X$ where $S = \{gcd, input, in, output, out\}$;
- $M_3 \approx_{\{in,out\}} X$.

Moreover, some properties characterising the innovation can be expressed using a temporal logic. For example, no division operation (action div) is performed by the new process All, obtained by replacing the process M_3 with X. This property can be expressed using, for example, mu-calculus as $\nu Z.\, [div]\, \mathtt{ff} \wedge [-div]\, Z$ (see [14]). All the above three checks guarantee that M_3 can be safely replaced by X, obtaining an innovative process.

5 Conclusion and Related Work

An approach is presented for process improvement through the adoption of innovative software components informally proposed in different sources. The paper shows how to use formal methods for modelling and understanding the integrability degree of an innovative process component in an operative software process. As far as we know, this is the first attempt to exploit process algebras for process innovation. In specific contexts, such as service-oriented computing area, formal methods have already been used to improvement. First, unambiguous semantics for the languages WS-BPEL and WS-CDL, used to describe service compositions and interaction protocols (called *choreography*), has been defined. An overview of the various formalisms proposed, including process algebras, is contained in van Breugel and Koshkina [3]. Once a formal model of the system is available, it is possible to use it to innovate and compose web services [7], where Petri nets are used. One of the current research issues in the web service field deals with providing (semi)automatic support to web service composition for correctly defining the service interaction model respect some predefined goal [12], representing an innovative system requirement.

The applicability of the proposed approach has been discussed through an example that nevertheless its simplicity, describes aims and uses. Further analysis is needed in a real software process and with innovative software components. In addition, concepts will be added to the proposed approach for better modelling a process component. In addition, the authors will work on the extension of the formal method techniques and approaches for offering a support for choosing in a set of candidate innovative process component the one that better meets the improvement exigencies of a software process, even with incomplete information.

References

1. Barbuti, R., De Francesco, N., Santone, A., Vaglini, G.: Selective mu-calculus and Formula-Based Abstractions of Transition Systems. Journal of Computer and System Sciences 59(3) (1999)
2. Basili, V.R., Daskalantonakis, M.K., Yacobellis, R.H.: Technology transfer at Motorola. IEEE Software 11(2) (1994)
3. Breugel, F., Koshkina, M.: Models and verification of BPEL (2006), `http://www.cse.yorku.ca/~franck/research/drafts/tutorial.pdf`
4. Clarke, E.M., Grumberg, O., Peled, D.: Model Checking. MIT Press, Cambridge (2000)
5. Cleaveland, R., Sims, S.: The NCSU Concurrency Workbench. In: Alur, R., Henzinger, T.A. (eds.) CAV 1996. LNCS, vol. 1102, pp. 394–397. Springer, Heidelberg (1996)
6. Dyba, T.: An empirical investigation of the key factors for success in software process improvement. IEEE Transactions on Software Engineering 31(5) (2005)
7. Hamadi, R., Benatallah, B.: A Petri Net-based Model for Web Service Composition. In: Proceedings of the 14th Australasian Database Conference (ADC 2003), Adelaide, South Australia (February 2003)
8. Milner, R.: Communication and Concurrency. Prentice-Hall, Englewood Cliffs (1989)
9. Napier, N.P., Kim, J., Mathiassen, L.: Software Process Re-engineering: A Model and its Application to an Industrial Case Study. Software Process: Improvement and Practice 13(5) (2008)
10. Niazi, M., Ali Babar, M., Katugampola, N.M.: Demotivators of Software Process Improvement: An Empirical Investigation. Software Process: Improvement and Practice 13(3) (2008)
11. Paulk, M.C., Weber, C., Curtis, B., Chrissis, M.B.: The Capability Maturity Model: Guidelines for Improving the Software Process, p. 441. Addison-Wesley Publishing Co., Reading (1995)
12. Pistore, M., Traverso, P., Bertoli, P., Marconi, A.: Automated Synthesis of Composite BPEL4WS Web Services. In: Proceedings of the 3rd IEEE International Conference on Web Services (ICWS 2005), Orlando, Florida, USA, July 11-15 (2005)
13. Staples, M., Niazi, M., Jeffery, R., Abrahams, A., Byatt, P., Murphy, R.: An exploratory study of why organizations do not adopt CMMI. Journal of Systems and Software 80(6) (2007)
14. Stirling, C.: An Introduction to Modal and Temporal Logics for CCS. In: Boissonnat, J.-D., Laumond, J.-P. (eds.) Geometry and Robotics. LNCS, vol. 391. Springer, Heidelberg (1989)
15. Tortorella, M., Visaggio, G.: Evaluation of a scenario-based reading technique for analysing process components. Journal of Software Maintenance 13(3) (2001)

Abstracting Models from Execution Traces for Performing Formal Verification

Thierry Bodhuin, Federico Pagnozzi, Antonella Santone, Maria Tortorella, and Maria Luisa Villani

Dipartimento di Ingegneria, University of Sannio, Benevento, Italy
bodhuin@unisannio.it, fed.984@gmail.com,
{santone,tortorella,villani}@unisannio.it

Abstract. Because of its complexity, software system verification is a hard task and very often neglected for complex distributed component-based architectures with high degree of dynamism. Monitoring and verification of these systems are important even when they have to be running with a high level of availability and low halt time. Model checking is an automatic technique to verify compliance of the system implementation with respect to the requirements. In this paper we address the problem of abstracting a process model from a set of execution traces of a Java application with the aim of performing formal verification through model checking.

Keywords: Runtime instrumentation, bytecode, CCS, model checking.

1 Introduction

Modern software systems are becoming more and more complex with distributed component-based architectures and a high degree of dynamism enabled by object-oriented languages. This complexity reflects on the verification process, especially for critical systems where formal methods like model checking are necessary to assess reliability.

Model checking [7] is an automatic technique to verify compliance of the system implementation with respect to its defined requirements. It applies to a formal description of the system behaviour as a finite automata, and to a temporal-logic formula representing the requirement to be verified. Examples of such specification languages are, respectively, the Calculus of Communicating Systems (CCS) [18], which provides a Labelled Transition System (LTS) semantic of processes and it is especially powerful to describe concurrency, and the mu-calculus logic [22].

In the context of software verification, a non-trivial problem to be faced is the actual availability of the CCS description of the system to be analysed. This description has to provide a model of the behaviour of the system into a finite LTS that is enough faithful to the real system, so that the verification process is then feasible and useful. In the best cases, such models might have been realised in the design phase of the system development process, although usually other notations are used, such as UML dynamic diagrams from which a translation to

D. Ślęzak et al. (Eds.): ASEA 2009, CCIS 59, pp. 143–150, 2009.

CCS could be attempted. But, even then, design models are not always consistently updated in the implementation activities to reflect the realised behaviour of the system or in the subsequent phases of software maintenance and evolution. Therefore, reverse engineering methods [6] have to be used for supporting program comprehension and obtaining realistic models. These methods must include both static and dynamic analysis. In particular dynamic analysis is needed for capturing aspects like dynamic binding in object oriented systems, such as Java, and understanding process concurrency.

In this paper, we address the problem of abstracting a process model from a set of execution traces of a Java application to the aim of formal verification through model checking. In particular, given a class of safety properties, we are interested in checking whether these properties were satisfied in all of the runs of the system logged. We actually start from the Java byte-code so that the applicability of the method is widen to the cases where the Java source code is not available, or because generated from other bytecode-compiled languages. Using Java Instrumentation API [16], the Java byte-code is instrumented at runtime with instructions useful for generating logs containing just the necessary events for the verification of a specific set of properties.

We propose a technique to build appropriate models out of the system traces, preserving the behaviour with respect to the class of safety properties to be verified. This technique consists of an iterative procedure that starts from an initial raw main process, which includes all the system traces as alternative branches. Given a set of actions ρ, built from the actions appearing in the logical formulae, at each step, a more compact process is obtained, through (sub)processes merge and reduction, allowed for states not immediately reachable from actions in ρ. This new process is still capable to generate all the given traces, but may feature additional behaviour. However, this behaviour will not impact on the truth of the safety properties to be verified. The process transformation step is structured as a sequence of rules, including fold/unfold rules already used for optimisation of logic programs [21], to form a ρ-strategy. With this method, we intend to both ease the verification process and provide the user with an appropriate abstraction from the non-critical states identified through ρ. Indeed, the proposed method is parametric with respect to ρ (namely, the ρ-strategy); by changing this set, different process models can be obtained, featuring different levels of abstraction. The most abstract (or compact) process is obtained if ρ is the empty set, while a formula-based process model is built if ρ contains the actions occurring in the formula itself. Thus, this model can be used for the formal verification. Moreover, the transformation rules directly apply to the CCS processes, without the need for building the corresponding LTSs, contrary to other works [23] that propose to act on the automata.

Although our method cannot ensure that the system under consideration is correct (if it is) it can find an error if it is not correct. Thus, it holds that if the discovered model, obtained by applying the ρ-strategy does not satisfy a safety φ, with property that the actions occurring φ belong to ρ, then the application does not also.

The paper is organised as follows. In Section 2 instrumentation concepts are recalled. In Section 3 the Java byte-code instrumentation method and the logs-to-CCS traces conversion are briefly explained. Finally, considerations and comparisons with some related work are given in Section 4.

2 Instrumentation

Instrumentation refers to an ability of monitoring and measuring the level of a product's performance, diagnosing errors and writing trace information. Instrumentation is in the form of code instructions that monitor specific components in a system [19]. Instrumentation approaches can be of two types, source code instrumentation and binary instrumentation (http://asm.objectweb.org).

Instrumentation may be done in static way [19], without executing the code, or in a dynamic way [10,14], during code execution. The static approaches require the availability of the source code. While the dynamic approaches permit also to perform the instrumentation of code potentially downloaded on the fly from the network [2,3], such as Java applets or Java Web Start applications. Many software systems exist for applying dynamic instrumentation for different hardware/Operating system environments using run-time binary patching. With the Java era, the instrumentation can be performed directly in the running virtual machine by rewriting the Java bytecode [17] as it is loaded inside the virtual machine or when requested. The most flexible approach for instrumenting Java applications regards the use of instrumentation as dynamic transformation of bytecode during the software system execution.

The bytecode transformation, considered in this paper, is applied at runtime. It is based on the new Java instrumentation API [16] and use the ASM Library for parsing and applying modification to the Java byte code. The implemented instrumentation library is an agent entirely written in Java for the instrumentation and monitoring of Java applications. The Java Instrumentation API allows bytecode transformation when the Java bytecode is loaded by the class loader. It allows getting information regarding when and which class is loaded at a certain time and extracting information regarding class structure methods, fields and control flow, through some bytecode library. Both Java Instrumentation API and ASM were used for providing flexibility and lowest possible overhead during execution of the instrumented program.

3 The Method

The proposed method is based on two main steps:

1. obtaining execution traces from Java Bytecode-based programs by applying bytecode instrumentation;
2. discovering models from traces using program transformation for checking properties.

The following two subsections will discuss in a major detail each of this steps.

3.1 Obtaining Execution Traces from Java Bytecode-Based Programs

The execution traces, recovered during a software system execution, include both static information and dynamic information. For obtaining execution traces, software systems need to be instrumented adding some instructions called instrumentation code. The instrumentation of Java bytecode is applied when software is executed using the Java instrumentation API [16]. However, different execution of the same software systems will generally produce different traces depending on the execution order of the different instructions due to Thread scheduling or other software external context. For simplicity, we used XML files for storing the execution traces. Choosing the right model for execution traces depends on the objective of the system that will use them. This is a difficult task to be performed in a general way without affecting performance or generating too much unneeded information.

All the information at the static level and additional information at dynamic level needed to be kept. In particular, the information gathered at the dynamic level are only method calls from application level methods, calls to the wait and notify methods of Object instances and class/instance variables accesses either in read or write mode. During the static analysis, full class names are recorded together with the super class or interface name list, if needed. In addition, the signatures of all the methods are registered together with the exception class names that may be thrown.

The Java Instrumentation API allows to register a class called Agent, containing a premain method that is executed before the "main" class. The premain method gets as parameter an object implementing an interface called Instrumentation that allows the system to catch any class loading, thus permitting the bytecode redefinition for instrumentation purpose. The adopted instrumentation uses the ASM library for obtaining the class structure before instrumenting.

Three types of instrumentation that were used for obtaining dynamic information: method calls, field accesses and synchronisation events.

In the following, the approach will be illustrated with reference to the simple example shown in Table 3.1 which concerns the definition of a class including the factorial method. The method receives two integers y and n and calculates the factorial of y if $0 \leq y \leq n$, decrementing the value of the variable n, otherwise calculates the factorial of $y-1$. The program prints the value of the variable $fatt$ if $fatt$ is equal to n, otherwise prints 0.

In [4] the instructions inserted during the instrumentation phase in the small sample program and the traces obtained by the execution of the program for the static information are discussed.

3.2 Discovering Models from Traces Using Program Transformation for Checking Properties

The Unfold/Fold transformation approach was introduced in [5] to manage functional programs and then used for logic programs [21]. This approach is based

Table 1. A simple program

```
public class Factorial {
  private int y, n;
  public Factorial(int y, int n) {
   this.y=y;    this.n=n;
  }
  public void factorial() {
1     fatt=1;                        (k)
      if (y >=0 && y <= n)
2        n--;                        (a)
      else
3        y--;                        (c)
      while (y>0){
4       fatt *= y;                   (b)
5       y--;}                        (c)
      if (fatt == n)
6        System.out.println(fatt); (l)
      else
7        System.out.println(0);    (d)
  }}
```

on the construction, by means of a *strategy*, of a sequence $\{P_k\}$ of programs each obtained from the preceding ones by using a transformation rule. The rules are based on *Unfold* and *Fold*, i.e. expansion and contraction of a sub-expression of P_k using the definitions of P_k or a preceding program. Other rules are used, as, for example, *Definition Elimination* and *Introduction*. Each program in the sequence is related with the preceding ones by a particular semantic notion. Developments of the transformational approach for CCS can be found in [9], where it has been proved that all programs of a transformation sequence are strongly equivalent. In this paper, for lack of space, the basic concepts of CCS are not recalled. The reader can refer to [18]. We suitably define other new rules (*Substitution & Introduction* and *Simplification*) for the aim of building models starting from traces. In particular: the *Substitution & Introduction* rule substitutes constants with a new constant definition. The Substitution & Introduction rule does not preserve strong equivalence, but trace equivalence. The *Simplification* rule simplifies sub-processes, based on known properties of the operators. These rules allow to implement the synthesis procedure to CCS from traces which is mainly based on merging all states reached by the same transition. Further, we have defined a strategy, i.e. an order of application of the transformation rules, to obtain a CCS program from a given set of traces. Informally, the strategy merges states through the application of the Substitution & Introduction rule, it introduces new definitions only for states reachable from the same transition and it folds these states using the new definitions; subsequently, it unfolds the body of the new definitions, so that the simplification rule can be applied. The Simplification and the Elimination rules are applied as much as possible, in order to reduce the CCS model.

The aim is to obtain a CCS model over which to check properties. Following the classification in [22] of liveness, weak liveness, safety and weak safety properties, the properties we handle in this paper can be characterised as follows:

ρ-safety properties: no run with actions in ρ contains a bad feature. If we use the selective mu-calculus logic [1], a ρ-safety property is syntactically recognised as it contains only actions in operators, i.e. ρ. The ρ-strategy is parametric with a set of actions ρ that range from the empty set to the whole set of actions $\mathcal{A}$. The emptiness of the set ρ means that we want to obtain the most compact model. Thus, merge and reduction operations are unconditionally applied. This case falls in the traditional focus of process mining, that is, to reconstruct a possible model of the system by extracting knowledge from event logs. In this way, the discovered model is useful for human validation and for verifying compliance with the business process [20].

On the contrary, if ρ is not empty, merging and reduction operations are not applied whenever they involve actions belonging to ρ. Indeed, actions in ρ are relevant for checking the ρ-safety properties, and, to this aim, we have defined a ρ-strategy, see [4]. In general, it holds that the discovered model includes all initial traces, but additional traces may be added. On the other hand, suppose that we want to satisfy a ρ-safety property such that $\rho \subseteq \mathcal{A}$ and $\rho \neq \emptyset$. In this case it holds that for all traces containing actions in ρ no additional traces with actions in ρ are added in the model. Roughly speaking, the initial traces with actions in ρ are identical to those in the model. The proposed methodology guarantees that if a ρ-safety property does not hold in the discovered model then it does not hold also in the CCS program obtained directly applying the $\mathcal{T}$ operator for the given set of traces T (i.e. $\mathcal{T}(T)$).

Consider the program in Table 3.1 and suppose that we want to verify the following property: "it is not possible to print the variable $fatt$ (action l) if both the initialisation of the variable $fatt$ to 1 (action k) and the decrement of the variable n (action a) have not been performed". This property can be expressed in selective mu-calculus as $\varphi = \langle l \rangle_{\{k,a\}}\texttt{ff}$[1]. The set of actions occurring in the logic formula φ is $\rho = \{l, k, a\}$. Therefore, if we apply our methodology with $\rho = \{l, k, a\}$ we obtain a CCS program whose labelled transition system is shown in Figure 1.

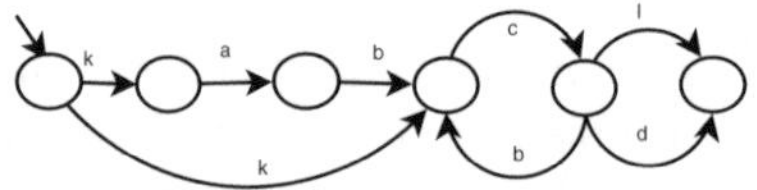

Fig. 1. Labelled transition system obtained applying the $\{l, k, a\}$-strategy

It holds that the property does not hold on the discovered model, thus we can deduce that it does not hold also on the program. In fact, when $n = 1$ an $y = 2$ the execution of the program produces the trace $k.c.b.c.l$, where l is performed without having previously performed the action a.

[1] For lack of space syntax and semantics of the selective mu-calculus logic are not reported. The reader can refer to [1] for details.

4 Conclusion and Related Work

Recently many modelling approaches have been proposed. They differ in the kind of properties they help reason about and in the level of precision or formality of the results one may obtain through them. In [12] the authors focus on models that may be used to reason about non-functional properties of the software-to-be. In this case models are heavily dependent on parameters that must be provided a-priori by domain experts or extracted by other similar systems. In [11] the formal foundations of model extraction process based on contexts is discussed. The correctness of the models is affected by the set of attributes used as the system state, while in our approach is guaranteed for safety properties. Moreover, our approach is completely automated. Thus no guidance from a process engineer is required.

Process mining from execution traces is an interesting and challenging research problem in many areas of computer science. In the information system context, this is referred to workflow mining. Quite a lot of research has been done in this setting ([15,23,13] to name just a few), with results focussing on different problems, such as log analysis through clustering, data cleaning from noise, or recognition of particular workflow patterns. The work in [8], uses a statistic-based technique to infer a Finite State Machine model of a system. Using metrics for the number, frequency, and regularity of event occurrences, they identify the likely concurrent behaviour being manifested by the system. Concurrency identification from traces is challenging, but in our case, we get it for grant from the instrumentation technique. The work closest to our is that presented in [23], which includes a strategy-based approach using the theory of regions to identify states to be merged on a Labelled Transition System. Differently to that, our approach works on the CCS syntax, so we do not have to generate the Labelled Transition System, which may be problematic for big-size processes, and it is modular, as new rules may be easily added.

The software engineering works address the problem of specification mining, aiming at deriving software specifications from the implementation through reverse engineering techniques [6]. Our tools and method follow the bytecode based approach to software model checking, as many other software model checkers. The Java PathFinder (JPF) (http://javapathfinder.sourceforge.net/) is an open source application and is a very successful software model checker for Java bytecode. It pioneered the concept of implementing a software model checker as a virtual machine that simulates the binary code of the application to be checked. Microsoft Research also developed a Tool (XRT) (http://research.microsoft.com/apps/pubs/default.aspx?id=77413) with similar goals as JPF for the .Net platform. XRT is an exploration framework, not currently publicly available, for programs represented in Microsoft's common intermediate language (CIL).

References

1. Barbuti, R., De Francesco, N., Santone, A., Vaglini, G.: Selective mu-calculus and Formula-Based Abstractions of Transition Systems. Journal of Computer and System Sciences 59(3), 537–556 (1999)

2. Bodhuin, T., Tortorella, M.: A Tool for static and dynamic Model extraction and Impact Analysis. In: Proc. of CSMR 2005, 9th European Conference on Software Maintenance and Reengineering, Manchester, UK, March 21-23 (2005)
3. Bodhuin, T., Di Penta, M., Troiano, L.: A Search-Based Approach for Dynamically Re-packaging of Downloadable Applications. In: IBM Centers for Advanced Studies Conference - CASCON 2007, Toronto, Canada, October 22 - 25 (2007)
4. Bodhuin, T., Pagnozzi, F., Santone, A., Tortorella, M., Villani, M.L.: Abstracting Models from Execution Traces for Performing Formal Verification. Technical Report
5. Burstall, R.M., Darlington, J.: A Transformation System for Developing Recursive Programs. J. ACM 24(1), 44–67 (1977)
6. Canfora, G., Di Penta, M.: New Frontiers of Reverse Engineering. In: Proc. of FOSE 2007, Future of Software Engineering, pp. 326–341. IEEE, Los Alamitos (2007)
7. Clarke, E.M., Grumberg, O., Peled, D.: Model Checking. MIT press, Cambridge (2000)
8. Cook, J.E., Wolf, A.L.: Discovering models of software processes from event-based data. ACM Trans. Softw. Eng. Methodol. 7(3), 215–249 (1998)
9. De Francesco, N., Santone, A.: A Transformation System for Concurrent Processes. Acta informatica 35(12), 1037–1073 (1998)
10. Dmiuiev, M.: Selective Profiling of Java Applications Using Dynamic Bytecode Instrumentation. IEEE, Los Alamitos (2004)
11. Duarte, L.M., Kramer, J., Uchitel, S.: Towards Faithful Model Extraction Based on Contexts. In: Fiadeiro, J.L., Inverardi, P. (eds.) FASE 2008. LNCS, vol. 4961, pp. 101–115. Springer, Heidelberg (2008)
12. Epifani, I., Ghezzi, C., Mirandola, R.: Model Evolution by Runtime Adaptation. In: Proc. of ICSE 2009, 31st International Conference on Software Engineering, pp. 111–121. IEEE, Los Alamitos (2009)
13. Greco, G., Guzzo, A., Manco, G., Saccà, D.: Mining unconnected patterns in workflows. Inf. Syst. 32(5), 685–712 (2007)
14. Hollingsworth, J.K., Miller, B.P., Gonalves, M.J.R., Naim, O., Xu, Z., Zheng, Z.L.: MDL: A language and compiler for dynamic program instrumentation. In: Proc. of the 1997 International Conference on Parallel Architectures and Compilation Techniques (November 1997)
15. Jansen-Vullers, M.H., van der Aalst, W.M.P., Rosemann, M.: Mining configurable enterprise information systems. Data Knowl. Eng. 56(3), 195–244 (2006)
16. Java Instrumentation API, `http://tinyurl.com/3htevy`
17. Lindholm, T., Yellin, F.: The Java Virtual Machine Specification. Addison-Wesley, Reading (1999)
18. Milner, R.: Communication and Concurrency. Prentice-Hall, Englewood Cliffs (1989)
19. Panzer, J.: Automatic Code Instrumentation. C/C++ Users Journal (1999)
20. Papp, R.: Introduction to Strategic Alignment. In: Papp, R. (ed.) Strategic Information Technology: Opportunities for Competitive Advantage, pp. 1–24. Idea Group, Hershey (2001)
21. Pettorossi, A., Proietti, M.: Transformation of Logic Programs: Foundations and Techniques. J. Logic Programming 19(20), 261–320 (1994)
22. Stirling, C.: An Introduction to Modal and Temporal Logics for CCS. In: Boissonnat, J.-D., Laumond, J.-P. (eds.) Concurrency: Theory, Language, and Architecture. LNCS, vol. 391, Springer, Heidelberg (1989)
23. van der Aalst, W.M.P., Rubin, V., Van Dongen, B.F., Kindler, E., Gunther, C.W.: Process Mining: A Two-Step Approach using Transition Systems and Regions. In: BPM Center Report BPM-06-30 (2006), `http://is.tm.tue.nl/staff/wvdaalst/publications/p359.pdf`

A Hybrid Model in Dynamic Software Updating for C

Mehdi Jalili[1], Saeed Parsa[2], and Habib Seifzadeh[3]

[1] Department of Computer Engineering, Islamic Azad University – Soofian Branch, Soofian, Iran
jalili.m@gmail.com
[2] Department of Computer Engineering, Iran University of Science and Technology, Tehran, Iran
parsa@iust.ac.ir
[3] Computer Engineering Faculty, Islamic Azad University- Najafabad Branch, Najafabad, Iran
seifzadeh@iaun.ac.ir

Abstract. The aim has been to develop a model for dynamic updating of software. A major difficulty with dynamic updating is the execution time overhead required for running the extra code embedded within the updatable version of the program. In order to resolve the difficulty, the dynamic updating model, suggested in this paper, activates the updatable version whenever updates are ready. When the updating is finished, the execution carries on with a newly updated program in which there is not any extra code for dynamic updating. Since the updatable version of the program is created at run-time, the proposed model not only increases the performance of the system, but also enables us to update programs that have been compiled and executed without any dynamic updating considerations, before. Our experimental results demonstrate the applicability and performance of the proposed model.

Keywords: dynamic software updating, state-transfer, programming language.

1 Introduction

In software maintenance phase, programs are updated to correct faults, improve functionality, and adapt the software to changes its execution environment. The typical software-update process consists of stopping the system to be updated, updating the code and restarting the system. Many applications, however, must run continuously and have maximum downtime requirements approximately a few minutes per year [15]. For ISPs, online transaction processing and life-support systems being available 24/7 is an important issue. Thus, the dynamic software updating (DSU) becomes more appealing, nowadays. Dynamic software updating is the task of updating parts of a program without having to terminate its execution.

There are two main models for dynamic updating, called interrupt [2], [3], [4], [6], [17], [18], [19] and invoke model [11], [20]. In an interrupt model, the running program can be interrupted at any time and any location within the running code [6]. However, it is not possible to update and carry on with the execution of a program at any location within the program. To resolve this problem, invoke models are offered.

D. Ślęzak et al. (Eds.): ASEA 2009, CCIS 59, pp. 151–159, 2009.

In an invoke model, updates can be applied at fixed locations, defined at compile time [11], [14], [20]. However, a major difficulty with invoke models is the overhead of executing code inserted for dynamic updating. In addition, in order to prepare a program for dynamic updating the structure of the program may be altered. These structural modifications also can slow down the program execution.

In the model proposed in this paper, the runtime overhead is removed by executing the updatable version whenever updates are required. In this way, it is possible to update any running code by preparing an updatable version of the code. The proposed model is a hybrid of invoke and interrupt models. It follows the interrupt model for switching between a running code and the updatable version of the code. An invoke model is applied for creating the updatable code. Before a program could be updated, the updatable version of the program is executed to carry on with the execution of the running code. The running code is terminated while the updateable code is executing. After all the modifications are applied to the updatable code, the code is automatically converted into the original program code.

The remaining parts of this paper are organized as follows: In Section 2, we provide a background on previous researches related to our work. Section 3 describes the hybrid model, a new model to dynamically update C programs, and briefly discusses its implementation issues. In Section 4 the hybrid model is evaluated and compared with the other DSU models. Finally, Section 5 gives a summary and discusses ongoing work.

2 Related Works

Over the past forty years, varieties of approaches have been proposed for dynamically updating running software. Fabry [2] provides a software dynamic update system. Motivated by the needs of large database systems, Fabry's scheme adds a level of indirection on module invocations, which allows the calls to be redirected and an update performed. Multics [16], DAS [3], DYMOS [4] were early systems that describe dynamic updating. Some systems have been developed to support dynamic updating in high-level language such as Erlang and Dynamic ML [18], [19]. In addition, some other approaches, Ksplice [8], K42 [9], LUCOS [10], [13], developed systems to provide dynamic updating of operating systems.

A number of general-purpose dynamic update systems, for applications written in C or C-like languages, have been developed. Gupta has developed an update system, which works on C programs [6]. His system could only update functions which are not on the stack. It also cannot update local variables. OPUS [17] is a dynamic update system for C programs specifically targeting security patches. It has some improves over Gupta's work such as the process of creating dynamic patches. Hjalmtysson and Gray have developed a system supporting dynamic replacement of C++ class implementations in a running program [12]. It supports any changes in class but it does not allow any modifications to the class interfaces. Hicks [14] attempts to address many of the limitations of previous dynamic updating systems, namely the flexibility of when and how programs may be changed, the robustness and correctness of the updated code and finally the ease of use of the system. In the Hicks's approach, programs have to be written in a type-safe variant of C known as Popcorn. This special language requirement is the system's greatest limitation. Ginseng [11] contains an implementation of the static updateability analysis from Proteus [20], which is used to determine and insert safe update points into a C program. Pending updates are applied when the running program reaches a safe update point. Ginseng also automatically adds indirections for types and functions, at compile time, to enable later updates. Ginseng provides safe, fine-grained dynamic updates for arbitrary C code, with a performance overhead measured between 5 and 32% [1].

A major difficulty with some of the above mentioned approaches, is that they [3], [4], [14], [16], [18], [19] can only apply runtime updates to the programs developed in a specific programming language. Most of the current approaches restrict dynamic updates to specific type of programming items under certain circumstances [6], [12], [17]. For instance, global variables cannot be dynamically updated in some of the approaches [6]. Another difficulty is to formally prove the correctness of the updates. Gupta [7] has proved that finding safe points to apply updates is in general undecidable. One more difficulty is runtime program execution overhead. Adding a relatively large number of indirections to convert a given program into an updateable format may result in runtime overhead to the program execution [11]. Another limitation with applying [11] is that it cannot be applied to update legacy code, not compiled with the Ginseng.

The above-mentioned problems with [11] are resolved in the approach presented in this paper.

3 Hybrid Model

In this section, the architecture and design of our model is described. Then, some issues about its implementation are discussed.

3.1 Architecture and Design

First, let us see some key definitions which are used throughout the paper. From now on, we refer to the archaic version of the running program as P_0. Note that P_0 runs now, but it will be replaced shortly. P_1 is the new version of the program which is desired to be a replacement for P_0. The goal is to replace P_0 with P_1 at run-time, but it is not a trivial task, at all. Therefore, P_{0u} and P_{1u} have been required to come. The letter "u" in P_{0u} and P_{1u} names stands for "Updatable".

P_{0u} does the same operations as P_0 and P_{1u} does the same operations as P_1. The only difference is that switching the execution from P_{0u} to P_{1u} at run-time is much simpler than switching the execution from P_0 to P_1. The reason is that P_{0u} and P_{1u} have some additional information such as type and function indirection, loop extraction, etc. Notions of P_{0u} and P_{1u} and the related concepts such as function indirection have been introduced by [13] in great detail. In Ginseng's compiler, P_{0u} and P_{1u} are generated automatically. Therefore, there is just a little more labor imposed on the programmer to generate any other code rather than P_0 and P_1 codes.

As it was mentioned, the aim that the paper is looking for is to replace P_0 with P_1 at run-time. In [11], which is more similar to our model than the other works, P_{0u} is used in place of P_0 and P_{1u} is used in place of P_1, all along. The replacement takes place in the means of switching the execution from P_{0u} to P_{1u}. If an update request is received during P_{0u} execution, [11] generates a patch using P_1 and P_0 codes. The patch then can be applied to P_{0u} and converts it to P_{1u}.

In contrast, in our model P_0 and P_1 themselves are executed and the replacement takes place by replacing P_0 with P_1. P_{0u} and P_{1u} are created during the replacement process to simplify replacing process, but they are discarded when the replacement is completed. Thus, in our model there is no need to do anything at compile-time. After the program starts it work by P_0 execution, when an update request is received, (1) P_{0u} and P_{1u} are generated, (2) P_0 is paused, (3) the corresponding point in P_{0u} is found, (4) the program's state is transferred from P_0 to P_{0u}, (5) the execution is switched from P_{0u} to p_{1u} in a safe update point, (6) the corresponding point in P_1 is found, (7) the program's state is transferred from P_{1u} to P_1, and (8) finally P_1 continues to run. These steps are shown in Figure 1.a. In the above steps, steps 3 and 6 are trivial because P_0 and P_1 have the same functionalities as P_{0u} and P_{1u}, respectively. Moreover, step 5 is trivial because the conversion can be done using the techniques introduced in [13].

It's obvious that in compare with [11] our approach does more when an update request is received. So, the performance may be decreased in the dynamic replacement times. However, at the times other than dynamic replacement process, it's shown that performance of our approach is higher than the other approach. The reason is that in our method, P_0 and or P_1 are executed while in the other method, their twins (P_{0u} and P_{1u}), which have worse performance, are executed. Since update requests are received infrequently, the dynamic replacement times are negligible in compare with the whole program execution. Therefore, it sounds that performance of our approach is higher than the other approach as a whole. Performance comparison of our model with other works will be discussed in detail, later.

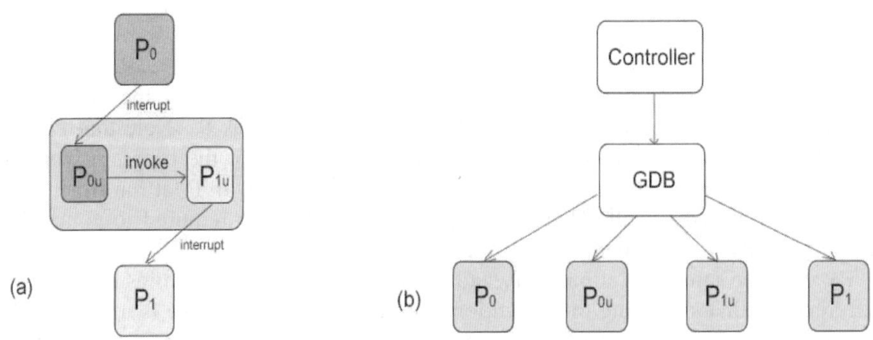

Fig. 1. a. The Hybrid model. **b.** Components of Hybrid model.

Figure 1.b shows main components of the hybrid model. System has a controller which controls other components. This controller has an interface that the user can write some updates commands and set variables to do updating. It uses GDB [5] to control processes. Controller uses piping technology to send commands to GDB and receive the results from it. GDB can then manipulate any running process.

3.2 Implementation and Its Issues

The main architecture of our system that was provided in the previous section was a little coarse-grained and the implementation details had been dismissed. Here, we would like to provide the main algorithm of our system in more detail: At first, P_0 is executed as the current version of the program. It's important to notice that long running programs usually have a main infinite loop in which the program executes. Therefore, P_0 has such a loop in its main function. When an updated version of the program (P_1) is ready, P_{0u} is generated by Ginseng's compiler, loaded into the memory and a stack frame for main function of it is created. In order to state transformation, the hybrid system should access to all global variables and main's local variables of P_0. This can be achieved via GDB. P_0 is stopped at the end of its main loop, though it can be stopped at any points. The system reads all of global and local variables of P_0 via GDB and sets them in P_{0u} by running an initialize function on P_{0u}. If the state transformation is successful, the hybrid system kills P_0 and executes P_{0u} from the start of its main loop. P_{0u} continues running to meet a safe update point. Some safe update points are determined in the code at the compile-time [14]. When such a point met, P_{0u} is allowed to apply patch and is upgraded to P_{1u}. Since P_{1u} and P_1 have the same functionalities, it can be assumed that the update was finished. However, due to P_1 is more polished than P_{1u}, if the update carries on and P_1 is replaced with P_{1u}, the performance becomes higher. So, P_1 is loaded into the memory, P_{1u} is stopped at the end of its main loop, and the state is transferred from P_{1u} to P_1 by calling an initialize function on P_1. If the state transformation is successful, the system kills P_{1u} and resumes the program execution toward P_1.

In continuation of this section, issues of implementation and some suggestions for resolving them are described.

Compiling in the Debug Mode. In order that the GDB can control the programs during their executions, P_0, P_{0u}, P_{1u} and P_1 should be compiled in a mode called "debug mode". Compiling in the debug mode, GCC adds some additional information to the object code. The most important one is symbol table. Unfortunately, in some circumstances, P_0 might not be compiled in the debug mode. GDB has a feature that can attach the symbol table to a running process to help us in such cases. Moreover, compiling programs in the debug mode can result in increasing size of the program and it causes the performance to decrease. However, the performance decrement is not significant in many programs.

Reading Variables. In the hybrid system, the state transformation from P_{1u} to P_1 is not trivial. The reason is that the structures of the variables in P_{1u} have been modified by Ginseng compiler so that they cannot be understood by GDB. The trick that was used in the system is to add some getter functions which are responsible for returning the values of P_{1u} variables. In this way, GDB calls these functions and reads values of the desired variables.

Pointers. When the state is transferred from an old version to an updated version of a program, it is necessary to preserve to consistency of pointers [6]. GDB provides some functions with which we can find corresponding address of each old program's variable in the updated program. The obtained address then must be set to the pointer in the updated program. This step is done in the *Initialize function* of updated program.

Initialization Function. In order to transfer values of variables from P_0 to P_{0u}, an initialization function has been added to P_{0u} which is called after reading values of P_0 variables. This function has simple assignments, each of which sets a value into a global, local or a pointer variable in P_{0u}. Initialization functions are invoked by the controller during state transformation. Similarly, to transfer variable values from P_{1u} to P_1, there should be an initialization function in P_1.

Complex Data Types Transfer. Some of data types such as linked lists cannot be transferred using the regular method performed in the initialize functions. As an alternative, we can use IPC mechanisms like shared memory to transfer data items. In this method, the complex data item is copied to a shared memory and then the target program reads the desired values from that shared memory. Note that there must be a function in the target program to redirect memory access commands to the shared memory. The methods described here can be applied to transfer arrays, liked lists, records, etc.

Time of Update. As in the main algorithm of hybrid model was mentioned, updating P_0 to P_{0u} and P_{1u} to P_1 are not actual updates and they are performed due to improve the performance. Hence, they can be done not only at the update requests reception but also at any other time that the system workload is low. For instance, an intelligent system may figure out that an update request should be received in the next day. So, it can update P_0 to P_{0u} this night, just a couple of hours before any update request is received.

4 Comparison and Evaluation

In this section, the hybrid model is evaluated by 3 measures: (1) the performance of the system when it runs normally, (2) the memory footprint of the system when multiple versions of it is arrived during a long period of time, and (3) the service disruption time when the system is being updated.

The model has been implemented in Fedora core 2.6.23, GCC 3.4.2, GDB 6.2 and Ginseng 1.2.1 have been used for creating programs and patches.

4.1 Performance

Performance is one of the most important measurements in software, especially long-life, systems. Since applications with capability of dynamic updating are usually long-life, the mentioned measurement becomes more important. Therefore, in the hybrid system, it has been tried to avoid techniques that are common in dynamic updating systems and have a significant impact on the performance. In our system, they are used only when we employ Ginseng model to update P_{0u} to P_{1u}, which is very short time.

The first technique which causes the performance to decrease is function indirection. In systems which use such mechanism, all of function call requests go through a function or a pointer which is called function wrapper; The function wrapper is then responsible to call the correct function [6], [10], [11], [14], [15], [21]. As it can be easily seen, the mechanism increases the number of function calls in the system. If a program has one function-call in each x command, x+1 (one extra command is for function indirection) will be executed (i.e., if x=20 then we have 5% overhead in running an updatable program).

The second technique is type wrapping. When a data item like a *struct* is updated, its dependants may fail in accessing the data item. To prevent this failure to occur, some systems use a mechanism called type wrapping [10], [11], [13], [14]. In this method, a function called type wrapper is employed to return the data item's value. Each type wrapper function typically has three commands: (1) Accessing the data item, (2) converting data item for its dependants, and (3) returning the calculated value. Therefore, updating a data item causes that each data item access becomes four commands. If there is one data access in x command, program will run x+4 commands. Overhead in running is 400/x percent. For example if x=5, run's overhead is 80%.

To examine how much overhead the function indirection can impose to the performance, we constructed a simple program which calls an empty function one billion times. Then, we run the program using a normal compiler and a complier that uses function indirection and measured the total time that the program takes each time. For measuring the type-wrapping overhead, the program was modified so that it accesses to a variable instead of calling a function one billion times. The results are shown in Figure 2.

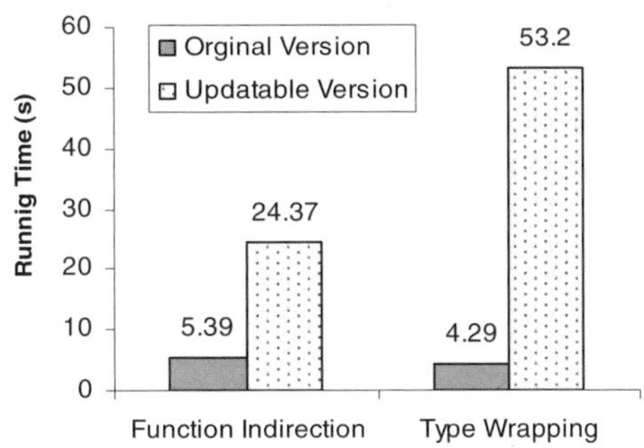

Fig. 2. Run time overhead in Orginal and updatable version of a sample program

4.2 Memory Footprint

The important reason for memory leakage in DSU systems is dynamic patches that be attached to a running application. In many systems, the original program remains in memory and updated parts are added to it; nothing is unloaded. So, DSU systems that leverage dynamic patches for updating their systems can suffer from memory footprint issues [1], [9], [10], [11], [14]. In contrast, in our model, all of the unnecessary programs are unloaded from memory.

4.3 Service Disruption Time

Since there are three steps in the update process (updating P_0 to P_{0u}, P_{0u} to P_{1u}, and P_{1u} to P_1), a simple formula for calculating the service disruption time can be equal to:

Service Disruption Time = Updating P_0 to P_{0u} Time + Updating P_{0u} to P_{1u} Time + Updating P_{1u} to P_1 Time

"Updating P_{0u} to P_{1u} Time" comes from the updating disruption time imposed by the Ginseng model. [11] has shown that for a sample application that works with data items of a linked list, this time is less than 5 ms. Results of executing the same application in the hybrid model indicate that service disruption time for all the three stages is less than 16ms. It means that the service disruption time of our model is 10ms more than the similar model. Since the update process usually occurs infrequently, 10ms can be negligible.

5 Conclusion and Future Work

A hybrid model as an updating system for C programs is presented. In contrast to previous systems, this model is capable of updating legacy systems or already running programs, and has much less overhead at run-time and memory footprint. However, the limitation of our model is that it has a bit more service disruption than the previous models.

As some works like [11] can update multi-threaded programs in addition to single-threaded applications, work is ongoing to extend this model to update multithread programs, as well.

Since Ginseng, which is a part of our model, is a large system, it is more generic and has a structure more than it is required in the hybrid system. Therefore, another extension can be streamlining Ginseng model so that it has only the functions required in the hybrid model.

References

1. Baumann, A.: Dynamic Update for Operating Systems. PhD thesis, Department of Computer Science and Engineering, University of New South Wales, Australia (2007)
2. Fabry, R.S.: How to design a system in which modules can be changed on the fly. In: Proceedings of the 2nd ICSE, San Francisco, CA, USA, pp. 470–476 (1976)
3. Goullon, H., Isle, R., Lohr, K.P.: Dynamic restructuring in an experimental operating system. In: Proceedings of the 3rd ICSE, Atlanta, GA, USA, pp. 295–304 (1978)
4. Lee, I.: DYMOS: A Dynamic Modification System. PhD thesis, University of Wisconsin-Madison (1983)
5. GNU Debugger, `http://www.gnu.org/software/gdb/documentation/`
6. Gupta, D., Jalote, P.: On-line software version change using state transfer between processes. Software - Practice and Experience 23(9), 949–964 (1993)
7. Gupta, D., Jalote, P., Barua, G.: A formal framework for on-line software version change. IEEE Transactions on Software Engineering 22(2), 120–131 (1996)
8. Ksplice: Rebootless Linux kernel security updates, `http://web.mit.edu/ksplice/`
9. Baumann, A., Heiser, G., Appavoo, J., Silva, D.D., Krieger, O., Wisniewski, R.W., Kerr, J.: Providing dynamic update in an operating system. In: USENIX Annual Technical Conference, General Track, pp. 279–291 (2005)

10. Chen, H., Chen, R., Zhang, F., Zang, B., Yew, P.C.: Live updating operating systems using virtualization. In: VEE 2006: Proceedings of the 2nd international conference on Virtual execution environments, New York, NY, USA, pp. 35–44 (2006)
11. Neamtiu, I., Hicks, M., Stoyle, G., Oriol, M.: Practical dynamic software updating for C. In: Proceedings of the ACM SIGPLAN Conference on Programming Language Design and Implementation, Ottawa, Canada (2006)
12. Hjalmtysson, G., Gray, R.: Dynamic C++ classes—a lightweight mechanism to update code in a running program. In: Proceedings of the 1998 Annual USENIX Technical Conference, pp. 65–76 (1998)
13. Neamtiu, I.: Practical Dynamic Software Updating for C. PhD thesis, Department of Computing Science, University of Maryland, USA (2008)
14. Hicks, M.: Dynamic Software Updating. PhD thesis, Department of Computer and Information Science, University of Pennsylvania, USA (2001)
15. Segal, M.E., Frieder, O.: On-the-fly program modification: Systems for dynamic updating. IEEE Software 10(2), 53–65 (1993)
16. Organick, E.I.: The Multics System: An Examination of its Structure. MIT Press, Cambridge (1972)
17. Altekar, G., Bagrak, I., Burstein, P., Schultz, A.: OPUS: Online patches and updates for security. In: Proceedings of the 14th USENIX Security Symposium, Baltimore, MD, USA, pp. 287–302 (2005)
18. Armstrong, J., Virding, R., Wikstrom, C., Williams, M.: Concurrent Programming in ERLANG, 2nd edn., vol. 9, pp. 121–123. Prentice Hall, Englewood Cliffs (1996)
19. Gilmore, S., Kírlí, D., Walton, C.: Dynamic ML without dynamic types. Technical Report ECS-LFCS-97-378, Department of Computer Science, The University of Edinburgh (1997)
20. Stoyle, G., Hicks, M., Bierman, G., Sewell, P., Neamtiu, I.: Mutatis Mutandis: Safe and predictable dynamic software updating. In: Proceedings of the 32nd ACM SIGPLAN-SIGACT Symposium on Principles of Programming Languages, Long Beach, USA (2005)
21. Orso, A., Liang, D., Harrold, M.J., Lipton, R.: Gamma system: Continuous evolution of software after deployment. In: Proc. of the International Symposium on Software Testing and Analysis, pp. 65–69 (2002)

A Function Point Logic File Identification Technique Using UML Analysis Class Diagrams

José Antonio Pow-Sang[1], Loretta Gasco[1], and Arturo Nakasone[2]

[1] Pontificia Universidad Católica del Perú,
Av. Universitaria 1801, San Miguel, Lima 32, Peru
japowsang@pucp.edu.pe
[2] National Institute of Informatics
2-1-2 Hitotsubashi, Chiyoda Ku, Tokyo 101-8430, Japan
arturonakasone@nii.ac.jp

Abstract. Since the introduction of object-oriented (OO) development techniques into industrial practices for software development, many Function Point (FP) technique adaptations have been proposed to improve estimations on the size of a software application. Most research works only deal with OO modifications to the previous version of the FP Counting Practices Manual (4.1) or they do not include some important UML specifications such as the composition relationship between classes. In this paper, we propose rules to identify Internal Logic Files (ILF) and External Interface Files (EIF) using analysis class diagrams. These rules were defined in accordance with the recommendations included in the FP Counting Practices Manual 4.2.1. We also present the results obtained by applying our rules to software size estimation case studies performed with undergraduate and graduate students. These results have proved our proposal to be at least equally accurate and consistent with the original FP technique.

Keywords: Function Points, Object Oriented, UML, Conceptual Model, software engineering experimentation.

1 Introduction

Function Point (FP) [7] is a software measurement technique created by Allan Albrecht at IBM, and has gradually become a sounder alternative to other popular size metrics methods (e.g. source lines of code (SLOC)), making it one of the most widely used techniques nowadays. Given the widespread promotion of the Unified Modeling Language (UML) [16] developed by the Object Management Group, many object-oriented approaches to calculate function points have been proposed. However, the majority of these proposals do not take into consideration the changes included in the last FP Counting Practices Manual and important UML specifications such as the composition relationship between classes.

For this reason, in this paper we propose an approach to identify Logic Files (i.e. Internal Logic Files (ILF) and External Interface Files (EIF)) from UML analysis class diagrams that make use of association, aggregation, composition, generalization,

D. Ślęzak et al. (Eds.): ASEA 2009, CCIS 59, pp. 160–167, 2009.

and association-class relationships. This work constitutes an improvement of the rules presented in [14]. In addition, we tested our approach against the standard Function Points Counting Practices Manual, version 4.2.1 [7] proposed by the International Function Points User Group (IFPUG), obtaining interesting and promising results.

The rest of the paper is organized as follows: Section 2 describes the related work in the FP measurement technique area, Section 3 details our proposed rules to identify logical files, Section 4 presents the background scenario for the empirical study, Section 5 shows the obtained results for each case study; Section 6 discusses those results. Finally, a summary and our plans for future research will conclude our paper.

2 Related Work

In order to deal with object-oriented software measurement, several methods to calculate FPs are being promoted and used. These methods reformulate the IFPUG rules in terms of OO concepts to facilitate the function point counting process, and their final results are similar to what is obtained by directly applying IFPUG Function Point Analysis (FPA). Fetcke [6] defined rules for mapping the OO-Jacobson method [10] to concepts from the IFPUG Counting Practices Manual (CPM) 4.0 and the results obtained from three case studies have confirmed that these rules can be applied in a consistent way. Uemura et Al. [17] proposed FPA measurement rules for design specifications based on UML (Unified Modeling Language), developing a FP measurement tool. Cantone et Al. [4] and Caldiera et Al. [3] defined rules to map OO concepts to FPA and performed pilot studies to demonstrate the feasibility of their approaches. Finally, Abrahao et Al. [1] presented a FP-based method called OOmFP and its evaluation through an empirical study.

All the proposals described above define rules for mapping OO concepts taken from older versions of the IFPUG CPM. Although Abrahao considers the composition relationship, some mapping rules to calculate Logic Files (LF) are not in accordance with the latest version of the IFPUG CPM (currently, version 4.2.1).

Lavazza et al. [12] considers the composition relationship in their proposal but they do not agree with the recommendations of the IFPUG CPM 4.2.1. For instance, they count one file with one record element type (RET) for two classes joined by a composition relationship. When following the IFPUG CPM, we would normally count one file with two RETs for the same case. The Netherlands Software Metrics User Association (Nesma) [13] presents its own FPA rules and its composition rules agree with the indications of the IFPUG CPM 4.2.1, but its generalization rules differ from the IFPUG rules.

3 Rules to Identify Logical Files

The input for our proposed rules is the analysis class diagram included in the Jaaksi's method [9] or the domain model mentioned by Larman [11]. In this model transformation, we consider the following relationships among classes: *association*, *aggregation*, *composition*, *association class*, and *generalization*, and we do not take into account the difference between ILF and EIF. Our rules only deal with the identification of logic files and their number of RETs and data element types (DET). In contrast, the IFPUG CPM 4.2.1 defines rules to identify logic files and their number of RETs and DETs based on Entity-Relationship (E-R) diagrams.

Coad's patterns [5] describe the majority of the classes and relationships that are present in most information systems. Hence, we designed our model transformation in such a way that our rules would cover all these patterns. The rules we considered for our model are:

Rule 0: Number of DETs

Count one DET for each attribute in a class. If the class is connected by an association relation to another class, count one additional DET if a many-multiplicity relation type exists.

Rule 1: Composition

For this rule, we have considered four cases:

a) If there are two classes A and B connected through a composition relation (A is composed of B), and class B is not connected to any other class, then they must be mapped to one logic file for the composition relation with 2 RETs. In addition, one DET for each attribute for both classes must be counted.

b) If there are three classes A, B, and C, with two of them (A and B) connected through a composition relation as shown in Fig. 1, and the multiplicity attribute of C is either 0..1 or 1, then they must be mapped to one logic file for the composition relation with 2 RETs and another logic file for class C. This rule also applies if B has an aggregation relationship with C.

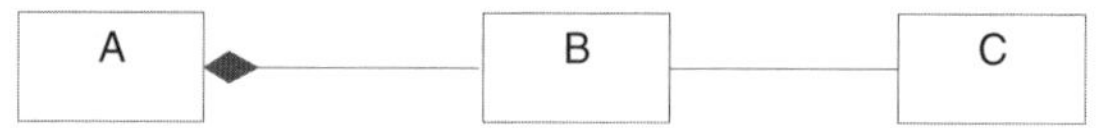

Fig. 1. UML Class Diagrams for Rule 1.b and 1.c

c) If there are three classes A, B, and C, with two of them (A and B) connected through a composition relation as shown in Fig. 1, and the multiplicity attribute of C is many, then they must be mapped to one logic file for the composition relation with 2 RETs. After this, use Rule 2 to determine if C should be treated as another file or as a RET for the file created for A and B.

d) If there are three classes A, B, and C, connected through composition relations (A is composed of B, and B is composed of C), then they must be mapped to one logic file with 3 RETs.

Rule 2: Association and Aggregation

If there are two classes, A and B, which are connected through an association or aggregation relation, the indications shown in Table 1 must be followed. The table is an adaptation from the IFPUG CPM 4.2.1 for OO development.

Table 1. Rules to identify Logic Files from classes without composition relationships

Multiplicity A	Multiplicity B	When this condition exists	Then Count as LFs with RETs and DETs as follows:
0..*	0..*	A and B are independent	2 LFs
0..1	0..*	A and B are independent	2 LFs
1	1..*	If B is independent of A	2 LFs
		If B is dependent on A	1 LFs, 2 RETs
1	0..*	If B is independent of A	2 LFs
		If B is dependent on A	1 LFs, 2 RETs
0..1	1..*	If A is independent of B	2 LFs
		If A is dependent on B	1 LFs, 2 RETs
0..1	0..*	A and B are independent	2 LFs
1	1	A and B are dependent	1LF, 1RET
0..1	0..1	A and B are independent	2 LFs
1..*	1..*	If B is independent of A	2 LFs
		If B is dependent on A	1 LFs, 2 RETs
1..*	0..*	If B is independent of A	2 LFs
		If B is dependent on A	1 LFs, 2 RETs

Rule 3: Generalization

If there are classes that are connected through a generalization relation and there are unique attributes among their child classes, count one logic file with two RETs (one for the parent class and one for the child classes). If not, count one logic file with one RET.

Rule 4: Association Class

If business requirements indicate that the association class belongs to only one of the logic files, the RET would be counted only with that logic file. If not, the association class must be mapped to one independent logic file with one RET.

4 Experimental Design

Since our proposal describes similar rules to the ones presented in E-R diagrams (IFPUG rules) with the exception of the composition rules, we decided to use an experiment setting similar to the one used in [15]. The study participants (students) had to apply IFPUG rules first and then our proposed rules in order to prevent the learning effect due to the composition relationships.

The formulated research question was: Does our approach produce measurements of Logic Files at least equally accurate to those found in the IFPUG FPA?

Since the objective of the experiment was to determine the accuracy measure obtained by the application of the counting rules and not the performance of the students in modeling with E-R or class diagrams, we provided them with descriptions and diagrams for each case study.

4.1 Variables Selection and Participants

Our independent variable was the method used by the students to estimate the size of the software on a case study, and our dependent variable was its accuracy: the agreement between the estimated measurement and the true value. To obtain "true values" for comparison, we took the values from similar case studies included in the IFPUG CPM 4.2.1.

The undergraduate students who participated in the experiment were fourth year students of the Informatics program at the Pontificia Universidad Católica del Perú (PUCP) that were enrolled in the Spring '09 Software Engineering course. These undergraduate students were trained in previous courses on E-R and class diagrams.

The practitioners were students of the 2009 Postgraduate Diploma in Software Engineering course at PUCP. They had at least two years of experience in software projects and, these students took an OO analysis and design course previous to the elaboration of the experiment.

4.2 Materials and Case Studies

The materials used in the experiment were the description of the case studies with E-R diagrams, the description of the case studies with class diagrams, forms to fill in the number of Logic Files and their RETs and DETs for each case study, and a questionnaire to know the students' opinion regarding the clarity of each technique.

At first, the students had to apply the IFPUG counting rules in seven case studies. Each case study included a description and an E-R diagram. Then, the students had to apply our proposed rules in other seven case studies. In this case, each case study included a description and a class diagram. Only one case study was used for both techniques, whereas the other case studies were different. In other words, the group of case studies that were analyzed with the IFPUG rules was almost totally different from the group where our rules were used. The descriptions of the case studies and further details of the used instruments can be found at http://macareo.pucp.edu.pe/japowsang/pf/oo-adaptation.html.

5 Results

For each case study, we graded it with "1" (one) if the student correctly identified the number of Logic Files and RETs, and "0" (zero) if he/she did it incorrectly.

Since the case studies used for each technique were not the same, we had to categorize each case study according to the type of relationship that would be used in a class diagram: association, aggregation, composition, association class or generalization in order to compare the obtained results. Because E-R diagrams do not make use of aggregation and composition relationships, we had to classify into the aggregation-composition category the case studies that would use these relationships in an analysis class diagram.

For both techniques, we applied two case studies for the association category, three case studies for the composition/aggregation category, one case study for the association-class category and one case study for the generalization category. Therefore, since we graded a student with "1" (one) every time he/she correctly identified the number of LFs and RETs in a case study, the student could obtain a grade up to "2" in the association category, "3" in the aggregation/composition category, "1" in the association-class category and "1" in the generalization category.

Table 2. Wilkoxon signed rank test results for undergraduate and graduate students

Variable	Categories							
	Association		Aggregation /Composition		Generalization		Association Class	
	Undergr. Students	Grad. Students	Undergr. Students	Grad. Students	Undergr. Students	Grad. Students	Undergr. Students	Grad. Students
Observations	22	15	22	15	22	15	22	15
V	135	45.5	0	7.5	0	12.5	20	0
Expected value	112.5	49.5	112.5	45	11	25	50	30
Variance (V)	843.75	235.125	856.875	238.125	121	156.25	500	180
p-value (one-tailed)	0.785764	0.41	< 0.0001	0.008	0.169903	0.169	0.093537	0.014

A significance level of 0.05 was established to statistically test the obtained results. Since these results follow a non-normal distribution, the paired samples t-test could not be used and, thus, we chose the Wilkoxon signed rank test, a non-parametric alternative. The statistical hypotheses formulated to test both techniques are:

H0: The distribution of the two sample sets is not significantly different.

Ha: The distribution of the IFPUG CPM 4.2.1 sample set is shifted to the left of the distribution of our proposed FPA sample set.

According to the results presented in Table 2, the computed p-value is lower than the significance level of 0.05 on the aggregation/composition category for undergraduate and graduate students and, therefore, we can reject the null hypothesis H0 and accept the alternative hypothesis Ha in this case. This means that we can empirically corroborate that our proposal produces more accurate assessments than the IFPUG CPM 4.2.1 approach for composition relationships.

In contrast, we cannot reject H0 for association and generalization categories, which empirically corroborates that our proposal and the IFPUG CPM 4.2.1 approach produce the same assessments. This could be explained by the similarity of rules between the IFPUG CPM 4.2.1 and our proposal for these cases.

From what can be observed from the result values presented, the students obtained better results when they had to apply composition rules and almost the same results when they had to apply rules for association and generalization. Based on these results, we can conclude that our proposal produces more accurate assessments than the IFPUG CPM 4.2.1 technique.

6 Discussion

The dependent variable (i.e. accuracy) that we used is proposed in the ISO/IEC 14143-3 [8].

By analyzing the results of the experiment, we can conclude that an empirical evidence for the relationship between the independent and the dependent variables exists. We have dealt with different aspects that could threaten the internal validity of the study:

Differences among subjects. The subjects had similar background knowledge. Students were trained in E-R and class diagrams on previous courses.

Learning effects. The application of two different case studies cancelled the learning effect due to similarities. We had to apply the IFPUG technique first and then our proposal in order to cancel the learning effect due to the composition rules.

Knowledge of the universe of discourse. We used the same case studies (with the same type of information system) with all the participants.

Fatigue effects. Each student took one hour on average per session to apply both case studies and answer questionnaires. Fatigue was not a relevant factor in this case.

Persistence effects. The students had never done a similar experiment before.

Subject motivation. Undergraduate students were motivated because they had to apply FP techniques in order to estimate the required effort in their assigned projects for the semester. Graduate students were also motivated because they wanted to apply FP techniques in their jobs.

Two threats to external validity were identified which limited the ability to apply any generalization of our conclusions:

Materials. We used representative case studies in which students had to apply the rules for association, aggregation, composition, association class, and generalization relationships between classes. However, more empirical studies that make use of software requirement specifications are needed.

Subjects. We are aware that more experiments with practitioners must be carried out in order to generalize these results. Although the graduate students (practitioners) had experience in software development projects, they had not used FP techniques in their projects before the experiment.

7 Conclusions and Future Work

This paper presented a conversion model to determine FP logic files using an analysis class diagram. This model takes into consideration the IFPUG CPM 4.2.1 rules and the association, aggregation, composition, association class and generalization relationships between classes. In addition, we took Coad's patterns as a reference in order to define the rules of our proposal.

We also described two controlled experiments with undergraduate and graduate students in order to determine the accuracy of our approach compared to the IFPUG CPM 4.2.1 technique. The students had to analyze case studies with E-R and class diagrams to identify logic files and their DETs and RETs. The results of the experiments show that our approach produces more accurate results than the original IFPUG CPM 4.2.1 technique. Although the results obtained from the experiment are very encouraging, we are aware that more experiments are needed to confirm them.

As future work for this research, we plan to conduct experiments with software requirements specifications in order to obtain more precise results and opinions about the applicability of our model in the industry and to include our proposed rules in the Tupux tool [2] to facilitate the counting of FPs based on analysis class diagrams.

Acknowledgments

This research work has been performed with the support of Dirección Académica de Investigación of Pontificia Universidad Católica del Perú, under project DAI-4051.

References

1. Abrahão, S., Poels, G.: Experimental evaluation of an object-oriented function point measurement procedure. Information & Software Technology. Elsevier, Amsterdam (2007)
2. Balbin, D., Ocrospoma, M., Soto, E., Pow-Sang, J.A.: TUPUX: An Estimation Tool for Incremental Software Development Projects. In: Proceedings AST 2009. IEEE Computer Society, Los Alamitos (2009)
3. Caldiera, G., Antoniol, G., Fiutem, R., Lokan, C.: Definition and Experimental Evaluation of Function Points for Object-Oriented Systems. In: Proceedings METRICS 1998. IEEE Computer Society, Los Alamitos (1998)
4. Cantone, G., Pace, D., Calavaro, G.: Applying Function Point to Unified Modeling Language: Conversion Model and Pilot Study. In: Proceedings of METRICS 2004. IEEE Computer Society, Los Alamitos (2004)
5. Coad, P., North, D., Mayfield, M.: Object Models: Strategies, Patterns and Applications. Prentice-Hall, Englewood Cliffs (1997)
6. Fetcke, T., Abran, A., Nguyen, T.: Mapping the OO-Jacobson Approach into Function Point Analysis. In: Proceedings of TOOLS-23 1997. IEEE Computer Society, Los Alamitos (1997)
7. IFPUG, Function Points Counting Practices Manual (version 4.2.1), IFPUG: International Function Point User Group, Westerville Ohio (2004)
8. ISO. ISO/IEC 14143-3 - Information technology – Software measurement – Functional size measurement – Part 3: Verification of functional size measurement methods (2003)
9. Jaaksi, A.: A Method for Your Object-Oriented Project. Journal of Object-Oriented Programming 10(9) (1998)
10. Jacobson, I.: Object-Oriented Software Engineering. A Use Case Driven Approach. Addison-Wesley, USA (1992)
11. Larman, C.: Applying UML and Patterns: An Introduction to Object-Oriented Analysis and Design and Iterative Development, 3rd edn. Addison-Wesley, Reading (2004)
12. Lavazza, L., Del Bianco, V., Garavaglia, C.: Model-based functional size measurement. In: Proceedings ESEM 2008. ACM, New York (2008)
13. NESMA, FPA Applied to UML/Use Cases Version1.0 (2008), `http://www.nesma.nl`
14. Pow-Sang, J.A., Imbert, R.: Including the Composition Relationship among Classes to Improve Function Points Analysis. In: Proceeding VI Jornadas Peruanas de Computación-JPC 2007, Trujillo, Peru (2007)
15. Pow-Sang, J.A., Nakasone, A., Imbert, R., Moreno, A.M.: An Approach to Determine Software Requirement Construction Sequences based on Use Cases. In: Proceedings ASEA 2008, Sanya, China. IEEE Computer Society, Los Alamitos (2008)
16. Object Management Group, Unified Modeling Language USA (2005), `http://www.uml.org`
17. Uemura, T., Kusumoto, S., Inoue, K.: Function Point Measurement Tool for UML Design Specification. In: Proceedings METRICS 1999. IEEE Computer Society, Los Alamitos (1999)

Reliable Mobile Application Modeling Based on Open API*

Sera Jang and Eunseok Lee

School of Information and Communication Engineering, Sungkyunkwan University, Suwon 400-746, South Korea
{jangsera,eslee}@ece.skku.ac.kr

Abstract. Today, the expectations placed on the mobile environment is getting high to the point that users want access to the internet at any time and in any place, exceeding functionality of simple voice chat and SMS to include search, service, and blogging. Amidst this kind of change, big companies such as Microsoft, Symbian, Google, and Apple are jumping into the mobile platform market, and open platforms and open APIs are being introduced left and right. In step with this, countless applications are being developed using open APIs. Open APIs allow developers to develop services closely tied to the device more easily. However, generally there are many difficulties when constraints from application requirements are considered in the design stage when developing applications using open APIs. In this paper, constraints when using open APIs in the modeling stage are defined, and code generation technique for which reliability verification through an appropriate model is possible is proposed. By verifying the reliability by applying the proposed methodology to existing applications developed using open APIs, the proposed methodology was validated.

Keywords: Reliability, Open API, Mobile Application Modeling.

1 Introduction

With the rapidly changing mobile environment, various platforms and APIs have been made public to previously closed development environment, changing into a development environment in which open platforms and open APIs are used. Such open platforms and APIs allow developers to develop systems or applications more easily and rapidly than ever before.

However, when developing applications using open platforms and open APIs, it's difficult to consider in detail the platform or API in the design stage. Therefore, it's difficult to predict the impact of the platform or the API on the final system or application from the aspects of performance or functionality. Not only that, there are difficulties in finding a clear cause and solution to errors that occur in the execution stage.

* This work was supported by the Korea Science and Engineering Foundation(KOSEF) grant funded by the Korea government(MEST) (No. 2009-0077453).

D. Ślęzak et al. (Eds.): ASEA 2009, CCIS 59, pp. 168–175, 2009.

In order to solve these problems, it is necessary to clearly analyze the open platform or the open API in the modeling stage, reflecting the results obtained. Furthermore, constraints regarding the final application need to be reflected in the design so that reliability of the application can be verified.

This problem is also caused by the fact that the open API is not developed by the developer who develops the application but other developers and provided. Because of this, there is a need for quickly verifying whether the problem is not with the application but the open API.

In this paper, constraints resulting from using open APIs in the modeling stage are defined, and a mechanism for defining a fault model that can verify the reliability of the application through an appropriate model is proposed. Furthermore, a methodology for generating executable code from the created model so that possible errors that may occur during execution can be discovered is proposed based on the fault model.

In this paper, to apply modeling to open platform and open API, API profile was used. Also, to verify constraints and reliability, Test Profile[12] from OMG was extended and used. These profiles are used not only in modeling but in converting to executable code through the created model.

Also, test cases of the application are extracted using the created model and based on the test cases a fault model is defined. Based on the fault model, the application's reliability can be verified and improved.

In this paper, a modeling methodology is proposed centered on the case of developing applications using open APIs when it comes to open platform and open API use.

2 Related Research

The mobile OSs of today are gradually being made open, in contrast to the closed terminal OSs of the previous era. Especially, platforms and OSs used for smart phones have been made open strategically by key manufacturers or suppliers, leading to OS API (Application Program Interface), SDK (Software Development Kit), and even the entire source code being released to the public[1].

In contrast to poor expandability and flexibility when developing a RTOS (Real Time OS), for an open OS, the UI is user-centric and provision of applications is superior, leading to increase in its necessity[1].

For mobile device OSs, particularly ones being used for smart phones, there are the following examples[1]: "Synbian", the mostly widely used OS for smart phones and which Nokia uses a lot; "Windows Mobile", developed by Microsoft and which has excellent compatibility with the PC; "Mac OS X" which is being used for Apple iPhones; RIM OS from RIM and used for Blackberry phones; "Limo", Linux-based and developed for the mobile; "Android", set up by Google and developed by OHA (Open Handset Alianc).

Applications developed for these kinds of open platforms need to guarantee their reliability as well. The most important stage for realizing a reliable mobile application is the monitoring stage where the types of the fault are detected[2]. The reason is that because software faults are depended on the application domain, in the monitoring stage, classifying the fault types is very important[2].

The type of fault can be classified as syntactic fault, semantic fault, service fault, communication/interaction fault, and exception[3][4]. Among the fault types, the discovery of semantic fault, non-functional fault, and communication/interaction fault are considered as important factors in securing reliability. These faults are important factors in securing reliability of systems in which open platforms and open APIs are used as well.

Many methodologies for securing the reliability of these systems have been proposed and being researched. However, research on verifying reliability for the application of open platforms and open APIs is still in the beginning stage.

3 Proposed Approach

In this paper, constraints resulting from open API use in the modeling stage are defined when it comes to application development using open APIs, and a methodology that can be used to define a fault model through an appropriate model is proposed. Furthermore, a methodology for improving the reliability of the system is proposed by proposing an executable code generation technique for which reliability can be verified using a model[9].

The proposed methodology is a 5 stage process as shown below (Fig. 1).

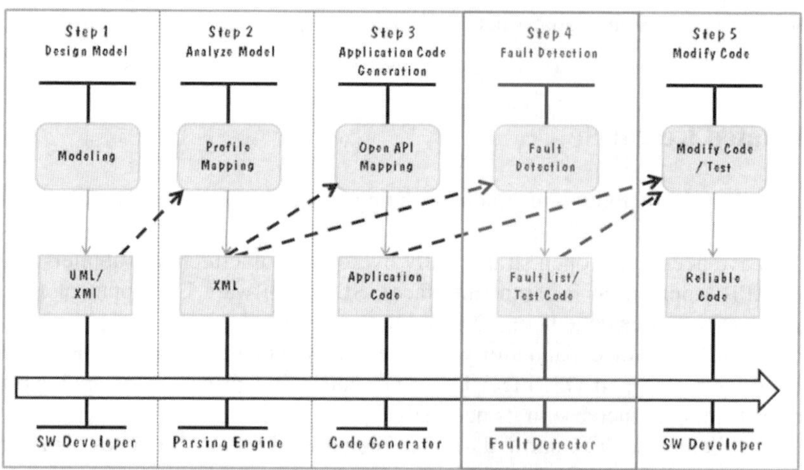

Fig. 1. This shows the process stage of proposed methodology

3.1 Design Model

A software system can be described in many aspects using UML profiles, and a clear architecture can be modeled through the profile[7][8]. To develop a reliable application in which open API is used, UML profile was expanded and applied to modeling in this paper. The applied UML profile is divided into the two items.

One is open API profile. The open API profile is a profile regarding technology and requirements resulting from applying open API. It is composed of stereotypes, tagged values, and constraints. Mapping is done to the open API and application functionality in the UML modeling stage. It is applied to the open API technology at the time of XML conversion for executable code generation.

The other is test profile. The test profile is a profile regarding constraints of the system, and composed of stereotypes, tagged values, and constraints. Mapping is done to constraints of the open API in UML modeling stage. At the time of XML conversion for executable code generation.

3.2 Analyze Model

The XMI created through model design gets converted into XML for executable code generation by undergoing a parsing process. It is converted into the two forms of XML as shown below.

Application XML is factors for executable code generation for the application are extracted based on the open API profile and XML is generated.

Test XML is factors for test case and test code generation are extracted based on the test profile and XML is generated[5][6].

3.3 Application Code Generation

The code generator generates executable application code based on the application XML information generated by a model. The code structure is based on the open API template.

Typically, open APIs are object-oriented, and have a common structure following the application platform. The Open API template is organized according to this kind of structure.

3.4 Fault Detection

In this paper, a methodology for verifying reliability when developing applications using open APIs is proposed. This methodology is carried out by the following process: 1) test cases are extracted; 2) in the appropriate test case, a fault model is defined; 3) test code is generated; 4) fault validation is done using the code.

3.5 Modify Code

As the last step, the application developer resolves the faults found according to the strategy defined in the fault model.

4 Implementation and Evaluation

In this paper, a modeling method in which open API is applied through UML profile expansion was proposed. For evaluation of the proposed methodology, a service that uses the open API of Google's Android was realized.

The service developed is a MapViewer Application, and is composed of the following services (Table 1).

Table 1. Services of Target Application

Service	Discription
S1	Display Default Map
S2	Move(Up/Down/Left/Right)
S3	Zoom In
S4	Zoom Out
S5	Home

In this paper, for UML modeling and XMI conversion, Borland Together was used. Fig. 2(a) shows an example of a sequence diagram on the zoom out function from the model of the system which used Together. The UML modeled like this was converted into application XML and test XML by being processed by the parse engine after being converted into XMI. The application XML was generated as executable code based on open API template through the code generator. Fig. 2(b) shows the generated application configuration file, and Fig. 2(c) shows a part of the generated code.

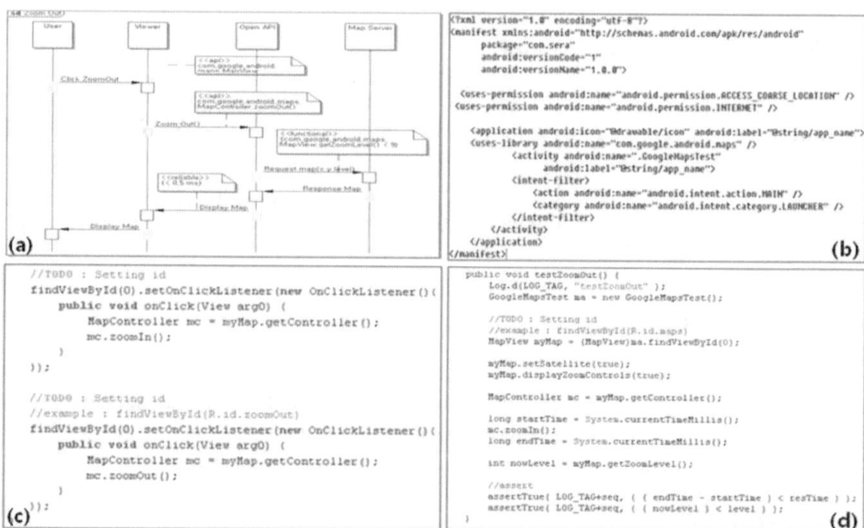

Fig. 2. This shows the example of generated target application: (a) a sequence diagram of the Zoomout function, (b) a generated configuration file of target application, (c) a generated application code of target application, (d) a generated test code of target application

Along with the source code generation of the application, a fault model was created by undergoing a fault discovery process based on the test XML, and test code for verifying the fault model was generated. Table 2 shows the fault model generated targeting the application. Because zoom in and zoom out functions adjust the size of the map data according to the requested zoom level of the map, it is an important part for which the performance of the device needs to be considered. Therefore, it was defined as fault model. Based on the fault model, test code was generated. The test code was generated by applying the test code template which applied the JUnit structure of Java. Fig. 2(d) shows a part of the generated test code.

For the generated application code and test code to run successfully, the software developer has to complete the tasks described by TODO messages, which are environment configuration information such as authentication information, and UI-related areas such as UI and event mapping.

In this paper, in order to verify the validity of the proposed methodology, Google Android platform's map service API (com.google, android.maps) were created as API template, and Android's junit.framework was applied as the test template.

The evaluation was carried out from the following two aspects. The first is on the degree of completion of the application code generated by a model. When application code was generated using the model created by applying the open API profile, the code generated had about 80% degree of completion for parts of code outside the UI(Table 3). Secondly, the degree of inclusion of stated constraints in the design stage by the extracted test cases through the model was assessed, as well as the degree of completion for the generated test code. In this case, the constraints defined in the design stage were all included by the test cases. However, when converting the test cases defined by the fault model to test code, about 70% completion ratio was shown(Table 4). Test code was often incorrectly generated when the types of passed parameters or their number was changed and when the start and end were ambiguously stated in the UML for duration time measurement.

Table 2. The System Fault Model

Service	Fault/Failure	Monitoring	Diagnosis	Strategy
Common	No response	Response	Open API server is down Authentication error	Simple module test
	Delay in response time	Compare the difference between request time and response time	Insufficient end point resource Open API server is overloaded	Adjust map level Adjust map size
ZoomIn	Levels below 0 is requested for the map	Response	No constraints check	Add a constraints check module
ZoomOut	A higher level than the maximum possible level is requested	Response	No constraints check	Add a constraints check module

Also, in order to verify the reliability of application, we apply verification process: 1) Fault injection ; 2) Fault detection; 3) Fault repair. We had confirmed what defined functional faults and non functional faults were detected all by applying verification process. Also we had confirmed what detected functional faults were repaired strategically by itself. But, almost strategies of non functional faults couldn't perform by itself, the self repairing about non functional faults was impossible.

In future, the self repairing of non functional faults must be improved by applying self reconfiguration methodology. These evaluation results are not absolute because they depend significantly on how well the open API template and test template, need for code generation, are defined. However, if the templates are well defined, the proposed methodology can reduce the amount of burden placed on the developer in developing an application which uses open API, which would not only lead to decrease in development time, but development of reliable software would be made possible.

Generally speaking, because when developing mobile applications short development times are required, shortened development time is quite important. Furthermore, because the mobile environment has more constraints than the PC environment, application quality is very important. From this aspect, the proposed methodology is useful in increasing the reliability of the application.

Table 3. Completion Ratio of Application Code

Application	Number of Class	Line of Code (LOC)	Added/Modified Code	Completion ratio
MapViewer	1	40	10	75
Animation	2	165	25	85
MediaPlayer	1	90	20	78
DateWidget	1	130	25	81
Average				**80**

Table 4. Completion Ratio of Test Code

Application	Number of Class	Line of Code (LOC)	Added/Modified Code	Completion ratio
MapViewer	3	115	15	87
Animation	4	180	60	67
MediaPlayer	2	60	20	67
DateWidget	5	135	40	70
Average				**73**

5 Conclusion

With the advent of open platforms and open APIs for the mobile environment, the application development environment is getting easier and simpler more and more, and based on such environment, a lot of applications are being developed. However, the reality is that as more applications are developed, their completion rates and quality are decreasing. What is more, developers often jump right into development skipping the design stage.

However, for applications developed in such way, many problems that weren't considered in the design stage appear and the time it takes to solve the problems often exceeds the original development time. This can be attributed to the fact that because APIs released third-party developers are used, so the developer doesn't make correct use of them, or if there is a problem with the API itself, it is impossible for the developer to fix it.

In order to solve these kinds of problems, a modeling methodology which applied open API in the modeling stage was proposed. And based on the model, test code generation methodology for verifying the reliability of the application was proposed. The proposed methodology not only makes possible short development time when applying open APIs for development, but through extraction of test cases regarding constraints, a fault model can be defined, and through the model faults that may occur in the application are discovered and the reliability of the application is therefore increased.

However, in order to generate application code and test code with high degree of completion in the proposed system, the template regarding the open API has to be well composed. The problem regarding API template composition is left for future research.

References

1. Mobile Platform/OS Open Trend. Korean Electronics Technology Institute (2008)
2. Jiang, M., Zhang, J., Raymer, D., Strassner, J.: A Modeling Framework for Self-Healing Software Systems. Models@Run.time (2007)
3. Avizienis, A., Laprie, J.-C., Randell, B., Landwehr, C.: Basic concepts and taxonomy of dependable and secure computing. IEEE Trans. on Dependable and Secure Computing 1(1), 11–33 (2004)
4. Mariani, L.: A fault taxonomy for component-based software. In: International Workshop on Test and Analysis of Component-Based Systems (TACoS), ENTCS, vol. 82(6) (2003)
5. James, G.: Applying test driven development to embedded software. Instrumentation & Measurement Magazine 10(6), 20–25 (2007)
6. Kim, S.-K., Choi, J., Lee, D., Noh, S.H., Min, S.L.: Virtual Framework for Testing the Reliability of System Software on Embedded Systems. In: The 2007 ACM symposium on Applied computing, pp. 1192–1196 (2007)
7. Bernardi, S., Merseguer, J.: A UML Profile for Dependability Analysis of RealTime Embedded Systems. In: The 6th international workshop on software and performance, pp. 115–124 (2007)
8. Jurjens, J., Wagner, S.: Component-Based Development of Dependable Systems with UML. In: Atkinson, C., Bunse, C., Gross, H.-G., Peper, C. (eds.) Component-Based Software Development for Embedded Systems. LNCS, vol. 3778, pp. 320–344. Springer, Heidelberg (2005)
9. Hsiung, P.-A., Lin, S.-W., Tseng, C.-H., Lee, T.-Y., Fu, J.-M.: Win-Bin See: VERTAF: An Application Framework for the Design and Verification of Embedded Real-Time Software. IEEE Trans. on Software Engineering 30(10), 656–674 (2004)
10. `http://www.embedded-computing.com`
11. `http://www.omg.org/technology/documents/formal/test_profile.html`
12. `http://code.google.com/intl/ko/android`

An Improved Steganography Covert Channel

Md Amiruzzaman[1], Hassan Peyravi[1], M. Abdullah-Al-Wadud[2], and Yoojin Chung[3,⋆]

[1] Department of Computer Science
Kent State University, Kent, Ohio 44242, USA
{mamiruzz,peyravi}@cs.kent.edu

[2] Department of Industrial and Management Engineering,
Hankuk University of Foreign Studies, 89 Wangsan, Mohyun, Cheoin,
Kyonggi, 449-791, South Korea
wadud@hufs.ac.kr

[3] Department of Computer Science,
Hankuk University of Foreign Studies, 89 Wangsan, Mohyun, Cheoin,
Kyonggi, 449-791, South Korea
chungyj@hufs.ac.kr

Abstract. An improved steganographic method is proposed in this paper. Two distinct methods are combined to achieve possibly high data hiding capability with high visual quality. The proposed method shifts the last n nonzero AC coefficients from S JPEG block, and changes the magnitude values of the first n nonzero AC coefficients from T JPEG blocks. S and T blocks are determined by the number of nonzero JPEG coefficients in the block. Zero run-length modification method improves the robustness against statistical attack based on magnitude histogram. Magnitude modification method improves the visual quality. This combination complements each other.

Keywords: Steganography, JPEG image, information hiding.

1 Introduction

Steganography and Steganalysis are advancing at the same time. The history of steganography and steganalysis is a history of rat races. Whenever a steganographic method has been proposed, the method is about to be broken soon by new steganalysis methods. Therefore, steganographers try to develop new methods secure fully or partially from the existing steganalysis methods. However, it is not possible all the time to be able to take all security issues into account and solve in one method. It is known that steganography is one of the oldest arts or techniques for hiding data to establish a secure covert communication channels. However, it is not so long since the ground of digital steganography techniques has been formed. Many innovative steganographic algorithms are available now [4], [5], [6], [7], [8].

⋆ Corresponding author.

D. Ślęzak et al. (Eds.): ASEA 2009, CCIS 59, pp. 176–187, 2009.

The most important goal of steganography is to conceal the existence of a secret message. However, researchers are also having interest to break steganographic schemes. There are many available attacks [3] invented by several researchers. Among them statistical attack [9] is one of the most popular and effective attacks in steganographic world. Another famous attack is the calibrated statistics attack [1], [2]. Data hiding methods have to be designed to make them secure from statistical attack because this attack is relatively easy to combat. Simple solution against this attack is keeping the same or similar histogram to the original histogram. However, keeping the same shape of a magnitude histogram is not easy to achieve as long as the coefficient magnitudes are modified. Note that one branch of steganography methods is inventing schemes to preserve the original histogram perfectly. Least significant bit overwriting methods including OutGuess [4] can preserve the original histogram almost perfect, but not absolutely perfect. This method modifies half of the nonzero coefficients and corrects the distorted histogram by adjusting with the rest of unused coefficients. In general, perfect preservation is not possible because of unideal data pattern.

F5 [9] also tries to narrow the gap between original and modified histograms by decrementing nonzero JPEG coefficients towards 0 and applying matrix embedding and permutative straddling. Sallee models the marginal distribution of DCT coefficients in JPEG-compressed images by the generalized Cauchy distribution [5]. Thus, the embedded message is adapted to the generalized Cauchy distribution using arithmetic coding. Arithmetic coding transforms unevenly distributed bit streams into shorter, uniform ones. This procedure is known as MB1. One weak point of this method is that block artifact increases with growing size of the payload. MB2 has presented a method to overcome this weakness [6]. The MB2 embeds message in the same way as MB1 does, but its embedding capacity is only half of that of MB1. The other half of the nonzero DCT coefficients is reserved for de-blocking purpose.

Preserving the perfect shape of histogram of stego image has been a primary target in the field of steganography. For the first time, one method can preserve the shape of histogram exactly between original and stego images. The main drawback of this method is low embedding capacity with poor image quality. In this paper, a combined approach is introduced to overcome low embedding capacity and poor image quality.

The rest of this paper is organized as follows: In Section 2, coefficient magnitude and run-length histograms are defined. Data hiding method based on the run-length histogram is presented. Section 3 summarizes experimental results. Section 4 concludes the paper.

2 Proposed Approach

As the proposed method works with a combination of two different approaches, two methods have to be discussed one by one: each method to hide data into either S or T JPEG blocks. The S and T blocks are separated on the basis of the number of nonzero AC coefficients. To select the S and T blocks, a threshold value is used. Before further discussion, it is necessary to define S and T JPEG blocks.

2.1 S and T JPEG Blocks

An image can be divided into 8×8 non-overlapping blocks and processed in the frequency domain by transforming using discrete cosine transform (DCT) and quantization block by block. Each block consists of integer values where the leftmost and topmost value is a DC coefficient value, and the other 63 coefficients are AC coefficient values. The DC coefficient plays an important role: it maintains an average luminance value of the block. Hence, the DC coefficient is not used for embedding data due to serious possibility of blocking effects among neighboring blocks.

The S and T blocks are determined by the number of nonzero AC coefficients. The leftmost and topmost AC coefficients close to the DC coefficient are considered to be more important than the rightmost and bottommost AC coefficients far from the DC coefficient. Importance of the coefficients can be measured by the magnitudes of the associated quantization coefficients. In addition, in general, it is believed that low-frequency components are more important than high-frequency components in data compression. The proposed method uses a threshold value to determine S and T JPEG blocks. If a JPEG block has less or equal to T_v number of nonzero AC coefficients, then that block is treated as an S block. Similarly, if the numbers of nonzero AC coefficients are more than the threshold value T_v, then that block is a T JPEG block (see Figure 1).

Let the DC coefficient in a block be denoted as DC, the AC coefficients as AC_i, (where, i =1, 2, $\cdots$, $n-1$, n), and the threshold value as T_v. In general, $n \leq 63$, where AC_n is the last nonzero AC coefficient in the block, where an end-of-block (EOB) marker follows. Assume that a JPEG block has AC coefficients

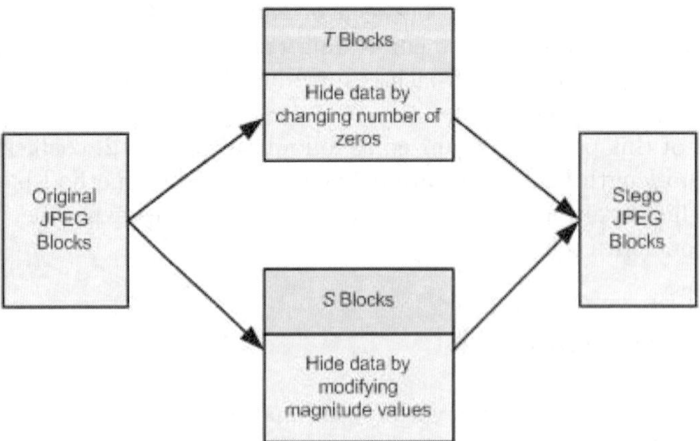

Fig. 1. Block diagram of the encoding phase

(i.e., both nonzero and zero)as follows: for example, [16 1 0 0 0 -2 1 0 0 -1 2 EOB]. Then, we denote them as DC = 16, AC_1 = 1, AC_2 = 0, AC_3 = 0, AC_4 = 0, AC_5 = -2, AC_6 = 1, AC_7 = 0, AC_8 = 0, AC_9 = -1, AC_{10} = 2, and the EOB marker follows. For the efficiency of compression, zero elements after the EOB marker are not considered as regular coefficients.

The nonzero AC coefficients are easily identified. In this example, there are 5: AC_1 = 1, AC_5 = -2, AC_6 = 1, AC_9 = -1, and AC_{10} = 2. If the threshold value T_v is 3, then the number of nonzero AC coefficients in this toy example is more than T_v, which means that this JPEG block is a T block (see Figure 2). Again, in another toy example with zigzag-scanned JPEG coefficients [32 5 0 0 0 2 EOB], we can denote them as DC = 32, AC_1 = 5, AC_2 = 0, AC_3 = 0, AC_4 = 0, AC_5 = 2, and EOB. The number of nonzero AC coefficients is 2: AC_1 = 5 and AC_5 = 2. Note that this block is an S block when T_v is 3 (see Figure 3) by the definition of S and T blocks. There is no special meaning in the name of S and T. For the convenience of definition, S and T blocks are used. If the number of nonzero coefficients (except DC value) in a block is larger than T_v, the block is just considered as a T block; otherwise, the block is an S block.

2.2 Shifting Nonzero AC Coefficients

The proposed method allows shifting of nonzero AC coefficients to make either even or odd number of zeros in between two nonzero coefficients in order to hide data. This method has excellent features. Since this method does not change the magnitude of coefficients, the resulting histogram is totally unchanged. Thus, existing statistical attacks cannot find any clue of steganography. This kind of histogram is called magnitude histogram. Existing statistical attack takes the magnitude histogram into consideration.

In this paper, run-length histogram is introduced to cope with the shifting nonzero AC coefficients by adjusting run-lengths to hide data. If there is no zero coefficient between two consecutive nonzero coefficients, the run-length of zero coefficient is 0 by definition. Similarly, if there are 10 zero coefficient between two consecutive nonzero coefficients, the run-length of zero coefficient is 10 by definition. The run-length histogram shows the number of run-lengths from 0 to 63. In general, this run-length histogram shows an exponentially decaying distribution. However, when a stego image has excessive number of hidden messages, its run-length histogram may be far away from an exponentially decaying distribution.

Serious drawback of the coefficient shifting method is its poor image quality. The reason is obvious: Assume that one coefficients is shifted to the left or right by one position, this operation results in change of at least two nonzero AC coefficients. Consider an example with [... 5 0 0 0 6 0 ...] where one more zero coefficient has to be inserted between nonzero coefficients 5 and 6 to make even number of zeros. Then, the changed coefficients have the form [... 5 0 0 0 0 6 0 ...]. Note that the position of 6 is changed to 0 while the position of 0 next to 6 is changed to 6. One is changed from 6 to 0 and the other one from 0 to 6. Subsequent changes may follow due to all nonzero coefficients in the right-hand

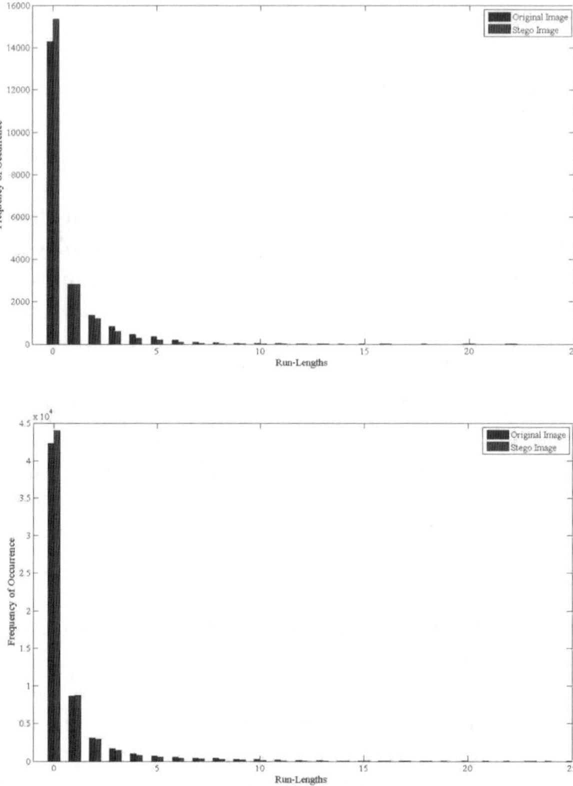

Fig. 2. Run-Length histogram of the original Lena image and stogo Lena image (top). Run-Length histogram of the original Baboon image and stogo Baboon image (bottom).

side of 6. In case of traditional JPEG steganography, the maximum error due to magnitude is, in general, ± 1 in a single position. However, the position shifting method causes significant errors at least in two positions.

Thus, inserting or deleting zero coefficients everything in a block is a bad idea. One solution is inserting or deleting T_c number of zero coefficients in between the last nonzero coefficients. Of course, this solution may cause serious image degradation. However, this method is much better than shifting nonzero coefficients everywhere. In general, T_c should be as small as possible such as $T_c = 1$.

This kind of shifting operation results in the change of number of zero AC coefficients while nonzero coefficients are unchanged. If the number of AC coefficients in between nonzero AC coefficients is odd and the message to hide is odd (i.e., 1), this method does not need to make any change. But if the number of zero coefficients is odd but the message to hide is even (i.e., 0), this method has to make the number of zero coefficients even by either removing or inserting one zero so that the next nonzero AC coefficient shifts from its original position either to the left or right, respectively. There are two more cases to make four possible cases: odd-odd, odd-even, even-odd, and even-even. The other two cases are similar to the previous two cases in nature. The overall four cases are summarized in Subsection 2.3. Note that in case of odd-odd (i.e., odd run-length with odd message to hide) and even-even pairs encoder does not need to insert or delete zeros. However, in any case, zeros are inserted or deleted intentionally to minimize distortion.

In this paper, coefficient shifting method is applied to the T block. For the decoder, odd or even number of zeros indicates the hidden message information. The following block [16 1 0 0 0 -2 1 0 0 -1 2 EOB] is a T block. Embedding of the secret message "01" into this T block changes last two run-lengths like [16 1 0 0 0 -2 1 0 0 -1 0 2 EOB] (see Figure 2). Note that one zero is forcefully inserted in between AC_9 and AC_{10}. Therefore, the position of the last nonzero AC coefficient (i.e., 2) has to be shifted to the right and has a new position AC_{11}.

2.3 Modifying Magnitude Nonzero AC Coefficients

Magnitude changing method is an ugly duckling. Magnitude changing method also has its merits. Thus, this method is applied to the S blocks. The magnitude of the first T_c nonzero coefficients is modified by a very simple rule. When the hidden bit is even (i.e., 0) and the magnitude value of nonzero AC coefficient is odd, then the method reduces or increases the magnitude value by 1 in order to make it even. Similarly, when the method has to hide 1 and the magnitude

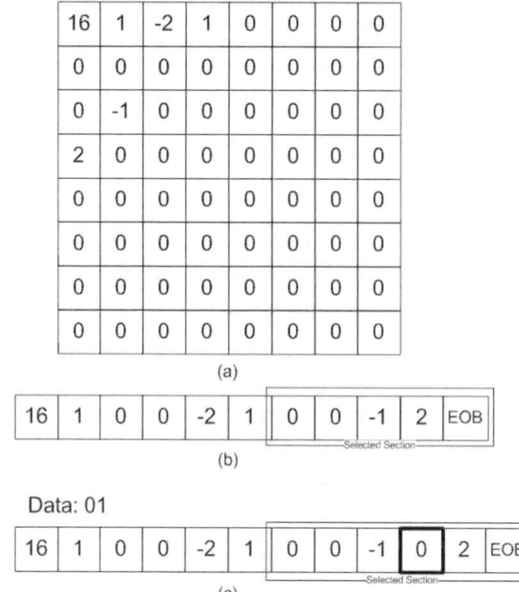

Fig. 3. An original T JPEG block (a), the zigzag scanned array of the T block (b), and the changed array after embedding binary data "01" (c)

is even, this method increases or reduces the magnitude by 1 to make it odd. Always the magnitude value 0 was skipped for modification. If zero coefficient is changed from 0 to 1 or -1, decoding becomes wrong. In addition, modification from 1 or -1 to 0 also causes wrong decoding. Thus, magnitude change inwards to 0 is not so good, which has been used traditionally. This method changes a nonzero coefficient to a smaller one by 1 in absolute magnitude. For example, 6 can be changed to 5.

In this paper, magnitude change from 0 outwards is introduced as a baseline method. Outward change increases absolute magnitude by 1. For example, 6 can be changed to 7. It is easy to show that there is not significant difference between inward modification and outward modification. Thus, there is no objection to use outward modification. However, in order to minimize distortion, both inward and outward modification methods are used interchangeably.

In case of odd-even (i.e., odd magnitude with even message to hide) or even-odd pairs, magnitude of coefficients have to be modified. However, in case of odd-odd or even-even pairs, magnitude of coefficients are left unchanged. However, changing all nonzero coefficients gives the hint of data hiding. Thus, in order to fight against statistical attack, not all nonzero coefficients are changed. In this paper, encoder changes T_c number of nonzero coefficients near from the DC coefficient. It is easy to show that magnitude of distortion or magnitude of error after data hiding is almost proportional to the magnitude of the quantization coefficients. It is obvious that most of quantization coefficients are smaller as far as they are closer from the DC coefficient.

An example block [32 5 0 0 0 2 EOB] is an S block (see Figure 4). There are two nonzero AC coefficients: $AC_1 = 5$ and $AC_5 = 2$. After embedding a message string "01" with two bits, the block becomes either like [32 4 0 0 0 1 EOB] or [32 6 0 0 0 3 EOB]. We can choose one of them that produces smaller magnitude of distortion.

2.4 Embedding Algorithm

Embedding algorithm of this paper combines two different methods: modification of both magnitude of nonzero coefficients in S blocks and run-length of zero coefficients in T blocks. The algorithm is summarized as follows:

Encoder

(1) Separation of S blocks from T blocks by T_v: If a block has less AC coefficients than or equal to T_v, this block is an S block, and otherwise, a T block.

(2) Change the magnitude values in the S block from the first T_c nonzero coefficients from the DC coefficient.

(a) If the message to hide is 0 and the nonzero coefficient magnitude is odd, make it even by either increasing or reducing the magnitude value by 1. Choice is determined by the smaller magnitude of distortion.

(b) If the message to hide is 1 and the nonzero coefficient magnitude is even, make it odd by either increasing or reducing the magnitude value by 1. Choice is determined by the smaller magnitude of distortion.

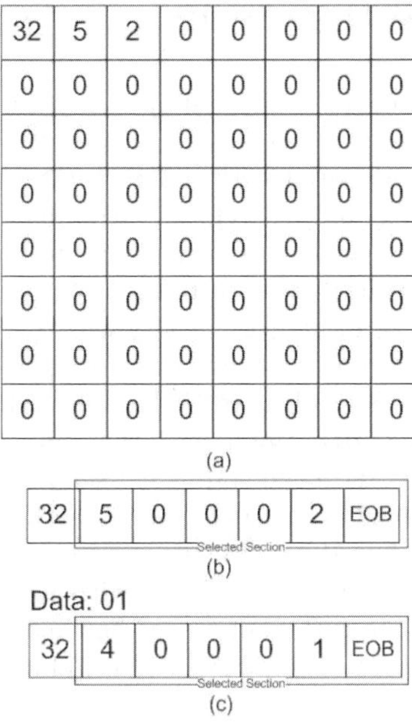

Fig. 4. An S JPEG block (a), the zigzag scanned array of the S block (b), and the changed array after embedding binary data "01" (c)

(3) Change the number of zeros in between the nonzero AC coefficients from the last T_c) run-lengths in the T block.
(a) If the hidden message is 0 and the number of zeros between two nonzero AC coefficients is odd, then make it even by either adding or deleting additional zeroes. Choice is determined by the smaller magnitude of distortion.
(b) If the hidden message is 1 and the number of zeros between two nonzero AC coefficients is even, then make it odd by either adding or deleting additional zeroes. Choice is determined by the smaller magnitude of distortion.

Decoder

The decoding algorithm is also simple. Checking magnitudes of run-lengths if they are odd or even and checking a block if it is an S block or a T block are the role of decoder. The decoding algorithm is given bellow.

(1) Determine whether a block is an S block or a T block by T_v.
(2) In an S block, the magnitude values of first T_c nonzero coefficients from the DC value are checked to see if they are odd or even. The odd magnitude values represent 1 and even numbers represent 0.
(3) In a T block, the number of zeros in between last T_c nonzero coefficients are counted. If the number is odd or even, then the hidden message is 1 or 0, respectively.

3 Experiment and Discussions

Implementing the proposed method is simple and easy. For the encoder and decoder, the proposed method was tested on four images. Performance of the data hiding methods is compared with different threshold values. The sample images are 512×512 in size and, therefore, have 4,096 8×8 DCT blocks. With different threshold values, various numbers of S and T blocks are obtained to hide data. The threshold values are used to control the capacity as well as image quality (i.e., PSNR). In case of higher capacity with $T_v = 4$ and $T_c = 4$, different images achieve different hiding capacity due to different number of S and T blocks. Lena image allows 8,658 bits to be hidden with 34.05 dB, and Barbara image 10,284 bits with 27.87 dB. Again, with the same threshold value, Gold-hill and Baboon images achieve data embedding capacity with 11,667 bits and 12,131 bits with 35.47 dB and 26.69 dB, respectively (see Table 1). After changing the threshold values as $T_v = 4$, and $T_c = 3$, the proposed method achieves different hiding capacity. Lena image embeds 6,575 bits with 36.05 dB, and Barbara image 7,466 bits with 29.83 dB. Since Baboon image has many nonzero AC coefficients due to its rich high-frequency components, the hiding capacity is significantly

Table 1. Performance over Hiding Capacity, Measured by different T_v, and T_c value

		PSNR [dB]	Capacity [bits]	in S [bits]	in T [bits]
Lena	$T_v = 4, T_c = 4$	34.06	8,658	6,099	2,559
	$T_v = 4, T_c = 3$	36.05	6,558	4,066	2,509
	$T_v = 4, T_c = 2$	38.49	4,560	2,527	2,033
	$T_v = 3, T_c = 3$	35.95	6,467	1,791	4,676
	$T_v = 3, T_c = 2$	38.49	4,119	1,781	2,338
	$T_v = 2, T_c = 2$	38.49	4,679	3,734	945
Barbara	$T_v = 4, T_c = 4$	27.88	10,284	1,776	8,508
	$T_v = 4, T_c = 3$	29.8329	7,466	1,774	5,692
	$T_v = 4, T_c = 2$	33.28	4,615	1,767	2,848
	$T_v = 3, T_c = 3$	29.73	7,283	1,109	6,174
	$T_v = 3, T_c = 2$	33.28	4,200	1,103	3,097
	$T_v = 2, T_c = 2$	33.28	3,914	542	3,372
Gold-hill	$T_v = 4, T_c = 4$	35.48	11,667	2,373	9,294
	$T_v = 4, T_c = 3$	36.88	8,552	2,356	6,196
	$T_v = 4, T_c = 2$	39.14	5,471	2,353	3,108
	$T_v = 3, T_c = 3$	36.71	8,010	876	7,134
	$T_v = 3, T_c = 2$	39.14	4,461	874	3,587
	$T_v = 2, T_c = 2$	39.14	4,121	327	3,794
Baboon	$T_v = 4, T_c = 4$	26.69	12,131	275	11,856
	$T_v = 4, T_c = 3$	28.29	8,162	258	7,904
	$T_v = 4, T_c = 2$	31.21	4,222	270	3,952
	$T_v = 3, T_c = 3$	28.35	8,144	100	8,044
	$T_v = 3, T_c = 2$	31.21	4,128	96	4,032
	$T_v = 2, T_c = 2$	31.21	4,088	24	4,064

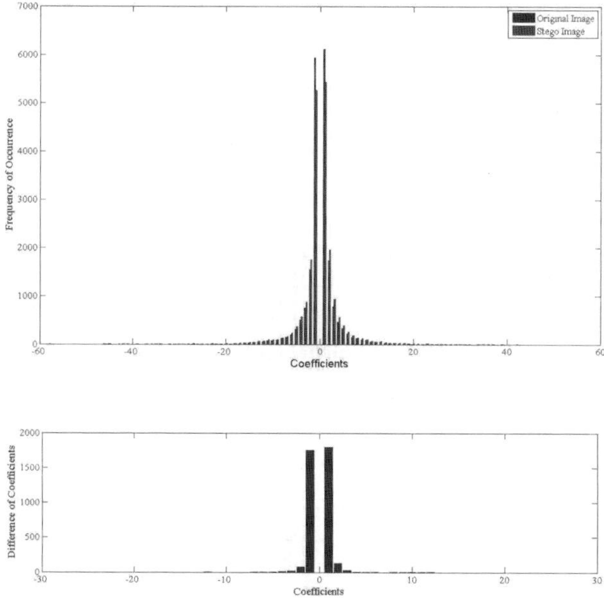

Fig. 5. Histogram of the original Lena image (top) and that of the difference between original and stego images (bottom) with $T_v = 4$ and $T_c = 4$

higher than other images. Note that with $T_v = 4$, and $T_c = 3$, the embedding capacity of Baboon image is 8,162 bits with 28.29 dB of visual quality.

After hiding data by the proposed method, small changes are observed in the magnitude histogram of the stego image compared with original image. Two graphs of histogram for original image and the difference between original and stego images are shown in Figures 5 and 6. It is observed that the difference is almost negligible, and, hence, the stego image is relatively secure due to its capability to keep almost the same as original original histogram. Histogram of the original image compressed by JPEG has a Cauchy-like distribution as shown in Figures 5 and 6. Difference between two histograms is almost equal to the number of total nonzero coefficients changed in the T blocks. By adjusting the threshold values T_v and T_c, histogram of the difference can be controlled. Note that the differences between magnitude histograms depend on images. However, most differences are occurred at 1 and -1.

4 Conclusions

The proposed method provides significantly higher embedding capacity with slightly worse image quality in comparison with a method of shifting nonzero coefficients only. In terms of security issue, this method is less weaker than traditional methods that modify magnitude of coefficients, but still can produce

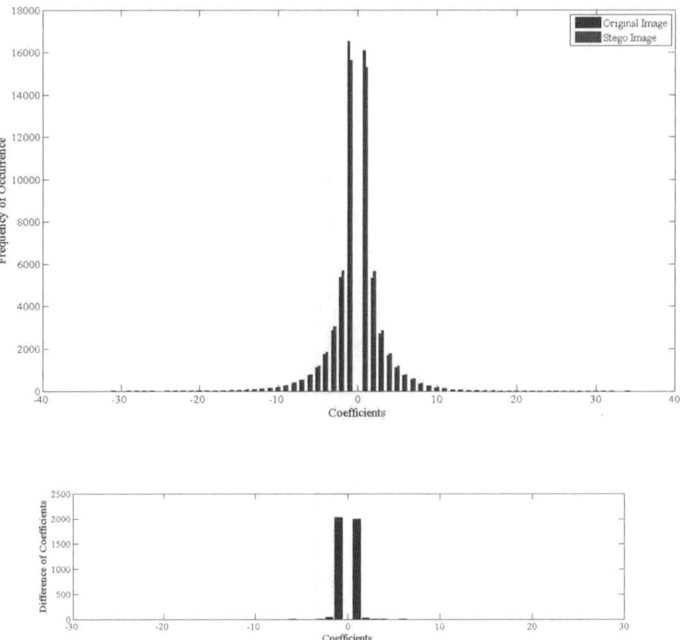

Fig. 6. Histogram of the original Baboon image (top) and that of the difference between original and stego images (bottom) with $T_v = 4$ and $T_c = 4$

almost the same magnitude histogram and less distortion in visual quality. For the future work, optimization can be used to improve performance and security level. Many variations are possible in combination of two methods.

Acknowledgements

The authors would like to thank the reviewers for their valuable comments and suggestions, which have improved the paper.

References

1. Fridrich, J., Goljan, M., Hogea, H.: Attacking the Out-Guess. In: Proceedings of the ACM Workshop on Multimedia and Security, pp. 967–982 (2002)
2. Fridrich, J., Goljan, M., Hogea, H.: Steganalysis of JPEG image: Breaking the F5 algorithm. In: Petitcolas, F.A.P. (ed.) IH 2002. LNCS, vol. 2578, pp. 310–323. Springer, Heidelberg (2003)
3. Fridrich, J.: Feature-based steganalysis for JPEG images and its implications for future design of steganographic schemes. In: Fridrich, J. (ed.) IH 2004. LNCS, vol. 3200, pp. 67–81. Springer, Heidelberg (2004)
4. Provos, N.: Defending against statistical steganalysis. In: Proceedings of the 10th USENIX Security Symposium, pp. 323–335 (2001)

5. Sallee, P.: Model-based steganography. In: Kalker, T., Cox, I., Ro, Y.M. (eds.) IWDW 2003. LNCS, vol. 2939, pp. 154–167. Springer, Heidelberg (2004)
6. Sallee, P.: Model-based methods for steganography and steganalysis. International Journal of Image and Graphics 5(1), 167–190 (2005)
7. Solanki, K., Sarkar, A., Manjunath, B.S.: YASS: Yet another steganographic scheme that resists blind steganalysis. In: Furon, T., Cayre, F., Doërr, G., Bas, P. (eds.) IH 2007. LNCS, vol. 4567, pp. 16–31. Springer, Heidelberg (2008)
8. Westfeld, A., Pfitzmann, A.: Attacks on steganographic systems. In: Pfitzmann, A. (ed.) IH 1999. LNCS, vol. 1768, pp. 61–75. Springer, Heidelberg (2000)
9. Westfeld, A.: F5: A steganographic algorithm: High capacity despite better steganalysis. In: Moskowitz, I.S. (ed.) IH 2001. LNCS, vol. 2137, pp. 289–302. Springer, Heidelberg (2001)

Software Test Data Generation Based on Multi-agent

Siwen Yu, Jun Ai, and Yifu Zhang

Department of System Engineering of Engineering Technology,
Beihang University, Beijing 100191, China
applifish126@gmail.com, aijun@buaa.edu.cn

Abstract. Software test data generation is an important part of software testing. This paper presents a multi-agent cooperation framework for software test data generation. The framework is constituted by Graph Miner, Method Selector and test data generation method agent group. Graph Miner extracts software information sequences from UML graphs, and sends them to Method Selector. Then Method Selector selects out relevant method agents to generate test data. This framework can solve the problems of test data generation methods extension and low level of intelligence exists in traditional methods. Based on the framework proposed in this paper, a software prototype is developed. It is proved that this framework is feasible.

Keywords: Agent; software test data; UML.

1 Introduction

UML is a semi-formal modeling language, which is well defined and easy to express. It is an effective resource to generate software test data. The UML based test data generation method is a type of black box testing method. The black box testing method includes equivalence class classification, boundary value analysis, causal mapping, statistical test method, pairs test method and various test methods based on artificial intelligence. But the traditional UML based software data generation methods are poor to extend and can not impose a variety of testing methods, which can not be effective in the discovery of software defects.

Agent refers to the entity present in a particular environment to carry out its own action to meet the goal, with the characteristics of scalability, flexibility and high degree of autonomy. By setting the relevant rules, Agent can impose a wide range of software test data generation methods in accordance with the actual needs. By adding the rules, new software test data generation method can be added. This overcomes the shortcomings of poor scalability and method oneness. This paper uses the cooperation of the multi-Agent to complete the generation of software test data.

2 The Principles of the Framework

2.1 The Principles of the Framework

The framework proposed by this paper can be described by the following formula: S={U,C,D,V,f}[1].U represents UML models. R=C∪D represents the property set of

D. Ślęzak et al. (Eds.): ASEA 2009, CCIS 59, pp. 188–195, 2009.

the framework, in which C is the conditional properties and D is the result condition. V is the value set of property, V=∪ vr, $r \in R$. f is information function, f: U×R→V. f defines how to select test data generation method in accordance to the specified UML diagrams.

Based on the UML model Up, the framework can choose the test data generation methods agent set D according to conditional property C. The agents which is selected are then to execute method to generate test data.

According to the process of test data generation, the principles above can be summarized into the following three steps:
Extract software test information from UML diagrams;
Select agent set Di from rule set Ci;
Execute the selected agents to get software test data.

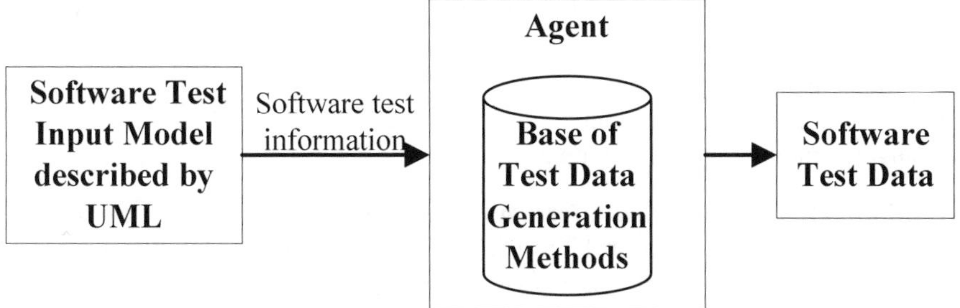

Fig. 1. The framework of agent based software test data generation

2.2 The Design of the Framework

This paper introduced in two agents and one agent group. They are Graph Miner, Method Selector and test data generation method agent group. There are many kinds of method agent in test data generation method agent group.

Graph Miner extracts test information from UML diagrams to provide information to the generation of test data.

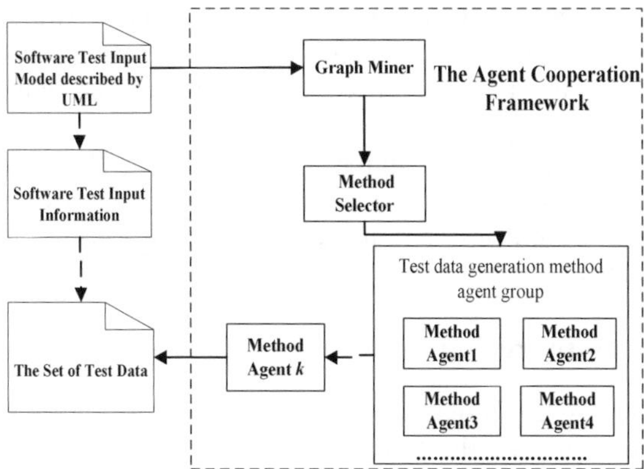

Fig. 2. The agent cooperation framework

Through the knowledge base in Method Selector, the agent k is selected from the test data generation method agent group according to C. Then agent k is executed to generate test data. Fig 2 shows framework of the design.

3 Test Input Information Extraction

3.1 Test Input Information

It is necessary to clarify the concept of software test input information. For this, the paper defines software testing input package and software testing information sequence.

Definition 1 (Software testing input package): Let InputPackage represents software testing input package, which is a triple vector. InputPackage={Var,VarType, VarRange}, the definition of elements in the vector is as follows:

Var: variable name in the test input;
VarTye: variable type in test input;
VarRange: variable scope in test input.

Definition 2 (Software testing information sequence): Software testing information sequence is a quaternion group STS={Start, Final, Restriction, InputPackage }.The meaning of the elements in the vector is as follows:

Start: the start point of the UML diagram;
Final: the final point of the UML diagram;
Restriction: the conditions of the migrations;
InputPackage: oftware testing input package.

The content and format of software testing information sequence has nothing to do with the specific UML diagrams. This provides the information source to generate test data.

3.2 The Coverage Criteria of UML Diagrams

In order to ensure the adequacy of software testing, we must consider the validity of test data and coverage criteria. Based on the concept of the software testing information sequence, the constraints, nodes and variable information should be extracted from the diagrams. So, this paper defines criteria to cover these elements. The criteria are as follows:
Constraint coverage criterion: cover all the constraints in the UML diagrams;
Node coverage criterion: cover all the nodes in the UML diagrams;
Variable information coverage criterion: cover all the information of variable in the UML diagrams, such as variable name, variable scope and variable type.

3.3 Extraction of Software Test Input Information

Graph Miner traversals UML diagram Up to generate software testing information sequence in accordance with the test coverage criteria. The specific process is as follows:

Read the type mark of the UML diagram Tp;
Select UML diagram traversal methods based on mark Tp;
Implement traversal method rules, obtain the software testing information sequence.

Through the process, the software testing information sequence STSp can be generated from model Up. The following is the algorithm to generate software testing information sequence from UML activity diagram.

```
typedef struct migration{
        int adjvex;//the position of the node
 string Restriction;//restrict condition
 struct migration *next;//point of the next edge
}Elink;
typedef struct node{
string var;//name of variable
string varitype;//type of variable
int varrange[M];//range of variable
Elink *link;}VNode;
```

Algorithm: Generate test information of activity diagram
Input: UML activity diagram T
Output: Test information of activity diagram
Algorithm design:

```
travel_Activity_Diagram(VNode G[], int vnode)
{ int w;
        Visit(vnode);//visit the information in vnode, extract test information
        w=FIRSTNODE(G,vonde);//look for the first adjacent point of V, return -1
if no adjacents exist
while (w!=-1)
{if(vistited[w]= =0)
travel_Activity_Diagram(G,w);
w=NEXTNODE(G, vonde);// look for the next adjacent point of V, return -1 if no
adjacents exist}}
```

4 Software Test Data Generation

After the software testing information sequence is generated, Method Selector chooses the relevant software test generation method Agent to generate software test data. Method Selector completes the task by the knowledge base of software test data generation method internal. In fact, Method Selector is the executor of the mapping U×R to V.

The value table Y of R is in the Method Selector. The generation of test data is based on the software testing information sequence. Therefore, the elements of the sequence should be the conditional elements for the test data generation. In this paper, table Y is realized by the table of software test information sign-Agent name-Agent ID (Table TST-AN-AID for short). In table 1, Bi, $i \in N$ represent the set of the name

Table 1. TST-AN-AID table

C	*D*	
Test information sign	Agent name	Agent ID
*Var:T*1	*B*1	*Ag*1
VarType:T2	*B*2	*Ag*2
VarRange:T3	*B*3	*Ag*3
Start:T4	*B*4	*Ag*4
Final:T5	*B*5	*Ag*5
Restriction:T6	*B*6	*Ag*6

of the Agents be selected. Bi={Lij|i,j∈N, Lij is the name of the method}. Agi, i∈N represent the set of IDs of the Agents. Agi={Gij∈G | G is the set of ID of the Agents}.

Based on the table of TST-AN-AID, test data generation method agent Bi is selected out to generate test data. The steps are as follows:

Graph Miner extracts software testing information sequence from UML diagrams;
Trough TST-AN-AA table software test data generation Agent k is selected out;
Agent k generates software test data based on the software testing information sequence.

In order to complete the cooperation between the agents, this paper uses Indirect / Active termination model [2]. The principle of the model is showed in Fig 3.

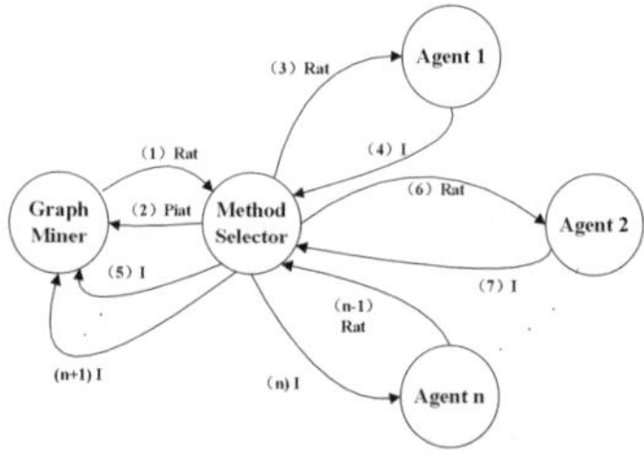

Fig. 3. Indirect / Active termination model

5 Case Study

In this paper, an aircraft plug-weapon management system is used as an example to illustrate the principle. There are six use case diagrams, three activity diagrams and one sequence diagrams. Figure 4 is the system's system-level use case diagram. Due to the restrictions on article length, can not all of the diagrams be listed.

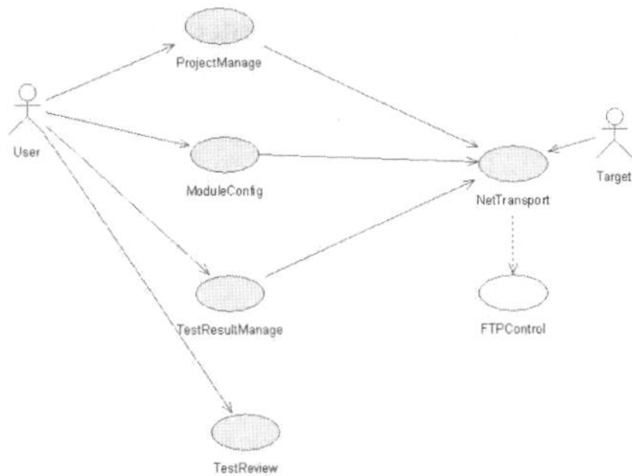

Fig. 4. Indirect / Active termination model

Graph Miner traverses through the use case diagram, to generate the software testing requirement tree C, Figure 5. The node types of Tree C are listed in Table 2.

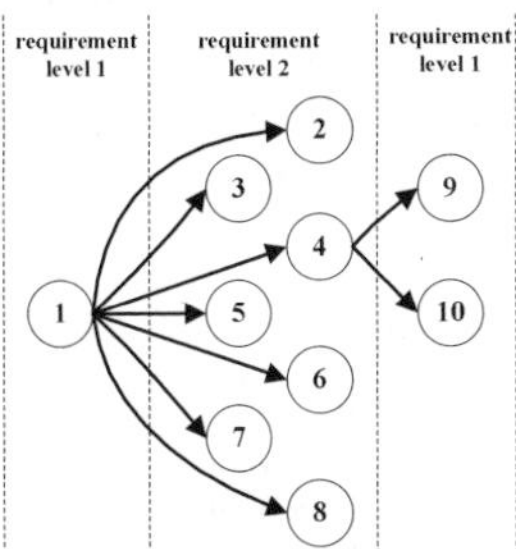

Fig. 5. Test requirement tree

Table 2. The diagram type and mark of test requirement tree

Diagram type	Node	Diagram type mark
Use case diagram	1, 4, 5, 6, 7, 8	$P1$
Activity diagram	2, 9	$P2$
Sequence diagram	3, 10	$P3$

After the requirement tree is generated, the corresponding rules are found to generate software test information sequences through Table 3.

Table 3. The generation of test information sequences

Diagram type mark	Node	Rules	Software test information sequence
$P1$	1, 4, 5, 6, 7, 8	Ap1	STS p1, STS p4, ,…, STS p8
$P2$	2, 9	Ap2	STS p2
$P3$	3, 10	Ap3	STS p3, STS p10

Based on the software test information sequence, test method agents are selected to generate test data through table 4.

Table 4. The generation of software test data

STS	Element	Agent name	Agent ID	Software test data set
*STS*1, *STS*2, .., *STS*10	*Var*	*B*1	*Ag*1	*D*11~ *D*110
	VarType	*B*2	*Ag*2	*D*21~ *D*210
	VarRange	*B*3	*Ag*3	*D*31~ *D*310
	Start	*B*4	*Ag*4	*D*41~ *D*410
	Final	*B*5	*Ag*5	*D*51~ *D*510
	Rrestriction	*B*6	*Ag*6	*D*61~ *D*610

The framework proposed by this paper can solve the problem of test data generation method extension. New method Agent can be added by add new elements in TST-AN-AA table. At the same time, the extension of test data generation method is realized. The principle is showed in Fig 5.

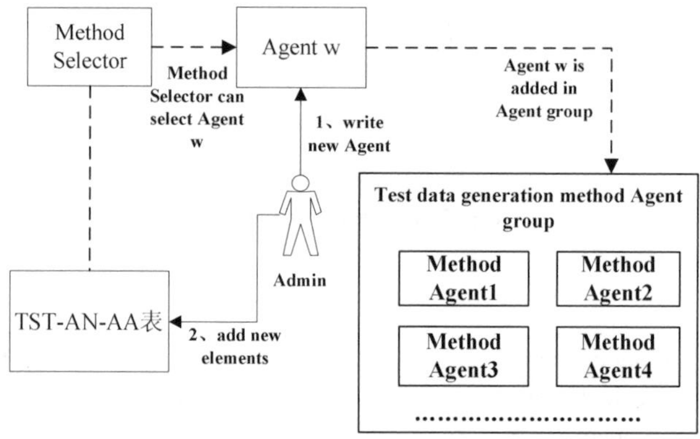

Fig. 6. The principle of software test data generation method extension

6 Conclusion

Through using multi-Agent cooperation method in software test data generation, this paper proposes a framework of software test data generation. Based on the test information extraction and test data generation, the principle and process of the Agent-based framework is elaborated. According to the framework proposed in this paper, a prototype is developed to verify the feasibility of the framework. In addition, the framework is easy to extend test method, can generate test data based on multiple UML diagrams and high level of intelligence.

References

1. Linzhang, W., Jiesong, Y., Xiaofeng, Y., et al.: Generating test cases from UML activity diagram based on Gray-box method. In: 11th Asia-Pacific on Software Engineering Conference, November 30-December 3, pp. 284–291 (2004)
2. Li, B.-L., Li, Z.-s., Qing, L., et al.: Test case automate generation from UML sequence diagram and OCL expression. In: 2007 International Conference on Computational Intelligence and Security, December 15-19, pp. 1048–1052 (2007)
3. Chevalley, T.-F.: Automated generation of statistical test cases from UML state diagrams. In: Computer Software and Applications Conference COMPSAC 2001, 25th Annual International, October 8-12, pp. 205–214 (2001)
4. Bai, X., Dai, G., Xu, D., et al.: A multi-agent based framework for collaborative testing on Web services. In: Software Technologies for Future Embedded and Ubiquitous Systems, 2006 and the 2006 Second International Workshop on Collaborative Computing, Integration, and Assurance. SEUS 2006/WCCIA 2006. The Fourth IEEE Workshop on April 27-28, 2006, 6 p. (2006)
5. Huanglin, Z.: Intelligent Computing, vol. 204, pp. 2–4. Chongqing University Press (2004)
6. Xinjun, M.: Agent Oriented Software Development, p. 140. Tsinghua University Press, Beijing (2005)

Knowledge Creation and Creativity in Agile Teams

Broderick Crawford[1,2] and Claudio León de la Barra[1]

[1] Pontificia Universidad Católica de Valparaíso, PUCV, Chile
[2] Universidad Técnica Federico Santa María, Valparaíso, Chile
{broderick.crawford,cleond}@ucv.cl

Abstract. Knowledge has been called the only meaningful economic resource of the Knowledge Society. Then, Knowledge Creation in organizations is a very important issue. Particularly, the development of new software products requires the generation of novel and useful ideas. In this paper, software development approaches are analyzed from the perspective of Knowledge Management and Creativity. Here too, we apply these concepts to enhance the creative performance of eXtreme Programming introducing a new role wich can stimulate the Knowledge Creation and Creativity of the developers.

Keywords: Creativity, Knowledge Management, Software Development, Agile Methodologies, eXtreme Programming.

1 Introduction

Software engineering is a knowledge intensive process that includes some aspects of Knowledge Management (KM) in all phases: eliciting requirements, design, construction, testing, implementation, maintenance, and project management. No worker of a development project possess all the knowledge required for fulfilling all activities. This underlies the need for knowledge sharing support to share domain expertise between the customer and the development team [7]. The traditional approaches (often referred to as plan-driven, task-based or Tayloristic), like the waterfall model and its variances, facilitate knowledge sharing primarily through documentation. They also promote usage of role based teams and detailed plans of the entire software development life-cycle. It shifts the focus from individuals and their creative abilities to the processes themselves. In contrary, agile methods emphasise and value individuals and interactions over processes. Tayloristic methods heavily and rigorously use documentation for capturing knowledge gained in the activities of a software project life-cycle [6]. In contrast, agile methods suggest that most of the written documentation can be replaced by enhanced informal communications among team members internally and between the team and the customers with a stronger emphasis on tacit knowledge rather than explicit knowledge [5].

The study in [3] claim that the adaptation of agile methods is facilitated by a high degree of knowledge creation, enabled by interaction of developers

D. Ślęzak et al. (Eds.): ASEA 2009, CCIS 59, pp. 196–203, 2009.

and users. They examined knowledge sharing in an eXtreme Programming (XP) project and a traditional project, founding that when the XP model was used, the creation of tacit knowledge improved as a result of frequent contacts.

Increasing knowledge can influence creativity because knowledge drives creative self-efficacy [28,27]. People with more knowledge and skills are more likely to feel confident that they can be creative. We believe that creativity is the only way to manage software development in organizations trying to maintain their advantages. Consequently, we are interested in the study of techniques to foster creativity in software engineering. In this work, we address the improvement of creativite performance in XP.

This paper is organised as follows: Section 2 gives a brief overview of XP and its roles. Section 3 briefly shows Software Engineering from KM perspective. In section 4 we explain the relevance of Creativity in Software Development. Section 5 is about central aspects in Creativity. Section 6 presents a comparison between roles in creative teams and roles in XP teams. Finally, in Section 7 we conclude the paper and give some perspectives for future research.

2 eXtreme Programming

A new group of software development methodologies has appeared over the last few years. For a while these were known as lightweight methodologies, but now the accepted term is Agile methodologies. The most common of them are: eXtreme Programming, the Crystal Family, Agile Modeling, Adaptive Software Development, Scrum, Feature Driven Development, Dynamic System Development Method [10]. There exist many variations, but all of them share the common principles and core values specified in the Agile Manifesto [6]. Extreme Programming is an iterative approach to software development [4]. The methodology is designed to deliver the software that customer needs when it's needed. This methodology emphasizes team work. Managers, customers, and developers are all part of a team dedicated to deliver quality software. XP implements a simple, yet effective way to enable groupware style development. XP improves a software project in four essential ways; communication, simplicity, feedback, and courage. XP defines the following roles [4]: Programmer, Customer, Tester, Tracker, Coach, Consultant and Big boss.

3 Knowledge Creation and Software Engineering

It has been said that Knowledge Management implementations in Software Engineering can extract knowledge from its sources of knowledge: documentation, artifacts, objects, components, patterns, templates and code repositories, exploiting this knowledge in future software developments. But, software reuse is not a technology problem, nor is it a management problem. Reuse is fundamentally a Knowledge Management problem. In [17] Jim Highsmith explains how over the last ten or so years, by packaging objects into components and components into templates, we have made the problem bigger, not smaller. Objects, patterns, templates, and components are packaged (explicit) knowledge Ů the larger the package, the greater the encapsulated knowledge. The greater the encapsulated knowledge, the harder it is to transfer. Additionally, the essence of problem solving, innovation, creativity, intuitive design, good analysis, and effective project management involves more tacit knowledge, the harder it is to transfer. By putting tacit knowledge in a principal role and cultivating tacit knowledge environments, KM can play an important role in software development. An understanding of knowledge sharing and transfer issues offers important insights about Reusability and Software Engineering.

4 Creativity in Software Development

Since human creativity is thought as the source to resolve complex problem or create innovative products, one possibility to improve the software development process is to design a process which can stimulate the creativity of the developers. There are few studies reported on the importance of creativity in software development. In management and business, researchers have done much work about creativity and obtained evidence that the employees who had appropriate creativity characteristics, worked on complex, challenging jobs, and were supervised in a supportive, noncontrolling fashion, produced more creative work. Then, according to the previous ideas the use of creativity in software development is undeniable, but requirements engineering is not recognized as a creative process in all the cases [23]. In a few publications the importance of creativity has been investigated in all the phases of software development process [11,12,8] and mostly focused in the requirements engineering [26,24,25]. Nevertheless, the use of techniques to foster creativity in requirements engineering is still shortly investigated.

5 Creativity: Purposes, Performance and Structure

The creativity definitions are numerous [2,21,31], therefore, considering the object of analysis in the present paper: a software development teamwork, that must respond to the requirements of a specific client for a particular problem, a suitable definition is the one raised by Welsch [30]:

Creativity is the process of generating unique products by transformation of existing products. These products, tangible and intangible, must be unique only to the creator, and must meet the criteria of purpose and value established by the creator.

More specifically, and from an eminently creative perspective, it is possible to distinguish three aspects at the interior of a group developing new products:

1) *The purposes* that the team tries to reach, which demand two scopes of results [9,13,14,15,16]; those related to the creative result that must be original, elaborated, productive and flexible and those related to the creative team, so that it reaches its goals, developing cognitive abilities and presenting an improved

disposition to the change. All this in order to obtain a better creative team performance in the future.

2) *The performance* shown by the team in connection with the main aspects of the complex dynamics that the persons build inside a team. We describe three aspects, the personal conditions of the members of the team, in terms of the styles and cognitives abilities, the personality, their intrinsic motivation and knowledge [31,1,2,9], the organizational conditions in which the creative team is inserted, and that determines, at least partly, its functioning. These conditions, in the extent that present/display certain necessary particular characteristics - although non sufficient - for the creative performance. They emphasize in special the culture (communication, collaboration, trust, conflict handle, pressure and learning) [31,20,18]; the internal structure (formalization, autonomy and evaluation of the performance) [31,20,18,1]; the team available resources (time disposition) [31,20,2] and the physical atmosphere of work [21], and the conditions of performance of the creative team, mainly the creative process realized, which supposes the set of specific phases that allow to assure the obtaining of a concrete result (creative product) [21,29].

3) *The structure* of the creative team, particularly the group characteristics, such as norms, cohesiveness, size, diversity, roles, task and problem-solving approaches [31].

Of the mentioned aspects, we deepen in those referred to the structure and performance of the team for the development of new products, specially considering the roles surrounding the creative process [29,21].

5.1 Roles in a Creative Team

Lumsdaine and Lumsdaine [22] raise the subject of the required cognitives abilities (mindsets) for creative problem resolution. Their tipology is excellent for the creative team, and the different roles to consider. These roles are the following ones:

- Detective. In charge of collecting the greatest quantity of information related to the problem. It has to collect data without making judgements, even when it thinks that it has already understood the problem exactly.
- Explorer. Detects what can happen in the area of the problem and its context. It thinks on its long term effects and it anticipates certain developments that can affect the context (in this case, the team). The explorer perceives the problem in a broad sense.
- Artist. Creates new things, transforming the information. It must be able to break his own schemes to generate eccentric ideas, with imagination and feeling.
- Engineer. Is the one in charge of evaluating new ideas. It must make converge the ideas, in order to clarify the concepts and to obtain practical ideas that can be implemented for the resolution of problems.
- Judge. Must do a hierarchy of ideas and decide which of them will be implemented (and as well, which ones must be discarded). Additionally, it must

detect possible faults or inconsistences, as well as raise the corresponding solutions. Its role must be critical and impartial, having to look for the best idea, evaluating the associated risks.
- Producer. In charge of implementing the chosen ideas.

Leonard and Swap [21] have mentioned additional roles, possible to be integrated with the previous ones, because they try to make more fruitful the divergence and the convergence in the creative process:

- The provoker who takes the members of the team "to break" habitual mental and procedural schemes to allow the mentioned divergence (in the case of the "artist") or even a better convergence (in the case of the "engineer").
- Think tank that it is invited to the team sessions to give a renewed vision of the problem-situation based on his/her experticia and experience.
- The facilitator whose function consists in helping and supporting the team work in its creative task in different stages.
- The manager who cares for the performance and specially for the results of the creative team trying to adjust them to the criteria and rules of the organization (use of resources, due dates).

Kelley and Littman [19], on the other hand, have raised a role tipology similar to Lumsdaine and Lumsdaine [22], being interesting that they group the roles in three categories: those directed to the learning of the creative team (susceptible of corresponding with the detective, explorer, artist, provoker and think tank roles), others directed to the internal organization and success of the team (similar to the judge, facilitator and manager roles) and, finally, roles whose purpose is to construct the innovation (possibly related to the role of the engineer and judge).

6 Creativity in eXtreme Programming

Regarding to the structure dimension of a new product development team (in particular software), it is possible to relate the roles in creativity to the roles defined in the XP methodology distinguishing: base roles, that is, those directly related to the creative processes and software development, and support roles, whose function is to support or lead the other roles for a better performance.

6.1 Team Structure (Base and Supporting Roles)

The base roles are directly related to the creative and software development process and the supporting roles support or lead the base roles to a better performance. The following is the correlation between creative and XP roles:

- The detective function consisting in collecting information related to a problem is made by the client himself in XP, because this one generates the first contact with the software development team.

- The function of explorer consisting in defining completely the problem is made in XP as much by the client as the manager of the team, all together they appreciate the reach of the identified problem, as well as of the possible solutions. The function of the artist consisting in transforming the information, creating new relations, and therefore generating interesting solutions is made by the developer, that in XP methodology is in charge of the analysis, design and programming of software.
- The function of the engineer referred to clarify and to evaluate the new ideas, in terms of its feasibility is made in XP by the tester and the tracker.
- The function of the judge, understood as the definitive selection of the solutions to implant, is made in XP by the tracker and the client.
- The function of the producer, referred to the implementation of the selected ideas (strictly speaking it is working software) is made in XP by the client in his organization, including the processes and procedures that this function implies.

The supporting roles considered are:

- The provoker; creativity demands that the divergence as well as convergence in the solutions be maximum and complete. There is not explicit reference in XP methodology about divergent thinking.
- The think tank who helps the team work "from outsid" is equivalent completely to the role of the consultant.
- The facilitator whose function is helping the team, corresponds in XP to the coach role.
- The manager whose function is to lead to the team in terms of its general efficiency and its effectiveness corresponds with XP's big boss or manager.

7 Conclusions

Agility is about creating and responding to change. Today, Agile Teams addresses the need for innovative approaches, particularly, the eXtreme Programming methodology includes implicitly central aspects of a creative teamwork. These aspects can be organized according to the structure that the team adopts and the performance that characterizes to the team.

The structure that the team adopts and specially the different roles that the methodology advises to define, nearly correspond with the roles at the interior of a creative team. The performance that characterizes the team through certain advisable practices, from the perspective of creativity, constitutes the necessary basic conditions, although nonsufficient, in order to favor the group creative performance. These conditions - called practices in XP methodology - are accompanied by concrete phases of constituent activities of an agile software development process, which is possible to correspond with the creative process, which is fundamental to the creative performance.

In spite of the previous comments, we think that XP methodology should have a more explicit reference to:

- The provoker role that is thoroughly described in creativity as a fundamental factor to generate innovation. This can be explained because, in general, agile methodologies do not aim, as a central element, to generate an original software, but an effective one.
- The distinction and formalization of the creative phases to generate options incubation and option choices (that are fundamental in creativity). It is assumed that they take place in the iterative and production process. Again, XP is not focused in "originality", resulting that the divergence is not so fundamental in XP.
- A more direct mention to the physical atmosphere of work, that in creativity are considered as highly relevant to enhance the performance. These aspects should have a greater consideration since software development is a special case of product development.

References

1. Amabile, T.: How to kill creativity. Harvard Business Review, 77–87 (September-October 1998)
2. Amabile, T., Conti, R., Coon, H., Lazenby, J., Herron, M.: Assessing the work environment for creativity. Academy of Management Journal 39(5), 1154–1184
3. Bahli, B., Zeid, E.: The role of knowledge creation in adopting extreme programming model: an empirical study. In: Proc. ITI 3rd International Conference on Information & Communication Technology (ICICT), Cairo, Egypt, December 2005, pp. 75–87 (2005)
4. Beck, K.: Extreme programming explained: embrace change. Addison-Wesley Longman Publishing Co., Inc., Boston (2000)
5. Beck, K., Beedle, M., Bennekum, A.V., Cockburn, A., Cunningham, W., Fowler, M., Grenning, J., Highsmith, J., Hunt, A., Jeffries, R., Kern, J., Marick, B., Martin, R.C., Mellor, S., Schwaber, K., Sutherland, J., Thomas, D.: Manifesto for agile software development (2001), http://agilemanifesto.org
6. Chau, T., Maurer, F.: Knowledge sharing in agile software teams. In: Lenski, W. (ed.) Logic versus Approximation. LNCS, vol. 3075, pp. 173–183. Springer, Heidelberg (2004)
7. Chau, T., Maurer, F., Melnik, G.: Knowledge sharing: Agile methods vs tayloristic methods. In: Twelfth International Workshop on Enabling Technologies: Infrastructure for Collaborative Enterprises, WETICE, pp. 302–307. IEEE Computer Society, Los Alamitos
8. Crawford, B., de la Barra, C.L.: Enhancing creativity in agile software teams. In: Concas, G., Damiani, E., Scotto, M., Succi, G. (eds.) XP 2007. LNCS, vol. 4536, pp. 161–162. Springer, Heidelberg (2007)
9. Csikszentmihalyi, M.: Creativity: Flow and the Psychology of Discovery and Invention. Harper Perennial, New York (1998)
10. Fowler, M.: The new methodology (2001), http://www.martinfowler.com/articles/newMethodology.html
11. Glass, R.L.: Software creativity. Prentice-Hall, Inc., Upper Saddle River (1995)
12. Gu, M., Tong, X.: Towards hypotheses on creativity in software development. In: Bomarius, F., Iida, H. (eds.) PROFES 2004. LNCS, vol. 3009, pp. 47–61. Springer, Heidelberg (2004)

13. Guilford, J.P.: Intelligence, Creativity and Their Educational Implications. Edits Pub. (1968)
14. Hallman, R.: The necessary and sufficient conditions of creativity. Journal of Humanistic Psychology 3(1) (1963); Also reprinted in Gowan, J.C., et al.: Creativity: Its Educational Implications. John Wiley and Co., New York (1967)
15. Hallman, R.: Aesthetic pleasure and the creative process. Journal of Humanistic Psychology 6(2), 141–148 (1966)
16. Hallman, R.J.: Techniques of creative teaching. Journal of Creative Behavior I (September 1966)
17. Highsmith, J.: Reuse as a knowledge management problem, `http://www.awprofessional.com/articles/article.asp?p=31478`
18. Isaksen, S.G., Lauer, K.J., Ekvall, G.: Situational outlook questionnaire: A measure of the climate for creativity and change. Psychological Reports (85), 665–674
19. Kelley, T., Littman, J.: The Ten Faces of Innovation: IDEO's Strategies for Defeating the Devil's Advocate and Driving Creativity Throughout Your Organization, Currency (2005)
20. Kotler, P., Armstrong, G.: Principles of Marketing, 10th edn. Prentice-Hall, Englewood Cliffs (2003)
21. Leonard, D.A., Swap, W.C.: When Sparks Fly: Igniting Creativity in Groups. Harvard Business School Press, Boston (1999)
22. Lumsdaine, E., Lumsdaine, M.: Creative Problem Solving: Thinking Skills for a Changing World. McGraw-Hill, Inc., New York (1995)
23. Maiden, N., Gizikis, A., Robertson, S.: Provoking creativity: Imagine what your requirements could be like. IEEE Software 21(5), 68–75 (2004)
24. Maiden, N., Robertson, S.: Integrating creativity into requirements processes: Experiences with an air traffic management system. In: 13th IEEE International Conference on Requirements Engineering (RE 2005), Paris, France, August 29 - September 2, pp. 105–116. IEEE Computer Society, Los Alamitos (2005)
25. Mich, L., Anesi, C., Berry, D.M.: Applying a pragmatics-based creativity-fostering technique to requirements elicitation. Requir. Eng. 10(4), 262–275 (2005)
26. Robertson, J.: Requirements analysts must also be inventors. IEEE Software 22(1), 48–50 (2005)
27. Sternberg, R., Lubart, T.: Defying the Crowd: Cultivating Creativity in a Culture of Conformity. Free Press, New York (1995)
28. Tierney, P., Farmer, S.: Creative self-efficacy: Its potential antecedents and relationship to creative performance. Academy of Management Journal 45(6), 1137–1148 (2002)
29. Wallas, G.: The art of thought. Harcourt Brace, New York (1926)
30. Welsh, G.: Personality and Creativity: A Study of Talented High School Students. Unpub. doctoral dissertation. University of North Carolina, Chapel Hill (1967)
31. Woodman, R.W., Sawyer, J.E., Griffin, R.W.: Toward a theory of organizational creativity. The Academy of Management Review 18(2), 293–321 (1993)

TEST: Testing Environment for Embedded Systems Based on TTCN-3 in SILS

Hochang Chae[1], Xiulin Jin[1], Seonghun Lee[2], and Jeonghun Cho[1]

[1] School of Electrical Engineering and Computer Science, Kyungpook National University, 1370 Sankyuk-dong, Buk-gu, Daegu, Korea
[2] Daegu Gyeonbuk Institute of Science & Technology, Daegu Technopark Venture 1 Plant, 75 Gongdanbuk 2gil, Dalseo-gu, Daegu, Korea
hc23chae@knu.ac.kr, kimsuelim@knu.ac.kr, shunlee@dgist.ac.kr, jcho@ee.knu.ac.kr

Abstract. The Testing and Test Control Notation Version 3 (TTCN-3) is an internationally standardized language for defining test specifications for a wide range of computer and telecommunication systems. Since embedded systems software is frequently used in case that safety is a primary issue and reliability is critical in the systems, it is necessary for the embedded systems software to use a systematic testing method such as TTCN-3. Unfortunately, the difference of testing environment between embedded and PC-based software makes developers hard to test the software, and hence products not tested thoroughly could be released in the market, which can be a potential disaster. In this paper, we review the TTCN-3 testing system and suggest a modified TTCN-3 testing environment for embedded systems software in Software In the Loop Simulation (SILS). A simple example shows our demonstration of testing embedded systems software based on the proposed TTCN-3 testing system.

Keywords: testing environment, TTCN-3 testing system, embedded system software.

1 Introduction

As embedded systems industry is rapidly developed, software for the embedded systems is getting more complex and sophisticated. Embedded systems in the past were used for trivial purposes, but modern embedded systems have various functionalities and have significantly advanced purposes. For example, automotive computing systems have radically come to the forefront of the industry. About 100 Electronic Control Units (ECU) consist of the automotive system recently, and the system has a plenty of interactions. It means that the software of the embedded systems is inevitably getting complex and sophisticated.

Handling highly complicated systems has unavoidably large possibility of occurring errors. These errors imported in the system can be a serious hazard for the user when it comes to safety-critical system. A small error and trivial fault originated from the embedded software can result in tremendous accident such as car crash and

D. Ślęzak et al. (Eds.): ASEA 2009, CCIS 59, pp. 204–212, 2009.

spaceship explosion. Therefore, improving the reliability of embedded software is the most important factor facing modern embedded systems software.

In this paper, we focus on the way to test a system to improve the reliability by using a TTCN-3 which is standardized for testing system, particularly in the SILS testing environment. To satisfy the property of embedded systems, we suggest a modified structure of TTCN-3 testing environment with SILS by inserting two additional software parts, so that the TTCN-3 testing method can be applied to the embedded systems.

The rest of this paper is organized as follows: Section 2 introduces brief surveys related to this paper, and the TTCN-3 testing system environment and typical embedded systems testing methods are mentioned. The two approaches that we suggest for the testing of embedded systems software in TTCN-3 are explained in Section 3. In Section 4, we provide an example of implementing the TTCN-3 testing system where two our approaches are applied. We conclude our work in Section 5 and propose additional work for the future in Section 6.

2 Related Work

Testing methods for embedded systems have been introduced in previous work. A work that embedded software is tested by using simulated hardware has done [1]. This work presents an approach to testing software-intense embedded systems using simulations of the target hardware instead of actual target hardware.

VMLab is a tool for simulating AVR processor-based hardware systems [2]. This tool allows system developers to connect certain peripherals with AVR processors and test embedded systems on the simulating environment. This provides SILS environment for AVR processor-based system. However, this tool does not provide any other methods to investigate many test cases.

TTCN-3 lacks continuous signals to test a system as a language construct. Based on this limitation, continuous TTCN-3 has been introduced [3]. It presents the concepts for specifying continuous and hybrid test behavior and the TTCN-3 extensions are demonstrated in the research.

TTCN-3 for distributed testing embedded software is suggested because of the limitation of real-time behavior on host-based testing [4]. Prior to testing embedded software in a target environment, the software is usually tested on the host. It means that the host environment can affect timing problems. This research provides a semantic for host-based testing with simulated time and shows which kind of timing constraints can be adequately tested with simulated time.

TTCN-3 Runtime Interface (TRI) is essential to implement TTCN-3 test systems. A research shows how to implement TTCN-3 test systems using TRI [5]. It presents different kinds of testing systems which can be built from the conceptual model provided by the TRI.

2.1 TTCN-3 Testing System

The Testing and Test Control Notation Version 3 (TTCN-3) is a language for specifying test suites and test control [6]. It was first published as a standard in 1992 by the

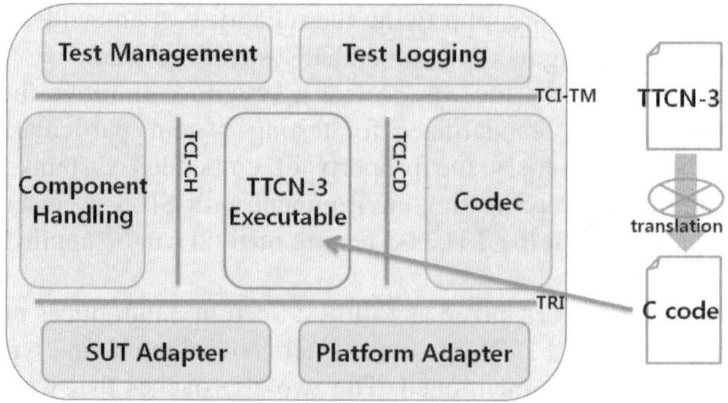

Fig. 1. An overview of a TTCN-3 test system

International Organization for Standardization (ISO) and recently has been standardized by European Telecommunications Standards Institute (ETSI) as a new test specification language beyond protocol testing. The previous version, TTCN-2, has been used mostly in testing telecommunication systems. But in the third revision of TTCN, the best parts of its previous version have been integrated with new features for extension of the testing language using a new textual syntax. This improvement allows the application area of TTCN-3 not to be restricted to just testing telecommunication systems.

TTCN-3 code segments make up a collection for testing simple cases which are referred to as a test suite and, in particular case, as an abstract test suite [1]. The word, "abstract" means that there is no system-specific information in TTCN-3 code, like how messages should be encoded and decoded or how messages could actually communicate with the System Under Test (SUT).

A TTCN-3 code cannot be executed by itself. There must be an interpretation and translation to generate an executable code. In addition, some parts, which support the TTCN-3 code, have to be provided to complete the testing by making up the testing system.

2.2 Testing an Embedded Systems Software

There are some differences between the testing of embedded systems software and that of general software.

One primary difference is that embedded systems software is heavily dependent on hardware of systems. When testing embedded systems software, the testing scheme has to include a part for considering the structure of hardware. To find out problems which are inherent in the embedded system, more structured and more hardware-specific testing methods are indispensable.

Another is that the testing scheme of embedded system is dualized. As shown in Fig.2, when testing general software, the host that carries out testing and the target that is tested are in the same environment. On the other hand the host and target are not on the same side, in other words, dualized. There must be proper consideration for this feature when developing a testing environment.

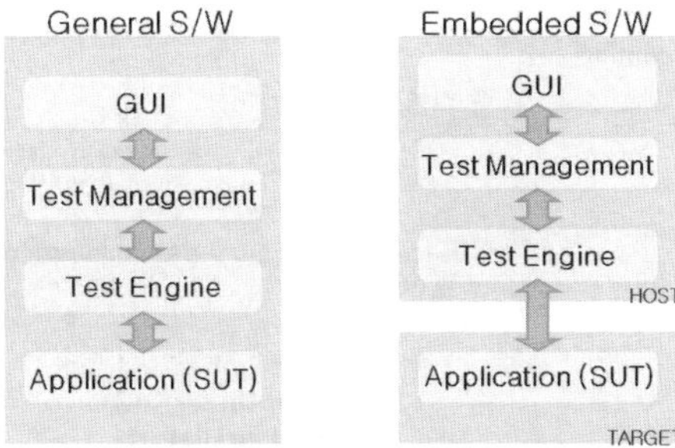

Fig. 2. The difference between general and embedded software testing

2.3 Testing on SILS

Simulation as a tool for testing and debugging software has a long history. Simulating a system has always carried the advantage of increased insight and flexibility, at a cost in execution speed and timing fidelity with compared to real machine.

There are many simulating tools that can handle the entire system including the processor. Long time ago, using a simulation technology for developing software of the large scale embedded systems and testing had been fairly limited [1]. Because the simulating technology could provide only instruction-set simulation for the target systems, such solutions were limited to simulating the processor, not the surrounding hardware components. However, until recently, testing and debugging the system to develop has been commonly done by simulation. In particular, system developers can gain a lot of advantages by making up the whole system as a software implementation, SILS. It can also be useful to test embedded systems software.

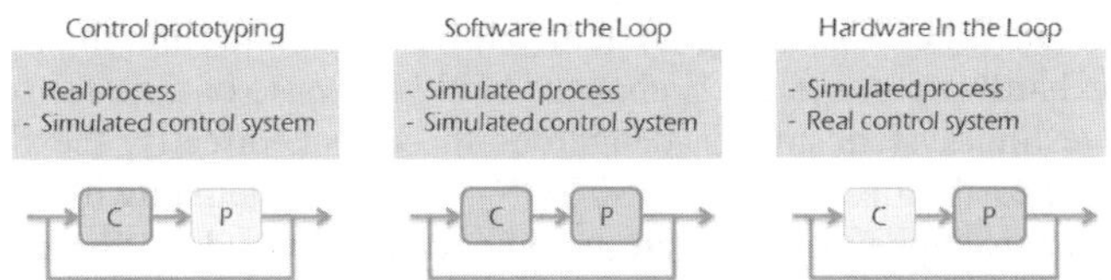

Fig. 3. Classification of the simulation methods

3 TTCN-3 for Testing Embedded Systems Software

TTCN-3 testing scheme originate from testing telecommunication systems. Though it can be extended to broad domains to test any system, there are still some limitations for applying TTCN-3 testing schemes to general software testing.

There must be a specific approach that allows TTCN-3 testing system to be applied to testing general features of embedded systems beyond testing telecommunication systems. TTCN-3 provides many standardized operations that is used to link between TTCN-3 Executable code and the SUT Adapter. In other words, a developer of testing environment is supposed to make it proper with modifying TRI operations.

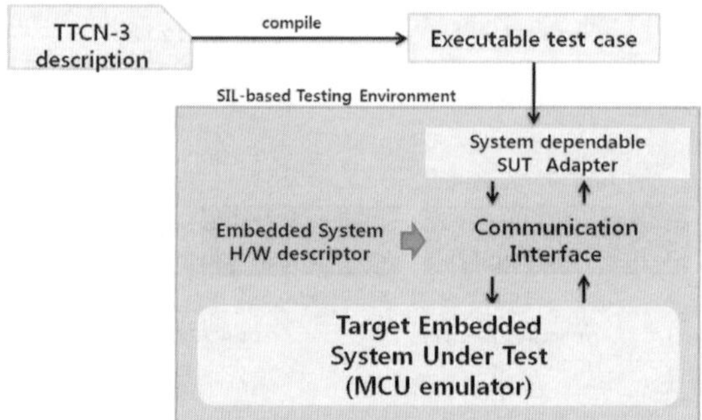

Fig. 4. TTCN-3 test system suitable to embedded system on SILS

In the original method of TTCN-3 testing, the SUT Adapter is directly connected to the SUT. But some other components in the testing environment are needed for applying TTCN-3 to embedded systems. In this paper, we suggest two components to handle TTCN-3 testing system for embedded systems.

3.1 Hardware Description of the Embedded Systems

Testing environment for embedded software should consider hardware of the system being tested because embedded systems software is highly dependent on hardware. The structure of the system hardware could frequently changes while developing embedded systems. Every change of the embedded system should be reflected to the testing system, unlikely with normal software which is run on unchangeable system environment such as PC.

The SUT Adapter needs to be separated from the part that plays a role of reflecting the changed hardware. Reflecting changes of hardware can be done by modifying the SUT Adapter in TTCN-3 testing system. However, modifying the SUT Adapter whenever the hardware of system is changed could be waste of time for recompilation of TTCN-3 testing system and be dangerous to correct, directly, the SUT Adapter because of the possibilities that ruin the TTCN-3 testing system unwillingly.

In this paper, we append a software module, called Embedded Systems Hardware Descriptor (ESHD) which contains information of how the hardware of the system is made up. With the ESHD, the SUT Adapter has no reason to be modified whenever there is any changing of the hardware. All the thing that the SUT Adapter needs to do is referring to the information of ESHD such as which pins are configured as input or output, which port is used for communication and what kind of peripherals are used. By describing the hardware of the system in the ESHD suggested, the SUT Adapter can be automatically modified.

3.2 Communication Interface with SUT

There is another software abstraction layer for interfacing between the TTCN-3 testing system and SUT. Testing environment could be interfaced with many systems to be tested. And, sometimes, the target to be tested is not on the same side with the host, testing environment. By inducing Communication Interface (CI) between TTCN-3 testing system and SUT, more flexible and SUT-friendly testing system could be possible to implement.

More flexible and compatible testing system could be acquired by putting the CI abstraction layer between the SUT Adapter and SUT. To create the method of testing embedded systems software, simulation approach can be used. In this paper, SILS is taken for the testing environment. But another simulation which includes real hardware components in the simulating cycle, called Hardware In the Loop Simulation (HILS), can be used as well, even though the system to be tested is exactly the same as it to be tested by SILS. Without CI layer, the SUT Adapter of the TTCN-3 testing system should be modified depending on the simulation method. But CI provides consistency to the SUT Adapter with regardless of simulation method. Whatever the testing environment is, SILS or HILS, there is no need to change the SUT Adapter for the testing system developer.

4 Implementation of the Testing System

The most important thing to develop the testing system is implementation of TTCN-3 Runtime Interface (TRI) operations. TTCN-3 provides means to make a testing system suitable to any system to be tested. Especially, TRI operations must be set up in a specific way at the boundary between the testing system and SUT.

4.1 Automatic Update of SUT Adapter Using Hardware Descriptor

How the hardware of the system is compromised must be considered when testing based on TTCN-3. In other words, it must be taken into consideration which IO pin is connected to the button and which communication port of the Microcontroller is used for sending and receiving data.

We use a simulation tool for 8-bit AVR core processor, ATmega128 and extended this tool to simulate the whole system which uses this processor. Based on this simulation tool, we set up the SILS environment of testing system for this work. The part for describing the hardware of the system is suggested for simulating because the tool that we made had extended features beyond just emulating instructions of the AVR processor. It has provided system simulation including processor. So we can connect the ATmega128 processor with some peripherals such as LEDs, buttons, communication ports and so on. An example of the hardware description code is as follows.

```
;Button
  B1 PA0
  B2 PA1
  B3 PA2
  B4 PA3
;LED
  L1 PB0
  L2 PB1
  L3 PB2
  L4 PB3
;UART Setting,9600bps, 8bit data
  RS232 TTY1(9600 8)
```

```
;UART Setting,19200bps, 8bit data
  RS232 TTY2(19200 8)
```

The system consists of 4 buttons, 4 LEDs and 2 ports of UART. Buttons are connected to pins 0,1,2,3 of the IO port A and LEDs are connected to pins 0,1,2,3 of the I/O port B. UART has two ports for communication and each has different settings. This description of the system hardware can be used for simulating the system in our simulation tool and also for making up the testing system to apply for embedded systems.

Because the CI refers to the hardware description above, the SUT Adapter does not have to care the changing of the embedded systems to be tested. And, especially in the SILS testing environment, the hardware description itself can be useful to implement the TTCN-3 testing system as well as simulation tool.

4.2 Interface between Testing System and SUT

The CI we suggest in this paper provides an interfacing layer to the SUT and deals with the changes of the hardware by referring to ESHD. CI refers to the hardware description to manage the flexible interface to the SUT and this can make it possible for the SUT Adapter to sustain itself without being modified for composing the testing system.

The example of CI source code is as follows.

```
public void SetPort()
{
  StreamReader sr = new StreamReader("hwconfig.ini");
  string str = sr.ReadLine();
  string[] strArr = str.Split(' ');
  if (strArr[1] == "PA0")
  {
    Console.WriteLine("Button1 connected to PA0");
     AT128.DM.dataMemory[0x39] = 0;
     AT128.DM.dataMemory[0x39]= (byte)
                        (AT128.DM.dataMemory[0x39] | 0xFE);
     if (AT128.DM.dataMemory[0x39] == 0xFE)
     {
       Console.WriteLine("Set PORTA.0");
     }
  }
  else if (strArr[1] == "PA1")
  … //omit
  else if (strArr[1] == "PA7")
  {
    Console.WriteLine("PA7");
     AT128.DM.dataMemory[0x39] = 0;
     AT128.DM.dataMemory[0x39] = (byte)
                        (AT128.DM.dataMemory[0x39] | 0x7F);
           if (AT128.DM.dataMemory[0x39] == 0x7F)
                 Console.WriteLine("Set PORTA.7");
  }
}
```

The above example shows a function of the CI. The function is used to set a pin in an I/O port. TTCN-3 code does not have any information about the hardware of the system. Some functions of TRI interface called by TTCN-3 Executable (TE) code should use the functions which are implemented in CI. Even at this moment, the SUT Adapter has no idea which IO port has to be set or reset. The file, hwconfig.ini, which describes the hardware of the system to be tested, is referred in the functions of CI so that the testing system can be made properly to specific hardware without any consideration of the SUT Adapter.

4.3 Example of the Testing Result

Based on the hardware descriptor and CI, we make up the testing environment for embedded systems software. The testing system is implemented on the SILS environment. We have done many scenarios to test a system and confirmed that the TTCN-3 testing system we suggested is making good progress.

One of the scenarios that we have run through is as follows. At first, the button of the system is pushed to trigger that SUT sends a message as a response to the testing environment. The SUT should send a message in a specific time and testing environment would wait to receive the message sent from SUT at a certain time. With this scenario, testing has done and notice whether an error happens or not.

The following is the execution result of testing.

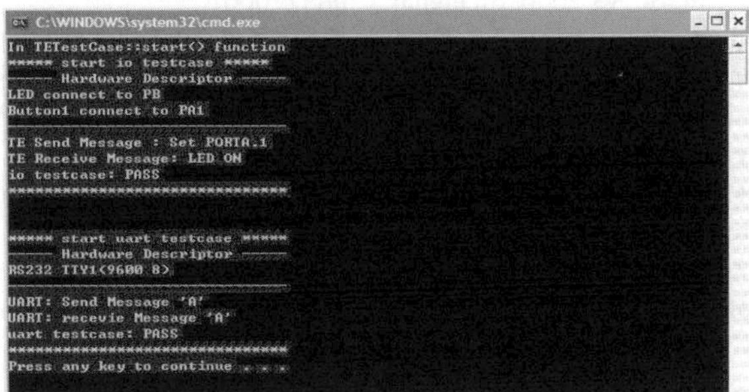

Fig. 5. Execution result of testing system

5 Conclusion

We have discussed the way to implement testing environment for embedded systems based on TTCN-3 in SILS. Additional parts are added to make the testing environment more flexible and suitable for embedded systems. The embedded systems software is so dependent on hardware that the testing environment should consider it and reflect the change of it. By adding hardware descriptor and CI to the testing environment for embedded software, we could achieve our goal. Especially in this work, our SUT is built on the SILS platform. So hardware descriptor is used for simulating the system as well as making up the testing system.

From this work, we might have a chance to go one step forward in the making of more flexible and reliable testing system solution for embedded systems. We have considered only the SILS environment for testing embedded systems software. But the HILS environment is also valuable when considering testing embedded systems, because HILS might guarantee more accurate and dependable result for testing embedded systems software in some aspects. It might be possible to apply the TTCN-3 test system to embedded systems of HILS environment. Finally, we will try to implement the testing system that we suggest on the TTworkbench tool [7].

Acknowledgement

"This research was supported by the MKE(The Ministry of Knowledge Economy), Korea, under the ITRC(Information Technology Research Center) Support program supervised by the NIPA(National IT industry Promotion Agency)" (NIPA-2009-C1090-0902-0020).

References

1. Engblom, J., Girard, G., Werner, B.: Testing Embedded Software using Simulated Hardware. In: ERTS, Toulouse (2006)
2. Advanced Micro Tools, VMLab, http://www.amctools.com
3. Schieferdecker, I., Bringmann, E., Großmann, J.: Continuous TTCN-3 Testing of Embedded Control Systems. In: SEAS 2006, Shanghai, China (2006)
4. Blom, S., Deiß, T., Ioustinova, N., Kontio, A., van de Pol, J., Rennoch, A., Sidorova, N.: TTCN-3 for Distributed Testing Embedded Software: Perspectives of Systems Informatics. In: Virbitskaite, I., Voronkov, A. (eds.) PSI 2006. LNCS, vol. 4378, pp. 98–111. Springer, Heidelberg (2007)
5. Schulz, S., Vassiliou-Gioles, T.: Implementation of TTCN-3 Test Systems using the TRI. In: IFIP Conference Proceedings, vol. 210, pp. 425–442. TestCom (2002)
6. ETSI: Testing & Test Control Notation, http://www.ttcn-3.org
7. Testing Technologies IST GmbH: TTworkbench, http://www.testingtech.com

A Framework for Measuring the Alignment between Business Processes and Software Systems

Lerina Aversano, Carmine Grasso, and Maria Tortorella

Department of Engineering University of Sannio
Via Traiano 1
82100 Benevento Italy
aversano@unisannio.it, carmine.grasso@gmail.com,
tortorella@unisannio.it

Abstract. The alignment degree existing between a business process and the supporting software systems strongly affect the performance of a business process execution. Methods are needed for messuring the alignment and keeping a business process aligned with a supporting software system even when one of the two evolves. Actually, any modification performed in the business process activities and/or supporting software system, may impact the process activities and/or software system component and, therefore, cause misalignment. This paper proposes a framework including a set of metrics codifying the alignment concept with the aim of measuring it and detecting misalignment if it occurs. The application of the framework is shown through an example.

Keywords: Measurement framework, Modelling, Metrics.

1 Introduction

The alignment of business processes and software system is a critical concern for the organizations, as it directly affects their performance. In general terms, a view of business and technological alignment defines at which degree the information technology mission, objectives, and plans, support and are supported by the business mission, objectives, and plans [1, 2, 3]. The alignment between software system and business process involves software system, and all its components, for evaluating at which extent they were designed and implemented for adequately supporting a business process when it is executed [10].

Software engineers very often have to deal with cases in which some misalignment occur, and, as a consequence the business process is not effectively supported by a software system. In addition, understanding what business and information systems alignment is and how maintain it, is a "problem" [11]. This cause the decreasing of the performance of the business process. Then, software innovation activities have to consider the alignment between business processes and supporting software systems.

In the best of the authors' knowledge, research and industry scarcely address these aspects. In [9], criteria and associated generic metrics are proposed to quantify at which extent there is a fit between the business and the system which supports it. In [5], a framework is presented for analyzing the alignment problem and proposing an

D. Ślęzak et al. (Eds.): ASEA 2009, CCIS 59, pp. 213–220, 2009.

approach to application architecture design with reference to a business context. The Business and Information Systems MisAlignment Model (BISMAM), is proposed in [6, 8], to understand, classify and manage misalignments. Unfortunately, this approaches have not been adequately are experimented in an operative context and are not always easily applicable.

Even if business processes and supporting software systems appear aligned in a certain operation context, modifications in this context can cause a misalignment between them. This can be due to either technological and/or management innovations, or unchecked change of the way the activities are executed or the supporting software systems are exploited. Furthermore, a modification may not only regard the considered object but also impact other objects having a dependence relation with the modified ones.

Detected a misalignment, the re-alignment consists of interventions that involve one or more objects of the analyzed business process. The modification impacts must be analysed and changes must be planned. For example, a change of an activity may require modifications in the software system components supporting it and/or dependent activities, or modifications of a software system component may require the analysis and modifications of the activities it supports and/or other software components.

Monitoring the existing alignment degree between business process and software systems involves measurement activities that have to be continuously executed in the operative business context. This requires the definition of a monitoring approach introducing suitable metrics regarding both business process and software system.

In [4], a coarse grained strategy was proposed for detecting misalignment between software systems and supported business processes if a change was executed. The alignment degree was expressed by the evaluation of two attributes expressing the *Technological Coverage* of a business process and *Technological Adequacy* with which each business activity was technologically supported. This paper uses the previous work and proposes a framework for alignment detection by defining a set of fine-grained metrics whose aggregation allows evaluating the two attributes previously introduced.

The rest of the paper is organized as follow: Section 2 describes the proposed misalignment detection framework; Section 3 presents an example aiming at highlighting how the approach can be applied; and final remarks are given in the last section.

2 Measuring the Alignment

A quantitative codification of the alignment existing between a business process and the supporting software systems is required. To this aim suitable metrics are needed for codifying the alignment level.

The evaluation of the Technological Coverage and Technological Adequacy, proposed in [4], is considered for alignment degree existing between business process and supporting software system, but a fine-grained analysis is proposed for obtaining more objective and precise measures. With this in mind, a measurement framework, defined on the basis of the Goal Question Metrics (GQM) paradigm [5], is proposes.

The following goal defines the conceptual level of the measurement framework:

> *Analyse a business process and the supporting software systems with the aim of evaluating the alignment level existing between them from the point of view of the software engineer.*

The logical level is defined by the following questions to be answered for achieving this goal above :

> *Q1. Which is the Technological Coverage (TC) of the business process?*
> *Q2. Which is the Technological Adequacy (TA) of the business process?*

Other questions can be formulated on the basis of the business process complexity and characteristics of the activities.

Answering questions Q1 and Q2 requires the definition of the operative level of the measurement framework consisting on a set of metrics to be evaluated for answering the questions. The identified metrics needed for evaluating the TC and TA regard the essential components of the business processes and software system, that is activities, artifacts, resources and control flow.

The following subsections introduce the metrics that have to be identified for each question.

2.1 Q1. Evaluating the Technological Coverage

For answering question Q1, the measurement framework analyses the coverage level of the software component respect the business components. In particular, the metrics considered are: *Activity Coverage* (*AC*), *Actor Coverage* (*ActorC*), *Artefact Coverage* (*AtfC*). They are evaluated from the technological support point of view, basically expressed in terms of number of supported activities, actors and artifact. In addition, the *Transition Coverage* (*TrC*) is considered for evaluating the offered support form a dynamic point of view.

This metrics are described in the following:

- *Activity Coverage* (*AC*). It is evaluated as the percentage of the automatically supported process activities, considering the number of the business process activities supported by software systems and the number of the business process activities.
- *Actor Coverage* (*ActorC*). It is measured as the percentage of the actors whose activities are automatically supported. It can be evaluated by analyzing the number of actors involved in the business process activities and the number of those whose activities are supported by the software systems.
- *Artefacts Coverage* (*AtfC*). It measures the percentage of the automatically supported process artifact. Its evaluation involves the detection of the number the artefacts used/defined in the Business Process Activities and that one of Artefacts used/defined in the Process Activities that are also managed by the software systems.

- *Transition Coverage* (*TrC*). It evaluates the Technological Coverage of the business transitions, and is determined by considering the set of the transitions that models the control flow among the Business Process Activities and that one of the transitions that are automatically controlled by the software system.

The final value of the Technological Coverage is achieved by aggregating the listed metrics. In particular, it is computed as the average of *AC*, *ActorC*, *AtfC* and *TrC*:

2.2 Q2. Evaluating the Technological Adequacy

Answering question Q2 of the measurement framework involves the analysis of the adequacy of the support provided by the software systems to the business components in terms of activities, artifacts and actors of the business process. In particular, the metrics identified are referred to the full process, but their measurement involves the evaluation of of similar metrics involving each singular activity, artifact and actor. The considered metrics are the following:

- *Artefact Adequacy* (*AtfA*). It expresses how adequate is the automatic support offered to the business process artifacts. It is evaluated as the average of the automatic support adequacy offered to each business artifact. The automatic support offered to a business artifact is measured on the basis of the percentage of business operations that have to be performed on an artifact and that can be executed with the support of the analysed software system.
- *Actvity Adequacy* (*AA*). It expresses how adequate is the automatic support offered to the business activities. It is evaluated as the average of the automatic support adequacy offered to each business activity. This aspect involves the rate of business elementary operations that are efficiently supported by the analysed software system. This calculation entails the analysis of the automatic support degree of artifacts and resources involved in the activity.
- *Actors Adequacy* (*ActorA*). It measures how adequate is the automatic support offered to the business actors. It is evaluated as the average of the adequacy of the automatic support offered to each business actor. The level of support offered by the software system to one actor is evaluated by analyzing which are the activities that involve the actor and measuring the technological adequacy of each of these activities.

Once evaluated the adequacy of the automatic support offered to each activity, actor and artifact, it is possible to calculate the final value of the Technological Adequacy. In particular, the obtained values, *AA*, *AtfA*, *ActorA*, are aggregated by an average formula.

$$TA = \frac{AA + AtfA + ActorA}{3}$$

It is worthwhile noticing that the level of technological coverage and adequacy also depends on the nature of the analysed business process. In fact, business activities that are intrinsically manual can exist. Obviously, this kind of processes cannot reach the highest values of technological coverage and adequacy. Then, the achievement of the goal of the measurement framework has also to consider this aspect.

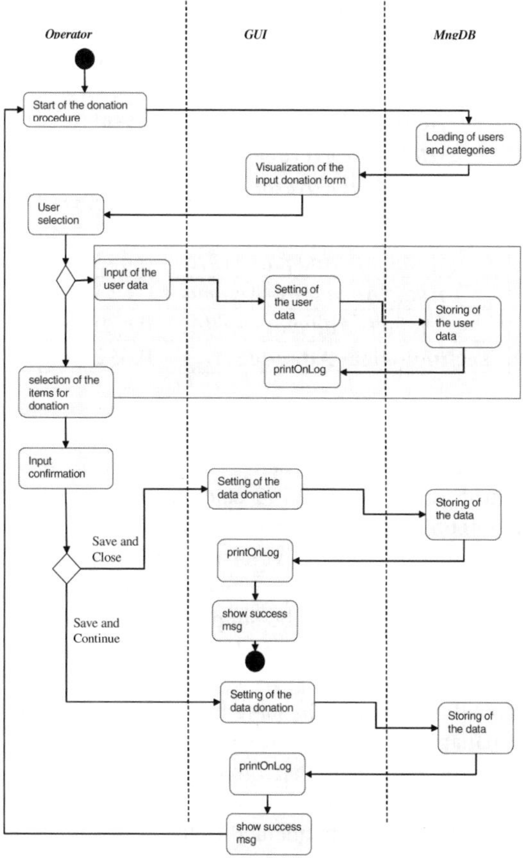

Fig. 1. Model of the business process where SantaClaus is used

3 An Example

In order to evaluate the applicability of the proposed framework, a fragment of a business process has been analysed. In particular, the example is referred to the business process executed by a voluntary association, named BENESLAN, to manage object donations for needy children (http://santaclaus.beneslan.it/). Fig. 1 shows the full business process, even if, for the purpose of the example, only the highlighted activities have been analysed.

The business process shown in Fig. 1 is supported by a software system, named SANTACLAUS (http://santaclaus.beneslan.it/santaclaus/), a web application written in PHP and Java.

All the concepts required for evaluating the different metrics were identified and the definition specified above were applied.

Table 1. TA and TC values obtained by the example

METRIC NAME	VALUE
Activity Coverage (AC)	0.750
Actor Coverage (ActorC)	1.000
Artefacts Coverage (AtfC)	0.670
Transition Coverage (TC)	0.670
Technological Coverage	**0.772**
Activity Adequacy (AA)	0.643
Actor Adequacy (ActorA)	0.833
Artefacts Adequacy (AtfA)	0.479
Technological Adequacy	**0.652**

Table 1 shows the results obtained by analyzing the selected four activities and the software system components supporting them.

The evaluation leaded to a value of 0.772 calculated for the Technological Coverage, *TC*, and a value of 0.652 computed for the Technological Adequacy, *TA*. The low obtained results indicate that the four activities are not adequately supported by SANTACLAUS software system. In particular, considering the values of the metrics, it is possible to notice that the main lack of the support is related to the way the artifacts are managed. In fact, the Artefact Coverage (*AtfC*) and Adequacy (*AtfA*), are the metrics that reach the lowest values.

Table 2 shows the analytical data. The table highlights that: some artifacts (address and PrintOnlog) are managed by the business activities, but the software system does not implement classes for their automatic management; some artifact (Town and User) are considered by the business process, but not all the operations needed for automatically managing them are implemented in the corresponding software classes.

Table 2. Analytical measures

Metrics	Values
Actors Adequacy: ActorA$_i$	
Actor$_1$: gesDB	1.000
Actor$_2$: Operator	1.000
Actor$_3$: Gui	0.500
Artefact Adquacy : AtfA$_i$	
AtfA$_1$: address	0.000
AtfA$_2$: District	1.000
AtfA$_3$: Town	0.500
AtfA$_4$: account	1.000
AtfA$_5$: user	0.375
AtfA$_6$: PrintOnlog	0.000
Activity Adequacy: AA$_i$	
AA$_1$:Input of the user data	0.570
AA$_2$:setting of the user data	1.000
AA$_3$:storing of the user data	1.000
AA$_4$:printOnLog	0.000

This cause the low level of the corresponding metrics at the process level, even if some other artifacts are adequately supported (District and account). Analogous considerations can be formulated with reference to activities and actors.

4 Conclusions

This work presents a framework for measuring alignment between business processes and supporting software systems. The framework involves the execution of some activities and the evaluation of a set of metrics.

In particular, the framework evaluates the Technological Coverage and Technological Adequacy of a software system with reference to a business process. Its application involves the analysis of all the activities, artifacts and actors of the business process.

The results of the evaluation of the metrics allow for the identification of a possible misalignment. In particular, they provide a misalignment degree giving a measure of the extent at which the software systems used in a business process supports it. If misalignment emerges, evolution activities need to be planned and executed for reestablishing alignment and guaranteeing the most efficient and effective execution of the business process.

The application of the measurement framework was described with reference to an example, referring to a business process and related supporting software system.

Obviously, the evaluation of the adequacy of the way a software system support a business process could depend also on the way the actors execute it. Therefore, the adequacy measurement should also consider the actors' opinion. This can be considered in the technological adequacy evaluation and affects the measurement process discussed in this paper.

The future work to be performed in the described context will refer the completion of the experimental activities aiming at understanding the framework applicability and refining the set of chosen metrics and mechanisms for their computation.

For making more objective and effective the application of the measurement framework a formalism will be defined for modeling both business process and software system, so to make directly and graphically comparable the two modeled entities. In this direction, further study will also regard the development of an automatic detection methods helping to evaluate the impact of an evolution strategy. The aim is to offer a decision support when a business or software concept need to evolve in an operative context.

References

1. Henderson, J.C., Venkatraman, N.: Strategic Alignment: Leveraging Information Technology for Transforming Organizations. IBM Systems Journal 32(1), 4–16 (1993)
2. Papp, R.: Introduction to Strategic Alignment. In: Papp, R. (ed.) Strategic Information Technology: Opportunities for Competitive Advantage, pp. 1–24. Idea Group, Hershey (2001)
3. Reich, B., Benbasat, I.: Factors That Influence the Social Dimension of Alignment Between Business and Information Technology objectives. MIS Quarterly 24(1) (March 2000)

4. Aversano, L., Bodhuin, T., Tortorella, M.: Assessment and Impact Analysis for Aligning Business Processes and Software Systems. In: Proc. of the 2005 ACM Symposium on Applied Computing, pp. 1338–1343. ACM Press, New York (2005)
5. Wieringa, R.J., Blanken, H.M., Fokkinga, M.M., Grefen, P.W.P.J.: Aligning application architecture to the business context. In: Eder, J., Missikoff, M. (eds.) CAiSE 2003. LNCS, vol. 2681, pp. 209–225. Springer, Heidelberg (2003)
6. Carvalho, R., Sousa, P.: Business and Information Systems MisAlignment Model (BISMAM): an holistic Model Leveraged on Misalignment and Medical Sciences Approaches. In: Proceedings of BUSITAL 2008 (2008)
7. Korherr, B., List, B.: A UML 2 Profile for Event Driven Process Chains. In: Proceedings of the international Conference on Research and Practical Issues of Enterprise Information System (Confenis 2006), Vienna, Austria. IFIP Series. Springer, Heidelberg (2006)
8. Thevenet, L., Salinesi, C., Etien, A., Gam, I., Lasoued, M.: Experimenting a Modeling Approach for Designing Organization's Strategies in the Context of Strategic Alignment. In: AWRE 2006 Adelaide, Australia (2006)
9. Etien, A., Rolland, C.: Measuring the fitness relationship. Requirements Engineering Journal (REJ) 10(3), 184–197 (2005)
10. Society for Information Management: IT Management Concerns Survey. What keeps CIO awake at night? (2006)
11. Pereira, C., Sousa, P.: Getting into the misalignment between Business and Information Systems. In: 10th European Conference on Information Technology Evaluation. Madrid (2003)

Service Composition System in Consideration of the Characteristics of Services

Jai-Kyung Lee[1], Seong-Whan Park[1], Moohyun Cha[1], Seung Hak Kuk[2], and Hyeon Soo Kim[2]

[1] Korea Institute of Machinery and Materials
171 Jang-dong, Yuseong-gu, Daejeon 305-343, Rep. of Korea
{jkleece,swpark,mhcha}@kimm.re.kr
[2] Dept. of Computer Science and Engineering, Chungnam Nat'l Univ.
220 Gung-dong, Yuseong-gu, Daejeon 305-764, Rep. of Korea
{triple888,hskim401}@cnu.ac.kr

Abstract. The product development in mechanical industry can be modeled as an engineering process defined on the collaboration of various engineering services. An e-Engineering framework aims to integrate engineering services, so as to promote collaboration within the context of product development. The collaboration of engineering services is very similar to a business process, in terms of web service composition. By using the web service composition, the e-Engineering framework can be operated in an open environment. However, the existing web service composition methodology shows some limitations when dealing with engineering services. This paper presents a service composition system for the engineering services in consideration of their characteristics.

Keywords: Service Composition, Engineering Process, QoS, BPEL.

1 Introduction

In the areas of automotive, railway vehicle, shipbuilding and other mechanical industry the development process of a complex product can be modeled as an engineering process defined on the collaboration of various engineering services [1].

To provide such collaboration, an integrated and collaborative engineering environment (called e-Engineering framework) is constructed by KIMM (Korea Institute of Machinery and Materials). The e-Engineering framework provides flexible integration and automation of an engineering process in a distributed environment [2]. The collaboration of the engineering services within the framework, the engineering process, and the service compositions are very similar to the processing of the business logic in e-business environments. Thus the service compositions are realized by Web service compositions. By introducing Web service compositions into the e-Engineering framework, we expect that the framework can be operated in an open environment, and provide better engineering services.

To process the collaboration of engineering service using web service composition, the modeling power of BPEL (Business Process Execution Language) is sufficient for the representation of the scientific workflow [3]. However, BPEL does not allow for

D. Ślęzak et al. (Eds.): ASEA 2009, CCIS 59, pp. 221–228, 2009.

the modeling of the non-functional characteristics of service (Quality of Service, QoS). A study for extending BPEL to express QoS [4,5] and QoS-based web service composition [6,7] cannot cover the non-functional characteristics of an engineering service, which is usually related to numerical analysis.

In this paper, we propose a web service composition system for the e-Engineering framework. We analyze the characteristics of the engineering service, and propose an extended BPEL system for the framework.

2 An e-Engineering Framework and the Engineering Process

The e-Engineering framework was designed as a distributed system with a 3-tier structure. It consists of a presentation layer that enables users (designer, project builder, etc.) to access the system to define, manage, monitor and perform the engineering projects, a business processing layer that performs the business processes for solving engineering problems, and an engineering resource layer that includes a number of engineering software used to obtain concrete solutions to the problems. The Web services technologies are applied to integrate and utilize the engineering resources effectively [2].

The engineering process is modeled as a sequential or parallel workflow that consists of the engineering services (CAD modeling, structural analysis, dynamics analysis, and others) necessary to solve engineering problems. Each engineering service generally is modeled using mechanical engineering software (for instance, CATIA, NASTRAN, ANSYS, and etc). Fig. 1 shows the typical process of durability analysis from CAD Modeling. It had been applied to an automobile suspension module in our previous work [2].

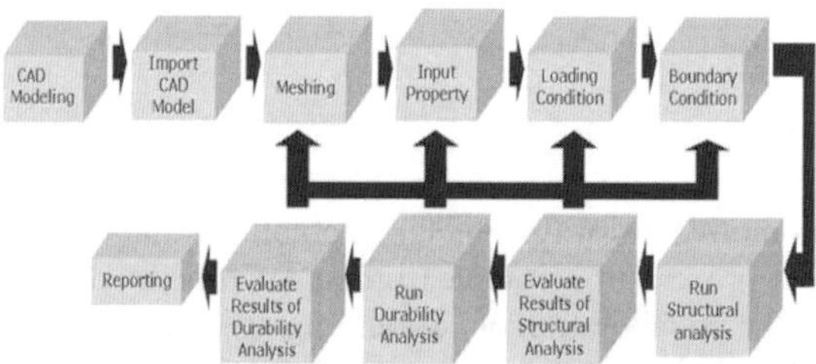

Fig. 1. Engineering process of durability analysis for automobile suspension module

3 Characteristics of Engineering Service

Compared with conventional web services, engineering services have long execution duration and are sensitive to the execution environment. These make the selection of engineering services with the same functionality more important.

In the e-Engineering framework most of the engineering services perform the analysis works in the mechanical engineering problem. Thus they deal with diverse numerical methods. In this paper, numerical methods are roughly classified into three

Table 1. Classification of numerical methods

	Linear equation	Time-integration	Non-linear equation
Typical application	Structural analysis, fatigue analysis, noise analysis.	Dynamics analysis, computational fluid dynamics analysis, crash analysis.	Kinematic analysis
Features	Dimension of problem space (array) is large, but solution is computed at once.	Dimension of problem space (array) is small, but computation of solution is proportional to time history and time interval.	Solution is computed by iteration and the linear equation is computed at each step of iteration
Performance factor	Memory-bound	CPU-bound	CPU-bound & memory-bound

types: linear equation, time-integration and non-linear equation. Table 1 shows the typical application areas, the features, and the factor that govern the performance.

To explain the characteristics of engineering services, two numerical methods described in Table 1 are selected. Here, only their memory and CPU usage are presented for discussion. Fig. 2 shows the results of measurement in the execution of the linear equation method for the structural analysis. The needed memory size is 1002 MB. If there is not sufficient physical memory (less than 1002MB), execution times can be consumed by page fault. This fact means that this is a memory-bounded service. Since the ratio of maximum CPU usage to average CPU usage is 0.36, this service is not CPU-bound.

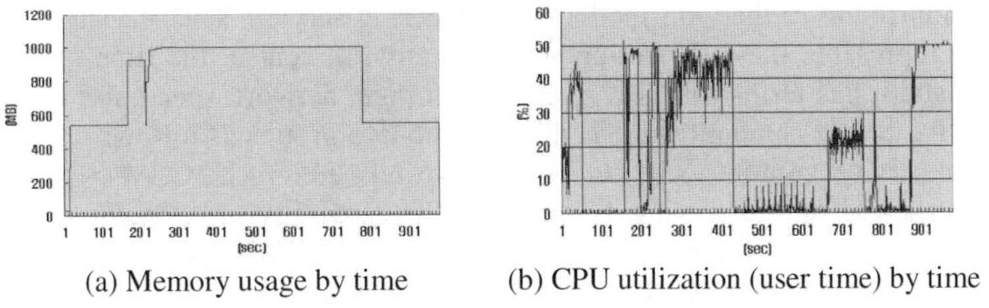

(a) Memory usage by time (b) CPU utilization (user time) by time

Fig. 2. Measurement results from example of linear equation

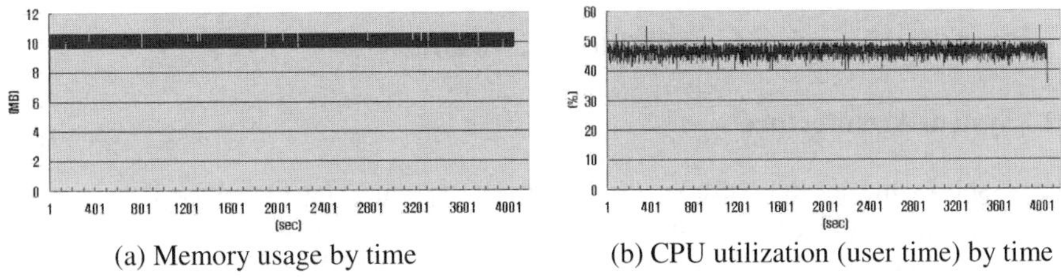

(a) Memory usage by time (b) CPU utilization (user time) by time

Fig. 3. Measurement results from example of time-integration

Fig. 3 shows the results of measurement in the execution of the time-integration method for the dynamics analysis. Since the needed memory size is 10.5 MB, the memory size is less relevant. However the ratio of the maximum CPU usage to an average CPU usage is 0.84, this fact means that this service is CPU-bound.

To reflect the characteristics of engineering services, they are expressed in the form of constraint and selection specification by the designer. The constraint specification describes the minimum requirement of the execution environment to satisfy the QoS requirement of the service. For example, in order to process the engineering service in Fig. 2, the environmental constraint requires at least 1002 MB of memory to avoid bottlenecks on performance. The selection specification describes the preference of selection for getting better performance, lower cost, or preferable QoS, when the service candidates satisfy the constraint specification. For example, the engineering service in Fig. 3 requires very high CPU usage. So, if there are multiple candidates for the service, the one with a higher CPU capacity is preferable.

Previous studies related to the QoS-based web service compositions have already introduced QoS attributes to serve as preference criteria for selecting from the candidates with the same functionality [6,7]. We have chosen some of these for the engineering service.

- Execution time: It is defined as the required time to execute the service.
- Execution cost: It represents the expense to be paid in using the service. It is computed by multiplying the execution time by the use rate of the service.
- Availability: It is computed in this paper as the ratio of service uptime to total service time.
- Reliability: We compute reliability by using the ratio of successful service execution to total service requests.

By considering the characteristics of the engineering service, we add the service context QoS attribute to the QoS model of engineering service. The service context QoS attribute represents the engineering service's environment at the time of the service request, and it has terms for CPU, memory, storage, network speed, use rate, and etc. The service context QoS attribute is divided into two groups as follows:

- Static service context (SSC) QoS group is defined as <U, C, Ms>, where U denotes the use rate of service, C denotes CPU capability in MOps/Sec, and Ms denotes the system memory size (physical + virtual) in MBytes.
- Dynamic service context (DSC) QoS group is defined as <Md, PMd>, where Md denotes the available system memory size in MBytes and PMd denotes the size of available physical memory in MBytes.

4 Proposed Service Composition System

4.1 System Architecture

Fig. 4 shows the architecture of the proposed system. The QoS-based web service orchestration system extends the existing BPEL system (denoted by the white box) using QoS Service, QoS Broker, and QoS Registry. BPEL engine invokes the QoS Broker when QoS-based service selection is needed. QoS Registry manages the QoS information of the system. The QoS Service attached to the atomic service or the service composition provides the QoS information of the service.

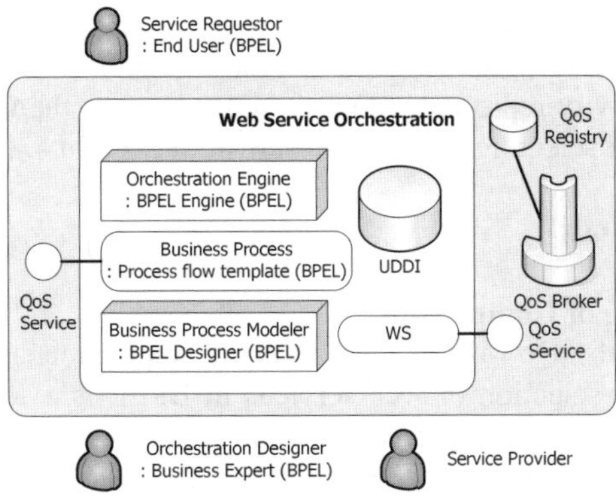

Fig. 4. Architecture of Service Composition System

■ Classification of QoS attributes

For the computation of the QoS value, QoS attributes are classified into three categories: static, dynamic, and statistical. Static QoS attributes are fixed at registration time, and are immutable unless the service changes. Dynamic QoS attributes are those that are changeable during the lifetime of service. Statistical QoS attributes are computed based on the history of QoS attributes. Table 2 shows the classification of QoS attributes.

Table 2. Classification of QoS attributes

QoS name	Type	CS	SS
Use rate	Static	O	O
CPU capability	Static	X	O
System memory	Static	O	X
Available system memory	Dynamic	X	O
Available physical memory	Dynamic	X	O
Execution time	Dynamic	X	X
Execution cost	Dynamic	X	X
Availability	Statistical	O	O
Reliability	Statistical	O	O

Note. CS: Constraint Specification, whether used or not.
SS: Selection Specification, whether used or not.

■ System usage scenario

The usage scenario of a system is divided into three steps: the registration step of atomic service is similar to the registration of the conventional web service, except that the QoS Service also is registered to UDDI, and it sends static QoS information in Table 2 to QoS Broker. In the modeling step of service composition, the orchestration designer defines a control flow of engineering service, the functional aspect of the engineering process, and creates the business process using modeling elements of BPEL. The designer should describe not only the interface of the service but also the QoS-based selection of service. Section 4.2.1 explains how to describe the QoS-based selection of service. The runtime step of service composition can be initiated when the service requester invokes the Orchestration Engine. The Orchestration Engine performs its function by processing the business process. When the Orchestration Engine finds the activity represented QoS-based selection, the QoS Broker is called. The detailed steps for selecting services are shown in Section 4.2.2.

4.2 Proposed Methods

4.2.1 The Modeling of Composition

In order to express the QoS-based web service composition, the <invoke> activity which stands for the selection of web services in BPEL is extended. Extended <invoke> activity has the <QoS-Based> tag to denote QoS-based service selection. Fig. 5 shows the structure of the proposed BPEL modeling.

The <QoS-Based> tag consists of <QoS-Constraints> and <QoS-Selection> tag. The <QoS-Constraints> is used for constraint specifications of service. It can contain multiple <QoS-Constraint> tags, to denote each constraint specification. The <QoS-Constraint> has three sub-tags: <QoS-Name>, <QoS-Op>, and <QoS-Value>. The <QoS-Name> represents the QoS attribute selected in Table 2, and the <QoS-Op> is the relational operator: EQ, NE, GT, LT, GE, and LE. The <QoS-Value> represents the value as a constraint. The upper part in Fig. 6 shows an example of the constraint specification for engineering service in Fig. 2.

The <QoS-Selection> tag is used for selection specifications of service. Multiple <QoS-WeightTerm> tags can be used for selection specification. The <QoS-WeightTerm> has two sub-tags: <QoS-Name> and <QoS-Weight >. The <QoS-Name> is the same one in constraint specification. The <QoS-Weight> represents the weight value of each QoS attribute, and the sum of the values in <QoS-Weight> should be 1. The lower part in Fig. 6 shows the example of the selection specification for engineering service in Fig. 3.

```
<process>
 <!-- details ... -->
 <invoke>
   <QoS-Based>
     <QoS-Constraints>
       <QoS-Constraint>
         <QoS-Name> QoS name </QoS-Name>
         <QoS-Op> Relational Operator </QoS-Op>
         <QoS-Value> Constraint value of QoS </QoS-Value>
       </QoS-Constraint>
             ...
     </QoS-Constraints>
     <QoS-Selection>
       <QoS-WeightTerm>
         <QoS-Name>QoS name</QoS-Name>
         <QoS-Weight>Weighted value of QoS</QoS-Weight>
       </QoS-WeightTerm>
             ...
     </QoS-Selection>
   </QoS-Based>
 </invoke>
 <!-- details ... -->
</process>
```

Fig. 5. Structure of proposed BPEL model

```
<QoS-Constraints>
        <QoS-Constraint>
          <QoS-Name> Available Physical Memory</QoS-Name>
          <QoS-Op> GT </QoS-Op>
          <QoS-Value> 1002  </QoS-Value>
        </QoS-Constraint>
                <QoS-Constraint>
          <QoS-Name> Reliability </QoS-Name>
          <QoS-Op> GT </QoS-Op>
          <QoS-Value> 0.9  </QoS-Value>
        </QoS-Constraint>
</QoS-Constraints>
```

```
<QoS-Selection>
      <QoS-WeightTerm>
          <QoS-Name> CPU Capability  </QoS-Name>
        <QoS-Weight> 0.9 </QoS-Weight>
      </QoS-WeightTerm>
            <QoS-WeightTerm>
          <QoS-Name> Available Physical Memory </QoS-Name>
          <QoS-Weight> 0.1 </QoS-Weight>
      </QoS-WeightTerm>
</QoS-Selection>
```

Fig. 6. Examples of the constraint specification and the selection specification

4.2.2 The Execution of Composition

If the <QoS-Based> tag in <invoke> activity is found during execution of the engineering process, the orchestration engine calls the QoS Broker with the service's interface information. The detailed procedure for QoS-based service selection in QoS Broker is shown in Fig. 7.

1) Find the candidates from UDDI using the service's interface information.
2) Retrieve the static/statistical QoS information of UDDI candidates from QoS Registry.
3) Generate 1st candidates by applying the static and statistical QoS part of constraint specification to UDDI candidates.
4) Request dynamic QoS information from the 1st candidates.
5) Generate 2nd candidates by applying the dynamic QoS part of constraint specification to 1st candidates.
6) Perform a service selection by applying selection specification to the 2nd candidates, and pick the best one.
7) Return to Orchestration Engine with the selected service's interface information

Fig. 7. Procedure for service selection

5 Related Researches

Many studies [4-7] for QoS-based service composition have assumed that the execution cost and execution time of a service can be estimated, or that the history of these values can be used as values for quality of service, and have used these as a criterion of selection and comparison of services. However, the e-Engineering framework uses engineering services, such as parts of QoS attributes, with characteristics that cannot be expressed as conventional web services.

Regarding the selection of web service, [8] has proposed that the consideration of resources is required, as it affects the quality of service. The system context information of the service requester, such as processor load, memory usage, and network bandwidth should be maintained at the time of service request. The service provider's contextual information is not dealt with, and it does not address service composition. In the consideration of the service provider's environment, the use of a limited resource raises the cost of the service [9], and it does not consider the failure of service due to the resources.

6 Conclusion and Future Work

The proposed QoS-based web service composition enables the composition of engineering services and efficient product development that satisfies the limitations of time and cost. Thus, the collaboration of engineering processes can be processed in a more efficient manner, and the reduction of time and cost for product development can be achieved in a range of industries. Future work will be devoted to the analysis of numerical methods not covered by this paper, and the survey of engineering services that perform non-numerical analysis. In addition, the relationships between QoS attributes within atomic services will be dealt with.

Acknowledgement. This work was carried out with the financial support of the Ministry of Knowledge Economy of Korea.

References

1. Wang, L., Shen, W., Xie, H., Neelamkavil, J., Pardasani, A.: Collaborative conceptual design—state of the art and future trends. Computer-Aided Design 23(13), 981–996 (2002)
2. Kuk, S.H., Kim, H.S., Lee, J.K., Han, S.H., Park, S.W.: An e-Engineering Framework Based on Service-Oriented Architecture and Agent Technologies. Computers in Industry 59(9), 923–935 (2008)
3. Akram, A., Meredith, D., Allan, R.: Evaluation of BPEL to scientific workflows. In: Proc. of the 6th IEEE Int'l Symp. on Cluster Computing and the Grid, pp. 269–274 (2006)
4. Baligand, F., Botlan, D.L., Ledoux, T., Combes, P.: A language for quality of service requirements specification in web services orchestrations. In: Georgakopoulos, D., Ritter, N., Benatallah, B., Zirpins, C., Feuerlicht, G., Schoenherr, M., Motahari-Nezhad, H.R. (eds.) ICSOC 2006. LNCS, vol. 4652, pp. 38–49. Springer, Heidelberg (2007)
5. Canfora, G., Penta, M.D., Esposito, R., Perfetto, F., Villani, M.L.: Service composition (re)binding driven by application-specific QoS. LNCS, vol. 4652, pp. 141–152. Springer, Heidelberg (2007)
6. Zeng, L., Benatallah, B., Ngu, A.H., Dumas, M., Kalagnanam, J., Chang, H.: QoS-Aware Middleware for Web Services Composition. IEEE Transactions on Software Engineering 30(5), 311–327 (2004)
7. Jaeger, M.C., Goldmann, G.R, Muhl, G.: QoS Aggregation for Service Composition using Workflow Patterns. In: Proc. of the 8th Int'l Enterprise Distributed Object Computing Conf. (EDOC 2004), pp. 149–159 (2004)
8. Day, J., Deters, R.: Selecting the best web service. In: Proc. of the Conf. of the Centre for Advanced Studies on Collaborative Research, pp. 293–307 (2004)
9. Tosic, V., Patel, K., Pagurek, B.: WSOL – Web Service Offerings Language. In: Bussler, C.J., McIlraith, S.A., Orlowska, M.E., Pernici, B., Yang, J. (eds.) CAiSE 2002 and WES 2002. LNCS, vol. 2512, pp. 57–67. Springer, Heidelberg (2002)

Business Viability Assessment of Potential Software Projects: An Empirical Study with the CASSE Framework

Joseph Kibombo Balikuddembe and Antoine Bagula

Department of Computer Science
University of Cape Town
Private Bag Rondebosch 7701
South Africa
{jbalikud,bagula}@cs.uct.ac.za

Abstract. The opportunity cost decision of selecting a software project is dependent, among other things, on how a given project best meets a company's business goals and overall competitive strategy. Remaining competitive in the agile software market today requires selecting only those projects that position a business strategically in the market place and that render it competitive over time. Using an industrial case study, we demonstrate the role of the Complex Adaptive Systems Software Engineering (CASSE) framework in supporting value-based project selection. We apply Actor Object Dependencies (AOD) analysis and Functional Points (FP) sizing techniques to predict the overall project value before incurring any actual costs of implementing such a project. The overall contribution of this work therefore lies in demonstrating that alternative engineering approaches that analyze AODs can enhance how we select software projects and how we plan project schedules optimally so as to increase business value derived on projects.

Keywords: Project Selection Techniques, CASSE Framework, Software Economics.

1 Introduction

The software project value differentiator in a market place is primarily dependent on process engineering approaches that optimize the scope, schedule, cost and budget constraints of the project, thus ensuring that stakeholder benefit is realized on completion of the project [1].

Studies such as [2] and [3] have shown that project requirements are complex; they are volatile, they evolve, and they require deeper scrutiny to assess dependencies between them, and at the same time to gauge the right level of effort to deliver a product on time, within scope and within budget. Consequently, there is a clear need in this changeable software market for integrated approaches, tools and techniques that make it possible to select viable projects, based on their scope, their requirements, and their complexity.

D. Ślęzak et al. (Eds.): ASEA 2009, CCIS 59, pp. 229–236, 2009.

This work draws from available literature in value-based software engineering, such as [4 and 5] to provide an integrated approach for assessing overall value on a software project. We perceive value as the benefit realised in terms of profit or long-term business benefit that the software vendor derives from a project, given the project's overheads.

2 Purpose

We aimed at examining how the emergent AOD analysis technique of the CASSE framework can be applied to support viable project selection. Such a mechanism would eventually enhance evaluation of the probability distribution of profits and losses on a software project before investment costs on such a project are incurred.

3 The CASSE Framework Approach

This technique is based on understanding and modeling the entire project as a complex adaptive system in which patterns of interrelationships emerge from local interrelationships between requirements and their artefacts. As modifications for value matrices on the project occur, new patterns are continuously emerging. These could have a huge impact on the profit-loss and distribution curve for the project. The belief is that the emerging patterns must be projected to a management dashboard so as to aid effective decision making in real time. This technique is built around the AOD modelling facets which we describe in our previous work [6 and 7].

We infer that as a time saving mechanism, the visibility of the project status must be projected in a simple format and must be easily interpretable. In this approach, we suggest a project value evaluator as a sufficient option. This mechanism was developed and tested as a feedback channel to management. Its overall aim is to highlight the business status of any potential project in comparison to the established business strategy in the company.

Over the years, our industrial experience has enabled us realize the growing need for informed feedback on projects especially when it comes to selling ideas to management or even convincing management about taking certain decisions that are strategic to business. Decisions makers often don't have much time to read long project reports prepared by the technical people. Rather, they only require brief information which at the same time is informed enough to give them a wider view of what is being presented.

3.1 The Project Value Evaluator

Our conviction is that the project value evaluator would offer this visibility. It is used to broadly asses projects and their value within a given project portfolio. It compares project benefit against investment in the project as illustrated in Fig. 1.

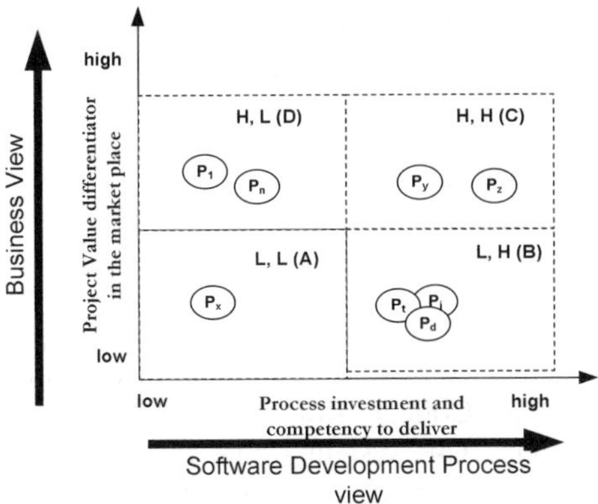

Fig. 1. Project value evaluator

The X-axis represents the software process development view in which measurement is done on the process investment and competency required to deliver a project within time, scope and budget. The Y-axis represents the business view in which the project value differentiator in the market is evaluated.

Projects that have low value and low process investment to deliver are displayed in *L, L (A)*. This implies that such projects will yield low return on investment and may not necessarily be valuable to the business, both in the short and long run. They should therefore be exited and potential resources that would have been invested on such projects be channelled to other investment options. Projects that have high process investment to deliver yet with low business value are displayed in *L, H (B)*. This implies that the development process will be constrained with high investment required to implement and complete the project gracefully. This could be in terms of time or cost. The value axis in this quadrant indicates that there will be low value for that project in both the short term and in the long term. Therefore, projects in this quadrant are highly susceptible to project failure with high losses. However, they have significant promise and can easily be fixed.

On the other hand, projects that have high development process investment as well as high business value will be displayed in *H, H (C)*. This could be for both the short and long run time frames. This quadrant characterises new technology development projects which requires time to mature but have high value in the long run. Thus, these projects must be managed and exploited for the fact that cash flow from these projects can be used to fund more attractive investments. Projects that have high value and low process investment will be displayed in *H, L (D)*. This is the most viable quadrant that every business would want to operate in. It reflects maturity in the software development process. It may imply that you have the right competency to deliver and that most of the features proposed already exist in your project database or software platform. It is very favorable for customizable software products. Whence, such projects exhibiting significant opportunity for growth must be given first priority as such projects hold the greatest potential for value creation.

As a profitability objective function, the framework requires that at project selection, the entire project is scored against the business value threshold. This threshold is always described in the business operations model. The output of this assessment and prediction is in turn projected to this dashboard.

4 Case Study Evaluation

4.1 Case Study Description

This specific case study entailed evaluating system needs as presented in the Request For Proposal (RFP) document for the development of an on-campus crime management system for Joliet Junior College, Illinois. The RFP call described it as a police records management system. This system would fulfil the College's need for documenting and managing crime records as well as overall crime control on the premises. By using a formal RFP process, Joliet Junior College management thus sent out an RFP to interested software companies that would provide a useful software solution to this problem. A copy of this RFP is available here [8].

This project had the following characteristics. The RFP was issued on March 7, 2008 and the deadline for interested companies to submit their questions in relation to the project, was set for March 14, 2008. This particular scenario meant that the client expected companies to investigate the proposal needs and submit the required quotation within 7 days after issuing the RFP. The anticipated announcement of the award was April 9, 2008. Any successful applicant for this job (based upon the lowest cost and the criteria set forth under the Evaluation section of the RFP) was expected to install the system by June 30, 2008. This would allow for a maximum of only 50 production days (about 400 man hours, excluding overtime) to analyse, design, implement, test and install the entire system. The client was strict on the final product delivery deadline. This meant that the project schedule was inflexible, requiring the optimisation of resources in order to meet the deadline.

This project thus assumed that any interested company would have the necessary capacity to deliver such a system within such a short period of time. It was assumed that vendors whose product-line fell within this ambit would only need to customise existing features to suit the desired functionality. New players in the market, if successful, would have to develop everything from scratch or to adapt existing open-source libraries to suit the desired functionality.

Having been a systems analyst employed by a company that was interested in responding to this RFP call, one of us was required by management to submit a quotation for this project proposal. This quotation had to take into account the high-level requirements given in the RFP document as well as other budgetary concerns. The company was initially using heuristic ways of quoting for projects without any major metric or tool used for estimation, but rather basing it on project characterises and experience.

As a result, the CASSE framework was particularly useful at this stage. The original estimate using traditional means was a round figure of R195, 000 (taking $1 = R10). The CASSE approach, however, came to a different result, although it was not far off from the estimated result.

The quoting process for this project was based on the last scenario describe above (new players) since this company had never developed any solution of this kind before. However, the company believed that it had the right competency to deliver the desired solution within the specified schedule. The results obtained by the CASSE approach were not final; they were only suggested to management as guidelines for informed decision making. They were thus forwarded to management who would make the final recommendation on the viability of the project. This eliminated bias in analysis, and gave management an opportunity to compare the suggested approach with the traditional means in order to ascertain if such an approach was worth integrating in the development process.

Given this background and using CASSE analytics (a tool born out of the framework), viability of the project based on the preliminary requirements in the RFP document was analysed. The idea for using this tool was that the results obtained would be benchmarked with the heuristic figure obtained using the traditional quoting methods adopted by the company. This would create a favourable situation to obtaining a reconcilable quotation for the envisaged project based on the two approaches. The biggest threat here was that the requirements were incomplete and lacking in clarity in the initial stage, thus any modelling and subsequent estimation would only be indicative of the likely project status. There was a significant chance that the project requirements would change as the client began more fully to understand the needs of the system. This would ultimately have cascading effects on the overall project budget, timelines and scope.

Consequently, CASSE analytics was specifically applied to illustrate how a company can fine-tune the project constraints to ensure that a viable project is selected, to predict a viable implementation time, to rank the project value and to prioritise the features in order to optimise a given production process.

4.2 Analysis Parameters

In this analysis, parameters of interest included the following: A UML Actor Object Graphical model (as a conceptual static structure) generated from the high-level requirements provided; the overall anticipated budget that would be obtained as a sum of expected development costs and other expenses on the project; expected income as derived from the overall project figure; expected net profit after budgetary expenses; overall time span as provided for in the RFP document; predicted time according to the CASSE analytics; and expected slack/overrun time as a difference between available and predicted time.

The highest investment value of R700 (as the hourly rate for this project) per functional point was proposed. This value represents the actual costs incurred in analysing, designing, developing and testing each functional point on an hourly basis. Conversely, the proposed highest return on investment was R2,500 per functional point. This meant that anticipated profit per Functional Point (FP) amounting to R1,800 would be realised as a mark-up difference between high return on investment and high investment.

Making any adjustments of any of these parameters would result in assessing the most suitable operating point. This point would be used in making investment decisions on this project.

4.3 Case Study Analysis Results

The following results were obtained, as shown in Table 3 (the figures have been adjusted for confidentiality purposes but do reflect the project status).

Table 1. Project viability status

Item	Quantity
Total project costs (budget)	R125,000
Expected development costs	R50,760
Other project expenses	R74,240
Expected project income	R211,500
Expected gross profit	R160,740
Net profit expected	R86,500
Time span	400hrs
Predicted time	194hrs
Expected slack/overrun	206hrs

With a budget estimate of R125,000 (as the sum of development costs of R50,760 and other budgetary expenses of R74,240), the model predicted 194 hours of project time out of the expected 400 hours derived from the RFP document. This left 206 hours of slack time. The expected income in this regard (as the overall quoted figure) was R211,500. The difference between expected income and expected development costs resulted in R160,740 as profit, before the deduction of other budgetary expenses. The net income would thus be R86,500 being the difference between the expected project income and the anticipated total project budget. This was the expected profit on this project.

4.4 The Quadrant Analysis

Mapping this project to the project value evaluator revealed that this project fell into Block A, the risky quadrant of low investments and low returns, as illustrated in Fig.2.

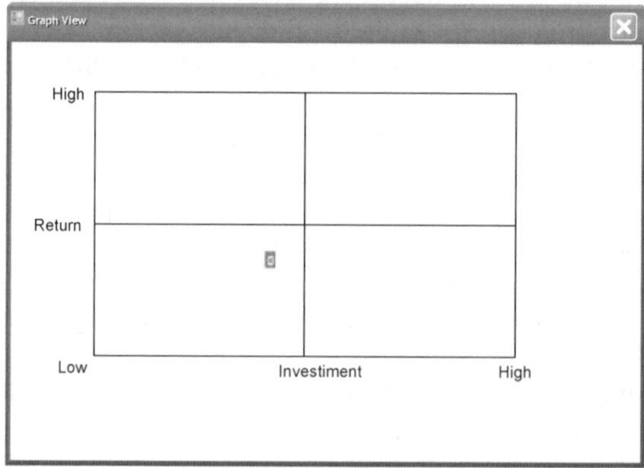

Fig. 2. RFP project mapping

The red dot on the graph above shows the position of the project on the value graph. This implies that this given project was likely to be risky in that it attracted fewer profits than the expected profitability threshold for any project taken on by this company. As illustrated above, given the current budget, this project would yield only 51.81% profitability levels on the overall (R86,500 of R160,740), yet the targeted profit on any project for this company must be above 70%. Although this can be considered as a very high level profit margin in the commercial arena, it was highly likely that these projected profits would be eroded by change management bottlenecks and evolving project needs, among others. Overcoming such fixed price quotation issues would entail having good project management skills (which were lacking in this regard), which would limit changes or charge for them separately.

4.5 Case Study Implications

According to the project data published on the college website, the tender for this project was awarded to the successful vendor for about R400,000 and was completed on time. However, the basis for awarding this tender to the successful company was not published. Comparing the analysis results against the amount awarded resulted in the following observations. When the anticipated profitability was adjusted in accordance with the award amount, the project status shifted into a different quadrant of the project value evaluator, as illustrated in Fig. 3.

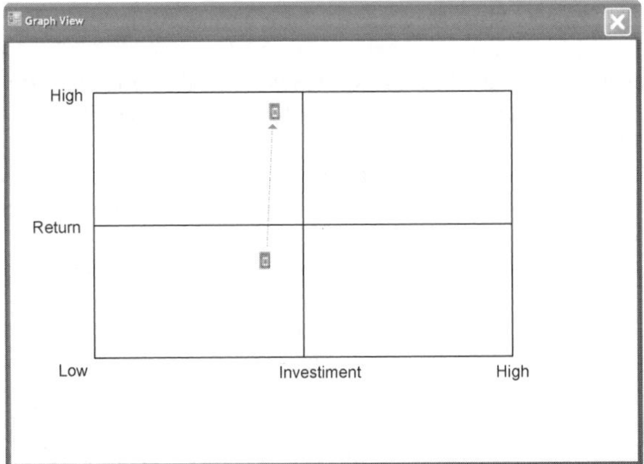

Fig. 3. Quadrant shifting

If this R400, 000 was the original amount quoted on this project, this project would be located in quadrant D, which is a favourable quadrant for investment. In this regard, if the company had submitted an even higher quotation (up to the award amount of R400,000), then they might not only have been awarded the contract, but they would also have been more profitable.

These results demonstrate that various investment questions can be answered by means of guiding tools such as CASSE Analytics. Business viability assessments of potential software projects require such tools if informed decisions are to be made.

Information provided by such tools not only aids business case assessment and evaluation of the project, but it also identifies risky projects before investment commitments are made.

5 Conclusion and Future Work

This study therefore offers a capability for increasing the predictability and evaluation of a viable risk-balanced favourable operating point on any project before this project is added to a potfolio. This in return would lead to minimizing the selection of unprofitable projects. Therefore, alternative engineering approaches such as these can enhance how we select software projects and how we plan project schedules optimally so as to increase business value derived on projects.

In future we intend to investigate how any given project that has been scored against the business threshold at the initial selection stage is tracked through the lifetime of the project. Such trends would make it possible to analyse the lessons learnt on a project and to assess whether the anticipated profitability could be sustained or not. The patterns detected in this way would provide a mechanism for improving both the estimation process on projects as well as the quoting process over time.

References

1. Barnett, L.: Agile Projects Must Measure Business Value. Agile Journal (2007), http://www.agilejournal.com/content/view/211/76
2. Nikula, U., Sajaniem, J.: Tackling the Complexity of Requirements Engineering Process Improvement by Partitioning the Improvement Task. In: ASWEC, pp. 48–57. IEEE CS, Washington (2005)
3. Karlsson, L., Dahlstedt, A.G., Regnell, B., Dag, J.N., Persson, A.: Requirements Engineering Challenges in Market-driven Software Development – An Interview Study with Practitioners. Info. and Soft. Tech. 49(6), 588–604 (2007)
4. Boehm, B., Huang, L.G.: Value-based Software Engineering: a Case Study. Computer 36(3), 33–41 (2003)
5. Saliu, M.O., Ruhe, G.: Bi-Objective Release Planning for Evolving Software Systems. In: The 6th Joint Meeting of the European Software Engineering Conference and the ACM SIGSOFT Symposium on the Foundations of Software Engineering, pp. 105–114. ACM, New York (2007)
6. Balikuddembe, J.K., Potgieter, A.E.: Using Actor Object Operations Structures to Understand Project Requirements Complexities. In: The 3rd International Conference on Software Engineering Advances, pp. 290–294. IEEE Press, Los Alamitos (2008)
7. Balikuddembe, J.K., Potgieter, A.E.: Predicting Value-creation in Software Project Complexity. In: The 10th IASTED International Conference on Software Engineering and Applications – Dallas, p. 514. ACTA Press (2006)
8. Joliet Junior College, http://www.jjc.edu/about/operational/business-auxiliary/purchasing/Documents/R08003.pdf (last accessed on July 30, 2009)

Aligning the Software Project Selection Process with the Business Strategy: A Pilot Study

Joseph Kibombo Balikuddembe and Antoine Bagula

Department of Computer Science
University of Cape Town
Private Bag Rondebosch 7701
South Africa
{jbalikud,bagula}@cs.uct.ac.za

Abstract. This report aims to present the significance of requirements engineering approaches in guiding the project selection process with an overall objective of ensuring that selected projects align fully with an established business strategy. We analyze software practitioners' views on managing the software project selection process in Cape Town, South Africa. We designed this empirical study following on from our previous literature survey. Using data categorization techniques, our findings suggest that software vendors ought to ensure that organizational business strategy is well explained to all stakeholders, including the technical personnel who produce the software. Similarly, the engineering approaches directed towards mitigating selection of risky business must be utilized and integrated into the development process. Failure to take these factors into perspective renders the organizational competitive strategy ineffective. Detailed research methods used in the study are given as well as approaches undertaken for data collection and analysis.

Keywords: Software Process Improvement, Effective Business Strategy Formation, Value-based Software Engineering.

1 Introduction

The value-based software engineering premise perceives value derivation on software projects as an integral notion, embracing a full range of existing and emerging software engineering principles and practices [1]. Pivotal to this are requirements engineering, project planning and control, as well as risk management mechanisms utilized in the development processes. Similarly, achieving project value and success requires that the engineering approaches utilized on such projects support both the project selection process and the business strategy [2]. We view this as a three-in-one cycle summarized in Fig. 1 below.

D. Ślęzak et al. (Eds.): ASEA 2009, CCIS 59, pp. 237–244, 2009.

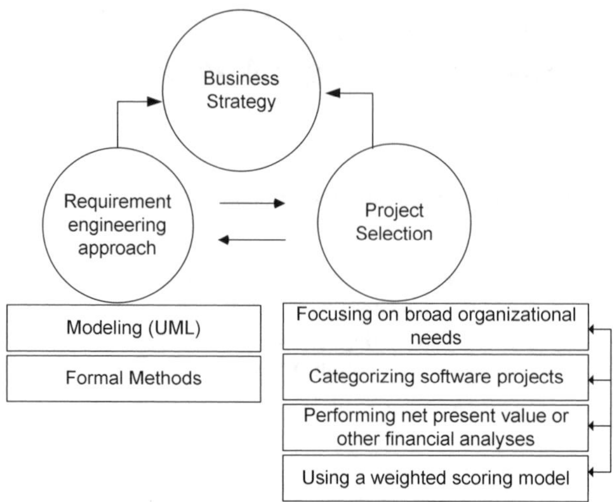

Fig. 1. Technical inputs to the business strategy

The project management theory provides that the project selection process is fundamentally driven by four principles, including: focusing on broad organizational needs, categorizing software projects according to organizational needs, performing net present value or other financial analyses on these projects and using a weighted scoring model to obtain a clear project value in terms of expected return on investment [3].

We infer that the engineering approaches utilized in understanding project needs and requirements must support these principles as bi-directional business functions impinging on the business strategy. This process can either be '*formal-method*' driven or carried out by use of modeling approaches such as the Universal Modelling Language (UML), thereby supporting the planning and control process on projects as well as identifying risk factors on the project. If well adapted (as project risk precaution drivers), support for identification of any risky business early on in the process, and even before resources are committed on such projects is ensured. As observed by Gregor *et al.*,[4], if neglected or in the absence of such business strategy- supporting mechanisms, profit-driven software businesses are likely to be edged out of the market easily

2 Purpose

Building on this view, we recently conducted an empirical study, over a four months period, with 70 software companies in Cape Town, South Africa. Our main objective was to examine whether project selection and requirements engineering processes (as technical inputs to the project selection process) employed in industry today align appropriately with organizational business strategies in general. Secondly, we wanted to examine how projects are selected in industry with or without the use of analytical tools, and if any requirement engineering techniques are used to assess risk on software projects.

Understanding the phenomena of prevailing project selection processes in industry and their alignment with the business strategy, would give us some insight in what is going on in business strategy formation and alignment and why it is indeed happening.

3 Methodology

Project Managers, Systems and Business Analysts in particular were targeted due to their strategic role in guiding management on project scoping and viability implications, especially during the software development life-cycle. While building on previous literature surveys, we applied the descriptive and analytical approach so as to identify presence of relationships among key factors found during the interview analysis.

A systematic process for survey development, as suggested by Sanchez *et al.* [5] was employed to develop the survey instrument. This 18 item instrument was divided into subscales of selected-responses centered on economic aspects of software development. It was designed to gather ordinal data on requirements engineering and project selection. The requirements engineering subsection was aimed at understanding current software development processes used today, by specifically analyzing the depth and breadth of requirements engineering techniques used in industry. The project selection subsection aimed at understanding how projects are selected in the various participating developing houses. The selection criteria used were instrumental in refining the study assertions and guiding conclusions to the research objective.

A 5 point Likert-type scale (i.e., 1 = Strongly Disagree, 2 = Disagree, 3 = Not sure, 4 = Agree, 5 = Strongly Agree) previously used by Guan *et al.* [6] was employed.

Seventy questionnaires were emailed to various software companies via the Software Process Improvement Network (SPIN) chapter in Cape Town. Participation in this study was voluntary. Of the 70 questionnaires emailed, only 50 questionnaires were returned, thus representing a 71% response rate from this targeted sample.

4 Presentation of Findings

Due to space limitations, we present a summarized analysis of how these findings impinge on the overall business formulation strategy. Based upon these findings we draw study conclusions. The assertions used in the study are given in table 1 below.

Table 1. Study asserstions used

Requirements engineering assertions	Project selection
RE 1: We usually first understand client requirements before project implementation	**PS 1**: Our projects are selected based on strategic business objectives
RE 2: We implement the requirements in parallel with requirement elicitation and validation	**PS 2**: We choose our projects based on profitability level anticipated
RE 3 We undertake systems modelling using OOSA using UML, etc.	**PS 3**: Our projects are in-house and my organisation is the direct recipient

Table 1. (*Continued*)

Requirements engineering assertions	Project selection
RE 4: We use a standardised process in collecting, documenting and validating our requirements	**PS 4**: We depend on feasibility assessment reports to determine project implementation
RE 5: We usually develop a traceability matrix for project requirements	**PS 5**: We use analytical tools that guide us in project selection
RE 5.1: The traceability matrix is generated using a matrix generation tool	**PS 6**: Our project selection is purely heuristic
RE 5.2: The traceability matrix is generated manually	**PS 7**: We just take on any project we get hold of
RE 5.3: We don't consider the traceability formulation important because of lack of time	**PS 8**: Our projects are for research and development
RE 6: It is part of our development procedure to undertake a requirement dependency assessment for risk assessment	
RE 6.1: There is generally less or no requirement dependency assessment undertaken	

Fig. 2 illustrated the response percentages of both categories. These findings are summarized and interpreted in the following section.

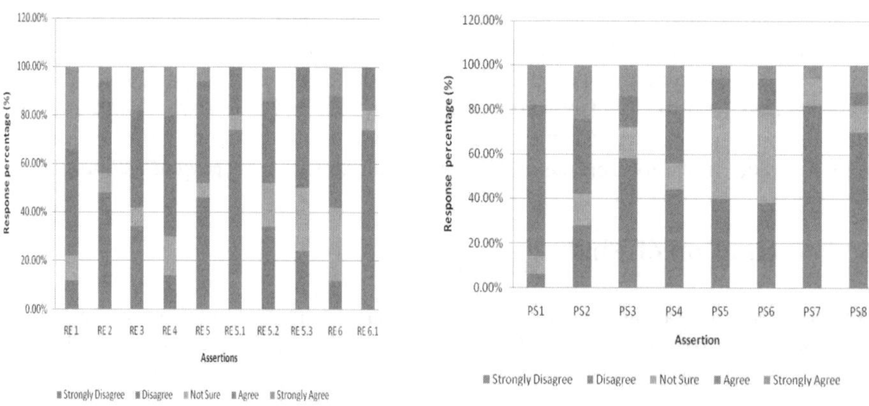

Fig. 2. Response percentages for both assertion categories

4.1 Interpretation Summary

The above findings are summarized as follows. Specific trends of interest were ranked according to a scale designed for overall results interpretation. This is illustrated in Table 2.

Table 2. Key for trends` scale

Prevailing trend	Scale
Not practiced at all	1
Require serious improvement	2
Occurs rarely	3
Satisfactory	4
Well practiced	5

It is upon this scale that conclusions were drown specifically looking at overall performance of a parameter of interest across the sample, majority responses to a parameter in comparison to the overall sample and a few or minority responses to a given parameter across the sample. The key parameters of interest are given in Table 3.

Table 3. Key parameters of interest

	Ranking parameters	Performance scale		
		Overall	Majority	A few
Overall business strategy formation	Aligning strategy with business	2	2	1
	technical personnel involvement	1	1	1
Requirement engineering	UML modelling	2	3	5
	tool usage in project selection	1	1	2
	tool usage matrix generation	1	1	1
	requirements traceability	1	1	2
	dependency analysis	1	1	2
Project selection	risk analysis on projects	2	3	4
	based on profitability & business goals	4	4	2
	Heuristic tendencies	3	1	3
	based on feasibility reports	5	4	3

As illustrated in the table above, for each parameter of interest, a scale ranking was attached arising from the statistical results obtained from the data.

4.1.1 Overall Strategy Formation

As illustrated from the figure above, it was observed that generally, aligning the selection and requirements engineering process with the business strategy requires serious improvement within the participating companies. The results also show that involvement of technical personnel in the formation of the business strategy is lacking across the board.

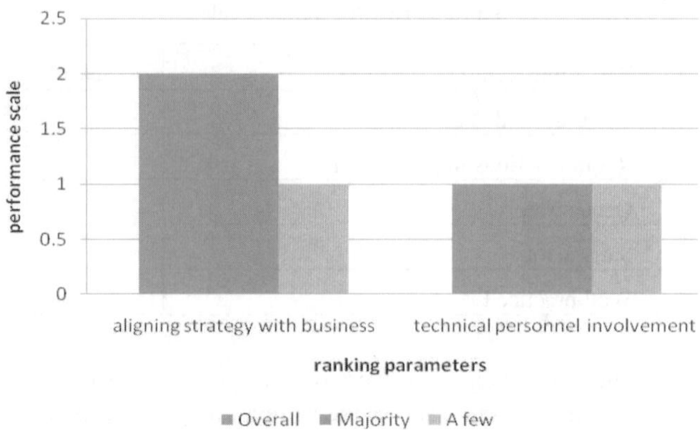

Fig. 3. Business strategy formation

4.1.2 Requirements Engineering Process

As illustrated in the figure above, UML modelling is well practised in only a few of the participating companies. In some companies however, it is used rarely, thus suggesting overall improvement in this area. On the other hand, tool usage in project selection and requirements matrix generation is not used at all. More still, requirements traceability as well as dependency analysis on software project requirements still scored poorly within this sample.

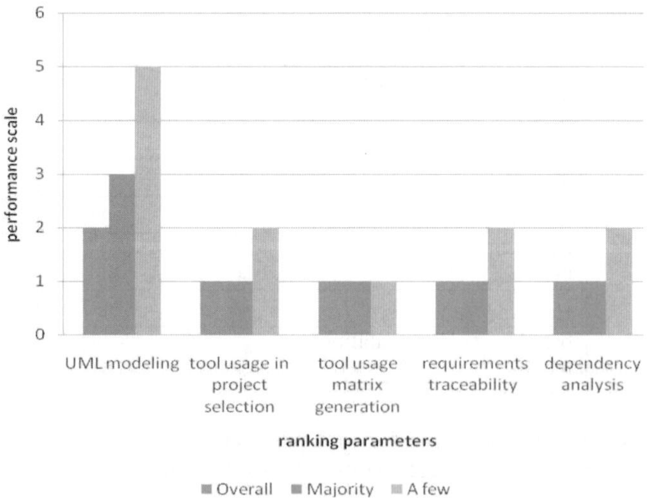

Fig. 4. Strategic requirement engineering

4.1.3 Project Selection

These results showed that, across this sample, projects are selected based on feasibility reports as well as on anticipated profitability and established business goals. However, risk analysis on these projects is only undertaken by a few of the

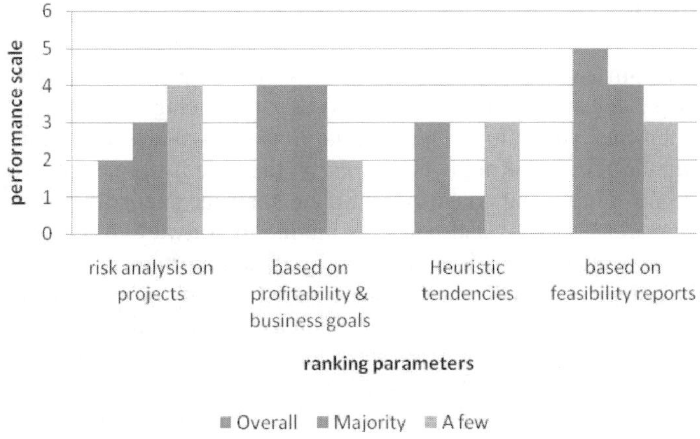

Fig. 5. Project selection parameters

respondents within this sample; majority of the respondents do not necessarily undertake this analysis.

4.2 Discussion

These results show that the need to realign engineering and project selection processes with business objectives is still evident. In instances where business objectives are not well integrated into the processes that produce the software, certain business elements may be sacrificed, such as productivity measurement, quality and risk detection in business selection and overall management. Although a given percentage of the participating companies undertake risk analysis, the extent to which it is done cannot be quantified. Tooling is not widely used in project selection, which implies that heuristic project selection approaches always suffice; although some companies often depend on feasibility assessment reports to determine viability of projects.

Requirement traceability is sacrificed due to time constraints, yet if well integrated it can aid decision-making to a reasonable extent, especially when enforcing reconcilable acceptance criteria establishment on projects. Lack of utilization of such techniques makes it difficult to track and interpret complexities embedded within project requirements. On the other hand UML as a modeling technique has not been adequately embraced; overall, less or no requirement dependency assessment is undertaken. More still, although projects are selected based on business objectives and anticipated profitability, these business objectives are not well explained to all stakeholders, including the technical personnel who execute the tasks on these projects. Interestingly, the anticipated profitability on projects is not often mapped to the processes which in turn impact its overall management during the project lifetime; thereby affecting sustainable business continuity and economic value realization at project completion.

5 Conclusion

While these results cannot be generalized across the entire spectrum, they are indicative of what is happening in most of the software-producing companies, irrespective of size and business direction. They are key business issues that require redress. Therefore, they offer a two-fold benefit. Firstly, they are instrumental in establishing baseline data for future comparison and problem analysis. Secondly, they can be used for identifying trends, issues and concerns unique to software development process, management and challenges. Similarly, a significant portion of most value-based engineering strategies available can be made operational by investing in and developing the process capabilities that can lead to increased competitiveness in the software business. The success of strategic project selection and engineering techniques utilized therefore requires reliable data in order to align improvements with strategy, and to understand precisely the processes with which the business needs to develop.

References

1. Egyed, A., Biffl, S., Heindl, M., Grünbacher, P.: A Value-based Approach for Understanding Cost-benefit Trade-offs During Automated Software Traceability. In: The 3rd international workshop on Traceability in emerging forms of software engineering, pp. 2–7. ACM, New York (2005)
2. Wu, W.Y., Sukoco, B.M., Li, C.Y., Chen, S.H.: An Integrated Multi-objective Decision-Making Process for Supplier Selection with Bundling Problem. Expert Sys. with App: An Inter. J. 36(2), 2327–2337 (2009)
3. Kerzner, H.: Project Management. In: A Systems Approach to Planning, Scheduling and Controlling. John Wiley, New York (1973)
4. Gregor, S., Hart, D., Martin, N.: Enterprise Architectures: Enablers of Business Strategy and IS/IT Alignment in Government. Information Technology and People 20(2), 96–120 (2007)
5. Sanchez, R.J., Truxillo, D.M., Bauer, T.N.: Development and Examination of An Expectancy-based Measure of Test-taking Motivation. Journal of Applied Psychology 85(5), 739–750 (2000)
6. Guan, J.C., Yam, R.C.M., Mok, C.K., Ma, N.: A Study of the Relationship Between Competitiveness and Technological Innovation Capability Based on DEA Models. European J. Oper. Res. 170(3), 971–986 (2006)

RE4Gaia: A Requirements Modeling Approach for the Development of Multi-Agent Systems*

David Blanes, Emilio Insfran, and Silvia Abrahão

ISSI Research Group, Department of Information Systems and Computation
Universidad Politécnica de Valencia, Camino de Vera, s/n 46022, Valencia, Spain
dablado@posgrado.upv.es, {einsfran,sabrahao}@dsic.upv.es

Abstract. This paper presents RE4Gaia, which is a requirements modeling approach for the development of multi-agent systems extending the Gaia methodology. The approach focus on dealing with the organizational structure as a means to adequately capturing and understanding required roles and associated functions, in the context of a organization, prior to the analysis and design of the MAS using Gaia. In addition, a traceability framework is introduced in order to facilitate moving from the requirements models to the analysis and design models proposed in Gaia.

Keywords: Requirements engineering, multi-agent systems, methodology, agent-oriented development.

1 Introduction

The Requirements Engineering (RE) process is recognized as being the most critical process of software development. Errors made during this process can have negative effects on the quality of the resulting software. A Multi-Agent System (MAS) is a specific type of system that is composed of multiple interacting intelligent agents used to solve problems that are difficult for an individual agent or monolithic system to solve. In the last few years, many agent-oriented methodologies [1][2][3][4][5] have been proposed to support the development of this type of systems.

Perhaps the most developed agent-oriented software engineering methodology is Gaia [2]. Gaia is based on the organizational metaphor and founded on the view of multi-agent systems as a computational organization. In Gaia, requirements are just *statements,* independent of the paradigm used for analysis and design, rather than a model oriented to capture requirements relevant to a MAS. Another drawback for Gaia, from our point of view, is the lack of explicit traceability from requirements to the artifacts produced along the MAS development. A better traceability mechanism could help to improve the overall quality of the developed software [3].

* This work is funded by the META project (TIN2006-15175-C05-05) and the Quality-driven model transformations project (UPV).

D. Ślęzak et al. (Eds.): ASEA 2009, CCIS 59, pp. 245–252, 2009.

In this work, we introduce RE4Gaia, which is a requirements modeling approach for the development of MAS extending the Gaia methodology. This approach focus on dealing with the organizational structure as a means to adequately capturing and understanding required roles and associated functions.

This paper is organized as follows. Section 2 presents the related work including characteristics of some methodologies for the development of MAS. Section 3 briefly introduces the Gaia methodology. Section 4 presents our requirements modeling proposal. Section 5 describes a case of study used to validate our approach. Finally, section 6 presents the conclusions and further work.

2 Related Work

As we presented in a previous work [3], we identified that the majority of MAS methodologies focus only on the analysis and design and do not give support to the requirements phase. This is the case of the Gaia methodology and the MASIVE [4]. Others MAS development approaches give a partial support to the requirements phase through use cases or scenarios, i.e. ROADMAP [6] or MaSE [7]. Perhaps the most developed and "well-accepted" approach in the community for dealing with the developing of MAS is Tropos [8]. Tropos is based on the i* framework following a goal-oriented approach. This fact reveals that there is a dearth of alternative methods and techniques for appropriately dealing with requirements for MAS development [3]. Moreover, most of the alternative requirements methodologies are focused in understanding the problem domain and communicate requirements among stakeholders. They lack traceability mechanisms to trace this requirements information towards analysis and design artifacts and backward. We believe that this fact is an important issue that constraints a wider use of these alternative proposals.

In summary, there are many attempts to provide techniques and methods to deal with some aspects of the RE process. However, there is a lack of solutions that allow developers to go systematically from well-defined requirements models to design models in a guided or automated way.

3 The Gaia Methodology

Gaia is a methodology with the purpose of guide the design of open systems using organizational concepts. Gaia is tailored the analysis and design of MAS. We describe only the analysis phase, which is directly related to our proposal.

This phase starts with the definitions of the *global organization goal*. It includes the decomposition of the global organization into sub-organizations. The next step is to build the *environmental model*. This model list all resources that one agent can access. The resources are represented as variables or tuples, where one agent can do three types of actions: sensing, effecting or consuming. The *preliminary role model* is build to capture the basic skills. In this model, a role is represented is represented with an abstract and semiformal description. There are two types of attributes to describe a role: *permissions* and *responsibilities*. The permissions are used to identify the resources accessed by the role and establish the limits for the role. The responsibilities are used to indicate the expected behavior of a role. They are divided in two types: liveness properties and safety properties. The *preliminary interaction model* determines dependencies and interaction between roles through protocols. The protocol is defined with a set of attributes: name, initiator role or roles, partner role or roles, inputs, outputs and a description to explain the purpose of the protocol. Finally, the organizational rules represent the responsibilities of the organization. They are two types of *organizational rules*: liveness rules and safety rules.

4 The Requirements Modeling Approach

The proposed requirements modeling approach (Figure 1) is aimed to deal with the organizational structure as a means to adequately capturing and understanding required roles and associated functions. It includes: i) A *Requirements Modeling Phase*. ii) *A Requirement Analysis Process*.

4.1 Requirements Modeling

The goal of the Requirements Model is to gather and represent the software requirements. This phase starts defining the Mission Statement (MS), the Functional Refinement Tree (FRT), the Requirements Role Model (RRM), and the Domain Model (DM). The MS set the goals of the global organization. The FRT helps to determine the sub-organizations forming the global organization and it participant roles. The RRM is used to detect intheritance relations between role and reason about their structural relationships, detecting possible inconsistencies. Finally the DM is used detect the entities that could be possible organizational resources.

The **Mission Statement** is the most general service (the main goal) that the system to be developed provides to its environment [13]. It is written in natural language with typically one or two paragraphs.

The **Functional Refinement Tree** is used to represent a hierarchical decomposition of the business functions independently of the software system structure. We put in the root of this tree the MS and then is successively refined looking for the functions of the system that are represented as leaf nodes in the FRT. In this process, we can find several levels. The nodes between the root and the leaf nodes are *intermediate nodes*. We distinguish two levels: i) *first*, we find sub-organizations. A sub-organization is part of the system which is oriented to achieve a goal in the system and that weakly interacts with other parts of the systems; ii) *second*, we find that sub-organizations are decomposed into roles. A role is a representation of an abstract entity that provides (several) functions for the system. A function is a task performed by a role in the organization independently if it needs to collaborate with other roles or not.

The **Requirements Role Model** describes the roles belonging to sub-organizations from the FRT. The purpose of this model is to represent the different roles discovered in the organization and create a hierarchy of roles using an inheritance relationship. In order to graphically represent this information, we use the UML Use Case diagram showing only the roles as actors, labeled with the stereotype «*role*», and the relationships among them. An example is shown in Figure 2 (b).

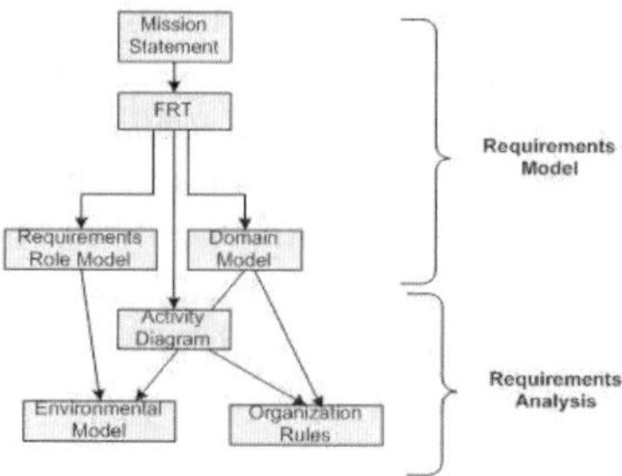

Fig. 1. Overview of RE4Gaia models and their relations

The **Domain Model** shows entities identified in the problem domain. The purpose is to gather key concepts and their relationships depicting a first structural view. These entities must make sense in the application domain. In addition, we represent associations among domain entities and inheritance relationships. In order to graphically represent all these information, we use the UML Class diagram as show the Figure 2 (a).

4.2 Requirements Analysis

The Requirements Analysis Process takes as input the identified functions in the FRT and decomposes them into: tasks and protocols with the help of the Activity Diagram (AD). Moreover, the AD is used to understand the internal flow of one role in order to determine its responsibilities into the Gaia role model. Next, we identify the resources (Environmental Model) refining the entities discovered into the DM. Once we have the internal task and protocols of a role and his accessed resources, we define the organizational rules to define the behavior and restrictions of the organization.

The **Activity Diagram** shows a sequence of steps showing a workflow necessary to realize the identified functions. A representation of the task flow can be useful to understand the logical flow of one role; helping to identify when a role needs to collaborate with others roles. Some guidelines regarding AD are: i) It's necessary to build at least one AD for each sub-organization identified in the FRT; ii) We suggest building one AD for each role that is the initiator of other protocols; iii) We create at least one Activity Partition. Each partition models the role logical flow. We suggest that the left partition is used for the role that starts the protocol. The others partitions represent the other roles that interacts with the initiator role; iv) If we identify that the role needs to interact with other roles, then we add a new activity partitions in the diagram.

The **Environmental Model** is a set of tuples with the following structure: *<role, resource, permission>*. For each **role** from the AM, we set the rightful resources accessed by the role. The information extracted from the AD will help to the analyst to identify which **resources** are accessed. Finally, we set the **permission** type for access to the resource between three types: *read*, *write,* and *consuming*.

Table 1. Excerpt of a FRT for the Settlement sub-organization

Sub-organization	Role	Function
Settlement	Buyer	Purchase good
		Take good away
	Buyer Manager	Update credit
		Send Buyer List
		Send result verify credit
		Sanction buyer
	Seller Manager	Update the credit

The last step in the Requirement Analysis phase is to define the **Organizational Rules**. They are written in natural language with the purpose to gather and represent general constraints for the Organizational behavior. These rules can be viewed as responsibilities of the organization as a whole and can be related to i) *Organization dynamics properties*, defining how should evolve the organization; ii) *Organization constraints*, defining restrictions that the organization must respect in every time.

5 Case Study

We introduce a case of study for an Auction System for a Fish Market. This case study was proposed in [14] and we adapted it in order to illustrate our proposal. The complete specification of the case study can be found at: http://www.dsic.upv.es/~einsfran/RE4Gaia/casestudy.html.

The first phase is the **Admission**. Here the guest can create a buyer account and the existing users can validate their credits. Meanwhile the buyers performs the admission, the sellers bring the goods. For each good the seller's admitter employed fix: the weight, the fish quality and the price and send the good list the Auctioneer. The second stage is the **Auction**, where auctioneer starts a new bidding round. He sends to each buyer: the list of buyers taking part in the round, the list of goods, and the next good to be auctioned. After that, the auctioneer starts broadcasting prices to all buyers in the auction room. The buyers bids for the goods offered by the auctioneer. When one good is sold, then the owner is informed of the new sale. The seller's earnings are updated. Finally In the **Settlements** buyers can collect a statement describing their purchases and pay them up, whereas sellers may collect their earnings at the settlements office once their lot of goods has been sold.

Applying our approach, we firstly build the ***Requirements Model***. The first step is to define the **Mission Statement**. The mission of the Fish Market system is to *automate the management of admission, register the incoming bids, give support to the Auction process and manage the sale of goods*. The next step is to build the **Functional Refinement Tree.** Table 1 represents an excerpt of the FRT showing the branch of the sub-organization Settlement (in a tabular format). The Buyer role does the functions Purchase good and Take good away. The Buyer Manager role does the functions: Update credit, Send Buyer List, Send result, Verify credit, and Sanction Buyer. Finally, the Seller Manager role does the Update credit task. Regarding the **Requirements Role Model**, we identified the following roles: *Guest, Buyer, Seller, Boss, Buyer Manager, Auctioneer, Seller Admitter, Buyer Admitter and Seller Manager*. There is an inheritance from *Buyer* and *Seller* roles to the *Guest*, representing the fact that everything that can be done by a *Guest* can also be done by a *Buyer* or by a *Seller*. This information is shown in Figure 2 (b). The main domain entities and relationships found are represented in Figure 2 (a). We identify a Person entity that shares common properties with the *Seller* and *Buyer*. A *Buyer List* is related to multiple Buyers, and an Item List is related to multiple Items. An Item belongs to one *Seller*, and a *Bidding Round* is composed by multiple *Bids*. Each *Bid* has *Buyer List*, multiple *Prices* and one *Item List* associated.

Secondly, we apply the ***Requirement Analysis Process***. This phase starts with the construction of the **Activity Diagrams**. In order to analyze the Settlement sub-organization, we should use build one AD for each role with proactive behavior, in this case: *Buyer* and *Seller*. Figure 3 shows the AD for the *Buyer* role. The *Buyer* when joining in the scenario can start the *Purchase*. When the *Buyer* finishes the protocol *Purchase*, then he exits from the scenario. In the other partition, Auctioneer, is the *Buyer Manager*, which is waiting for the *Purchase* protocol requests. The role checks if the *Buyer* role has enough credit. If it is true then the *Update Credit* task is performed, otherwise it starts the *Bad Credit* protocol to communicate a "bad purchase" to the Auctioneer role. For each role identified in the FRT, and also specified in the RRM, we set the resources with permission granted to the role to consider inheritance relationships. Table 2 shows a partial view of this model, representing two roles: *Auctioneer* and *Buyer Manager*.

Finally, we have the following organizational rules for our case study: i) One buyer must be registered before joining the auction; ii) One buyer cannot join in the settlement if he is not a bid winner; ii) The Auctioneer must wait if there not enough goods to auction; iv) The Auctioneer must wait if there are not enough buyers.

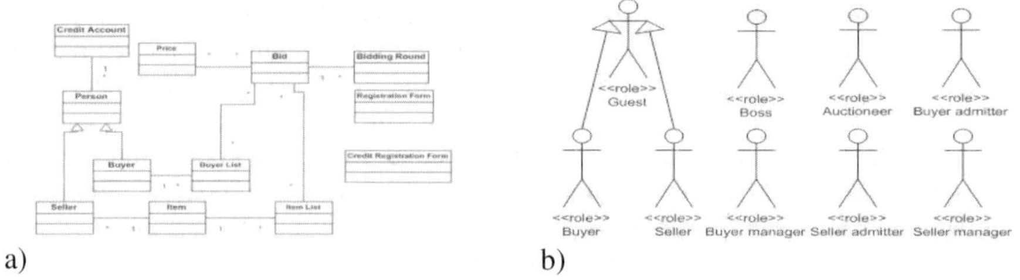

Fig. 2. a) Domain Model; **b)** Requirements Role Model

Fig. 3. Activity Diagram for the Buyer role in the Settlement sub-organization

5.1 Traceability Framework

In this section, due to space limitations, we briefly outline the traceability strategy. This traceability framework can be viewed from two perspectives: i) *inner,* which refers to the links established between elements in RE4Gaia; ii) outer, which refers to the links established between elements in RE4Gaia and the Gaia analysis models.

Related to the **inner** traceability, the main relationships are: i) The MS is related to sub-organizations identified in the FRT; ii) Each role identified in the FRT (and specified in the RRM) is related to its corresponding sub-organization in the FRT, iii) Each role identified in the FRT (and specified in the RRM) is related to one role into the EM, iv) Each entity identified in the DM is related to one resource into the EM. The user decides with which roles is related the resource and with which permissions have access granted; v) Each function in the FRT is related to a task or protocol in the AD, depending if the functions needs collaboration with others roles.

Related to the **outer** traceability, the main relationships are: i) Each resource from the EM is related to one resource in Gaia. As at this level the EM is preliminary, new resources can be identified at the Gaia analysis. The permissions are mapped for each role can access to the resource; ii) Each role identified in the RRM is related to a role in the Gaia Role Model. The information extracted from the AD helps to the user to fill the liveness, and safety properties; iii) Each task or protocol identified into the AD is related to one task or protocol in the Gaia Role Model, giving relevant information that is needed to specify in detail during the analysis and design; iv) The organizational rules in natural language are mapped to organization rules in the Gaia methodology. The user can decided if is converted into a liveness o safety rule.

Table 2. Partial Environment Model

Role	Resource	Permission
Auctioneer	Bid	Modify
	Bidding Round	Modify
	Price	Modify
Buyer Manager	Account	Read
	Buyer List	Modify

6 Conclusions and Further Work

We have presented a Requirements Modeling approach extending the Gaia methodology. The approach deals with the organizational structure as a means to adequately capturing and understanding required roles and associated functions, in the context of an organization prior to the analysis and design using Gaia. We believe that our approach fills the gap in the development of MAS providing a systematic approach to deal with requirements establishing better traceability mechanisms that help analysts to meet user needs, improve their understanding of the systems, facilitate the maintainability of produced artifacts, and improve the overall quality of the developed software.

Currently, we are applying the requirements modeling approach for the specification of other MAS with the intention to study the expressiveness and transformation capacities of our requirements models. We plan to perform controlled experiments with PhD students in order to empirically validate the effectiveness of our method. We are also working in the development of a tool using the Eclipse framework to implement the proposed approach. This tool will allow us to follow a model-driven development approach including model2model transformations from RE4Gaia models to Gaia models.

References

1. Penserini, L., Perini, A., Susi, A., Mylopoulos, J.: High Variability Design for Software Agents: Extending Tropos. ACM Trans. Autonom. Adapt. Syst. 2(4), Article 16 (2007)
2. Pavón, J., Gomez, J.: Agent Oriented Software Engineering with INGENIAS. In: CEEMAS, Prague, Czech Republic, pp. 394–403 (2003)
3. Bresciani, P., Perini, A., Giorgini, P., Giunchiglia, F., Mylopoulos, J.: Tropos: An Agent-Oriented Software Development Methodology. Autonomous Agents and Multi-Agent Systems 8(2), 203–236 (2004)
4. DeLoach, S., Wood, M., Sparkman, C.: Multiagent Systems Engineering. International Journal of Software Engineering and Knowledge Engineering 11(3), 231–258 (2001)
5. Lind, J.: Iterative Software Engineering for Multiagent Systems. In: The MASSIVE Method (2001)
6. Zambonelli, F., Jennings, N., Wooldridge, M.: Developing Multiagent Systems: The Gaia Methodology. ACM Transactions on Software Engineering and Methodology (TOSEM), 317–370 (2003)
7. Blanes, D., Insfran, E., Abrahão, S.: Requirements Engineering in the Development of Multi-Agent Systems: A Systematic Review. In: Accepted for publication in the International Conference on Intelligent Data Engineering and Automated Learning, Burgos, Spain (2009)
8. Cossentino, M.: From requirements to code with the PASSI methodology. In: Agent-Oriented Methodologies, pp. 79–106. Idea Group Inc., USA (2005)
9. Juan, T., Pearce, A., Sterling, L.: ROADMAP: extending the gaia methodology for complex open systems. In: AAMAS, Bologna, Italy, pp. 3–10 (2002)
10. Insfran, E.: A Requirements Engineering Approach for Object-Oriented Conceptual Modeling, Valencia, Spain (2003)
11. Napoli, C., Giordano, M., Furnari, M.: A PVM implementation of the Fishmarket. In: IX International Symposium on Artificial Intelligence, Cancun (1996)

Execution Traces: A New Domain That Requires the Creation of a Standard Metamodel

Luay Alawneh and Abdelwahab Hamou-Lhadj

Electrical & Computer Engineering Department, Concordia University

Abstract. Despite the fact dynamic analysis techniques of software systems have been shown to be useful in many software engineering activities such as software maintenance, software performance, testing, etc., there is no standard format for representing run-time information, which hinders interoperability and sharing of data. Runtime information is typically represented in the form of execution traces. Traces can contain different information, and can contain different types of information depending on what is being traced and the purpose of the trace. In this paper, we argue that traces represent vital knowledge about software that needs to be organized and modeled. We support our arguments by discussing the various types of traces used in the literature. We also discuss the challenges when dealing with execution traces and why a trace metamodel has to be carefully designed to overcome these challenges. We also discuss existing attempts to model execution traces. Finally, we discuss how the Knowledge Discovery Metamodel can be extended to support efficiently the modeling of large and complex execution traces.

Keywords: Execution Traces, Trace Metamodel, Knowledge Discovery Metamodel.

1 Introduction

An important issue in application modernization is the time it takes to understand how the application is built and why it is built this way. In an ideal situation, any change made to an existing software system must be based on information kept in up-to-date documentation. However, for a variety of reasons, it has been shown, in practice, that maintaining sufficiently good documentation is impractical in many organizations, which renders program comprehension a difficult and tedious task. Reverse engineering techniques aim at reducing the impact of this problem by recovering high-level views of the system from low-level implementation details. These views can be used by software engineers to understand the main aspects of the system before diving into the details.

Reverse engineering tools can be grouped into two categories depending on whether they focus on static analysis of the system or on the understanding of its dynamic characteristics. Static analysis techniques operate on the source code to extract a system's main components and their relations. Dynamic analysis, which is the focus of this paper, focuses on the analysis of the behavioural aspects of a system through the analysis of run-time information.

D. Ślęzak et al. (Eds.): ASEA 2009, CCIS 59, pp. 253–263, 2009.

Run-time information is typically represented using execution traces. There exist, however, many types of traces that vary in their structure, the contained information, and the level of abstraction of the contained information. An execution trace can be used to describe the interacting modules involved in a particular scenario, or may be detailed to capture the performed statements in each module's procedure. Examples of such traces include routine-call traces, statement-level traces, traces of inter-process communication, etc.

Although this paper focuses on reverse engineering, dynamic analysis has been shown to be useful in many software engineering activities such as program comprehension, runtime monitoring and performance analysis, testing, fault detection and intrusion detection, etc. There exist many tools for execution trace visualization and analysis. However, these tools use different format for representing traces, which hinders interoperability. This is attributable to a lack of a standardized way for representing execution traces despite the increasing attention to dynamic analysis techniques of software in recent years.

In this paper, we argue that execution traces form a new domain knowledge that needs to be organized and modeled. We discuss the most important types of execution traces, their applications, and their structures. We also discuss how these approaches deal with the trace size problem. Finally, we discuss existing metamodels such as the Knowledge Discovery Metamodel [1] from OMG [2], the UML metamodel [3], etc., and their limitations.

2 Execution Traces as a New Domain

Execution traces represent the sequence of execution in a running software system at different levels of abstraction. Traces may exist in different structures according to the degree of abstraction requested by the program analyzer. For example, statement-level traces are linear and contain single executed statements. Routine-level traces depict the sequence of routine calls for a program run and are often represented as a tree structure. Inter-process execution traces capture the interactions between different processes in terms of message passing, and they can be modeled using a graph.

In the following, we present an overview of different types of execution traces, their structure and their application.

2.1 Statement-Level Traces

Statement-level traces contain the executed statements of a program run according to a coverage that is usually specified by the user. This type of traces can profile a complete behaviour of the software system and can be used to extract information regarding the flow of control during execution and the dependencies among the executed statements. Also, it helps in maintenance activities such as bug fixing by identifying the cause of the problem.

One of the main challenges when using statement-level traces is the sheer size of the generated trace which can reach millions of events. Therefore, a metamodel that represents this type of traces must be built with scalability in mind. One simple approach to achieve this is to represent the repetitive information contained in a trace only once.

Zhang et al. present a more advanced trace compaction technique called Whole Execution Traces (WET) [4]. WET represents a compressed whole execution trace which captures complete profile information that covers control flow, variable values, variable memory addresses, and control and data dependencies. The framework can respond to a wide range of queries that may require single or multiple types of profile information in a fast and easy manner.

WET is a labelled graph that assigns a unique timestamp to every single instance for each executed statement in order to track the ordering of execution. Furthermore, the paper presents compression techniques that, according to the authors, reduce the size of WET effectively. Moreover, the paper shows some benchmark values that prove the efficiency of the used compression techniques.

2.2 Routine Call Traces

Routine-call traces and their object-oriented counterpart "method-call traces" capture the sequence of routine calls in an execution path. This type of traces is at a higher level of abstraction compared to statement-level traces and can be used to reveal significant information about the system's different scenarios. Routine-call traces, which are represented as tree structures, can be used in many maintenance activities such as bug-fixing [5], and feature-location [5]. Moreover, they can provide useful information that can enable software engineers to perform many activities in an efficient manner including restructuring, refactoring, and code optimization. Like any other type of execution trace, routine-call traces can grow dramatically in size and complexity. Therefore, compression and reduction techniques should be applied in order to utilize them effectively. In the following we present several research studies related to routine and method call traces.

Taniguchi et al. [7] proposed a new method for reverse engineering of UML sequence diagrams based on method-call execution traces. The purpose of this technique is to facilitate the understanding of object-oriented systems. Furthermore, the paper presents a set of four compaction rules in order to solve the problem of large execution traces. The proposed rules can be summarized as follows:

1. Rule 1 finds identical method-call subtrees and represents them in one subtree. Identical method-call subtrees share the same objects. By using this rule, the original call tree can be reconstructed.
2. Rule 2 finds repetitive method calls structures that correspond to different objects and then compacts them by unifying the objects. Although this method can detect repetitive structures that cannot be captured by the first rule, the original subtrees cannot be reconstructed using this rule.
3. Rule 3 detects similar subtrees that may not have the same exact method calls, i.e. one subtree may include one or more method calls than the other. In this case, the compaction is done by using the subtree that contains more method calls.
4. Rule 4 targets the compaction of recursive method calls by combining different recursive calls into one node.

In [8], Wang et al. proposed a new approach for threat model-driven security testing in order to detect threats at runtime. The approach uses UML sequence diagrams in order to model threats to security policies. A security policy defines what actions should be permitted or refused by the system. In the design phase, threat scenarios are constructed using sequence diagrams. These scenarios depict any expected threat to the system. . In order to reduce the size of the trace, the source code is only instrumented with essential information relevant to threat scenarios. Finally, these constructed scenarios are used to verify if any execution trace matches any of the threat scenarios.

Salah et al presented a study [9] that targets program comprehension. It presents a hierarchy of dynamic views composed of different tools for program execution trace analysis. The hierarchy includes feature-interaction, feature-implementation, class-interaction, and object-interaction views. In the same field of program comprehension, Apiwattanapong et al. [10] proposed a new approach for impact analysis of software changes based on dynamic analysis. The presented technique uses only essential dynamic information collected from method-call execution traces.

Finally, Hamou-Lhadj and Lethbridge [11] presented a technique for large execution trace summarization that can be applied to enable top-down analysis of traces as well as the recovery of the behavioural design model of the system. Additionally, the paper proposes a new metric for detecting utility methods which are considered as implementation details that can be removed in the process of abstracting out the main content for large traces.

2.3 Inter-process Level Traces

Inter-process communication execution traces capture the interactions among different processes in a software system. Processes may reside on the same computer or different computers. Also, this type of traces captures the communication among threads living within the same process. The main challenge when analyzing this type of execution traces, in addition to size and complexity, is that different executions for the same scenario could generate different traces, which makes it difficult to study this type of traces. The variation in the generated execution traces is due to the non-deterministic behaviour of multi-threaded applications.

Moe et al. [12] apply dynamic analysis through runtime execution traces in order to understand the behaviour of distributed software systems. They propose a method to support the understanding of distributed systems based on the analysis of execution traces at the remote procedure calls level. Also, the work provides a tool for the visualization of the processed execution traces. According to the authors, this work, when applied during the maintenance phase, can help in detecting design flaws, configuration and performance problems.

Bensalem et al. [13] presented an algorithm that uses a single execution trace of multithreaded programs in order to detect occurrences of deadlocks. An advantage of the proposed algorithm is the ability to detect deadlocks in running programs even when examining a deadlock-free execution trace.

2.4 System Call Level Traces

A system-call is a request to the kernel by a user-level program in order to be permitted to perform a set of predefined operations that the requesting program does not possess the required permissions to execute on its own. A system call trace is the sequence of calls made to the system by a running process.

System-call traces can be used to detect and control programs by verifying that each system call conforms to a policy that confirms a program's normal behaviour. Many research works on intrusion detection such as [14-16] use system-call level traces in order to detect and determine anomaly behaviour.

Another application for system-call traces is performance monitoring. Burns et al. [17] used system call execution traces to extract the logical block addresses of a file which are generated over a long period of time in order to evaluate the file system performance.

2.5 Execution Traces for Performance Analysis

The increasing size and complexity of software systems require planning for better memory management and CPU processing times. This led to the development of software analysis tools, usually known as profilers, which help in pinpointing execution bottlenecks and aid code optimization consequently. Moreover, the analysis provided by these tools can benefit in decreasing the execution time and reducing the resource utilization such as physical and virtual memory. The main weakness of this type of tools is the overhead introduced from the statically instrumented executed statements. However, Dynamic instrumentation [18] can be used in order to obtain a very low profiling overhead.

Harkema et al. [19] presented a Java Performance Monitoring Toolkit (JPMT) for analyzing the performance of Java applications. It uses event traces such as thread creation, method invocations and locking contention which are annotated by performance attributes such as timestamps in case of method invocations. Instrumentation overhead is overcome by only instrumenting for the types of events requested by the user. Additionally, JPMT supports visualization of event traces and provides the ability of querying for certain types of events.

In his work [20], Putrycz presents a novel approach for analyzing performance in COTS-based systems which uses low-level trace analysis in order to understand the interactions between the communicating components. Pahl et al [21] presents a service-specific approach for performance evaluation of model-driven developed services. This work presents a new approach for instrumentation of model-based languages in order to collect performance-relevant time information at execution time from specific model elements such as services and flow operators.

3 Existing Metamodels

There exist several metamodels that are used to capture runtime execution traces such as Compact Trace Format (CTF) [28] and UML [3]. UML sequence diagrams can be used to capture procedure calls among different objects. The problem with the existing metamodels is their inability to model all types of execution traces captured from different software architectures and the lack of support to trace compaction techniques. In this section, we present some of the existing metamodels that are being used or can be used to model different types of execution traces.

3.1 Compact Trace Format

Hamou-Lhadj et al. [28] developed a metamodel called the Compact Trace Format (CTF) to model traces of routine (method) calls. CTF was designed to deal with the enormous size of typical traces based on the idea that dynamic call trees can be turned into ordered directed acyclic graphs, where repeated sub-trees are factored out. CTF supports traces defined at different levels of abstraction including object, class and package level. It also supports the specification of threads of execution. Additional information such as timestamps and routine execution time are added to enable profilers to use CTF.

Trace data conforming to CTF can be expressed using GXL [29] or any other data 'carrier' language. However, the authors suggest using a compact representation in order to support the compactness objective of CTF. CTF is lossless such that the original trace can be reconstructed from its compact form.

3.2 Unified Modeling Language

UML is a modeling language adopted by OMG in 1997 that enables software designers to specify, visualize, and document software models. These models are abstract representations of the implementation details of software systems. The UML metamodel is based on the Meta Object Facility [30] (MOF) language. MOF defines an abstract language and framework for specifying, constructing and managing technology neutral metamodels.

UML diagrams are classified into two categories: structural and behavioural diagrams. The latter includes a subset known as interaction diagrams. The structural diagrams include those that capture the static structure of software systems such as class and package diagrams. The class and package diagrams help in building metamodels that capture execution traces. On the other hand, behavioural diagrams depict the dynamic behaviour of software systems. Behavioural diagrams include use case diagram, activity diagram, state machine diagram, sequence diagram and others.

The sequence diagram shows object interactions arranged in a time sequence. Sequence diagrams identify the communication required to fulfill an interaction. Moreover, they show the objects that participate in an interaction and the messages used to trigger the interactions among the objects.

There exist some research works that used UML sequence diagram to model runtime execution traces. Briand et al [31] proposed a framework for reverse engineering of UML sequence diagrams using execution traces. This work defines a metamodel for execution traces and maps the execution trace elements to its corresponding sequence diagram elements. The work uses code instrumentation to probe the parts of code that will be used to generate the execution trace. In [32], Delamare et al. used UML 2.0 sequence diagrams to capture the program state from its execution traces for the purpose of program understanding.

In [33], the authors used UML State Machine diagrams as the basis for their approach to runtime verification of Java programs. The approach studies the temporal order of message receiving based on consistency checking between the behaviour of state machine diagrams and the program execution traces.

3.3 Knowledge Discovery Metamodel

The Knowledge Discovery Metamodel (KDM) [1] is a metamodel that targets a widespread set of software applications, platforms and programming languages such as modern enterprise applications which involve multiple technologies and programming languages. The goal of KDM is to facilitate the integration between different tools that capture information about complex enterprise applications. The structure of KDM offers a common interchange format, using XMI schema, which allows interoperability between existing tools and their models. Moreover, KDM captures the physical and logical software assets at various levels of abstraction as entities and relations. This nominates it as a favorable basis for different software domains.

KDM is designed based on the separation of concerns principle in order to enable different compliant tools to support the same or compatible metamodel subsets. This modular structure of the metamodel allows a tool vendor to select only its desired or needed parts of the metamodel. Furthermore, the structure of KDM consists of different packages that represent each domain in enterprise applications. This modular structure allows for the extensibility of the KDM metamodel by adding new domains to the metamodel as needed.

This structure of KDM means that users need only to learn about the domain of their interest. For example, the Structural domain provides users with information about the architectural elements from the source code of the target system. On the other hand, the Business Rules domain provides users with behavioural elements of the system such as features or process rules.

The KDM metamodel is organized in four different layers. The KDM infrastructure layer defines the basis for the KDM metamodel. Its packages are used by the packages in the other layers. The Program Elements Layer defines a large set of metamodel elements whose purpose is to provide a language-independent intermediate representation for various constructs determined by common programming languages. The Runtime Resource Layer describes common patterns for representing the operating environment of existing software systems. Finally, the Abstraction Layer defines a set of metamodel elements whose purpose is to represent domain-specific and application specific abstractions, as well as the engineering view of the existing software system.

4 Proposed Execution Trace Metamodel

Runtime execution traces represent a separate domain in software modernization. They provide proper understanding of the different parts of the system under study. Also, they can facilitate different software maintenance and performance monitoring activities. Execution traces may exist in different levels of abstraction. The objective of this work is to support execution traces in all levels of abstraction and to define a standardized form for execution traces that supports meaningfulness, abstraction and expressiveness.

Execution traces can be generated using a technique known as program instrumentation. Instrumentation of the source code should be performed properly in order to generate an execution trace, at a certain level of abstraction, which can be applied feasibly in order to achieve the goal of the analysis task.

The proposed metamodel should be flexible to cover the aforementioned types of execution traces. Therefore, it should be based on a metamodel that supports extensibility in order to cope with newer types of traces. Our discussion on KDM shows that it can be a proper candidate for our proposed metamodel because of the following advantages:

1. KDM is a metamodel that targets a widespread set of software applications, platforms and programming languages such as modern enterprise applications which involve multiple technologies and programming languages.
2. Separation of concerns concept. This helps in extending KDM to support different domains by adding new packages to the metamodel.
3. KDM uses the XMI schema to store the software artifacts. XMI is an OMG standard for exchanging metadata information via Extensible Markup Language (XML). It can be used for any metadata whose metamodel can be expressed in Meta-Object Facility (MOF) such as UML.
4. KDM captures the physical and logical software assets at various levels of abstraction as entities and relations.
5. KDM metamodel defines program element entities and their relationships which can play a main role in building a comprehensive execution trace metamodel. Executed traces can be mapped easily to their corresponding program elements since KDM assigns a unique identifier for each program element.

We are interesed in the KDM Runtime Resource Layer because it represents the dynamic structures, instances of logical entities and their relationships, which exist at runtime such as processes and threads. Therefore, a new package to represent the Runtime Execution traces can be created in this layer. Figure 1 depicts the structure of KDM packages along with our new Trace package that will represent the execution traces domain.

The advantages of our approach are manifold and can be summarized as:

1. Our metamodel will utilize the structure of KDM. Therefore, runtime execution traces can be exchanged easily among different analysis tools.
2. The new Trace package will reuse various KDM packages such as Core, Code and Action.
3. The execution trace model can follow the Directed Acyclic Graph structures. Therefore, different graph reduction and summarization techniques can be applied to our metamodel.
4. Polymorphism and dynamic binding in object oriented systems will be supported in our metamodel easily since KDM assigns a unique identifier to every element in the source code. Therefore, each method will be instrumented with its KDM unique identifier. Thus, a method call in the execution trace can be linked to its class using its unique identifier.
5. Processes and Threads are already supported in KDM and will be reused in our Trace package.
6. The Trace package can be extended to support newer types of execution traces easily due to the extensibility nature of KDM.
7. The new metamodel can be integrated easily with several visualizations schema such as GXL.

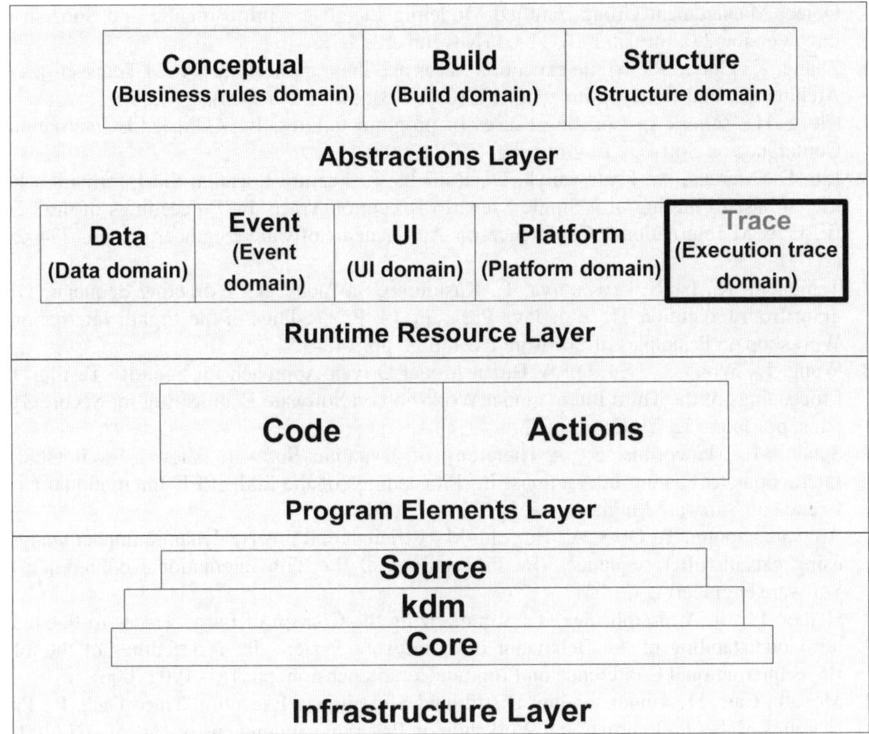

Fig. 1. Updated KDM Structure with Trace Package

5 Conclusion and Future Work

This paper presented runtime information through execution traces as a new domain in software engineering supported by several research studies that target or utilize execution traces to achieve their objectives. We discussed a few metamodels that are used to capture execution traces. Our discussion showed that the available metamodels lack the possibility of capturing all types of execution traces. Moreover, these metamodels except for [28] do not apply trace compaction techniques. Finally, we proposed building a new metamodel based on KDM for its numerous advantages. The resulting metamodel should be able to model any type of execution traces in a compact form.

Our future work will focus on building the new metamodel for the execution trace domain. We will continue studying all the available types of execution traces in order to support them in our metamodel.

References

1. Object Management Group. Knowledge Discovery Metamodel: KDM Version 1.1 Beta 3 (March 2008)
2. OMG: Object Management Group, `http://www.omg.org/`

3. Object Management Group. Unified Modeling Language: Infrastructure and Superstructure, Version 2.0, formal/2007-11-04 (November 2007)
4. Zhang, X., Gupta, R.: Whole execution traces and their applications. ACM Transactions on Architecture and Code Optimization (TACO) 2(3), 301–334 (2005)
5. Cleve, H., Zeller, A.: Locating causes of program failures. In: ACM/IEEE International Conference on Software Engineering, ICSE (2005)
6. Liu, D., Marcus, A., Poshyvanyk, D., Rajlich, V.: Feature Location via Information Retrieval based Filtering of a Single Scenario Execution Trace. In: Proceedings of the 22nd IEEE/ACM International Conference on Automated Software Engineering, pp. 234–243 (2007)
7. Taniguchi, K., Ishio, T., Kamiya, T., Kusumoto, S., Inoue, K.: Extracting Sequence Diagram from Execution Trace of Java Program. In: Proceedings of the Eighth International Workshop on Principles of Software Evolution, pp. 148–154 (2005)
8. Wang, L., Wong, E., Xu, D.: A Threat Model Driven Approach for Security Testing. In: Proceedings of the Third International Workshop on Software Engineering for Secure Systems, pp. 111–112 (2007)
9. Salah, M., Mancoridis, S.: A Hierarchy of Dynamic Software Views: From Object-Interactions to Feature-Interactions. In: Proceedings of the 20th IEEE International Conference on Software Maintenance, pp. 72–81 (2004)
10. Apiwattanapong, T., Orso, A., Harrold, M.: Efficient and precise dynamic impact analysis using execute-after sequences. In: Proceedings of the 27th international conference on Software engineering (2005)
11. Hamou-Lhadj, A., Lethbridge, T.: Summarizing the Content of Large Traces to Facilitate the Understanding of the Behaviour of a Software System. In: Proceedings of the 14th IEEE International Conference on Program Comprehension, pp. 181–190 (2006)
12. Moe, J., Carr, D.: Understanding Distributed Systems via Execution Trace Data. In: Proceedings of the 9th International Workshop on Program Comprehension, pp. 60–67 (2001)
13. Bensalem, S., Havelund, K.: Scalable deadlock analysis of multi-threaded programs. In: Proceedings of the Parallel and Distributed Systems: Testing and Debugging (PADTAD) Track of the 2005 IBM Verification Conference. Springer, Heidelberg (2005)
14. Varghese, S.M., Jacob, K.P.: Anomaly Detection Using System Call Sequence Sets. Journal of Software 2(6) (2007)
15. Fetzer, C., Suesskraut, M.: SwitchBlade: Enforcing Dynamic Personalized System Call Models. In: Proceedings of the 3rd ACM SIGOPS/EuroSys European Conference on Computer Systems (2008)
16. Goel, A., Feng, W., Maier, D.: Automatic high-performance reconstruction and recovery. The International Journal of Computer and Telecommunications Networking 51(5), 1361–1377 (2007)
17. Burns, R., Rees, R., Peterson, Z., Darrell, D.E.: Allocation and Data Placement Using Virtual Contiguity, iNIST/SSRC/01-001, pp. 1–6 (2001)
18. Cantrill, B.M., Shapiro, M.W., Leventhal, A.H.: Dynamic instrumentation of production systems. In: Proceedings of the USENIX Annual Technical Conference 2004 on USENIX Annual Technical Conference (2004)
19. Harkema, M., Quartel, D., van der Mei, R., Gijsen, B.: JPMT: a Java performance monitoring tool. In: Proceedings of the 13th International Conference on Modelling Techniques and Tools for Computer Performance Evaluation (2003)
20. Putrycz, E.: Using trace analysis for improving performance in COTS systems. In: Proceedings of the 2004 conference of the Centre for Advanced Studies on Collaborative research, pp. 68–80 (2004)
21. Pahl, C., Boskovic, M., Hasselbring, W.: Model-Driven Performance Evaluation for Service Engineering. In: Proceedings of the 2nd European Conference on Web Services Workshop on Web Services Technology (2007)

22. McGavin, M., Wright, T., Marshall, S.: Visualisations of Execution Traces (VET): An Interactive Plugin-Based Visualisation Tool. In: Proceeding of the 7th Australasian User Interface Conference, pp. 153–160 (2006)
23. Fischer, M., Oberleitner, J., Gall, H., Gschwind, T.: System Evolution Tracking through Execution Trace Analysis. In: Proceedings of the 13th International Workshop on Program Comprehension, pp. 237–246 (2005)
24. Cornelissen, B., Zaidman, A., Holten, D., Moonen, L., van Deursen, A., van Wijk, J.: Execution trace analysis through massive sequence and circular bundle views. Journal of Systems and Software 8(12) (2008)
25. de Kergommeaux, J.C., de Oliveira Stein, B.: Pajé: An Extensible Environment for Visualizing Multi-threaded Programs Executions. In: Proceedings of the 6th International Euro-Par Conference on Parallel Processing, pp. 133–140 (2000)
26. Roberts, J., Zilles, C.: TraceVis: An Execution Trace Visualization Tool. In: Proceedings of the Workshop on Modeling, Benchmarking, and Simulation (2005)
27. Malnati, G., Cuva, C.M., Barberis, C.: JThreadSpy: teaching multithreading programming by analyzing execution traces. In: Proceedings of the Parallel And Distributed Systems: Testing and Debugging Conference (2007)
28. Hamou-Lhadj, A., Lethbridge, T.C.: A Metamodel for Dynamic Information Generated from Object-Oriented Systems. Electronic Notes Theoretical Computer Science, vol. 94, pp. 59–69. Elsevier Press, Amsterdam (2004)
29. Winter, A., Kullbach, B., Riediger, V.: An Overview of the GXL Graph Exchange Language, Revised Lectures on Software Visualization. In: International Seminar, pp. 324–336 (2001)
30. Object Management Group. Meta Object Facility (MOF) Specification (2000)
31. Briand, L.C., Labiche, Y., Miao, Y.: Towards the Reverse Engineering of UML Sequence Diagrams. In: Proceedings of the 10th Working Conference on Reverse Engineering (2003)
32. Delamare, R., Baudry, B., Traon, Y.L.: Reverse-engineering of UML 2.0 Sequence Diagrams from Execution Traces. In: Workshop on Object-Oriented Reengineering at ECOOP (2006)
33. Li, X., Qiu, X., Wang, L., Lei, B., Wong, W.E.: UML State Machine Diagram Driven Runtime Verification of Java Programs for Message Interaction Consistency. In: Proceedings of the 23rd Annual ACM Symposium on Applied Computing (ACM SAC 2008), pp. 384–389 (2008)

Software Performability Measurement Based on Availability Model with User-Perceived Performance Degradation

Koichi Tokuno and Shigeru Yamada

Department of Social Management Engineering,
Graduate School of Engineering, Tottori University
4-101, Koyama, Tottori-shi, 680-8552 Japan
{toku,yamada}@sse.tottori-u.ac.jp

Abstract. This paper discusses software performability evaluation considering the real-time property. We assume that the software system has two operational states from the viewpoint of the end users: one is operating with the desirable performance level according to specification and the other is with degraded performance level. The time-dependent behavior of the system is described by the Markovian software availability model with performance degradation. Assuming that the system can process the multiple tasks simultaneously, we analyze the distribution of the number of tasks whose processes can be completed within the processing time limit with the infinite server queueing model. We derive several software performability measures; these are given as the functions of time and the number of debugging activities. Finally, we illustrate several numerical examples of the measures to investigate the impact of consideration of the performance degradation on the system performability evaluation.

Keywords: performability, real-time property, performance degradation, software availability model, infinite-server queueing model.

1 Introduction

The studies on performability evaluation methods for hardware-oriented computing systems have much been discussed. However, on the other hand, most of studies on software-oriented reliability evaluation have treated only the inherent reliability characteristics such as the residual fault content, the mean time between software failures (MTBSF), and the software reliability function. However, recently, software-conscious approaches extended to performability evaluation have also increased [1,2,3].

Most of the existing software-conscious approaches are discussed on the basis of performability measures in steady states and assume that the probabilistic or stochastic characteristics in system failure and restoration do not change even though the system is debugged or refreshed, i.e., the system returns to the initial condition in terms of the failure and restoration characteristics, neither better nor worse states. As to this point, the analytical framework in the above studies

D. Ślęzak et al. (Eds.): ASEA 2009, CCIS 59, pp. 264–271, 2009.

is basically similar to the hardware-conscious approach even though the authors of previous works often say that their works are software-oriented. Traditional stochastic software reliability modeling often considers the dynamic reliability/performance growth process. Musa [4] says that the above mention is one of main differences from the modeling for the hardware system.

In this paper, we discuss the user-oriented performability evaluation method for the software system considering the performance degradation in operation; this is the different approach from [1,2,3]. In particular, we consider the real-time property; this is defined as the attribute that the system can complete the task within the stipulated response time limit [5]. We assume that the software system can process the multiple tasks simultaneously and that the task arrival process follows a nonhomogeneous Poisson process (NHPP). Then the phenomenon of performance degradation, the dynamic software reliability growth, and the upward tendency of difficulty in debugging are described by the user-oriented Markovian software availability model [6]. The stochastic behavior of the number of tasks whose processes can be complete within the processing time limit is modeled with the infinite-server queueing model [7].

The organization of the rest of the paper is shown as follows: Section 2 states the Markovian software availability model with performance degradation. Section 3 defines the operating regulation of the system and analyzes the distribution of the number of tasks whose processes are complete within the processing time limit up to a given time point. Section 4 derives several software performability measures from the model. The measures are given as the functions of time and the number of debuggings. Section 5 illustrates the numerical example of the measures and examines the software performability analysis. Finally, Section 6 summarizes the conclusion of the paper.

2 Software Availability Model with Performance Degradation

We make the following assumptions for software availability modeling with performance degradation based on the model of [6]:

AI-1. When the software system is operating, the time-interval of operation with performance according to specification, T_s, and the holding time of performance degradation, T_d, follow the exponential distributions with means $1/\theta$ and $1/\eta$, respectively.

AI-2. The software system breaks down and starts to be restored as soon as a software failure occurs, and the system cannot operate until the restoration action completes.

AI-3. The restoration action includes the debugging activity and software reliability growth occurs if a debugging activity is perfect.

AI-4. Consider the imperfect debugging environment where the debugging activity may fail, i.e., it is probabilistic whether the debugging activity succeeds or fails. The debugging activity is perfect with perfect debugging probability

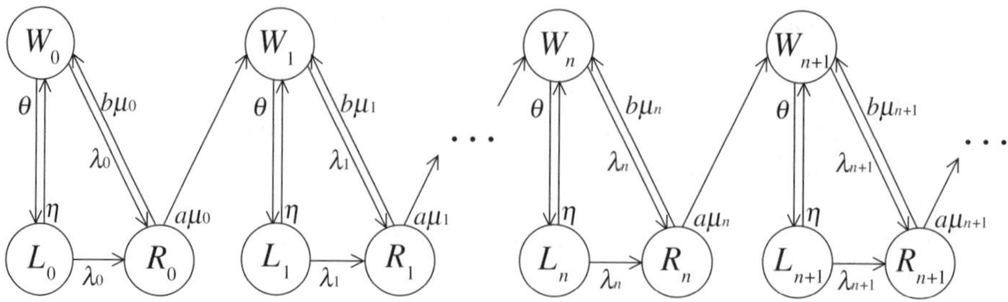

Fig. 1. Sample state transition diagram of $X(t)$

a $(0 < a < 1)$, while imperfect with probability $b(= 1 - a)$. A perfect debugging activity corrects and removes one fault from the system.

AI-5. When n faults have been corrected, the next software failure-occurrence time-interval, U_n, and the restoration time, V_n, follow the exponential distributions with means $1/\lambda_n$ and $1/\mu_n$, respectively.

AI-6. T_s, T_d, U_n, and V_n are mutually independent.

We introduce a stochastic process $\{X(t),\ t \geq 0\}$ representing the user-perceived state of the software system at the time point t. The state space of the process $\{X(t),\ t \geq 0\}$ is defined as follows:

$\boldsymbol{W} = \{W_n : n = 0, 1, 2, \ldots\}$: the system is operating with performance according to specification (desirable operational state),
$\boldsymbol{L} = \{L_n : n = 0, 1, 2, \ldots\}$: the system is operating with degraded performance,
$\boldsymbol{R} = \{R_n : n = 0, 1, 2, \ldots\}$: the system is utterly inoperable and restored,

where $n = 0,\ 1,\ 2,\ \ldots$ denotes the cumulative number of corrected faults. Figure 1 illustrates the sample state transition diagram of $X(t)$.

Let $P_{W_i,A}(t) \equiv \Pr\{X(t) = A|X(0) = W_i\}$ $(A \in \{W_n,\ L_n,\ R_n\};\ i, n = 0,\ 1,\ 2,\ \ldots;\ i \leq n)$ be the state occupancy probability representing the conditional probability that the system is in state A at the time point t on the condition that the system was in state W_i at time point $t = 0$. Then we can obtain $P_{W_i,A}(t)$'s as

$$\left.\begin{aligned} P_{W_i,W_n}(t) &\equiv \Pr\{X(t) = W_n|X(0) = W_i\} \\ &= B^0_{i,n} e^{-(\lambda_n+\theta+\eta)t} + \sum_{m=i}^{n} \left[B^1_{i,n}(m) e^{-d^1_m t} + B^2_{i,n}(m) e^{-d^2_m t}\right] \\ &\quad (i, n = 0,\ 1,\ 2,\ \ldots;\ i \leq n) \\ \left.\begin{matrix} d^1_i \\ d^2_i \end{matrix}\right\} &= \frac{1}{2}\left[(\lambda_i + \mu_i) \pm \sqrt{(\lambda_i + \mu_i)^2 - 4a\lambda_i\mu_i}\right] \\ &\quad \text{(double signs in same order)} \end{aligned}\right\}, \quad (1)$$

$$\begin{aligned} P_{W_i,R_n}(t) &\equiv \Pr\{X(t) = R_n|X(0) = W_i\} \\ &= \frac{g_{i,n+1}(t)}{a\mu_n} \quad (i, n = 0,\ 1,\ 2,\ \ldots;\ i \leq n)\,, \end{aligned} \quad (2)$$

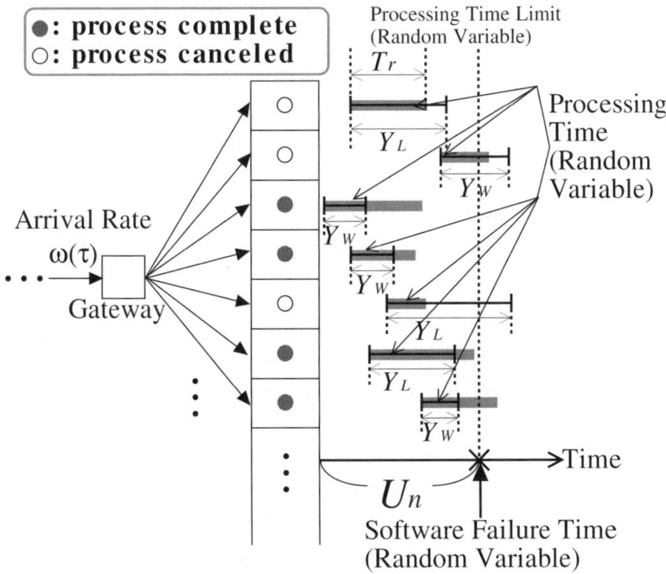

Fig. 2. Configuration of task processing

$$\begin{aligned} P_{W_i,L_n}(t) &\equiv \Pr\{X(t) = L_n | X(0) = W_i\} \\ &= G_{i,n}(t) - G_{i,n+1}(t) - P_{W_i,W_n}(t) - P_{W_i,R_n}(t) \\ &\quad (i, n = 0,\ 1,\ 2,\ \ldots;\ i \leq n)\ , \end{aligned} \tag{3}$$

respectively, where $B^0_{i,n}$, $B^1_{i,n}(m)$, and $B^2_{i,n}(m)$ $(m = i,\ i+1,\ \ldots,\ n)$ in Eq. (1) are constant coefficients, $G_{i,n}(t)$ in Eq. (3) is the distribution function of the first passage time of $X(t)$ from state W_i to state W_n $(i \leq n)$, and $g_{i,n}(t) \equiv \mathrm{d}G_{i,n}(t)/\mathrm{d}t$ in Eq. (2) is the density function of $G_{i,n}(t)$ (see [6] for the details of the derivation processes of $P_{W_i,A}(t)$'s).

3 Model Description and Analysis for Task Processing

We make the following assumptions for system's task processing:

AII-1. The number of tasks the system can process simultaneously is sufficiently large.

AII-2. The process $\{N(t),\ t \geq 0\}$ representing the number of tasks arriving at the system up to the time t follows the NHPP with the arrival rate $\omega(t)$ and the mean value function $\Omega(t) \equiv \mathrm{E}[N(t)] = \int_0^t \omega(x)\mathrm{d}x$.

AII-3. Each task has a processing time limit, T_r, which follows a general distribution whose distribution function is denoted as $F_{T_r}(t) \equiv \Pr\{T_r \leq t\}$.

AII-4. The processing times of a task in state $\boldsymbol{W}$, Y_W, and in state $\boldsymbol{L}$, Y_L, are distributed generally; their distribution functions are denoted as $F_{Y_W}(t) \equiv \Pr\{Y_W \leq t\}$ and $F_{Y_L}(t) \equiv \Pr\{Y_L \leq t\}$ $(\mathrm{E}[Y_W] < \mathrm{E}[Y_L])$, respectively. Each of the processing times is independent. The distribution of the processing time is determined by the state of the system at the time point when the corresponding task has just arrived at the system. In other words, once a task process starts, its distribution does not vary even though the state of the system in operation may change afterward. Y_W, Y_L, and T_r are mutually independent.

AII-5. When the system causes a software failure in task processing or the processing times of tasks exceed the processing time limit, the corresponding tasks are canceled.

Here we derive the distribution of the number of tasks whose processes are complete within the processing time limit. Figure 2 illustrates the configuration of the system's task processing we consider. Hereafter, we set the time origin $t = 0$ at the time point when the debugging activity is complete and i faults are corrected.

Let $\{Z_i^1(t),\ t \geq 0\}$ be the stochastic process representing the cumulative number of tasks whose processes can be complete within the processing time limit out of the tasks arriving up to the time t. By conditioning with $\{N(t) = k\}$, we obtain the probability mass function of $Z_i^1(t)$ as

$$\Pr\{Z_i^1(t) = j\} = \sum_{k=0}^{\infty} \Pr\{Z_i^1(t) = j \mid N(t) = k\} e^{-\Omega(t)} \frac{[\Omega(t)]^k}{k!} . \tag{4}$$

From Fig. 2, the probabilities that the process of an arbitrary task is complete within the processing time limit when the system is in state W_n and state L_n are given by

$$\beta_{W_n} \equiv \Pr\{Y_W < U_n,\ Y_W < T_r \mid X(t) = W_n\} = \int_0^{\infty} e^{-\lambda_n y} \overline{F_{T_r}}(y) \mathrm{d}F_{Y_W}(y), \tag{5}$$

$$\beta_{L_n} \equiv \Pr\{Y_L < U_n,\ Y_L < T_r \mid X(t) = L_n\} = \int_0^{\infty} e^{-\lambda_n y} \overline{F_{T_r}}(y) \mathrm{d}F_{Y_L}(y), \tag{6}$$

respectively, where we denote $\overline{F}(\cdot) \equiv 1 - F(\cdot)$. Furthermore, from the property of the NHPP, given $\{N(t) = k\}$, k arrival times of tasks are independent and identically distributed random variables having the following probability density function [7]:

$$f(x) = \frac{\omega(x)}{\Omega(t)} \quad (0 \leq x \leq t) . \tag{7}$$

Therefore, the probability that the process of an arbitrary task having arrived up to the time t is complete within the processing time limit is obtained as

$$p_i^1(t) = \frac{1}{\Omega(t)} \sum_{n=i}^{\infty} \int_0^t \Big[\beta_{W_n} P_{W_i,W_n}(x) + \beta_{L_n} P_{W_i,L_n}(x)\Big] \omega(x) \mathrm{d}x , \tag{8}$$

from the infinite-server queueing theory [7]. Then from assumption AII-4,

$$\Pr\{Z_i^1(t) = j \mid N(t) = k\} = \binom{k}{j} [p_i^1(t)]^j [1 - p_i^1(t)]^{k-j}$$
$$(j = 0,\ 1,\ 2,\ \ldots,\ k)\ , \tag{9}$$

where $\binom{k}{j} \equiv k!/[(k-j)!j!]$ denotes the binomial coefficient. Equation (9) means that, given that $\{N(t) = k\}$, the number of tasks whose processes can be complete within the processing time limit follows the binomial process with mean $kp_i^1(t)$. Accordingly, from Eq. (4) the distribution of $Z_i^1(t)$ is given by

$$\Pr\{Z_i^1(t) = j\} = e^{-\Omega(t)p_i^1(t)} \frac{[\Omega(t)p_i^1(t)]^j}{j!}\ . \tag{10}$$

Equation (10) means that $\{Z_i^1(t),\ t \geq 0\}$ follows the NHPP with the mean value function $\Omega(t)p_i^1(t)$.

4 Derivation of Software Performability Measures

The expected number of tasks completable out of the tasks arriving up to the time t is given by

$$\Lambda_i^1(t) \equiv \mathrm{E}[Z_i^1(t)] = \sum_{n=i}^{\infty} \int_0^t \Big[\beta_{W_n} P_{W_i,W_n}(x) + \beta_{L_n} P_{W_i,L_n}(x)\Big] \omega(x) \mathrm{d}x\ . \tag{11}$$

Furthermore, the instantaneous task completion ratio is obtained as

$$\upsilon_i^1(t) \equiv \frac{\mathrm{d}\Lambda_i^1(t)}{\mathrm{d}t} \Big/ \omega(t) = \sum_{n=i}^{\infty} \Big[\beta_{W_n} P_{W_i,W_n}(t) + \beta_{L_n} P_{W_i,L_n}(t)\Big]\ , \tag{12}$$

which represents the ratio of the number of tasks completed within the processing time limit to one arriving at the system per unit time at the time point t. As to $p_i^1(t)$ in Eq. (8), we can give the following interpretations:

$$p_i^1(t) = \frac{\mathrm{E}[Z_i^1(t)]}{\mathrm{E}[N(t)]}\ . \tag{13}$$

That is, $p_i^1(t)$ is the cumulative task completion ratio up to the time t.

We should note that it is too difficult to use Eqs. (11)–(13) practically since this model assumes the imperfect debugging environment. However, we can convert Eqs. (11)–(13) into the functions of the number of debuggings, l, i.e., we obtain

$$\Lambda^1(t,l) = \sum_{i=0}^{l} \binom{l}{i} a^i b^{l-i} \Lambda_i^1(t) \quad (t \geq 0;\ l = 0,\ 1,\ 2,\ \ldots)\ , \tag{14}$$

$$\upsilon^1(t,l) = \sum_{i=0}^{l} \binom{l}{i} a^i b^{l-i} \upsilon_i^1(t) \quad (t \geq 0;\ l = 0,\ 1,\ 2,\ \ldots)\ , \tag{15}$$

$$p^1(t,l) = \frac{1}{\Omega(t)} \sum_{i=0}^{l} \binom{l}{i} a^i b^{l-i} \Lambda_i^1(t) \quad (t \geq 0;\ l = 0,\ 1,\ 2,\ \ldots)\ , \tag{16}$$

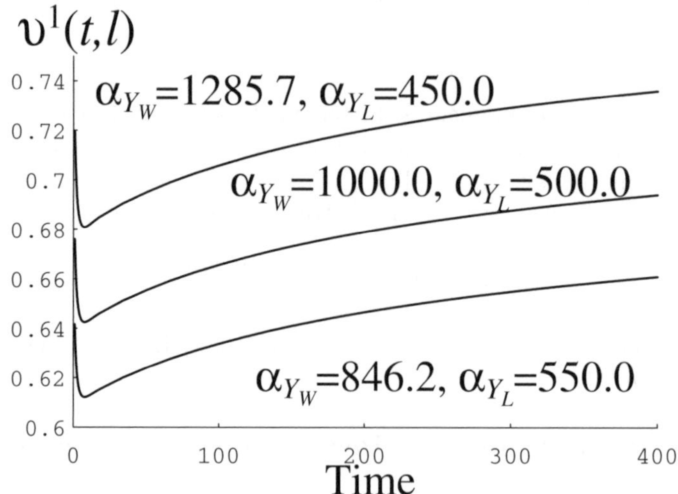

Fig. 3. Dependence of $\upsilon^1(t,l)$ on the values of α_{Y_W} and α_{Y_L}, given $1/\alpha_{Y_W} + 1/\alpha_{Y_L} = 0.003$ ($l = 0,\ \theta = 5.0,\ \eta = 48.0,\ \alpha_{T_r} = 400.0;\ a = 0.8,\ D = 0.246,\ c = 0.94,\ E = 1.114,\ r = 0.96$)

respectively. Equations (14)–(16) represent the expected cumulative number of tasks completable, the instantaneous and the cumulative task completion ratios at the time point t, given that the l-th debugging is complete at time point $t = 0$, respectively. It should be noted that Eq. (15) has no bearing on the task arrival process, $\Omega(t)$.

5 Numerical Example

Here we apply the model of Moranda [8] to the hazard rate λ_n and the restoration rate μ_n in the numerical example, i.e., $\lambda_n \equiv Dc^n$ ($D > 0,\ 0 < c < 1$) and $\mu_n \equiv Er^n$ ($E > 0,\ 0 < r \leq 1$), respectively. For the distributions of the processing times in state $\boldsymbol{W}$, $F_{Y_W}(t)$, and in state $\boldsymbol{L}$, $F_{Y_L}(t)$, and the processing time limit, $F_{T_r}(t)$, we apply the gamma distribution of order two denoted by

$$F_I(t) \equiv H(t|\alpha_I) = 1 - (1 + \alpha_I t)e^{-\alpha_I t}$$
$$(t \geq 0;\ \alpha_I > 0;\ I \in \{Y_W, Y_L, T_r\}) \,, \tag{17}$$

where α_I denotes the scale parameter, and the mean and the variance are given by $2/\alpha_I$ and $2/(\alpha_I{}^2)$, respectively.

Figure 3 shows the dependence of the instantaneous task completion ratio, $\upsilon^1(t,l)$, in Eq. (15) on the values of α_{Y_W} and α_{Y_L}, given the arithmetic average of the means of the processing times, i.e., the value of $(2/\alpha_{Y_W} + 2/\alpha_{Y_L})/2$ is constant. This figure displays that the case where the difference of performance levels between state $\boldsymbol{W}$ and state $\boldsymbol{L}$ becomes smaller decreases the performability evaluation of the whole system.

6 Concluding Remarks

In this paper, we have constructed the stochastic performability evaluation model for the software system with processing time limit, considering the performance degradation in system operation. Assuming that the cumulative number of the tasks arriving at the system up to a given time point follows the NHPP, we have analyzed the distribution of the number of tasks whose processes can be complete with the concept of the infinite-server queueing model. From the model, we have derived several software performability measures considering the real-time property. They have been given as the functions of time and the number of debuggings. We have also illustrated the numerical example of these measures.

Acknowledgments. This work was supported in part by Grants-in-Aid for Scientific Research (C) of Japan Society for the Promotion of Science under Grant No. 20510136 and Takahashi Industrial and Economic Research Foundation.

References

1. Okamura, H., Miyahara, S., Dohi, T.: Dependability Analysis of a Transaction-Based Multi-Server System with Rejuvenation. IEICE Trans. Fundamentals E86-A, 2081–2090 (2003)
2. Eto, H., Dohi, T.: Analysis of a Service Degradation Model with Preventive Rejuvenation. In: Penkler, D., Reitenspiess, M., Tam, F. (eds.) ISAS 2006. LNCS, vol. 4328, pp. 17–29. Springer, Heidelberg (2006)
3. Schwefel, H.-P., Antonios, I.: Performability Models for Multi-Server Systems with High-Variance Repair Durations. In: 37th Annual IEEE/IFIP International Conference on Dependable Systems and Networks, pp. 770–779 (2007)
4. Musa, J.D.: Software Reliability Engineering. McGraw-Hill, New York (1999)
5. Muppala, J.K., Woolet, S.P., Trivedi, K.S.: Real-Time-Systems Performance in the Presence of Failures. Comput. 24, 37–47 (1991)
6. Tokuno, K., Yamada, S.: User-Perceived Software Service Availability Modeling with Reliability Growth. In: Nanya, T., Maruyama, F., Pataricza, A., Malek, M. (eds.) ISAS 2008. LNCS, vol. 5017, pp. 75–89. Springer, Heidelberg (2008)
7. Ross, S.M.: Introduction to Probability Models, 9th edn. Academic Press, San Diego (2007)
8. Moranda, P.B.: Event-Altered Rate Models for General Reliability Analysis. IEEE Trans. Reliability R-28, 376–381 (1979)

An Experimental Evaluation of Error Rate in a Web Server System

Xiao Xiao and Tadashi Dohi

Department of Information Engineering, Graduate School of Engineering
Hiroshima University, 1–4–1 Kagamiyama, Higashi-Hiroshima, 739–8527 Japan
{xiaoxiao,dohi}@rel.hiroshima-u.ac.jp

Abstract. In this paper we focus on the relationship between the error rate which is one of the representative reliability measures in Apache web servers and the system parameters which reflect on the web server's system performance, and develop a probability model to describe it. More specifically, we implement a simple client server system and carry out an experiment to measure both the error rate and the system parameters. As the result on quantitative evaluation of the proposed logit model, it is shown that our model could fit the empirical error rate with varying the number of threads.

Keywords: web server reliability, Apache web server, system parameters, error rate, measurement-based approach, logit model.

1 Introduction

In the informational society where internet is widely spreaded, a very important issue is to keep the performance of web service systems. In this point of view, quantitative evaluation of the workload becomes necessary in operational web server performance assessment. Barford and Crovella [1] developed a tool that automatically measures six metrics that characterize the web server's workload such as the size of server file, the request size and so on. Hu, Nanda and Yang [2] focused on the Apache server that can operate on a single processor or 4-CPU-SMP (symmetric multi-processor) system, and executed the experimental performance evaluation of the Apache web server. van der Mei, Hariharan and Reeser [3] proposed an end-to-end performance evaluation model of the web server system which is based on a tandem type of queueing model, and investigated effectiveness of the model through simulation experiments. Nahum, Barzilai and Kandlur [4] also evaluated the performance of www server on UNIX platform, and developed a method that can efficiently reduce the server throughput. Cao *et al.* [5] considered analytically a queueing model that evaluates the performance of the web server, and derived the performance evaluation measures such as the average response time and the blocking probability, *etc.*

In this paper, similar to Hu, Nanda and Yang [2], we consider a quantitative evaluation of the Apache web server which is the most commonly used web server software. Due in good part to the broad utilization of Apache web server, it is

D. Ślęzak et al. (Eds.): ASEA 2009, CCIS 59, pp. 272–279, 2009.

considered that our challange in this paper may be capable of wide application. Moreover, we choose Apache web server, but not IIS or AN HTTPD, also for the following advantages; (i) it is a freeware, (ii) adequate responses for questions by the users are easily available from the Apache community when any technical problem occurred, (iii) the reliability as a server software is quite high, (iv) it possesses a variety of technical functions, (v) it corresponds to many kinds of operational circumstances. In this way, the Apache web server can demonstrate an enough performance even as it is, but a higher performance can be attained by ascertaining the bottleneck and by evaluating the performance through *load test*. Sugiki, Kono and Iwasaki [6] showed that the server throughput can be improved by the self-adjustment of the keep-alive time, and implemented it on a library of the Apache web server. Though a lot of tools have been developed up to now as load test tools, the Apache JMeter [7] is often used in the actual performance assessment of server systems.

In general, there are three performance evaluation measures in the Apache JMeter; mean response time, error rate and system throughput. In this paper, we focus on the error rate to assess the reliability of the Apache web server system. Unlike the general performance evaluation problem, there are very a few works related to the web server reliability. Shereshevsky *et al.* [8] constructed a simple client server system composed of two machines, and found the multifractal nature between software aging phenomenon [9] and the memory resource parameters. Also they examined the problem of forecasting the time to the system failure. Gokhale, Vandal and Lu [10] applied a stochastic model which is called *stochastic reward net* to carry out the throughput/reliability analysis based on the architecture of the Apache web server. However in the previous works, the system parameters which influence both the system performance and the error rate were not clarified. Hence the quantitative evaluation model to describe the error-occurrence mechanism of the web server system should be explored.

In this paperĄCwe take a measurement-based approach under the load test circumstance and propose a simple logit model which can describe the relationship between the error rate and the system parameters. The logit model is the well-known nonlinear regression model that is frequently used in the field of econometrics and the medical statistics. We construct an experiment system to measure the system parameters under the assumption that multiple clients send HTTP (Hypertext Transfer Protocol) requests to a web server randomly. We define the error rate as a ratio of the number of failed requests recognized as time-out errors when there is no response from the server for a constant response time period. Based on the logit model and its related standard techniques for statistical inference, we estimate the model parameters and perform the goodness-of-fit test on it. The rest part of this paper is organized as follows. In Section 2 we briefly explain the experimental setup in our study and describe the data sets collected in the experiments. Section 3 is spent for introduction of the logit model and its related parameter estimation with the least squares principle. The goodness-of-fit test result is presented in Section 4. Finally Section 5 contains some concluding remarks and the possible directions to the future research.

	Client	Server
	Request	index. jsp
OS	Windows XP	Windows 2000
Processor	2.59GHz	850MHz
RAM	2.00GB	128MB
Software	Apache JMeter (version 2.1.01082007)	Apache Server (version 2.2.4)

Fig. 1. Experimental setup

2 Experiments

2.1 Experimental Setup

In our experimental setup, the client-server system consists of an Apache server (version 2.2.4) on a Windows platform and a client connected via a local LAN. The system components and system structure are illustrated in Figure 1. In this experimental setup with only one client, we put the homepage, index.jsp, in the home directory of the web server and use the Apache JMeter [7] to generate HTTP requests that access the homepage randomly. In this way, we represent an environment where multiple clients randomly access the web server. Basically, there are three parameters we can use to control the workload of web server; (i) *number of threads* (users), (ii) *ramp-up period* (in seconds) and (iii) *loop count*. For instance, if these three parameters are set to be 20, 10 and 5, respectively, then it means that 20 clients send HTTP requests 5 times severally while all the 100 requests are started within 10 seconds. In our experiments, we fix the ramp-up period (in seconds) as 10 seconds and the loop count an infinity ("Forever" checkbox is selected) meanwhile the number of threads is set to be 30, 40 and 50. So, three kinds of workload environments are generated under this experiment.

2.2 Data Collection

We are interested in the error rate which is defined by

$$R_i = \frac{\text{the number of } HTTP \text{ requests failed by time } i}{\text{the number of } HTTP \text{ requests generated by time } i}, \tag{1}$$

where the failed HTTP requests are those caused by the time-out error and $i = 1, 2, \ldots$ denote the discrete time index. The error rate is automatically recorded on *the Aggregate Report* of the Apache JMeter, so we only need to collect the data of system parameters that reflect on the web server's performance. Since we focus on the system parameters concerned with memory resource usage, we employ the *Performance*, which is one of the Windows 2000 system tools, to take log files of these system parameters. Table 1 presents 9 system parameters

Table 1. System parameters

AB $(k=1)$	size of the virtual memory available currently
CaB $(k=2)$	number of bytes currently in use by the system cache
CoB $(k=3)$	size of virtual memory that has been committed
PNA $(k=4)$	number of calls to allocate space in the system nonpaged pool
PNB $(k=5)$	number of bytes in the nonpaged pool
PPA $(k=6)$	number of calls to allocate space in the system paged pool
PPB $(k=7)$	number of bytes in the paged pool
PPRB $(k=8)$	size of paged pool resident in core memory
SCRB $(k=9)$	number of bytes of system code total bytes currentlyresident in core memeory

which describe the momentary statement of the web server system, where for the notational convenience, we denote AB $\sim$ SCRB as system parameters $k = 1 \sim 9$ hereafter.

In our experiments, we set the operation time (time limit for web server system working per experiment) as 30 minutes and take the record every 10 seconds. Then since we obtain a sample with 180 data from one experiment, this procedure is repeated for $n = 30$ times when the number of threads is set to 30, 40 or 50. The main reason why the operation time is set to be 30 minutes is that the error rate tends to converge to a constant value after a while, so we stop the experiment every 30 minute which can be considered as a proper time limit.

3 Logit Model

3.1 Regression-Based Model

From the above discussion we know that system parameters concerned with memory resource usage may reflect the total performance of the web server. On the other hand, the error rate can be considered as one of the important reliability measures of the web server. Then the question is what the dependence of the system parameters on the error rate is. To this end, we propose a simple probability model to describe the relationship between multiple system parameters and the error rate. It is worth mentioning that in our situation the usual linear regression model is inappropriate because the error rate takes positive values less than one. The logit model under consideration can represent the error rate as a function of multiple system parameters used as explanatory variables and can bridge between them.

Let R_i $(0 \leq R_i \leq 1)$ and $\boldsymbol{x}_i = (x_{0,i}, x_{1,i}, \cdots, x_{9,i})$ denote the error rate and the system parameter vector observed at time i $(= 1,\ 2,\ \cdots)$ with $x_{0,i} = 1$. Then the error rate can be expressed as a function of system parameters by

$$R_i = R(\boldsymbol{x}_i) = \frac{\exp(\boldsymbol{\beta}\boldsymbol{x}_i^T)}{1 + \exp(\boldsymbol{\beta}\boldsymbol{x}_i^T)}, \tag{2}$$

where $\boldsymbol{\beta} = (\beta_0, \beta_1, \cdots, \beta_9)$ is the regression coefficient and T means transposition. Next, applying the logit transformation to function R_i yields

$$Y_i = Y(\boldsymbol{x}_i) = \log\left(\frac{R(\boldsymbol{x}_i)}{1 - R(\boldsymbol{x}_i)}\right). \tag{3}$$

Based on the above transform, we consider the following linear regression model:

$$Y_i = \boldsymbol{\beta}\boldsymbol{x}_i^T + \epsilon, \tag{4}$$

where ϵ is the Gaussian error term. More formally, we make the following assumptions:

(Assumption 1). The mean of error term is zero, *i.e.*, $\mathrm{E}[\epsilon] = 0$.
(Assumption 2). The variance of error term is constant, *i.e.*, $\mathrm{Var}[\epsilon] = \sigma^2$.
(Assumption 3). The covariance of error term is zero, *i.e.*, $\mathrm{E}[\epsilon_i \epsilon_{i'}] = 0$ $(i \neq i', i = 1, \cdots, n, i' = 1, \cdots, n)$.
(Assumption 4). The probability density function of ϵ is given by $p(y) = (2\pi\sigma^2)^{-1/2} \exp[-y^2/2\sigma^2]$.

At each observation time point, $i = 1,\ 2, \cdots,\ 180$, we repeat to observe Y_i and $\boldsymbol{x}_i$ $n = 30$ times and estimate the regression coefficients $\boldsymbol{\beta}$ by means of the well-known mean squares error method. It is noted that this statistical estimation method can be validated by the well-known Gauss-Markov Theorem, so an estimate of regression coefficient $\boldsymbol{\beta}$ is given by the solution of

$$\min_{\boldsymbol{\beta}} \sum_{j=1}^{n} \sum_{i=1}^{180} \left(y_{i,j} - \sum_{k=0}^{9} \beta_k x_{k,i,j} \right)^2, \tag{5}$$

where $y_{i,j}$ denotes the logit transformed value of the error rate observed at time i in the jth experiment, while $x_{k,i,j}$ denotes the value of system parameter k observed at time i in the jth experiment.

In order to predict the long-term behavior of the error rate, it is needed to know the future values of system parameters. If the system parameters are known in advance it is easy to estimate regression coefficients with the least squares method. In the case where system parameters can not be observed, on the other hand, we need to predict both of regression coefficients and the system parameters. In our experiences through the experiments, it is found that the system parameters, CoB, PPB and PPRB, almost take constant values, while the other parameters tend to show non-constant trends with stationary trend. To estimate the future system parameter values we apply a simple linear regression model and use the estimated values to predict the long-term behavior of the error rate.

Let $x_{k,i}$ denote the value of system parameter k observed at time $i = 1,\ 2, \cdots,$ 180. Define the time vector $I = (1, i)$ and assume that the system parameter is a function of time i. Then $x_{k,i}$ takes the following form:

$$x_{k,i} = \boldsymbol{\alpha}_k \cdot \boldsymbol{i}^T = \alpha_{k,0} + I \cdot \alpha_{k,1}, \tag{6}$$

Table 2. RSS with monitoring system parameters

(1) no. threads = 30

RSS	n= 5	n=10	n=15	n=20	n=25	n=30
SampleEva01	817.51	131.03	87.12	68.34	56.94	47.83
SampleEva02	1125.75	976.43	205.12	202.35	187.05	165.95
SampleEva03	2588.02	134.67	116.89	122.15	113.90	121.15

(2) no. threads = 40

RSS	n= 5	n=10	n=15	n=20	n=25	n=30
SampleEva01	2340.30	144.59	87.86	85.10	79.26	78.93
SampleEva02	764.98	150.68	101.08	86.74	117.78	95.78
SampleEva03	1850.64	160.73	101.68	83.56	69.95	69.77

(3) no. threads = 50

RSS	n= 5	n=10	n=15	n=20	n=25	n=30
SampleEva01	1069.71	182.56	161.20	160.84	141.05	149.22
SampleEva02	1552.62	322.55	227.00	189.76	254.09	205.14
SampleEva03	1990.38	182.71	177.87	172.81	156.76	154.76

where $\boldsymbol{\alpha}_k = (\alpha_{k,0}, \alpha_{k,1})$ is the regression coefficient of system parameter k. Then an estimate of system parameter is given by $\boldsymbol{\alpha}_k$ which is the solution of the following minimization problem:

$$\min_{\boldsymbol{\alpha}_k} \sum_{i=1}^{180} [x_{k,i} - (\alpha_{k,0} + I\ \alpha_{k,1})]^2. \tag{7}$$

Finally, from estimates of $\boldsymbol{\alpha}_k$ it is possible to obtain estimates of $x_{k,i}$ and the error rate in an arbitrary time.

4 Real Data Analysis

In this section, we apply the logit model to the measurement data. To evaluate the prediction performance of the logit model, we use the standardized residual sum of squares (RSS) as a criterion to quantify the estimation/prediction ability. For the fixed number of threads, we execute 33 experiments in parallel, where 30 data sets are used for estimation (training) and 3 data sets are used to investigate the prediction performance. The regression coefficients, $\boldsymbol{\beta}$ and $\boldsymbol{\alpha}_k$, are estimated 6 times while the number of experiment, n, is set to be n = 5, 10, 15, 20, 25 or 30. All the statistical analysis executed in this paper is employed with the well-known statistical analysis package, R [11].

Table 2 presents the goodness-of-fit result when the number of threads is fixed as 30, 40 or 50. The values in this table show the RSS between the observed error rate and its estimates via the least squares method, where n denotes experiment times in the estimation of regression coefficient $\boldsymbol{\beta}$. It is evident that as the number of samples increases, the estimation accuracy becomes much better. This is not a surprising result, because it is no wonder that the more available measurement

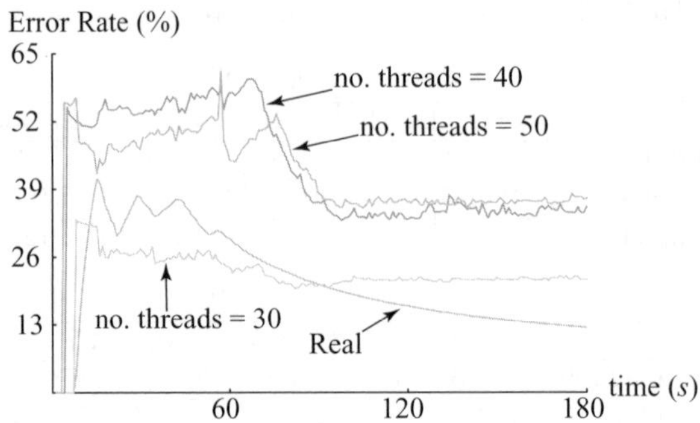

Fig. 2. Comparison among different no. threads

Table 3. RSS with predictions of system parameters

(1) no. threads = 30

RSS	n= 5	n=10	n=15	n=20	n=25	n=30
SampleEva01	464.18	236.39	133.81	117.20	92.96	98.53
SampleEva02	634.64	346.72	202.75	176.29	134.97	145.21
SampleEva03	382.46	196.86	122.98	113.23	100.74	103.08

(2) no. threads = 40

RSS	n= 5	n=10	n=15	n=20	n=25	n=30
SampleEva01	407.96	330.16	333.28	284.82	270.96	259.55
SampleEva02	539.67	434.92	439.24	367.98	344.96	366.02
SampleEva03	332.09	270.58	273.00	237.88	229.39	252.64

(3) no. threads = 50

RSS	n= 5	n=10	n=15	n=20	n=25	n=30
SampleEva01	286.90	322.69	283.32	247.02	239.25	252.74
SampleEva02	488.27	540.77	462.08	373.89	348.89	328.13
SampleEva03	287.03	318.50	294.24	277.60	276.34	314.75

data, the better the accuracy will be. However, it seems to be interesting to take notice on the results among different threads. SampleEva01 gives the smallest RSS when the number of threads is set to be 30, while SampleEva02 and SampleEva03 show smaller RSS in (2) than that in (3) of Table 3. This suggests that our logit model is more suitable for lower number of threads, or to say, it is more capable in a lighter workload situation. This result behaves much more clear in the following prediction part (refer to Table 3). As the result of parameter estimation, it can be checked that the error rate behaves as a multi-modal function of time and is right-skewed. This feature of error rate is captured by the proposed model rather excellently, and Figure 2 gives an obvious idea about this result.

Our next concern is the long-term prediction of the error rate as well as the system parameters. The RSS between the predicted and observed error rate is presented in Table 3, where the regression coefficient $\boldsymbol{\beta}$ is estimated by the least squares method. It should be noted that the value of system parameter $\boldsymbol{x}_i$ is a predictive one based on the linear regression model, but not the actual observations. It is a natural conclusion that $\boldsymbol{\alpha}_k$ can be estimated better as the number of experiments monotonically increases.

5 Conclusion

In this paper, we have proposed a simple logit model to describe the relation between the error rate, which is the representative reliability measure in the Apache web server, and the system parameters which reflect on the web server's system performance. By combining a simple linear regression model with the logit model, we have estimated the long-term behavior of the error rate and the system parameters simultaneously. It will be necessary, of course, to improve the estimation and prediction accuracy of the logit model in future. Especially, it is worth considering a novel approach to represent the situation where the workload varies dynamically.

References

1. Barford, P., Crovella, M.: Generating representative web workloads for network and server performance evaluation. In: Proceedings of 1998 ACM SIGMETRICS International Conference on Measurement and Modeling of Computer Systems (SIGMETRICS 1998), pp. 151–160. ACM, New York (1998)
2. Hu, Y., Nanda, A., Yang, Q.: Measurement, analysis and performance improvement of the Apache web server. In: Proceedings of 18th IEEE International Performance, Computing and Communications Conference (IPCCC 1999), pp. 261–267. IEEE CS Press, Los Alamitos (1999)
3. van der Mei, R.D., Hariharan, R., Reeser, P.K.: Web server performance modeling. Telecommunication Systems 16(3/4), 361–378 (2001)
4. Nahum, E., Barzilai, T., Kandlur, D.: Performance issues in www servers. IEEE/ACM Transactions on Networking 10(1), 2–11 (2002)
5. Cao, J., Andersson, M., Nyberg, C., Kihl, M.: Web server performance modeling using an $M/G/1/K^*PS$ queue. In: Proceedings of 10th International Conference on Telecommunications (ICT 2003), pp. 1501–1506. IEEE, Los Alamitos (2003)
6. Sugiki, A., Kono, K., Iwasaki, H.: Tuning mechanisms for two major parameters of Apache web servers. Software – Practice and Experience 38(12), 1215–1240 (2008)
7. JMeter - Apache JMeter, http://jakarta.apache.org/jmeter/
8. Shereshevsky, M., Cukic, B., Crowel, J., Gandikota, V., Liu, Y.: Software aging and multifractality of memory resources. In: Proceedings of IEEE/IFIP International Conference on Dependable Systems and Networks (DSN 2003), pp. 721–730. IEEE CS Press, Los Alamitos (2003)
9. Grottke, M., Trivedi, K.S.: Fighting bugs: remove, retry, replicate, and rejuvenate. IEEE Computer 40(2), 107–109 (2007)
10. Gokhale, S.S., Vandal, P.J., Lu, J.: Performance and reliability analysis of web server software architectures. In: Proceedings of 12th Pacific Rim International Symposium on Dependable Computing (PRDC 2006), pp. 351–358. IEEE CS Press, Los Alamitos (2006)
11. http://www.r-project.org/

A New Criterion for the Optimal Software Release Problems: Moving Average Quality Control Chart with Bootstrap Sampling

Mitsuhiro Kimura[1,⋆] and Takaji Fujiwara[2]

[1] Faculty of Science and Engineering, Hosei University,
3-7-2 Kajino-cho, Koganei-shi, Tokyo, 184-8584 Japan
kim@hosei.ac.jp
[2] Business Cube & Partners, Inc.,
1-20-18 Ebisu, Shibuya-ku, Tokyo, 150-0013 Japan
fujiwara.takaji@nifty.com

Abstract. This paper proposes a new practical method for determining when to stop software testing. This issue has been widely known as the optimal release problem of software product, and many researchers have been developing mathematical models for finding the solution.

We try to develop a new quality control charting to help making the right decision for it, by employing the moving average model and bootstrap scheme. After discussing the modeling, we show an example of the statistical decision making of the optimal software release time.

Keywords: software reliability, optimal release problem, moving average, control chart, bootstrap method.

1 Introduction

Recently, software systems have been becoming the integral part of computer systems. Since any software system could cause severe consequences due to software failures, the reliability of the software system is a primary concern for both software developers and users. Then, in the final stage of software development, testing is an important activity for detecting and removing software faults and improving reliability/quality of the software system. However, since it is impossible to detect and remove all the faults latent in the software system within a reasonable testing period, it needs a method for assessing and analyzing quantitatively the software reliability/quality during the testing. As one method for solving this problem, many software reliability growth models (abbreviated as SRGMs) reflecting testing- and operational-environment factors have been proposed. Especially, the SRGMs based on nonhomogeneous Poisson processes (abbreviated as NHPPs) have been widely and successfully applied to the practical

⋆ This work was partially supported by KAKENHI, the Grant-in-Aid of Scientific Research (C)(20500036).

D. Ślęzak et al. (Eds.): ASEA 2009, CCIS 59, pp. 280–287, 2009.

software development activities. For example, developers have used the assessment results derived by SRGMs in order to determine when to stop the testing and release the software product as an important management issue during the testing. We call this issue a software optimal release problem as developer's decision-making problem.

Until now, there have been optimal release problems considering the cost spent in the reliability growth processes in the testing-phase [1],[2], the difference of environment which surrounds the software between the testing- and operation-phase [3], and the reliability/safety requirements to the cost spent in the testing- and operation-phase [4] as assessment criteria. Furthermore, Fujiwara et al. [5] have proposed testing-termination criteria as a new paradigm. This has set up the allowable ratio of remaining faults as a targeted value by applying the common knowledge that all latent faults in the software system cannot be removed, and has proposed that it is the optimal release time. Here, the allowable ratio of remaining faults is determined in consideration of the characteristics of the software system. However, since this proposed method significantly depends on the analysts' experience, we have often observed that there exists a large deviation between a predicted value of the evaluation and its actual value. Based on this fact, we have found that the system analysts are anxious to obtain unbiased analysis results in terms of their experiences.

In this paper, we discuss a methodology to determine the optimal release time based on the allowable ratio of remaining faults without depending on the present analysts' experience. Especially, we propose the method of computing the achievement degree to the targeted value for the allowable ratio of remaining faults based on probability theory and statistics.

2 Concept of the Optimal Release Policy

In this section, we describe methodology of determining the optimal release time based on the allowable ratio of remaining faults.

In practical projects which we have experienced, we have usually grasped the validity and the severity of testing-activities by plotting past analysis records as shown in Fig. 1. Based on such a plot, we have judged whether it is releasable based on the time-dependent behavior by plotting past analysis-records, i.e., the achievement date of the allowable ratio of remaining faults could be obtained for every analysis and evaluation. Figure 1 sets the analysis-execution date for a horizontal axis and the releasable date based on analysis result for a vertical one. Here, the optimal release time based on the allowable ratio of remaining faults means the date that the estimated latent faults in the software system will reach below the targeted value. From Fig. 1, we can judge when to stop the testing and release the software product to a customer. That is, at the 'State 1' in Fig. 1, we need to make a judgment that the additional testing is still required, because the releasable date is scattered according to the insufficient information from the testing process to be performed. On the other hand, at the 'State 2' in Fig. 1, we can see that it is the right time when we should judge

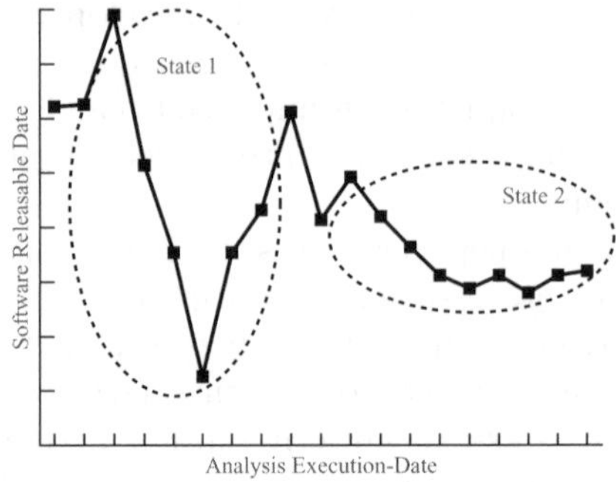

Fig. 1. Conceptual illustration of stabilizing behavior of an assessment measure

whether we can stop the testing, because the releasable date is in the converged state on a certain date, when the software faults are almost squeezed out.

Based on these concepts and ideas, we develop a new quality control charting methodology based on the moving average scheme in this paper, in order to help making the right decision of the optimal software release time.

3 Model Description

Consider that we have a time series of estimated values of software reliability assessment results in a software testing phase. These values might be obtained by, for example, software reliability growth models or some kinds of statistical ones. In this paper, we assume that such an estimated value is deeply related to the allowable ratio discussed in the previous section. First we explain the modeling.

Let X_i $(i = j, j+1, \ldots, n$; usually $1 \ll j)$ be the random variable representing the i-th estimator of a software reliability assessment measure, which is obtained at the testing time t_i. Therefore X_j denotes the estimator which is firstly obtained by a certain statistical estimation scheme for the data set. We assume X_i has a finite mean μ_i and variance σ_i^2.

Although it should be discussed which assessment measure is suitable for the aim of the software release problem, we choose the number of remaining software faults as the estimator in this paper. Thus, a realization of X_i, which is denoted by x_i, represents the i-th estimate of the number of remaining software faults.

One of the most simple quality control charting is to plot x_i itself along with the index i. The index i shows the time point of performing the estimation of X_i, and the time of estimation is t_i.

In principle, x_i contains some statistical errors even if t_i is close to the end of the planned testing schedule. In order to reduce the fluctuation of x_i on the control chart, we use a k-term moving average of X_i (at least $k < n$) for the evaluation. We think this is the second easiest way to plot the control chart, however, the variance of the moving average is affected according to the correlation of X_is.

Let $M_{i,k}$ be a random variable representing k-term moving average at t_i by

$$M_{i,k} = \frac{1}{k} \sum_{q=i-(k-1)}^{i} X_q. \tag{1}$$

Then the expectation and variance of $M_{i,k}$ are respectively given by

$$\mathrm{E}[M_{i,k}] = \frac{1}{k} \sum_{q=i-(k-1)}^{i} \mu_q, \tag{2}$$

$$\mathrm{Var}[M_{i,k}] = \frac{1}{k^2} \sum_{q=i-(k-1)}^{i} \sigma_q^2 + \frac{2}{k^2} \sum_{\substack{l,m=i-(k-1),\ldots,i \\ l \neq m}} \mathrm{Cov}[X_l, X_m], \tag{3}$$

where Cov$[X, Y]$ represents a covariance of the random variable X and Y.

3.1 Evaluation of Cov$[X, Y]$

In this paper, our software quality control chart employs the k-term moving average with its standard deviation (abbreviated by SD in the following). The realization of X_i, namely x_i, is the estimate of the number of remaining software faults. It is natural to consider that there exist the correlations between X_l and X_m in Eq. (3). However, since no one iteratively performs random (black-box) software test in the real situation, we obtain only one series of x_i $(i = j, j+1, \ldots, n)$ from the software faults detection process. This means that we cannot evaluate Cov$[X_l, X_m]$ in such a usual software testing environment.

Conversely, if we perform iteratively random software testing of K times, we will have K sets of the sequence x_i, like

$$\left.\begin{array}{ccccc} x_{j,1}, & x_{j+1,1}, & x_{j+2,1}, & \cdots, & x_{n,1} \\ x_{j,2}, & x_{j+1,2}, & x_{j+2,2}, & \cdots, & x_{n,2} \\ \wr & \wr & \wr & \cdots & \wr \\ x_{j,K}, & x_{j+1,K}, & x_{j+2,K}, & \cdots, & x_{n,K} \end{array}\right\}. \tag{4}$$

Thus we can evaluate the sample covariances for Eq.(3) by using these $K \times (n - (j-1))$ estimates. For example, we have

$$\widehat{\mathrm{Cov}}[X_l, X_m] = \hat{\mathrm{E}}[(X_l - \mu_l)(X_m - \mu_m)] = \frac{1}{K-1} \sum_{i=1}^{K} (x_{l,i} - \hat{\mu}_l)(x_{m,i} - \hat{\mu}_m), \tag{5}$$

where

$$\hat{\mu}_l = \frac{1}{K} \sum_{i=1}^{K} x_{l,i}, \quad \hat{\mu}_m = \frac{1}{K} \sum_{i=1}^{K} x_{m,i}. \tag{6}$$

In order to evaluate K sample sequences of the estimates shown by Eq. (4), we use a bootstrap sampling method based on the incomplete gamma function model [6].

3.2 Bootstrap Sampling with Incomplete Gamma Function Model

In this study, we assume that the original data set to be analyzed forms $(t_i,\ y_i)$ $(i = 1, 2, \ldots, n)$, where t_i means the i-th testing time recorded and y_i the cumulative number of detected (and removed) software faults up to t_i. We also assume that $0 < y_1 < y_2 < \ldots < y_n$ is satisfied.

In the incomplete gamma function model, a simple linear regression analysis is applied to the transformed data sequence as follows. That is, we prepare it by

$$z(c, d, t_i) = \begin{cases} \log\left[\frac{1}{2}\left\{\frac{y_{i+1}-y_i}{t_{i+1}-t_i} + \frac{y_i-y_{i-1}}{t_i-t_{i-1}}\right\}/y_i^c/t_i^d\right] & (1 \le i \le n-1) \\ \log\left[\frac{y_n-y_{n-1}}{t_n-t_{n-1}}/y_n^c/t_n^d\right] & (i = n) \end{cases}, \quad (7)$$

where $t_0 \equiv 0$ and $y_0 \equiv 0$, and two parameters c and d influence a performance of the model. By using $(t_i, z(c, d, t_i))$ $(i = 1, 2, \ldots, n)$, we apply the following linear regression model.

$$z(c, d, t_i) = A - Bt_i + \epsilon_i \quad (i = 1, 2, \ldots, n), \quad (8)$$

where A and B are the unknown constant parameters and ϵ_i represents an error term. Eq. (7) comes from the following modeling. Let $H(t)$ be a non-negative, increasing, and differentiable function to track the behavior of (t_i, y_i). Considering

$$\log\left\{\frac{dH(t)}{dt}/H(t)^c/t^d\right\} = A - Bt, \quad (9)$$

we obtain $H(t)$ as a solution of the differential equation above as

$$H(t) = \begin{cases} \left[(1-c)\{C_1 - \frac{e^A}{B^{d+1}}\Gamma[d+1, Bt]\}\right]^{\frac{1}{1-c}} & (\text{if } c \neq 1) \\ \left[C_1 \exp[-\frac{e^A}{B^{d+1}}\Gamma[d+1, Bt]\right] & (\text{if } c = 1) \end{cases}, \quad (10)$$

where C_1 is an arbitrary constant and $\Gamma[m, x]$ is the incomplete gamma function defined as

$$\Gamma[m, x] = \int_x^\infty s^{m-1}e^{-s}ds. \quad (11)$$

$H(t)$ can describe several growth curve models, e.g. exponential, delayed-S-shaped, Gompertz, logistic, and logarithmic-Poisson type models[6]. Note that we substituted the value of $\frac{dH(t)}{dt}|_{t=t_i}$ with the central difference which appears in Eq. (7). The unknown parameters c, d, A, and B can be estimated by the least squares analysis based on Eq. (8). However in the following discussion, we set $c = 0$ to simplify the model. Consequently, we can estimate the number of remaining software faults at t_i, x_i $(i = j, j+1, \ldots, n)$, by

$$x_i = \lim_{t\to\infty} \hat{H}(t) - y_i \quad (i = j, j+1, \ldots, n). \quad (12)$$

We show the procedure to obtain K bootstrap samples of x_j that is discussed previously as follows[7,8].

Step 1. Estimate $\hat{A}_0 = \hat{A}$ and $\hat{B}_0 = \hat{B}$ by a linear regression scheme with the data set $(t_i, z(0, \hat{d}, t_i))$ $(i = 1, 2, \ldots, j)$. This means the parameter d is also estimated.

Step 2. Calculate the residual, $w(t_i)$, by

$$w(t_i) = z(0, \hat{d}, t_i) - (\hat{A}_0 - \hat{B}_0 t_i) \quad (i = 1, 2, \ldots, j).$$

Step 3. Set the total number of iteration K. Let $p = 1$ $(p = 1, 2, \ldots, K)$.

Step 4. Generate a new $z_p(0, \hat{d}, t_i)$ by randomly choosing one value $w(t_*)$ from the set of $w(t_i)$ $(i = 1, 2, \ldots, j)$. Therefore we have

$$z_p(0, \hat{d}, t_i) = w(t_*) + (\hat{A}_0 - \hat{B}_0 t_i) \quad (i = 1, 2, \ldots, j).$$

Step 5. Estimate the parameters A_p and B_p by based on a new linear regression as

$$z_p(0, \hat{d}, t_i) = A_p - B_p t_i \quad (i = 1, 2, \ldots, j).$$

Step 6. Let $p = p + 1$ and go back to **Step 4** if $p < K$.

Step 7. We obtain K pairs of bootstrap estimates $(\hat{A}_p, \hat{B}_p)$ $(p = 1, 2, \ldots, K)$.

Step 8. Finally we have K samples of x_i $(i = j, j + 1, \ldots, n)$ shown in Eq. (4) by iterating the above steps with increasing j to n by 1. The value of j is the index of starting point of the quality evaluation.

4 Example of Data Analysis

In this section we show an example of moving average chart with SD. Figure 2 represents the behavior of the software fault count data ($n = 35$). Also we set $j = 25$ and $k = 3$, that is, we are going to plot 3-term moving average chart with SD. Figure 3 illustrates the first regression result along with $(t_i, z(0, 1.39837, t_i))$ $(i = 1, 2, \ldots, 25)$, where $\hat{A}_0 = 2.14289$ and $\hat{B}_0 = -0.126052$.

Under the configuration of the bootstrap by $K = 1000$, we have generated 1000 bootstrap samples for X_i $(i = 25, 26, \ldots, 35)$, where X_i means the number of residual software faults at t_i.

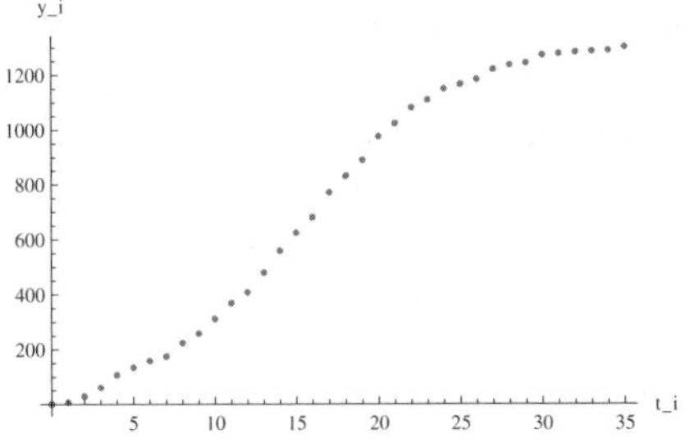

Fig. 2. Behavior of fault count data

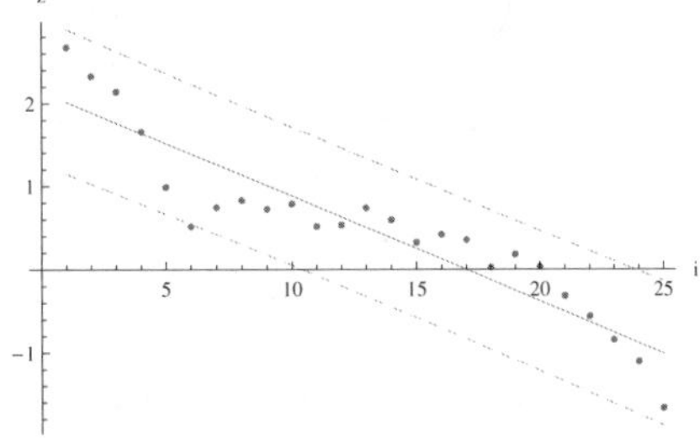

Fig. 3. Linear regression ($j = 25$)

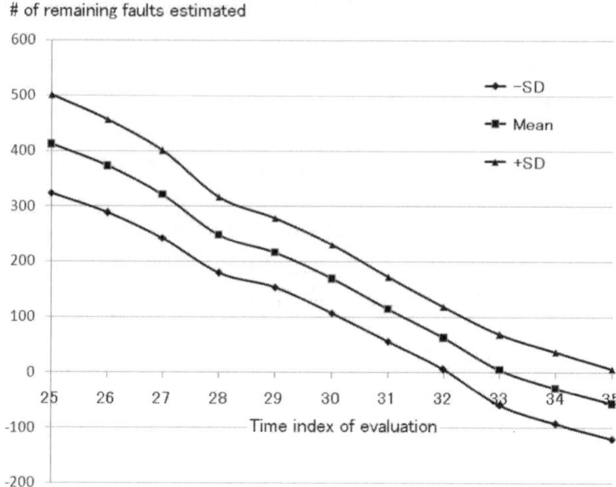

Fig. 4. A 3-term moving average chart $\mathrm{E}[M_{i,3}]$ with $\pm 1 \times$SD ($\hat{\sigma} = 63.4321$)

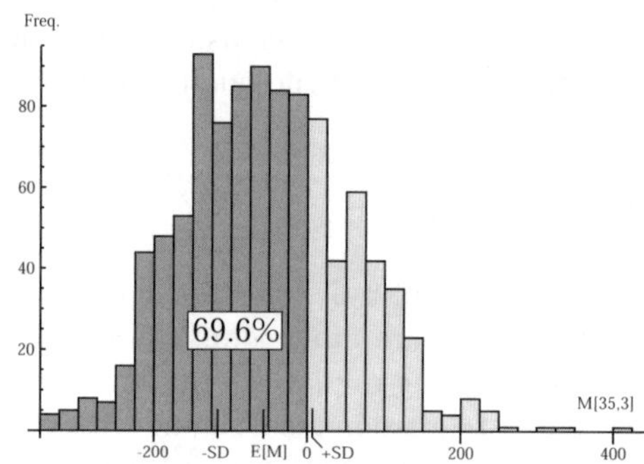

Fig. 5. Histogram of 1000 bootstrap samples of $M_{35,3}$

Finally, Fig. 4 is presented as a control chart for judging whether this software testing becomes enough and the software is releasable from the viewpoint of the number of residual software faults estimated. The estimated SD is $\hat{\sigma} = 63.4321$.

Now we recall the concept of the allowable ratio which was discussed in Section 2. If we denote the allowable ratio by a_r, therefore the maximum (allowable) number of remaining faults at the evaluation time t_i is given by

$$(\text{Max. \# of remaining faults at } t_i) = a_r \times (\text{\# of inherent faults, } \hat{H}(\infty)). \quad (13)$$

Thus the optimal software release time t^* can be given by

$$t^* = \inf_{t_i(i=j,\ldots,n)} \left\{ \Pr\left[M_{i,3} \leqq a_r \times \hat{H}(\infty) \right] \geqq \alpha \right\}. \quad (14)$$

That is, the target value upon the release is $a_r \times \hat{H}(\infty)$ and its achievement probability can be set by α. If we assume $a_r = 0$, i.e., no remaining fault is allowed under $\alpha = 0.7$, the optimal release criterion in this example is

$$t^* = \inf_{t_i(i=25,\ldots,35)} \left\{ \Pr\left[M_{i,3} \leqq 0 \right] \geqq 0.7 \right\}. \tag{15}$$

Hence we plotted a histogram of 1000 bootstrap samples of $M_{35,3}$ in Fig. 5. We calculated that $\Pr[M_{35,3} \leqq 0]$ is about 69.6% from the histogram. Under these assumptions for this data set and target values, this software test could be almost finished at t_{35}.

5 Concluding Remarks

In the practical judgment of software release time, it is almost impossible for the testing managers to grasp the total cost of software development, although it has been frequently discussed in the literature of software release problems. Our proposal in this paper can give one of the feasible solutions to make the right judgment on the software release time in the actual management environment, and will provide a method of online monitoring for the quality software.

References

1. Okumoto, K., Goel, A.L.: Optimum release time for software systems based on reliability and cost criteria. J. Systems and Software 1, 315–318 (1980)
2. Sando, H.: An optimal release problem in software tests of discrete-type software by quasi-error seeding. Trans. IEICE J72-A(6), 992–994 (1989) (in Japanese)
3. Yamada, S., Kimura, M., Tanio, Y., Osaki, S.: A note on optimum release problem based on software reliability assessment methods during operation phase. Trans. IEICE J75-D-I(1), 53–58 (1992) (in Japanese)
4. Yamada, S., Tokuno, K., Inoue, K.: Optimal release problems with software reliability/safety based on cost criteria. Trans. IEICE J82-A(1), 64–72 (1999) (in Japanese)
5. Fujiwara, T., Yamada, S., Gouda, H.: A method of product's reliability/quality analysis based on software reliability growth models. In: The 4th International Conference on Project Management, Alaska, USA (2008)
6. Kimura, M.: A study on bootstrap confidence intervals of software reliability measures based on an incomplete gamma function model. In: Dohi, T., Yun, W.Y. (eds.) Advanced Reliability Modeling II, pp. 419–426. World Scientific, Singapore (2006)
7. Gentle, J.E., Härdle, W., Mori, Y.: Handbook of Computational Statistics: Concepts and Methods. Springer, Heidelberg (2004)
8. Wu, C.F.J.: Jackknife, bootstrap and other resampling methods in regression analysis. Ann. of Statist. 14(4), 1261–1295 (1986)

An EM Algorithm for Record Value Statistics Models in Software Reliability Estimation

Hiroyuki Okamura and Tadashi Dohi*

Department of Information Engineering, Graduate School of Engineering,
Hiroshima University, 1–4–1 Kagamiyama, Higashi-Hiroshima 739-8527, Japan
http://www.rel.hiroshima-u.ac.jp/

Abstract. This paper proposes an EM (expectation-maximization) algorithm for record value statistics (RVS) models in software reliability estimation. The RVS model provides one of the generalized modeling frameworks to unify several of existing software reliability models described as non-homogeneous Poisson processes (NHPPs). The proposed EM algorithm gives a numerically stable procedure to compute the maximum likelihood estimates of RVS models. In particular, we focus on an RVS model based on a mixture of exponential distributions. As an illustrative example, we also derive a concrete EM algorithm for the well-known Musa-Okumoto logarithmic Poisson execution time model by applying our result.

Keywords: software reliability, non-homogeneous Poisson process, record value statistics, parameter estimation, EM algorithm.

1 Introduction

Software reliability is one of the most significant attributes for measuring software quality. The software reliability is quantitatively defined as the probability that there is no failure for a certain time period in operation. Thus, probabilistic models are applied to estimating software reliability with the field data. The software reliability community has developed a number of software reliability models (SRMs) from various points of view during the last four decades. Specifically, non-homogeneous Poisson process (NHPP) based SRMs have played a central role to estimate the number of remaining faults as well as the software reliability [1,2] due to their mathematically tractable properties.

Generally speaking, NHPP-based SRMs can be classified into finite and infinite failure models. The finite failure SRMs assume that there are a finite number of failure-causing faults in software, and that the expected total number of failures is always bounded even if a software lifetime goes to infinity. Since this property might be plausible to represent debugging activities for real software development, a large number of NHPP-based SRMs belonging to this category have

* This research was supported by the Ministry of Education, Science, Sports and Culture, Grant-in-Aid for Young Scientists (B), Grant No. 21700060 (2009-2011) and Scientific Research (C), Grant No. 21510167 (2009-2012).

D. Ślęzak et al. (Eds.): ASEA 2009, CCIS 59, pp. 288–295, 2009.

been proposed and extensively discussed in the literature. On the other hand, the infinite failure SRMs are stochastic models whose expected total numbers of failures go to infinity as time elapses. The infinite failure SRMs can be regarded as limiting models derived from the finite failure models. The well-known SRM belonging to this category is Musa-Okumoto logarithmic Poisson execution time model [3], which is also known as one of the most useful NHPP-based SRMs.

To understand the modeling assumption in a unified way, there are a few generalized modeling frameworks (meta-modeling frameworks) which provide either of existing finite or infinite NHPP-based SRMs [4, 5, 6]. Such a meta-modeling framework is quite important to discuss the parameter estimation and the model selection in the practical point of view. To the best of our knowledge, generalized order statistics (GOS) and record value statistics (RVS) models are two major modeling frameworks. In particular, GOS models have attractively been studied in terms of parameter estimation and model selection [7, 8, 9], since GOS models contain all of finite failure SRMs used in software reliability estimation. In contrast, RVS models have not fully discussed from the theoretical point of view.

This paper concerns a parameter estimation problem, and particularly proposes an EM (expectation-maximization) algorithm for RVS models in software reliability estimation. The EM algorithms for GOS models were proposed in [10, 13, 14, 15, 16], where the authors achieved practically more stable estimation procedures than general-purpose numerical algorithms. The proposed EM algorithm here also gives a numerically stable procedure to compute the maximum likelihood estimates of RVS models. In particular, we focus on an RVS model based on a mixture of exponential distributions. As an illustrative example, we also derive a concrete EM algorithm for Musa-Okumoto NHPP SRM [3] by applying our generalized EM framework.

2 Software Reliability Modeling

NHPP-based SRMs are widely accepted as stochastic models to estimate software reliability. Let $\{N(t); t \geq 0\}$ be a stochastic process which represents the number of software failures experienced before time t. The following assumptions are made on the cumulative number of software failures:

- $N(0) = 0$,
- $\{N(t);\ t \geq 0\}$ has independent increments,
- $P(N(t + \Delta t) - N(t) = 1) = \lambda(t)\Delta t + o(\Delta t)$,
- $P(N(t + \Delta t) - N(t) \geq 2) = o(\Delta t)$,

where $\lambda(t)$ is a failure intensity function and $o(\Delta t)$ is the second or higher order term of Δt. According to the above assumptions, $N(t)$ follows an NHPP having the probability mass function (p.m.f.):

$$P\left(N(t) = n\right) = \frac{\Lambda(t)^n}{n!} \exp(-\Lambda(t)), \quad t \geq 0,\ n = 0, 1, \cdots, \tag{1}$$

where $\Lambda(t) = \int_0^t \lambda(s)ds$ is called a mean value function representing the expected cumulative number of software failures experienced before time t.

A numerous number of NHPP-based SRMs have been proposed to estimate software reliability, and characterized by mean value functions. For example, when the mean value function is given by

$$\Lambda(t) = \omega(1 - e^{-\beta t}), \tag{2}$$

the corresponding NHPP-based SRM is the exponential SRM by Goel and Okumoto [11].

On the other hand, there are two generalized modeling frameworks that contain almost all existing NHPP-based SRMs. The first framework is based on generalized order statistics (GOS), which is called the GOS-NHPP model in this paper. The GOS-NHPP model is made on the following assumptions [4]:

- The number of failure-causing faults is finite with a Poisson distributed random variable.
- All software failure times are mutually independent random variables with an identical probabilistic law.

Let ω and $F(t)$ be an average number of failure-causing faults and the cumulative distribution function (c.d.f.) of a software failure time, respectively. Since the number of failure-causing faults follows the Poisson distribution with mean ω, the p.m.f. of the number of failures is given by

$$P(N(t) = n) = \frac{\{\omega F(t)\}^n}{n!} e^{-\omega F(t)}, \quad n = 0, 1, \ldots. \tag{3}$$

Equation (3) is equivalent to the p.m.f of NHPP-based SRMs. Substituting well-known statistical distributions into $F(t)$ yields many of existing NHPP-based SRMs in the GOS-NHPP model.

The second framework is based on record value statistics (RVS). The RVS model is a point process consisting of record-breaking times. Let $S_1, S_2, \ldots$ be IID (independently and identically distributed) random variables drawn from a p.d.f. $f(t) = dF(t)/dt$. Then the sequence of record-breaking times are defined as follows.

$$R_1 = 1, \tag{4}$$

$$R_k = \min\{i; S_i > S_{R_{k-1}}\}, \quad \text{for } k = 2, 3, \ldots, \tag{5}$$

$$T_k = S_{R_k}, \quad \text{for } k = 1, 2, \ldots, \tag{6}$$

where T_k is the k-th record-breaking time. In the RVS model, T_k corresponds to the k-th software failure time, and then the p.m.f. of the number of failures experienced before t becomes an NHPP with the mean value function [12]:

$$\Lambda(t) = -\log \int_t^\infty f(s)ds = -\log \overline{F}(t), \tag{7}$$

where $\overline{F}(t)$ is a survival function of $f(t)$. Similar to the GOS-NHPP model, we can represent a variety of NHPPs by substituting a statistical distribution defined on the positive domain into $f(t)$. For example, when $f(t)$ is given by an exponential density function, the resulting RVS model is coincide with a homogeneous Poisson process. If $f(t)$ is a Pareto distribution of the second kind;

$$f(t) = \frac{ab^a}{(b+t)^{a+1}}, \quad t > 0, \quad a, b > 0, \tag{8}$$

the corresponding RVS model is equivalent to the well-known Musa-Okumoto NHPP SRM [3]. The main difference between GOS-NHPP and RVS models is the expected number of total failures as $t \to \infty$. Since the GOS-NHPP model assumes a finite number of failure-causing faults, the expected number of total failures is also bounded, i.e., $\Lambda(\infty) < \infty$. On the other hand, RVS model gives the NHPP with unbounded failures, i.e., $\Lambda(\infty) \to \infty$.

This paper focuses on a class of the RVS model whose distribution is given by a mixture of exponential (ME) distributions [13]. Concretely, the p.d.f. of an ME distribution is generally given by

$$f(t) = \int_0^\infty u e^{-ut} g(u) du, \tag{9}$$

where $g(u)$ is a mixture ratio distribution. In the statistical sense, the ME distribution consists of exponential p.d.f.'s with different rates u. If the ratio is a deterministic value, i.e., $g(u)$ is the delta function $\delta(u - u_0)$, the corresponding RVS model is reduced into a homogeneous Poisson process with rate u_0. Also, when $g(u)$ is a gamma density;

$$g(u) = \frac{b^a r^{a-1} e^{-bu}}{\Gamma(a)}, \quad u > 0, \quad a, b > 0, \tag{10}$$

the corresponding model is Musa-Okumoto NHPP SRM, where $\Gamma(\cdot)$ is the standard gamma function. This paper abbreviates the RVS model with an ME distribution as the ME-RVS model.

3 Parameter Estimation

In this section, we discuss parameter estimation for the ME-RVS model. The commonly used method for parameter estimation is the maximum likelihood (ML) estimation.

Define the software failure time data as $D = (t_1, \ldots, t_{m_e}; t_e)$, where t_i denotes the i-th ordered failure time and t_e is the last of observation period, i.e., $N(t_e) = m_e$. Then the ML estimates of model parameters $\hat{\boldsymbol{\theta}}_{ML}$ are determined as the values maximizing the log-likelihood function (LLF):

$$\hat{\boldsymbol{\theta}}_{ML} = \underset{\boldsymbol{\theta}}{\operatorname{argmax}} \, \mathcal{L}(\boldsymbol{\theta}; D), \tag{11}$$

$$\mathcal{L}(\boldsymbol{\theta}; D) = \sum_{i=1}^{m_e} \log \lambda(t_i; \boldsymbol{\theta}) - \Lambda(t_e; \boldsymbol{\theta}), \tag{12}$$

where $\boldsymbol{\theta}$ is a parameter vector of NHPP-based SRM. To solve the above maximization problem, numerical techniques are needed since we cannot obtain closed-form solutions. However, general-purpose numerical methods like Newton-type methods are unstable to find the maximum due to their local convergence property. Therefore, in order to compute ML estimates stably, EM (expectation-maximization) algorithms are useful. In fact, [10, 14, 15, 16] developed the EM algorithms for GOS-NHPP models. This paper discusses the EM algorithm for the ME-RVS model.

The EM algorithm is an iterative method for computing ML estimates with incomplete data [17, 18]. Let D and Z be observable and unobservable data vectors, respectively, and we wish to estimate a model parameter vector $\boldsymbol{\theta}$ from only the observable data vector D. The problem corresponds to finding a parameter vector that maximizes a marginal LLF:

$$\hat{\boldsymbol{\theta}}_{ML} = \underset{\boldsymbol{\theta}}{\operatorname{argmax}}\, \mathcal{L}(\boldsymbol{\theta}; D), \tag{13}$$

$$\mathcal{L}(\boldsymbol{\theta}; D) = \log p(D; \boldsymbol{\theta}) = \log \int p(D, Z; \boldsymbol{\theta}) dZ, \tag{14}$$

where $p(\cdot)$ is any appropriate p.d.f. or p.m.f. The EM algorithm consists of E-step and M-step. E-step computes a conditional expected LLF with respect to the complete data vector (D, Z) using the posterior distribution for unobservable data vector with provisional parameter vector $\boldsymbol{\theta}'$, i.e., the conditional expected LLF is given by

$$\begin{aligned} Q(\boldsymbol{\theta}|\boldsymbol{\theta}') &= \mathrm{E}[\log p(D, Z; \boldsymbol{\theta})|D; \boldsymbol{\theta}'] \\ &= \int p(Z|D; \boldsymbol{\theta}') \log p(D, Z; \boldsymbol{\theta}) dZ. \end{aligned} \tag{15}$$

The posterior distribution for unobservable data can be obtained from Bayes theorem:

$$p(Z|D; \boldsymbol{\theta}) = \frac{p(D, Z; \boldsymbol{\theta})}{\int p(D, Z; \boldsymbol{\theta}) dZ}. \tag{16}$$

In M-step, we find a new parameter vector $\boldsymbol{\theta}''$ that maximizes the expected LLF:

$$\boldsymbol{\theta}'' := \underset{\boldsymbol{\theta}}{\operatorname{argmax}}\, Q(\boldsymbol{\theta}|\boldsymbol{\theta}'), \tag{17}$$

and $\boldsymbol{\theta}''$ becomes a provisional parameter vector at the next E- and M-steps. The E- and M-steps are repeatedly executed until the parameters converge to ML estimates. Here it should be noted that concrete EM algorithms depend on both model and unobserved data structures.

To develop the EM algorithm for ME-RVS model, we consider a pair of IID random variates (S_i, U_i) which are jointly drawn from the exponential distribution with rate U_i and the mixture ratio distribution $g(u)$. In addition, R_i denotes an index of the i-th record-breaking value. Then the LLF for (S_i, U_i) and R_i gives a complete LLF:

$$\log p(D, Z; \boldsymbol{\theta}) = \sum_{i=1}^{R_{m_e+1}} (\log U_i - U_i S_i) + \sum_{i=1}^{R_{m_e+1}} \log g(U_i; \boldsymbol{\theta}). \tag{18}$$

Then the E-step is represented as

$$Q(\boldsymbol{\theta}|\boldsymbol{\theta}') = \mathrm{E}\left[\sum_{i=1}^{R_{m_e+1}} \log g(U_i; \boldsymbol{\theta}) \middle| D; \boldsymbol{\theta}' \right]. \tag{19}$$

Here we can derive a useful formula to compute the above Q-function: For any function $h(\cdot)$, the expected value can be computed as follows.

$$\begin{aligned}
\mathrm{E}\left[\sum_{i=1}^{R_{m_e+1}} h(U_i) \middle| D; \boldsymbol{\theta} \right] &= \frac{\int_0^\infty h(u) u e^{-ut_1} g(u; \boldsymbol{\theta}) du}{\int_0^\infty u e^{-ut_1} g(u; \boldsymbol{\theta}) du} \\
&+ \sum_{k=2}^{m_e} \left(\frac{\int_0^\infty h(u) u e^{-ut_k} g(u; \boldsymbol{\theta}) du}{\int_0^\infty u e^{-ut_k} g(u; \boldsymbol{\theta}) du} + \frac{\int_0^\infty h(u)(1 - e^{-ut_{k-1}}) g(u; \boldsymbol{\theta}) du}{\int_0^\infty e^{-ut_{k-1}} g(u; \boldsymbol{\theta}) du} \right) \\
&+ \frac{\int_0^\infty h(u) e^{-ut_e} g(u; \boldsymbol{\theta}) du}{\int_0^\infty e^{-ut_e} g(u; \boldsymbol{\theta}) du} + \frac{\int_0^\infty h(u)(1 - e^{-ut_{m_e}}) g(u; \boldsymbol{\theta}) du}{\int_0^\infty e^{-ut_{m_e}} g(u; \boldsymbol{\theta}) du}.
\end{aligned} \tag{20}$$

On the other hand, since we find the parameter maximizing $Q(\boldsymbol{\theta}|\boldsymbol{\theta}')$, the M-step procedure can be derived from a usual ML procedure for $g(u)$. For example, $g(u)$ belongs to the exponential family, so that the ML estimates in the M-step are given in closed forms.

4 Illustration of EM Procedure for Musa-Okumoto SRM

We present concrete EM-step formulas for Musa-Okumoto NHPP SRM in this section. Suppose that the mixture ratio distribution is given by a gamma distribution with parameters a and b. Then the corresponding ME-RVS model becomes Musa-Okumoto NHPP SRM. The complete LLF for IID rate samples $\Lambda_1, \ldots, \Lambda_{R_{m_e+1}}$ can be written in the form:

$$\begin{aligned}
\log p(D, Z; (a, b)) = R_{m_e+1} a \log b + (a-1) \sum_{i=1}^{R_{m_e+1}} \log \Lambda_i - b \sum_{i=1}^{R_{m_e+1}} \Lambda_i \\
- R_{m_e+1} \log \Gamma(a).
\end{aligned} \tag{21}$$

Based on the EM formulas in the previous section, we have

$$\mu_1(a, b) := \mathrm{E}[R_{m_e+1} | D; (a, b)] = 1 + \sum_{k=1}^{m_e} \left(\frac{b}{b + t_k} \right)^{-a}, \tag{22}$$

$$\mu_\lambda(a, b) := \mathrm{E}\left[\sum_{i=1}^{R_{m_e+1}} \Lambda_i \middle| D; (a, b) \right] = \sum_{k=1}^{m_e} \left(\frac{1}{b + t_k} + \frac{a}{b} \left(\frac{b}{b + t_k} \right)^{-a} \right) + \frac{a}{b + t_e}, \tag{23}$$

$$\mu_{\log\lambda}(a,b) := \mathrm{E}\left[\sum_{i=1}^{R_{m_e+1}} \log \Lambda_i \,\middle|\, D; (a,b)\right]$$

$$= \sum_{k=1}^{m_e} \left(\frac{1}{a} + (\psi(a) - \log b) \left(\frac{b}{b+t_k} \right)^{-a} \right) + \psi(a) - \log(b + t_e), \quad (24)$$

where $\psi(\cdot)$ is the digamma function $\psi(a) = \frac{d}{da} \log \Gamma(a)$. Using $\mu_1(a,b)$, $\mu_\lambda(a,b)$ and $\mu_{\log\lambda}(a,b)$, the M-step for Musa-Okumoto NHPP SRM is given by

$$a = \inf \left\{ a > 0;\ \log a - \psi(a) = \log \frac{\mu_\lambda(a',b')}{\mu_1(a',b')} - \frac{\mu_{\log\lambda}(a',b')}{\mu_1(a',b')} \right\}, \quad (25)$$

$$b = \frac{a\mu_1(a',b')}{\mu_\lambda(a',b')}. \quad (26)$$

5 Discussions and Future Research

The proposed EM algorithm provides more stable procedures to compute ML estimates than general-purpose numerical methods, since the EM algorithm has a global convergence property. However, it should be noted that the convergence is slower than other methods like Newton-type methods. In general, the convergence rate of EM algorithm is known as a liner function of the number of iterations, whereas the convergence rate of Newton-type methods is a quadratic function of the number of iteration. In addition, the convergence speed of EM algorithm depends on the amount of unobservable information. In our EM framework for RVS models, we define unobservable data as the samples that do not break the current record value. Indeed, there are a huge number of such unobservable samples in our framework, except for the case where the total number of failures is small. Thus the proposed EM procedure is expected to be slow for the convergence when the number of failures becomes large, so that the EM algorithm for RVS models may not be applied to estimate software reliability from observed data. On the other hand, we also developed EM algorithms for GOS-NHPP models in [10,14,15,16] which gave a practically rapid convergence speed unlike the RVS case. Since several acceleration methods for EM algorithms have been proposed, e.g., [19], we will try to apply such acceleration techniques to improve the convergence speed of EM algorithm for RVS models in the future.

References

1. Musa, J.D., Iannino, A., Okumoto, K.: Software Reliability, Measurement, Prediction, Application. McGraw-Hill, New York (1987)
2. Lyu, M.R. (ed.): Handbook of Software Reliability Engineering. McGraw-Hill, New York (1996)
3. Musa, J.D., Okumoto, K.: A logarithmic Poisson execution time model for software reliability measurement. In: 7th International Conference Software Engineering, pp. 230–238. IEEE CS Press/ACM (1984)

4. Langberg, N., Singpurwalla, N.D.: Unification of some software reliability models. SIAM Journal on Scientific Computing 6, 781–790 (1985)
5. Dohi, T., Osaki, S., Trivedi, K.S.: An infinite server queueing approach for describing software reliability growth – unified modeling and estimation framework. In: 11th Asia-Pacific Software Engineering Conference, pp. 110–119. IEEE CS Press, Los Alamitos (2004)
6. Grottke, M., Trivedi, K.S.: On a method for mending time to failure distributions. In: International Conference on Dependable Systems and Networks, pp. 560–569. IEEE CS Press, Los Alamitos (2005)
7. Miller, D.R.: Exponential order statistic models of software reliability growth. IEEE Transactions on Software Engineering SE-12, 12–24 (1986)
8. Raftery, A.E.: Inference and prediction for a general order statistic model with unknown population size. Journal of the American Statistical Association 82, 1163–1168 (1987)
9. Wilson, S.P., Samaniego, F.J.: Nonparametric analysis of the order-statistic model in software reliability. IEEE Transactions on Software Engineering 33, 198–208 (2007)
10. Okamura, H., Watanabe, Y., Dohi, T.: An iterative scheme for maximum likelihood estimation in software reliability modeling. In: 14th International Symposium on Software Reliability Engineering, pp. 246–256. IEEE CS Press, Los Alamitos (2003)
11. Goel, A.L., Okumoto, K.: Time-dependent error-detection rate model for software reliability and other performance measures. IEEE Transactions on Reliability R-28, 206–211 (1979)
12. Kuo, L., Yang, T.Y.: Bayesian computation for nonhomogeneous Poisson processes in software reliability. Journal of the American Statistical Association 91, 763–773 (1996)
13. Okamura, H., Watanabe, Y., Dohi, T.: Estimating mixed software reliability models based on the EM algorithms. In: 2002 International Symposium on Empirical Software Engineering, pp. 69–78. IEEE CS Press, Los Alamitos (2002)
14. Okamura, H., Murayama, A., Dohi, T.: EM algorithm for discrete software reliability models: a unified parameter estimation method. In: 8th IEEE International Symposium on High Assurance Systems Engineering, pp. 219–228. IEEE CS Press, Los Alamitos (2004)
15. Okamura, H., Dohi, T.: Building phase-type software reliability models. In: 17th International Symposium on Software Reliability Engineering, pp. 289–298. IEEE CS Press, Los Alamitos (2006)
16. Okamura, H., Dohi, T.: Hyper-Erlang software reliability model. In: 14th Pacific Rim International Symposium on Dependable Computing, pp. 232–239. IEEE CS Press, Los Alamitos (2008)
17. Dempster, A.P., Laird, N.M., Rubin, D.B.: Maximum likelihood from incomplete data via the EM algorithm. Journal of the Royal Statistical Society, Series B. B-39, 1–38 (1977)
18. Wu, C.F.J.: On the convergence properties of the EM algorithm. Annals of Statistics 11, 95–103 (1983)
19. McLachlan, G.J., Krishnan, T.: EM Algorithm and Extensions. John Wiley & Sons, Chichester (1997)

Yet Another Metric for Predicting Fault-Prone Modules

Osamu Mizuno[1] and Hideaki Hata[2]

[1] Graduate School of Science and Technology, Kyoto Institute of Technology
o-mizuno@kit.ac.jp

[2] Graduate School of Information Science and Technology, Osaka University
h-hata@ist.osaka-u.ac.jp

Abstract. Recently, machine learning approaches have been widely used for fault-proneness detection. Introduction of machine learning approaches induces development of new software metrics for fault-prone module detection. We have proposed an approach to detect fault-prone modules using the spam-filtering technique. To treat our approach as the conventional fault-prone approaches, we summarize the output of spam-filtering based approach as a metric. In this paper, we show the effectiveness of our new metric comparing the conventional software metrics.

Keywords: Fault-prone module, Machine learning, Software metrics.

1 Introduction

Fault-prone modules prediction is one of the most traditional and important areas in software engineering. Detection of fault-prone modules has been widely studied[1,2,3,4]. Most of these studies used some kind of software metrics, such as program complexity, size of modules, or object-oriented metrics, and constructed mathematical models to calculate fault-proneness.

Recently, machine learning approaches have been widely used for fault-proneness detection[5]. Introduction of machine learning approaches induces development of new software metrics for fault-prone module detection. Thus, several new metrics have been proposed so far. For example, Layman et al. showed that change history data are effective for fault-prone module detection[6]. Kim et al. proposed a notion of "memories of bug fix" and showed that such memories of bug fix deeply related to the existence of faults in a module[7].

In order to mitigate such difficulties, we have introduced a spam filtering based approach to detect fault-prone modules, [8,9]. Inspired by the spam filtering technique, we tried to apply text-mining techniques to fault-proneness detection. A model is well-studied Bayesian model. Since the usefulness of Bayesian theory for spam filtering has been recognized recently, most spam filtering tools implement Bayesian theories. In fault-prone module detection, we treat a software module as an e-mail message, and classify all software modules into either fault-prone (FP) or non-fault-prone (NFP). However, using only one method may miss other important aspects of fault-proneness.

D. Ślęzak et al. (Eds.): ASEA 2009, CCIS 59, pp. 296–304, 2009.

In this paper, to treat our approach as the conventional fault-prone approaches, we summarize the output of spam-filtering based approach as a metric. We thus perform an experiment to confirm whether or not the combination with conventional metrics and other classification methods improves the accuracy of fault-prone module prediction.

2 Objective

The aim of this paper is to propose a new metric from a new viewpoint which can be used for fault-prone module prediction in source code modules. By an empirical experiment, we try to show the effectiveness of our proposed metric for the fault-prone module prediction.

The idea of the new metric comes from our previous work[8,9]. In the previous works, we proposed a new approach for fault-prone module prediction using spam-filtering technique. During the previous work, we considered that the output of our fault-prone module prediction approach can be regarded as a metric of fault-proneness. The approach itself has already been evaluated its accuracy in the previous work, and the result of evaluation showed that the approach has enough accuracy for the fault-prone module prediction. However, using only one method may miss other important aspects of fault-proneness.

Therefore, we guessed that combination with conventional metrics and the other classification methods improves the accuracy of fault-prone module prediction. In order to investigate our intuition, we conducted an experiment of fault-prone module prediction using the proposed metric as well as the conventional metrics. For the conventional metrics, we prepared 3 history metrics and 7 complexity metrics.

As for the classification methods, we prepared popular classifiers: naive Bayes, J48, Logistic, and NNge in Weka. For comparison purpose, we also prepared the fault-prone filtering method, which we previously proposed in [8].

3 Metrics Suit and Prediction Method

For a comparative study, we prepared three kinds of metrics suit: history, complexity, and text-filtering. We also prepared well-known classifiers for prediction methods.

3.1 History Metrics

- *FIX (Memories of bug fix)*[7]. This metric shows past existence of a fault in a module in the nominal scale. If a module had been reported bugs in the past revisions, *FIX* for the module becomes "yes"; otherwise *FIX* is "no".
- LOC_{add} *(Added lines of code from previous revision)*. This metric shows the amount of added code from the previous revision. This metric is the absolute scale.

- *LOC_{chg} (Changed lines of code from previous revision).* This metric shows the amount of changed code from the previous revision. This metric is the absolute scale.

3.2 Complexity Metrics

For the object-oriented design, Chidamber and Kemerer proposed an object-oriented metrics suit[10]. The metrics suit is called "CK metrics". CK metrics suit includes the following 6 metrics:

- *LCOM (Lack of Cohesion on Methods).* The number of pairs of member functions without shared instance variables, minus the number of pairs functions with shared instance variables. If this subtraction is negative, the metric is set to zero.
- *WMC (Weighted Methods per Class).* The number of methods defined in each class.
- *DIT (Depth of Inheritance Tree).* The number of ancestors of a class.
- *NOC (Number Of Children).* The number of direct descendants for each class.
- *CBO (Coupling Between Object classes).* The number of classes to which a given class is coupled.
- *RFC (Response For a Class).* The number of methods that can be executed in response to a message being received by an object of that class.

Many researchers used CK metrics suit for fault-prone module prediction[11,1,12]. For example, Gyimóthy et al. employed these metrics to fault prediction[12] and showed their effectiveness. Since the CK metrics suit is one of the most popular set of software metrics, we adopted it in this study.

Additionally, we used the most traditional complexity metrics for software:

- *LOC (Lines of code of a class file).* The lines of code is one of the oldest and most important software metrics. Here, *LOC* for a class file is measured.

All of above complexity metrics are the absolute scale metrics. For collection of these metrics, we utilized a tool, MASU, which is implemented by Miyake et al. [13].

3.3 Text-Filtering Metrics

- *P_{fpf} (A probability to be faulty for a module, which is calculated by a generic text filter*[8,9].

  This metric is implicitly related to information of frequency of words in a module. The computation of P_{fpf} is rather complex, but the basic idea is simple. Assume that you have corpuses of faulty and non-faulty modules. Here, a corpus contains tokens of source code modules decomposed by the lexical analysis. When you get a new module to see whether it has a fault or not, we can determine which corpus is appropriate to contain the tokens of the new module by the Bayes theorem. This mechanism is implemented in a generic text filter. Using such a text filter, we have developed a tool to calculate P_{fpf} for a module with given corpuses of faulty and non-faulty. For our implementation, P_{fpf} is calculated by a spam filter "CRM114[1]".

3.4 Fault-Prone Prediction Methods

In this study, we prepared 4 distinct classifiers for the fault-prone module prediction as follows:

naive Bayes: Naive Bayes is one of the simplest Bayesian classifier. Although many classifiers based on Bayes theorem, the naive Bayes is still a powerful classifier.

J48: J48 generates a pruned C4.5 decision tree. It is an implementation of famous tree classifier algorithm.

Logistic: Logistic is an implementation of logistic regression. Logistic builds a multinomial logistic regression model with a ridge estimator.

NNge: NNge is a nearest-neighbor-like algorithm using non-nested generalized exemplars (which are hyper-rectangles that can be viewed as if-then rules). NNge is one of the rule-based data mining method.

In the experiment, we compare the best accuracy measures between above classifiers.

4 Experiment

4.1 Target Project

For the experiment, we selected an open source software project, Eclipse BIRT[2]. This project is written in Java, and revisions are maintained by CVS. The source repository of CVS used in this study was uploaded on the Eclipse project Web site[3], and we obtained on the 1st of December, 2008. We treated a Java class file in each revision as a software module.

We also obtained bug reports from a bug-tracking system, Bugzilla on the 1st of January, 2009. We extracted reports from Bugzilla under the following conditions. The type of these faults is "bugs"; therefore, these faults do not include any enhancements or functional patches. The status of faults is "closed", and the resolution of faults is "fixed". This means that the collected faults have already been fixed and have been closed, and thus fixed revisions should be included in the entire repository.

4.2 Collection of Faulty Modules

We identify faulty modules with the SZZ algorithm[14,15]. Once modules are collected by the above procedure, we collect software metrics shown in Section 3 for each module. A part of collected metrics is shown in Table 1. Although P_{fpf} is a probability, most of values of P_{fpf} are 0 and 1.

[1] http://crm114.sourceforge.net/
[2] http://www.eclipse.org/birt/phoenix/
[3] http://archive.eclipse.org/arch/

Table 1. A part of collected metrics from BIRT

Module	FIX	LOC_{add}	LOC_{chg}	LOC	WMC	DIT	CBO	$LCOM$	RFC	NOC	P_{fpf}	Faulty?
BuildUtil.java	yes	0	1	108	7	6	11	0	18	0	0.1370	no
CheckDiskSpace.java	yes	33	42	623	62	5	68	161	182	3	0.0000	yes
DynamicProperty.java	no	32	0	61	7	6	3	8	8	0	0.0000	no
FeatureUpdater.java	no	0	1	188	17	4	21	41	37	1	0.0000	yes
...	...	...	...	...	...	...	...	...	...	...	...	...

Table 2. Train data and Test data from BIRT

	Train	Test
Version	2.1	2.2.0
Date	30th June, 2006	29th June, 2007
# of modules	2,445	2,927

For the experiment, we prepared 2 sets of metrics data: train data and test data. We used a snapshot of version 2.1 in 30th June, 2006 for train data and a snapshot of version 2.2.0 in 29th June, 2007 for test data. For this criteria, train data has 2445 modules and test data has 2927 modules.

4.3 Evaluation Measures

Table 3 shows a classification result matrix. True negative (TN) shows the number of modules that are classified as non-fault-prone, and are actually non-faulty. False positive (FP) shows the number of modules that are classified as fault-prone, but are actually non-faulty. On the contrary, false negative shows the number of modules that are classified as non-fault-prone, but are actually faulty. Finally, true positive shows the number of modules that are classified as fault-prone which are actually faulty.

In order to evaluate the results, we prepare two measures: recall, precision. Recall is the ratio of modules correctly classified as fault-prone to the number of entire faulty modules Recall is defined as Recall $= \frac{TP}{TP+FN}$. Precision is the ratio of modules correctly classified as fault-prone to the number of entire modules classified fault-prone. Precision is defined as Precision $= \frac{TP}{TP+FP}$. Since recall and precision are in the trade-off, F_1-measure is used to combine recall and precision. F_1-measure is defined as $F_1 = \frac{2\times\text{recall}\times\text{precision}}{\text{recall}+\text{precision}}$. In this definition, recall and precision are evenly weighted.

Table 3. Classification result matrix

		Classified	
		non-fault-prone	fault-prone
Actual	non-faulty	True negative (TN)	False positive (FP)
	faulty	False negative (FN)	True positive (TP)

4.4 Procedure

For the experiment, we used Weka[4] to conduct predictions of fault-prone modules. Using collected data shown in Table 2, we conducted the following two experiments.

(1) Ten-fold cross validation: For 10-fold cross validation, we used train data only. The 10-fold cross validation can show relatively fair results for a given data set. However, it cannot take into account important features such as the order of construction of the modules.
(2) Fault-prone module detection on post-release: Here, we used both train data and test data. Fault-prone modules are detected on test data using detection models trained with train data. On the test data, we evaluate the detection performance.

Generally speaking, the performance of fault-prone module detection varies according to the combination of these metrics used in a detection model. In order to find the best metrics subset for the train data, we prepared all ($= 2^{11} = 2,048$) combinations of metrics shown in Table 1. Then, we performed 10-fold cross validation for each combination, and obtained the best combination with the highest evaluation measurement, such as F_1.

Once we get the best combination of metrics, we construct a detection model using the best combination of metrics and the train data. We then apply the constructed model to the test data. This procedure is done for each classification method.

4.5 Results of Experiment

The result of experiment is shown in Table 4. For each classifier, recall, precision, F_1, and the best combination of metrics are shown. Note that the row "FPFiltering" is for comparison with the fault-prone filtering method. Remind that P_{fpf} is a value of probability to be fault-prone. Since P_{fpf} is a probability, the natural binary classification is $P_{fpf} \geq 0.5$ and $P_{fpf} < 0.5$. By this way, the evaluation measures in the row "FPF" are calculated.

As shown in Table 4, FPFiltering has high F_1 by itself. Therefore, all other classifiers uses the metric P_{fpf} in their model. Among them, we can see that J48 has the highest F_1 (=0.718) among 5 methods. We can also see that naive Bayes achieved higher F_1 than FPFiltering.

If we conduct the same experiment without P_{fpf}, the resultant F_1's become lower than that of Table 4. Since the space is limited in this article, we cannot show the result itself.

4.6 Discussion

In the experiment, J48 using P_{fpf} and LOC_{add} achieves the highest F_1. Let us show the detail of the constructed model. J48 constructs a decision tree from

[4] http://www.cs.waikato.ac.nz/ml/weka/

Table 4. Evaluation measures between classifiers

Classifier	Precision	Recall	F_1	Metrics
FPFiltering	.563	.952	.708	P_{fpf}
naive Bayes	.570	.947	.712	P_{fpf}
Logistic	.679	.542	.603	P_{fpf}, FIX, LOC_{add}, WMC, DIT
J48	.608	.877	.718	P_{fpf}, LOC_{add}
NNge	.590	.664	.676	P_{fpf}, LOC_{add}, LOC_{chg}, LOC, WMC, DIT, CBO, RFC

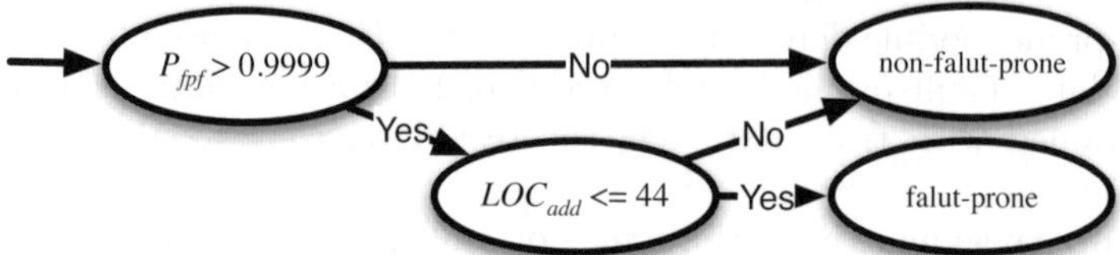

Fig. 1. A classification tree by J48

the given data. In this case, since two metrics P_{fpf} and LOC_{add} are adopted in the model, the tree is constructed as shown in Figure 1.

The tree says, "if P_{fpf} is greater than 0.9999 and LOC_{add} is smaller than or equal to 44, the module is fault-prone; otherwise the module is non-fault-prone." In other words, modules which have extremely high P_{fpf} value only considered to be fault-prone. This case shows an advantage of usage of other classifier with our proposed metric.

Next, in the case of naive Bayes, the metric P_{fpf} is only adopted, and achieve higher F_1 than FPFiltering. This means that some kind of calibration is applied to the result of FPFiltering by the naive Bayes classifier. We can say that this case shows an advantage of combining metrics.

FPFiltering still has the best result for the recall, but at the same time, it has the worst precision. High recall means that actual faults are not missed with the prediction, and low precision means that many non-faulty modules are predicted as fault-prone. Extremely imbalanced recall and precision are not good for a prediction system. From this point of view, the combination of several prediction methods can be one of the useful ways to achieving a good fault-prone module prediction method.

5 Threats to Validity

Generality of target projects is an external validity threat. In general, the Eclipse BIRT project does much better than other open source projects when using machine learning classifiers to predict fault-prone modules. We must study other projects and analyze performance across them. In addition, industrial projects may lead to different results.

There are two construct validity threats as follows:

- The SZZ algorithm adopted in this study has a limitation in that faults that are not recorded in revision logs cannot be collected. To make a complete collection of faulty modules from a source code repository, further research is required.
- It might turn out our implementation of the system contains faults.

6 Conclusions

We introduced a new metric for fault-prone module detection using the result of spam-filtering technique. Since the usefulness of the spam-filtering technique has already shown in the previous work, we tried to confirm whether or not the combination of the new metric and the conventional software metric can improve the quality of fault-prone module detection. The result of experiment shows that use of a certain convention of metrics can achieve higher accuracy measures.

Acknowledgments

This research is partially supported by the Ministry of Education, Science, Sports and Culture, Grant-in-Aid for Young Scientists (B), 20700025, 2009.

References

1. Briand, L.C., Melo, W.L., Wust, J.: Assessing the applicability of fault-proneness models across object-oriented software projects. IEEE Trans. on Software Engineering 28(7), 706–720 (2002)
2. Khoshgoftaar, T.M., Seliya, N.: Comparative assessment of software quality classification techniques: An empirical study. Empirical Software Engineering 9, 229–257 (2004)
3. Bellini, P., Bruno, I., Nesi, P., Rogai, D.: Comparing fault-proneness estimation models. In: Proc. of 10th IEEE International Conference on Engineering of Complex Computer Systems, pp. 205–214 (2005)
4. Menzies, T., Greenwald, J., Frank, A.: Data mining static code attributes to learn defect predictors. IEEE Trans. on Software Engineering 33(1), 2–13 (2007)
5. Catal, C., Diri, B.: Review: A systematic review of software fault prediction studies. Expert Syst. Appl. 36(4), 7346–7354 (2009)
6. Layman, L., Kudrjavets, G., Nagappan, N.: Iterative identification of fault-prone binaries using in-process metrics. In: Proc. of 2nd International Conference on Empirical Software Engineering and Measurement, pp. 206–212 (2008)
7. Kim, S., Pan, K., Whitehead Jr., E.J.: Memories of bug fixes. In: Proc. of 14th ACM SIGSOFT International Symposium on Foundations of Software Engineering, pp. 35–45 (2006)
8. Mizuno, O., Kikuno, T.: Training on errors experiment to detect fault-prone software modules by spam filter. In: Proc. of 6th joint meeting of the European software engineering conference and the ACM SIGSOFT symposium on the foundations of software engineering, pp. 405–414 (2007)

9. Mizuno, O., Kikuno, T.: Prediction of fault-prone software modules using a generic text discriminator. IEICE Trans. on Information and Systems E91-D(4) , 888–896 (2008)
10. Chidamber, S.R., Kemerer, C.F.: A metrics suite for object oriented design. IEEE Trans. on Software Engineering 20(6), 476–493 (1994)
11. Basili, V.R., Briand, L.C., Melo, W.L.: A validation of object oriented metrics as quality indicators. IEEE Trans. on Software Engineering 22(10), 751–761 (1996)
12. Gyimóthy, T., Ferenc, R., Siket, I.: Empirical validation of object-oriented metrics on open source software for fault prediction. IEEE Trans. on Software Engineering 31(10), 897–910 (2005)
13. Miyake, T., Higo, Y., Inoue, K.: Masu: Metrics assessment plugin-plutform for software unit of multiple programming languages. In: Proc. of Software Engineering Symposium 2008, pp. 63–70 (2008)
14. Śliwerski, J., Zimmermann, T., Zeller, A.: When do changes induce fixes (on Fridays). In: Proc. of 2nd International Workshop on Mining Software Repositories, pp. 24–28 (2005)
15. Kim, S., Zimmermann, T., Pan, K., Whitehead Jr., E.J.: Automatic identification of bug-introducing changes. In: Proc. of 21st International Conference on Automated Software Engineering, pp. 81–90 (2006)

Quantifying the Influences of Imperfect Debugging on Software Development Using Simulation Approach*

Chu-Ti Lin[1] and Chin-Yu Huang[2]

[1] Department of Computer Science and Information Engineering, National Chiayi University, Chiayi, Taiwan
chutilin@mail.ncyu.edu.tw
[2] Department of Computer Sicence, National Tsing Hua University, Hsinchu, Taiwan
cyhuang@cs.nthu.edu.tw

Abstract. Practical experiences indicate that imperfect debugging actually exists in software development. In addition to inherent faults, additional faults may be introduced into software system during debugging process. Therefore, the debugging team should be staffed with more personnel to fix the introduced faults and ensure the quality of software system. To address this problem, we apply *G/G/m* queueing model to describe debugging behavior under imperfect debugging environment. Based on the proposed simulation framework, we investigate the influences of imperfect debugging on staffing needs. The application of the proposed framework will be illustrated through a real data set. From the simulation results, project managers can be aware of the relationship between the staffing needs and the degree of imperfect debugging.

Keywords: Software Testing, Software Debugging, Software Reliability, Simulation-based Approach, Imperfect Debugging.

1 Introduction

The analyses of software failure processes are very important for ensuring the quality of the underlying software systems. Since 1970s, many software reliability growth models (SRGMs) have been proposed to predict software failure process [1], [2], [3], [4]. So far, more than 100 models exist in one form or another through numerous publications [5]. On the other hand, non-parametric techniques, such as artificial neural network (ANN), are also novel approaches for the prediction of software failure processes. Many researchers [6], [7], [8] have shown that neural networks offer promising approaches to software reliability modeling and estimation. Nevertheless, Tausworthe and Lyu [1] reported that most SRGMs only focus on the failure observation during the test phase or the operational phase, and the assumptions of most SRGMs may lead to over-simplification of failure process. Besides, most training algorithms for neural network approaches suffer from the overfitting problem [8]. That is, the

* The research work described in this paper was supported by the National Science Council, Taiwan, under Grant NSC 97-2221-E-007-052-MY3.

D. Ślęzak et al. (Eds.): ASEA 2009, CCIS 59, pp. 305–312, 2009.

fitting bias of the training set is very slight regarding known data, but the bias is unpredictably large when new data is presented to the network. Determination of the proper number of neurons is another common problem in the field of neural network research [9].

In recent years, Tausworthe and Lyu [1] proposed a novel rate-based simulation approach and showed that it can relax certain unreasonable assumptions which are common in most model-based approaches [1]. Nevertheless, most of existing simulation approaches assumes that, each time a failure occurs, the corresponding fault will be removed with absolute certainty [1], [10], [11]. This assumption can significantly simplify the simulation approaches. In fact, a debugging process may be complicated in a large-scale software system. It may be difficult to ensure that no new faults will be created when correcting a fault in practical software development. This phenomenon is often named imperfect debugging [12], [13] [14], [15]. If we ignore the influence of imperfect debugging when analyzing the failure processes, the number of fault counting and the staffing needs for software debugging may be underestimated. In this paper, we will incorporate the concept of imperfect debugging into the simulation-based approach, and analyze its influences on fault detection processes, fault correction processes and staffing needs.

The remainder of this paper is organized as follows: Section 2 gives the concept of rate-based simulation approaches, and reviews some existing methods which attempt to address the problem of imperfect debugging. In Section 3, we will propose a simulation procedure to analyze the fault detection and correction processes based on the concept of queueing theory. In the proposed simulation approach, the debugging behavior will take into account the influence of imperfect debugging. A numerical example based on real failure data is shown in Section 4. Finally, Section 5 concludes this paper.

2 Related Works

According to the concept of pure birth non-homogeneous continuous time Markov chain (NHCTMC), Tausworthe and Lyu [1], [16] proposed a set of simulation algorithms, which can be applied to different activities in software development, such as document construction, document inspection, code integration, code inspection, fault identification, fault repair, and so on. Later, based on Tausworthe and Lyu's work [1], Gokhale and Lyu [10] proposed a simulation technique to analyze the structure-based software reliability, and further extended the simulation to the reliability assessment on the application level. Besides, they also considered the explicit repair in the simulation approach, i.e. the removals of detected faults take non-negligible time. Recently, Lin and Huang [11] analyzed the staffing needs for software debugging teams through the use of simulation-based approaches based on the framework of *G/G/m* queueing model. To our understanding, most of existing simulation techniques are constructed under the assumption of perfect debugging. However, the problem of imperfect debugging should be considered in reality.

So far, there exist many researches that are dedicated to the problem of imperfect debugging. Ohba and Chou [13] ever investigated a large-scale system software development project, and reported that about 14 percent of faults detected and removed during the observation period were introduced. Thus, they integrated a parameter, fault introduction rate, into conventional SRGMs to parameterize the degree of imperfect debugging. Goel and Okumoto [17] also argued that an imperfect debugging model can perform well on the land-based radar system. In recent years, Pham et al. [14], [18] developed a series of imperfect debugging models in conjunction with some problems, such as multiple failure types [14], the change of fault introduction rate [18], etc. Based on the unified theory, Huang and Lin [4] generalized the NHPP-based SRGMs with multiple change-points under imperfect debugging environment. Apart from the framework of SRGM, Gokhale et al. [19] also ever considered the possibility of imperfect debugging in the simulation approach. But their work focused on some specific pending faults and ignored the testing process.

Existing works associated with imperfect debugging focus on not only the software reliability prediction, but also the estimation of software development cost. Xie and Yang [20] though imperfect debugging may affect the determination of the optimal software release time or operational budget. Therefore, they extended a commonly used cost model to address the case of imperfect debugging. However, we found most of related works do not discuss the influence of imperfect debugging on the staff needs for debugging systems.

3 Simulation Procedures

Dohi et al. [3] proposed a method to describe the software debugging behavior by using infinite server queueing models. Similarly, we can also use the queueing models to depict the debugging activities. Our assumptions are given as follows [1], [10]:

(1) The correction of each fault takes a debugger non-negligible time.
(2) Each time a failure occurs, there is no lag to allot a debugger to the detected fault if available debuggers exist. Otherwise, the detected fault is pending in the queue, and waits for a released debugger.
(3) The number of available debuggers is finite. The debugging system can be modeled by a *G/G/m* queue [21].
(4) A new fault may be introduced into the software system when removing a fault.

Based on these assumptions, a procedure *SIMULATION_PROCEDURE* is given in Fig. 1. It has four input parameters: the size of debugging team *personnel*, the total execution time duration denoted *end*, and the time length of each run denoted *dt*, and the degree of imperfect debugging *introduction_rate*, i.e. the probability of introducing a new fault when a detected fault is fixed. Note that each run should be short enough that the occurrence of multiple failures is rare [1], [2], [10]. In addition, there are other variables in the procedure. The variable *time* denotes the cumulative execution time till now, which increases when each run is finished. The queue Q keeps each detected fault which is currently pending and waiting for debuggers. Two sets C and R are used to keep track of the usage of debuggers. C contains the faults which were allotted to debuggers in current run while R holds the faults which have occupied debuggers prior to current run. When Q is not empty, it indicates that all debuggers are occupied and $|C \cup R|=$*personnel*. Set S includes the faults which were introduced into the software system but not detected yet. Finally, we use F to store all corrected faults. During the simulation, each run is composed of five steps: *Allocating step*, *Detecting step*, *Correcting step*, *Introducing step* and *Exposing step*.

Allocating step. In the beginning of each run, there may be some unoccupied debuggers. This step allocates the available debuggers to the faults pending in the queue. First, we check whether the following two conditions stand: (1) there exist the debuggers which were not assigned to fix some specific faults yet, i.e. $|C \cup R| \neq personnel$; (2) some faults are pending in waiting queue Q, i.e. $Q \neq \phi$. If both conditions are true, the fault pending at the tail of Q, $f_{pending}$, will be deleted from the waiting queue and assigned to a free debugger (i.e. Lines 06-07). The activities of debugger allocation (i.e. de-queue and assignment) will be repeated until Q becomes empty or all debuggers are occupied (i.e. none or only one condition stands).

Detecting step. In this step, we implement Function DETECTION( ) to determine whether a new inherent fault is experienced in this run. It will be executed one time in each run, and will compare $failure\_rate \times dt$ with a (0.0, 1.0)-uniform random number x, where $failure\_rate$ is the expected failure rate [10]. The condition that $failure\_rate \times dt > x$ means that a new inherent fault is detected. Then DETECTION( ) will return true, and will create a new element $f_{inherent}$ in the system (i.e. Lines 09-10). Besides, we should determine whether available debuggers exist once a new fault is detected (i.e. Line 11). If $|C \cup R| = personnel$, i.e., all debuggers are occupied, the fault $f_{inherent}$ will be inserted into Q (i.e. Line 12). Otherwise, the detected fault $f_{inherent}$ will be put into the set C (i.e. Line 13).

Correcting step. The number of service channels in a queue system can be considered as the number of allocated debuggers in a debugging team, and the service rate can be used to depict a debugger's efficiency. Similar to DETECTION ( ), CORRECTION( ) is implemented to check whether each fault $f_{correcting}$ (i.e. the fault which is being fixed by a debugger) can be removed in the current run. In CORRECTION( ), the success of fault removal relies upon the comparison between a (0.0, 1.0)-uniform random number x and $service\_rate \times dt$, where $service\_rate$ is the mean service rate of each debugger. If CORRECTION( ) return true, the fault will be removed from Set R to Set F (i.e. Lines 24-25). Please notice that, because the assumption of instantaneous repair is impractical, thus fault removal is assumed to be explicit in *SIMULATION_PROCEDURE*. That is, CORRECTION( ) is only invoked for the fault which was not detected in current run. Consequently, although faults in both C and R are currently being repaired by debuggers, CORRECTION( ) only checks the faults in R. If the removal is successful (i.e. Function CORRECTION( ) returns true), the fault $f_{correcting}$ will be moved from R to F.

Introducing step. This step is implemented to determine whether a new fault will be introduced by the current correction. Each time an fault is removed (i.e. Function CORRECTION( ) returns true), Function INTRODUCTION ( ) will be invoked to compare a random number x (ranging from 0 to 1) with $introduction\_rate$. The condition that $x < introduction\_rate$ indicates that the debugging process with respect to this fault is less than perfect. A new fault $f_{introduced}$ will be created and added into Set S (i.e. Lines 28-29); otherwise, the debugging process is perfectly finished without introducing new faults.

Exposing step. Similar to inherent faults, introduced faults may not be exposed by testers immediately. Hence, Set S only contains the faults which have been introduced into the system but not exposed yet. In this step, Function EXPOSING ( ) will determine whether each introduced fault in Set S, $f_{introduced}$, can be exposed by testers in current run. Similarly, a random number x (ranging from 0 to 1) will be compared with the value of $exposing\_rate \times dt$. If the condition that $exposing\_rate \times dt < x$ stands, it indicates that the fault will not be exposed in this run and will be reexamined in the next run. Conversely, if the condition is false, the fault $f_{introduced}$ will be removed from Set S (i.e. Line 17). Besides, similar to Detecting step, we should further check whether there exist unoccupied debuggers. $f_{introduced}$ will be pending in Q if all debuggers are busy (i.e. Line 19). Otherwise, $f_{introduced}$ should be added into Set C (i.e. Line 20).

At the end of each run, all faults in C will be removed to R (i.e. Lines 30-31). Note that above five steps will reiterate again and again until the end of simulation. In addition to the throughput of debugging system (i.e., the number of detected faults and removed faults), we can also have more statistics about the service level based on this skeleton, such as the average of waiting time, the average of response time, the debugger utilization, the average of queue length, etc.

```
SIMULATION_PROCEDURE (personnel, end, dt, introduction_rate)
01: time ← 0
02: Q ← C ← R ← F ← S ← φ
03: repeat
04:      Allocating step:
05:      while    |C∪R| ≠ personnel and Q ≠ φ
06:                  do   f_pending ← DEQUEUE(Q)
07:                       C ← C ∪ {f_pending}
08:      Detecting step:
09:      if   DETECTION() returns true
10:           then new an element f_inherent
11:                if |C∪R| = personnel
12:                     then ENQUEUE(Q, f_inherent)
13:                else C ← C ∪ {f_inherent}
14:      Exposing step:
15:      for  each element f_introduced ∈ S
16:           do   if   EXPOSING() returns true
17:                     then S ← S − {f_introduced}
18:                     if |C∪R| = personnel
19:                          then ENQUEUE(Q, f_introduced)
20:                     else C ← C ∪ {f_introduced}
21:      Correcting step:
22:      for  each element f_correcting ∈ R
23:           do   if   CORRECTION() returns true
24:                     then F ← F ∪ {f_correcting}
25:                          R ← R − {f_correcting}
26:      Introducing step:
27:                          if   INTRODUCTION(introduction_rate) returns true
28:                               then new an element f_introduced
29:                                    S ← S ∪ {f_introduced}
30:      R ← R ∪ C
31:      C ←φ
32:      time ←time + dt
33: until     time < end.
```

Fig. 1. Simulation Procedure

4 Numerical Example

In the experiment, the selected failure data were collected from a middle-sized software project in interval-domain format [22]. In the data set, 144 faults were totally observed during 17 weeks, and 143 out of the 144 observed faults were removed. In the simulation, we assume that all collected faults are inherent faults and simulate the introduced faults caused by different degrees of imperfection, i.e. *introduction_rate* ranges from 0 to 0.3. The experiment is set up as *end* = 17, *dt* = 0.001 and *service_rate* = *exposing_rate* = 4. The value of *failure_rate* was described using the rate function of the Goel-Okumoto model, and the statistics for the rate function are all one-week-ahead prediction [1]. In other words, all failure data prior to the specific time point are used to predict the number of failures in next time unit. In our simulation, we executed the procedures 5,000 times, and took the average.

Fig. 2 shows the number of open-remaining faults (detected but uncorrected faults) versus time. As seen from Fig. 2, if the debugging team contains at least 6 debuggers in Case 1, all detected faults will be removed at the end of 17 weeks. In Case 2, the teams with not less than 6 people can provide the same throughput by the end of 17 weeks. It is worth noting that, compared with 6 debuggers, more debuggers cannot improve the throughput in both Cases 1 and 2. Thus, 6 debuggers are suitable for the debugging systems of Case 1 and Case 2 under the given assumptions. From Figures 2(c) and 2(d), we can find that more faults are introduced during fault removals when the degree of imperfect debugging increases. As a result, the staffing needs increase as well. The staffing levels with 7 and 8 debuggers are recommended for Case 3 and Case 4, respectively.

Table 1 compares the service levels of debugging teams under different degrees of imperfect debugging when the staffing levels range from 4 to 10 or approach to infinite. The criteria related to throughput include the number of detected, introduced, removed, and remaining faults. As seen from Table 1, because more faults are introduced with the growth of the degree of imperfection, the number of detected faults (i.e. the total amount of inherent and introduced faults) will increase as well. However, the fault removals may be bound to the staffing level. That is, when the allocated debuggers are insufficient, the number of fault removals may not grow with the growth of introduction rate. Thus, given the same staffing level, the number of remaining faults may increase as the degrees of imperfect debugging increases.

Furthermore, it can be found that the waiting time and the response time increase with the growth of introduction rate, and decrease with the growth of staffing level. However, the changes are relatively minor when the allocated debuggers are adequate. Let's consider Case 1 and Case 2 as illustrations. When the staffing level is raised from 6 to 7, the changes on both waiting time and response time are less than 1. For Cases 3 and 4, the differences are also insignificant when the staffing levels are not less than 7 and 8, respectively. Finally, we can also find that the debugger utilization monotonously decreased with the growth of the debugging team size in all cases. Nevertheless, when the staffing level is low, all debuggers are busy at most time points, and the utilizations do not change clearly under different degrees of imperfection. On the whole, the best staffing levels are positively related to the degrees of imperfect debugging. The most cost-effective staffing levels for Cases 1-4 are 6, 6, 7 and 8, respectively.

In fact, debuggers' abilities and experience are both important factors for the degree of imperfect debugging. Therefore, the proposed framework can help to assess the staffing needs for the debugging system after evaluating the debuggers' abilities and experience. If most of the available debuggers are not experienced, assigning more debuggers may be necessary. On the other hand, if the debuggers are experienced, the possible introduction rate may be relatively low, and a lower staffing level may be a better recommendation.

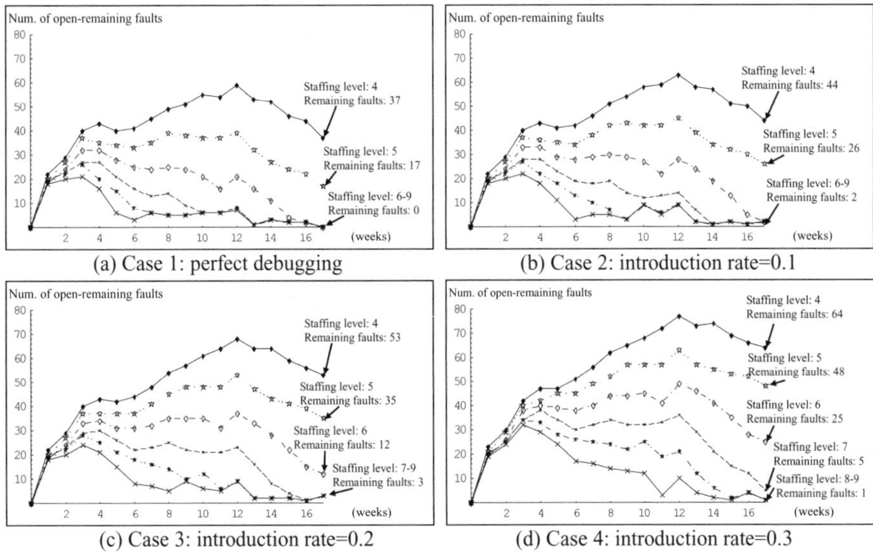

(a) Case 1: perfect debugging (b) Case 2: introduction rate=0.1

(c) Case 3: introduction rate=0.2 (d) Case 4: introduction rate=0.3

Fig. 2. Number of open-remaining faults versus time

Table 1. Service levels comparisons under different degrees of imperfect debugging

	Staffing Level	4	5	6	7	8	9	10	infinite
Case 1: Perfect debugging	Detected/introduced faults*	144/0	144/0	144/0	144/0	144/0	144/0	144/0	144/0
	Removed/remaining faults*	107/37	127/17	144/0	144/0	144/0	144/0	144/0	144/0
	Waiting/response time**	5.47/6.11	3.15/3.79	1.63/2.27	0.75/1.39	0.40/1.04	0.25/0.89	0.15/0.78	0.00/0.64
	Debugger utilization (%)	97.42	93.53	91.70	78.60	68.77	61.13	55.01	—
Case 2: Introduction rate=0.1	Detected/introduced faults*	151/7	153/9	154/10	154/10	154/10	154/10	154/10	154/10
	Removed/remaining faults*	107/44	127/26	152/2	152/2	152/2	152/2	152/2	152/2
	Waiting/response time**	6.20/6.84	3.72/4.36	1.97/2.61	1.03/1.66	0.50/1.13	0.29/0.93	0.17/0.81	0.00/0.64
	Debugger utilization (%)	99.50	99.40	97.36	83.48	73.05	64.93	58.44	—
Case 3: Introduction rate=0.2	Detected/introduced faults*	160/16	162/18	166/22	170/26	170/26	170/26	170/26	170/26
	Removed/remaining faults*	107/53	127/35	154/12	167/3	167/3	167/3	167/3	167/3
	Waiting/response time**	7.15/7.79	4.47/5.11	2.68/3.32	1.48/2.11	0.69/1.32	0.35/0.99	0.21/0.85	0.00/0.63
	Debugger utilization (%)	99.50	99.40	99.31	90.57	79.25	70.44	63.40	—
Case 4: Introduction rate=0.3	Detected/introduced faults*	171/27	175/31	179/35	187/43	189/45	189/45	189/45	189/45
	Removed/remaining faults*	107/64	127/48	154/25	182/5	188/1	188/1	188/1	188/1
	Waiting/response time**	8.94/9.57	5.89/6.52	3.85/4.48	2.40/3.03	1.39/2.02	0.75/1.38	0.43/1.06	0.00/0.63
	Debugger utilization (%)	99.50	99.40	99.31	99.10	88.18	78.39	70.55	—

*: It indicates the values evaluated by the end of 17 weeks. **: The time unit is weeks. Here the waiting time means the time of the fault pending in waiting queue, and the response time indicates the total time spent in the queueing system.

5 Conclusions

In this paper, we proposed a simulation approach based on *G/G/m* queueing model. The proposed simulation relaxes the perfect debugging assumption. In the numerical example, one real data set was selected to illustrate the use of our approach. Given different degrees of imperfect debugging, we analyzed the performance of debugging systems with various staffing levels. The performance is evaluated in terms of throughput, waiting time, response time, and debugger utilization. According to those criteria, we can have insight into the staffing needs for debugging teams under different conditions. Currently, we are enhancing the comparisons of service levels by evaluating more criteria. We plan to present the research results in the near future.

References

1. Lyu, M.R.: Handbook of Software Reliability Engineering. McGraw Hill, New York (1996)
2. Musa, J.D., Iannino, A., Okumoto, K.: Software Reliability, Measurement, Prediction and Application. McGraw Hill, New York (1987)
3. Dohi, T., Osaki, S., Trivedi, K.S.: An Infinite Server Queueing Approach for Describing Software Reliability Growth: Unified Modeling and Estimation Framework. In: 11th Asia-Pacific Software Engineering Conference, Busan, Korea, pp. 110–119 (2004)
4. Huang, C.Y., Lin, C.T.: Reliability Prediction and Assessment of Fielded Software Based on Multiple Change-Point Models. In: 11th IEEE International Symposium on Pacific Rim Dependable Computing, Changsha, China, pp. 379–3860 (2005)
5. Lyu, M.R.: Software Reliability Engineering: A Roadmap. In: 29th International Conference on Software Engineering, Future of Software Engineering, Minneapolis, pp. 153–170 (2007)
6. Su, Y.S., Huang, C.Y.: Neural-network-based Approaches for Software Reliability Estimation Using Dynamic Weighted Combinational Models. Journal of Systems and Software 80(4), 606–615 (2007)
7. Karunanithi, N., Malaiya, Y.K.: Prediction of Software Reliability Using Connectionist Models. IEEE Trans. on Software Engineering 18(7), 563–574 (1992)
8. Tian, L., Noore, A.: On-line Prediction of Software Reliability Using an Evolutionary Connectionist Model. Journal of Systems and Software 77(2), 173–180 (2005)
9. Cai, K.Y.: Software Defect and Operational Profile Modeling. Kluwer Academic Publishers, Dordrecht (1998)
10. Gokhale, S., Lyu, M.R.: A Simulation Approach to Structure-Based Software Reliability Analysis. IEEE Trans. on Software Engineering 31(8), 643–656 (2005)
11. Lin, C.T., Huang, C.Y.: Staffing Level Analysis of Software Debugging through Rate-Based Simulation Approaches. IEEE Transactions on Reliability (to appear in 2009)
12. Kapur, P.K., Younes, S.: Modelling an Imperfect Debugging Phenomenon in Software Reliability. Microelectronics and Reliability 36, 645–650 (1996)
13. Ohba, M., Chou, X.M.: Does Imperfect Debugging Affect Software Reliability Growth? In: 11th International Conference on Software Engineering, pp. 237–244 (1989)
14. Pham, H.: A Software Cost Model with Imperfect Debugging, Random Life Cycle and Penalty Cost. International Journal of Systems Science 27, 455–463 (1996)
15. Slud, E.: Testing for Imperfect Debugging in Software Reliability. Scandinavian J. Statistics 24, 555–572 (1997)
16. Tausworthe, R.C., Lyu, M.R.: A Generalized Technique for Simulating Software Reliability. IEEE Software 13(2), 77–88 (1996)
17. Goel, A.L., Okumoto, K.: An Analysis of Recurrent Software Errors in a Real-time Control System. In: 1978 ACM Annual Conference, Washington, D.C., USA, pp. 496–501 (1978)
18. Pham, H., Zhang, X.: An NHPP Software Reliability Model and Its Comparison. International Journal of Reliability, Quality and Safety Engineering 4(3), 269–282 (1997)
19. Gokhale, S., Lyu, M.R., Trivedi, K.S.: Incorporating Fault Debugging Activities into Software Reliability Models: a Simulation Approach. IEEE Trans. on Reliability 55(2), 281–292 (2006)
20. Xie, M., Yang, B.: A Study of the Effect of Imperfect Debugging on Software Development Cost. IEEE Trans. on Software Engineering 29(5), 471–473 (2003)
21. Gross, D., Harris, C.: Fundamentals of Queueing Theory. John Wiley & Sons, Chichester (1998)
22. Wu, Y.P., Hu, Q.P., Xie, M., Ng, S.H.: Modeling and Analysis of Software Fault Detection and Correction Process by Considering Time Dependency. IEEE Trans. on Reliability 56(4), 629–642 (2007)

Service Reliability and Availability Analysis of Distributed Software Systems Considering Malware Attack

Cheng-Jie Xiong, Yan-Fu Li, Min Xie, Szu-Hui Ng, and Thong-Ngee Goh

Department of Industrial and Systems Engineering, National University of Singapore, 119260, Singapore
{xiongchengjie,liyanfu,mxie,isensh,isegohtn}@nus.edu.sg

Abstract. Distributed systems are widely deployed in industries where high computational capability and low cost are required. Distributed software architecture is very important in the distributed system. However, since most distributed systems are designed based on a network structure, distributed software is very vulnerable to malware attacks. Due to the popularity of distributed system, it is vital to study the effects of malware attack on distributed systems. In this paper, we studied the malware attack behaviors by a Markov process model. The states of the object homogeneous distributed system can be derived by analyzing the Markov model, with which the service reliability and service availability can be further obtained. An illustrative demonstration is also presented.

Keywords: distributed system, service reliability, service availability, malware, Markov process.

1 Introduction

Distributed system, or sometimes referred to as "distributed computing", is a collection of multiple autonomous computers that communicate through a computer network [1] to solve a large computational task. The purpose of the distributed system is to coordinate the use of shared resources or provide communication services to the users [2]. Distributed system often consists of distributed hardware system and distributed software architecture. The distributed software architecture also has several layers: the local operating system on every autonomous computer, the distributed applications, and the middleware providing the buffer between computer network and distributed applications [4]. The distributed software architecture is of great importance, because without distributed software, the distributed system is of very limited function [5].

On the other hand, most failures occurred in distributed system can be classified as software problems. Reliability is a very important metric for distributed system performance. Many research efforts have been devoted into the reliability analysis of distributed systems, including both system/software reliability [6,13,14] and service reliability [7] of distributed systems. System availability is another important performance measure for complex systems and there are also plenty of literatures on the

D. Ślęzak et al. (Eds.): ASEA 2009, CCIS 59, pp. 313–320, 2009.

availability topics of distributed systems [7]. In summary, most of the related research concludes that distributed system's structure boosts both its reliability and availability, if compared to traditional computer systems. However, most of previous studies focused on failures caused by accidents or natural cataclysms. On the other hand, infective virus and malware become widely spread in the current computer networks including many distributed systems. Protecting the distributed system against the malicious attacks becomes an increasingly critical issue.

Malware is a general term used by computer professionals to refer a variety of forms of hostile, intrusive, or annoying software or program code [3]. Although different in forms, all malware aims to disturb the normal work of the target system and tries to spread and reproduce itself in other targets. According to Microsoft [3], over 90% of malware infections are direct consequences of network activities. If one computer in the distributed system is infected by malware, the infected node will attempt to attack other un-infected nodes via the network connection and will cause great lose of computational capability if the situation is not attended to. However, there are very limited resources in the existing literature to which we could refer.

As distributed system become more and more popular in human society, for example the internet reaches every corner of the world, while more and more malware are spreading over distributed systems; we are motivated to conduct a study of the effect of malware attack in distributed system. We regard malware attack as the major reason of computer crashing and the spreading of malware is modeled as a Markov process. The service reliability and availability is then derived as indicators of system status, which implies the consequences of malware attack.

This paper is organized as follows: in Section 2, the structure of common distributed systems is analyzed and malware attacks are considered. A Markov chain is built to model the malware spreading behavior with proper assumptions and we further derive the service reliability and availability from our proposed model. A simple but illustrative demonstration is then presented in Section 3. Section 4 summarizes this study with some possible further research directions.

2 Modeling of Malware Attack in Distributed Systems

2.1 Modelling of Distributed System under Malware Attack

In general, distributed systems are designed to coordinate node computers that are connected via certain types of network and provide computing services. In a typical distributed system, service request is usually received by a resource management server (RMS) and then the request is divided and dispatched to the computer nodes within the distributed system.

Various hardware and software architectures are used for distributed systems. If identical copies of application software run on the same type of computer nodes within a distributed system, then this kind of system is called a homogeneous distributed system. Homogeneous distributed system is the simplest while most widely used distributed system architecture [1,2,9] with many research and application studies [10]. In our study, we also focus on this type of distributed system.

The conceptual structure of a homogeneous N-nodes distributed system is shown in the figure 1.

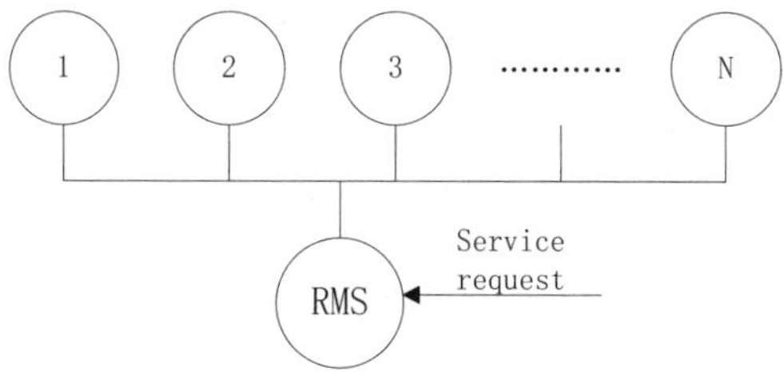

Fig. 1. Structure of a N-nodes homogeneous distributed system

Since all computer nodes within a distributed system communicate with each other, it is very easy for a malware-infected computer node to attack other computers. Malware disturbs normal operation of a computer node, which makes it unable to perform the assigned task anymore. In the mean while, malware utilizes all available resources of the infected computer node to attack other un-infected ones.

The attack of malware takes time and consumes resources such as CPU time and network bandwidth. Such malicious behaviors will deteriorate the overall performance of the distributed system. However, not all malware attacks are successful. The probability of a single successful malware attack is not high, but if the large amount of all target computer nodes is taken into consideration, some "unlucky" computer nodes still will get infected. In other words, if improper actions are taken, all nodes will ultimately become infected even if only one computer node was infected at the very beginning.

Luckily, complex systems such as distributed systems are usually taken good care of by professionals. Routine checking mechanisms are often deployed so that malfunctioning components can be restored to normal state. In order to model the behaviors of malware attacks and these restoring performances, a continuous Markov chain is built with proper assumptions. A list of notations is used in this paper.

Notation:

λ_i	failure rate of computer nodes
μ_r	restoration rate
λ_m	malware infection rate
λ_a	attacking rate of a malware-infected node
$X(t)$	the state of the distributed system at time t
$p_{(H,I,D)}(t)$	probability that the system is in state (H,I,D) at time t
α	service rate of each computer node of an exponential distribution
H	the number of normal computer nodes
I	the number of computers that are infected by malware
D	the number of computers that fail
N	the total number of computers: $N = H + I + D$.
T_E	required finishing time of a single service request
T	actual finishing time of a single service request
R_s	service reliability of the distributed system
A_s	service availability of the distributed system

We also made the following assumptions to facilitate our analysis in this research:

Assumptions:

1. A homogeneous N-nodes distributed system consists of N identical computer nodes, on which identical software applications are installed. Malware keeps attacking the system from outside the system.
2. Each computer nodes have the same service rate α . The work of each individual node is independent.
3. Each system node has an initial failure rate of λ_i and an initial infection probability λ_m that one computer node will fail or get infected, respectively. If a computer node is infected by malware, it can no longer perform the assigned task anymore. In the mean while, it keeps attacking other un-infected nodes with infection rate λ_a
4. Routine system checking is performed. After checking, a node can be restored with probability μ_r . If both infected nodes and failed nodes exist, failed nodes are dealt with first.
5. Only one un-infected node can be infected by malware attacking at a time.

All the above assumptions are easy to validate except for 2. There are cases where certain nodes have to wait for others' output as their input. Dai et al [8,11] discussed the problems of correlated nodes in distributed/grid systems. Since it's hard to estimate the level of correlation, which is normally low and the topic is not our main focus, this assumption is relaxed in our study.

Consider a stochastic process $\{X(t)\}$, where $X(t)=\{H,I,D\}$ is the state of the N-node distributed system. *H* denotes the number of healthy nodes, *I* denotes the number of infected nodes and *D* denotes the number of failed nodes. It can easily be proven that the Markov property holds in this process and $\{X(t)\}$ can be modeled as a continuous time Markov process. Due to the size limit of this paper, we only present the transition graph of a single state. Suppose that at least one computer node is infected by malware, and then the state transition diagraph is obtained in Fig.2.

Based on the transition graph in Fig.2, when there are infected nodes, for the state $\{H, I, D\}$ we could obtain a Kolmogorov differential equation listed below:

$$(I\lambda_i+\mu_r+H\lambda_m+I\lambda_a+H\lambda_i)\frac{d}{dt}p_{(H,I,D)}(t)=((H+1)\lambda_m+(I-1)\lambda_a)p_{(H+1,I-1,D)}(t)\\+\mu_r p_{(H-1,I,D+1)}(t)+\mu_r p_{(H-1,I+1,D)}(t) \tag{1}$$

The differential equations can be obtained similarly on other states. By consideration all the states, we can have a set of differential equations describing the transitions between different states.

If no malware infection has ever been reported, another type of equation can be obtained for the state $\{H, 0, D\}$:

$$(H\lambda_i+H\lambda_m)\frac{d}{dt}p_{(H,0,D)}(t)=\mu_r p_{(H-1,0,D+1)}(t)+\mu_r p_{(H-1,1,D)}(t) \tag{2}$$

Similar to (1), we can obtain a set of differential equations to describe the transitions between states without considering the malware infections.

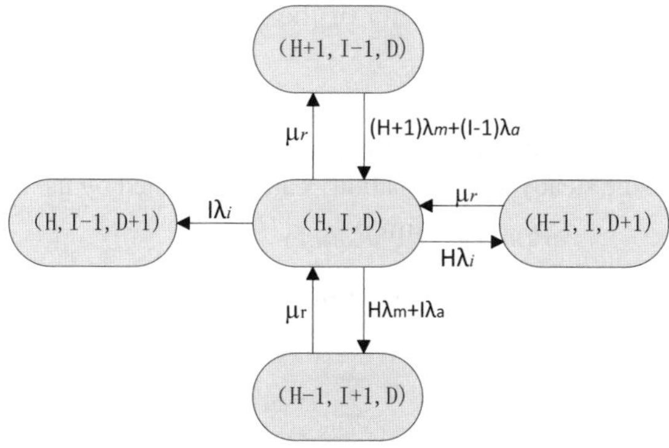

Fig. 2. Transition graph of state $\{H,I,D\}$

To solve the equation systems based on (1) and (2), we have to obtain the boundary conditions. We assume that the system starts from an all-healthy state, hence the boundary conditions are:

$$\sum p_{(H,I,D)}(t)=1,\ p_{(N,0,0)}(0)=1,\ p_{(N-1,0,1)}(0)=0,\cdots,\ p_{(0,N,0)}(0)=0,\ p_{(0,0,N)}(0)=0 \qquad (3)$$

The continuous Markov process can be explicitly solved with (1)~(3) and then we are able to get the transient state probability $p_{(H,I,D)}(t)$ of each state, which will greatly improve our capability of analyzing the system.

2.2 Derivation of Service Reliability and Availability

Software reliability of distributed systems has been studied by many authors, but only a few have ever considered the service reliability of distributed systems. There is still no precise definition of service reliability, but most authors [7,11] considered it as the probability of successfully finishing a target task within a required time interval. In this research, we also adopt this definition. According to our definition of service reliability, the service reliability of our target system at time t is the probability that it can finish the requested service within T_E time:

$$R_s(t)=\Pr\{T\le T_E\} \qquad (4)$$

We further assume that the finishing time of a certain requested service follows an exponential distribution. Then (4) can be further derived as

$$R_s(t)=\sum R_s(t\mid\{H,I,D\})\Pr\{H,I,D\}=\sum p_{(H,I,D)}(t)F(H\alpha T_E) \qquad (5)$$

where F is the CDF of an exponential distribution. The service availability can be defined as the probability that at least one computer nodes in the distributed system is still functioning:

$$A_s(t)=\Pr\{H>0\mid t\}=\sum_{\forall H>0} p_{(H,I,D)}(t) \qquad (6)$$

The above two equations give explicit forms of the transient service reliability and availability at a certain time. However, in some cases people are more interested in the situation when the system transition becomes stable. The steady state service reliability and availability can also be obtained with our proposed model.

Lemma1: The steady state probability of the Markov chain proposed in Section 2.1 exists.

Proof: Since all states communicates with each other, the Markov chain is irreducible and positive recurrent. Thus Lemma 1 is proven.

With Lemma1, the steady state probability can be obtained by the following equations:

$$p_{(H,I,D)} = \lim_{t\to\infty} p_{(H,I,D)}(t) \tag{7}$$

where $p_{(H,I,D)}$ is the steady state probability of state $\{H,I,D\}$. Then the steady state service availability can be derived as:

$$A_s = 1 - \sum_{\forall I,D} p_{(0,I,D)} \tag{8}$$

And the steady state service reliability can be derived as:

$$R_s = \sum_{\forall H,I,D} p_{(H,I,D)} F(H\alpha T_E) \tag{9}$$

3 Numerical Examples

In this section, two numerical examples will be presented and compared. We will first conduct a numerical analysis of service reliability and availability of a 3-node homogeneous distributed system without considering malware attack. Then we take the malware attack scenario into consideration. The results are compared and meaningful conclusions are made. Although we do not use real case data, our model and analysis approach can easily be adopted when real datasets are available.

Kondakci [12] conducted a similar study on malware analysis and provided some real data. However, his approach is different from ours and his data is based on single personal computers in an internet environment and may not be suitable for our study. In this research, some artificial data are generated for illustration purpose and are summarized in Table 1.

Table 1. Infection, restoration and failure probability

Notation	Value
λ_i	0.05
μ_r	0.8
λ_m	0.1
λ_a	0.3
α	0.5
T_E	2

If the distributed system is well protected and free of malware attack. As in this case, a duplet $\{H,D\}$ is enough for describing the system state. We define state 0~3 as {3,0}, {2,1}, {1,2} and {0,3}, respectively. If the distributed system is under malware attack, we have totally 9 states as {3,0,0} , {2,1,0}, {2,0,1}, {1,2,0}, {1,1,1}, {0,2,1}, {0,1,2},

{0,0,3} and {0,3,0}, respectively. Solving (1)~(3) we could obtain their transient state probability, based on which the system service reliability and availability can be obtained. Then the service reliability and availability can be plotted as follows:

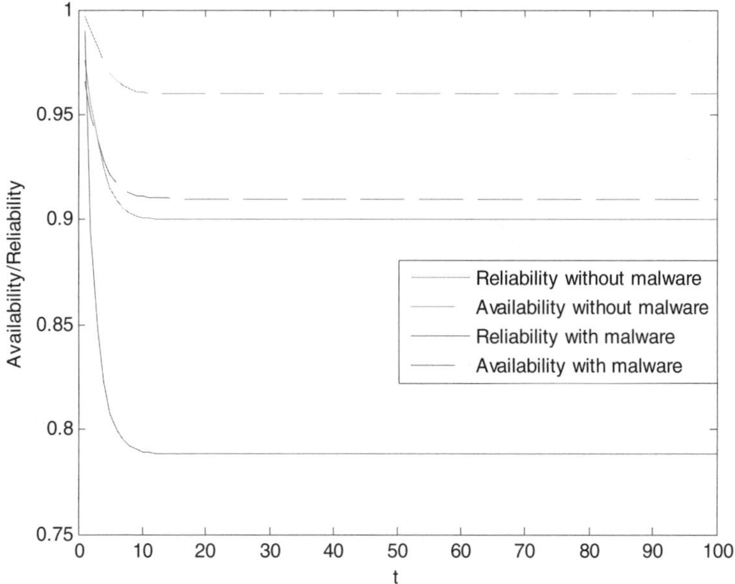

Fig. 3. Service reliability and availability plot over t

By comparing the different two sets of results that we obtained in analyzing two different scenarios, some meaningful conclusions can be made. An apparent decline of both service reliability and availability is observed if malware attack exists. This result indicates that the capability of a distributed system is obviously hampered by malware attack. Further comparison shows that the service reliability has been degraded more than availability has. In fact, even a distributed system is attacked by malware; it is hard for all its computer nodes to get infected at the same time. However, since the computational capability of a distributed system depends highly on the available computer nodes, it is expected that the service time for a certain task increases rapidly if malware attack exists. Our experimental analysis tallies with the real world cases.

4 Conclusions

In this research, the problem of malware attack in distributed software systems is considered. A Markovian approach is proposed to model the problem and we derived meaningful system metrics such as service reliability and availability from our proposed model. However, some strong assumptions are made in this research and further validation analysis is needed. For future research, we plan to take the different network structure of a distributed system into consideration. The sequential problem of computer nodes also interests us.

References

1. Andrews, G.R.: Foundations of Multithreaded, Parallel, and Distributed Programming. Addison-Wesley, Reading (2000)
2. Ghosh, S.: Distributed Systems–An Algorithmic Approach. Chapman & Hall/CRC3, Boca Raton (2007)
3. Defining Malware: FAQ, http://technet.microsoft.com/en-us/library/dd632948.aspx
4. Puder, A., Romer, K., Pilhofer, F.: Distributed Systems Architecture: A Middleware Approach. Morgan Kaufmann, San Francisco (2006)
5. Reza, H.: A methodology for architectural design of concurrent and distributed software systems. Journal of Supercomputing 37(3), 227–248 (2006)
6. Dai, Y.S., Levitin, G.: Optimal resource allocation for maximizing performance and reliability in tree-structured grid services. IEEE Transactions on Reliability 56(3), 444–453 (2007)
7. Dai, Y.S., Xie, M., Poh, K.L., Liu, G.Q.: A study of service reliability and availability for distributed systems. Reliability Engineering and System Safety 79, 103–112 (2003)
8. Dai, Y.S., Xie, M., Poh, K.L.: Availability modeling and cost optimization for the grid resource management system. IEEE Transactions on Systems Man and Cybernetics Part A-Systems and Humans 38(1), 170–179 (2008)
9. Agneeswaran, V.S., Janakiram, D.: Node-Capability-Aware Replica Management for Peer-to-Peer Grids. IEEE Transactions on Systems Man and Cybernetics Part A-Systems and Humans 39(4), 807–818 (2009)
10. Xie, M., Dai, Y.S., Poh, K.L., Lai, C.D.: Optimal number of hosts in a distributed system based on cost criteria. International Journal of Systems Science 35(6), 343–353 (2004)
11. Dai, Y.S., Wang, X.L.: Optimal resource allocation on grid systems for maximizing service reliability using a genetic algorithm. Reliability Engineering & System Safety 91(9), 1071–1082 (2006)
12. Kondakci, S.: Epidemic state analysis of computers under malware attacks. Simulation Modelling Practice and Theory 16(5), 571–584 (2008)
13. Huang, C.Y., Kuo, S.Y., Lyu, M.R.: An Assessment of Testing-Effort Dependent Software Reliability Growth Models. IEEE Transactions on Reliability 56(2), 198–211 (2007)
14. Tamura, Y., Yamada, S.: Optimisation analysis for reliability assessment based on stochastic differential equation modelling for open source software. International Journal of System Science 40(4), 429–438 (2009)

A Test Coverage-Based Model for Predicting Software Fault Content and Location during Multi-phase Functional Testing

Carol Smidts[1] and Ying Shi[2]

[1] Ohio State University, Columbus, OH 43210
smidts.1@osu.edu
[2] University of Maryland, College Park, Maryland 20742
yshi@umd.edu

Abstract. In this paper, we present a new test coverage-based model which allows 1) Description of software systems developed through multiple phases of functional testing, a practice common in industry, 2) Description of software systems where either the initial fault distribution is non-uniform with respect to location, or the repair and test and detection process favor certain locations, 3) Description of software systems which exhibit both characteristics.

Keyword: Software Reliability Prediction, Test Coverage, Multi-phase Test, Imperfect Repair, Defect Location Prediction.

1 Introduction

The relationship between test coverage (TC) and defect coverage (i.e. percentage of defects identified through test) has been highlighted by many and number of research efforts have been devoted to linking test coverage to the number of faults remaining and number of failures experienced. To cite only a few, Vouk [1] directly relates the number of detected faults and test coverage through a Weibull function. Piwowarsky et al. 2] predicts reliability based on the fact that the fault removal rate is a linear function of the code coverage. Malaiya et al. introduces a logarithmic model [3] that relates testing effort to TC and then estimates reliability using Musa's exponential model. Malaiya et al. [4] also develop a logarithmic-exponential model which differs from his earlier model by considering the linear relations between defect coverage and TC once a certain TC level is achieved. Gokhale et al. [5] [6] propose a unified definition of TC and incorporate explicitly the time-varying TC functions into the Enhanced Non-homogeneous Poisson Process (ENHPP) framework. In their model, variation in the number of failures experienced is proportional to variation in coverage via a detection rate function which varies with time. Pham and Zhang [7] revise the ENHPP reliability model by proposing *S*-shaped TC functions and by considering imperfect repair while assuming repairs take place as soon as the failure is experienced. Cai and Lyu [8] further integrate time and TC measurements together and present a hybrid reliability prediction model.

D. Ślęzak et al. (Eds.): ASEA 2009, CCIS 59, pp. 321–329, 2009.

Existing models assume that functional testing is a continuous single phase process where the software is run through a single predefined series of tests. For such cases the coverage function is a monotonically non-decreasing function of time as described in Figure 1a. While this assumption is appropriate for a large class of software development efforts, it fails to represent development efforts where functional testing is organized as a multi-phase process. In such case the software will undergo several series of functional tests and the coverage function will increase monotonically by phase while experiencing discontinuities between phases (see Figure 1b and 1c). Furthermore, repairs are not attempted as soon as failures are experienced but are deferred to the end of each phase. This process will in particular be found in the case of safety critical systems where one needs to ensure that the software will pass through an entire series of tests without experiencing faults (See Section B.3.1.12.4 of [9]; Section 5.4.2 of [10]; [11]). This leads to the existence of at least two phases: one with faults, and one without faults.

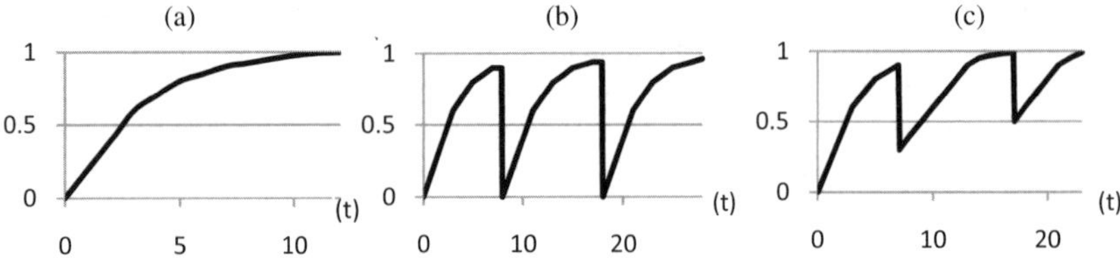

Fig. 1. Coverage is a continuous monotonic non-decreasing function of testing time (a); Coverage function for Multiple Phases of Functional Testing (b) (c)

In addition, these models make the assumption that faults are distributed uniformly in the code. There is no evidence that this might be true in practice (see for instance a recent study by [12]). While the uniformity assumption may not be critical for most software systems and as such is a very useful assumption, it needs to be carefully examined for safety critical systems which are more sensitive to the location of faults. Location is indeed an important contributing factor in the severity of faults.

This paper proposes analytical expressions for the number of failures remaining and the remaining fault location distribution which can be used for reliability prediction or to adjust testing efforts. In Section II we derive expressions for failures experienced and faults remaining for a software system undergoing multiple phases of functional test before being declared ready for fielding and operation. In Section III we account for the non-uniformity of the distribution of faults on fault sites. We conclude with possible applications of the extensions presented (see Section IV).

2 Number of Failures Experienced and Faults Remaining in the Case of Multiple Functional Test Phases

For software systems such as safety critical systems, a software component before being considered ready for release will need to undergo multiple phases of functional test. In phase 1, a first test plan will be used which contains a first set of functional tests. Failures are uncovered as testing progresses. Corresponding fixes are made at the end of the test phase. The modified code then undergoes another set of functional tests extract from a second test plan and so forth and so on. There may of course be some overlap between consecutive test plans. In such case the evolution of coverage with time will cease to be a continuous monotonic non-decreasing function of time as assumed in the models of section I and instead will take the form given in Figure 1b or 1c. Let us then try to express m(t), the number of failures experienced by time t. We will denote by t_{i-1} and t_i respectively the beginning and end of phase "i"; by $\Delta m_i(t)$ the number of failures experienced between t_{i-1} and t where $t_{i-1} \leq t < t_i$; by ã, the initial number of faults which exist in the code at the onset of functional testing, i.e. at the beginning of the first test phase.

Our assumptions are as follows: *1) Faults are uniformly distributed over all potential fault sites; 2) When a potential fault-site is covered, any fault present at that site is detected with probability K(t); 3) Repairs take place at the end of the phase and new faults may be introduced through repair errors. The repair rate is r and the probability of fault introduction given that a repair error has occurred is γ; 4) Coverage is a continuous monotonic non-decreasing function of testing time per phase as displayed in Figure 1b or 1c.*

Under those assumptions we obtain the following set of equations:

$$\frac{d\Delta m_1(t)}{dt} = \tilde{a}\, K_1(t)\, \frac{dc_1(t)}{dt}$$

for $0 \leq t < t_1$ where t_1 is the end of the first phase, $\Delta m_1(0) = 0$, and $c_1(t)$ is defined over $0 \leq t < t_1$ and is the coverage function over that interval of time.

$$\frac{d\Delta m_2(t)}{dt} = (\tilde{a} - \Delta m_1(t_1) \times r + \Delta m_1(t_1) \times (1 - r) \times \gamma) K_2(t) \frac{dc_2(t)}{dt}$$

for $t_1 \leq t < t_2$ where t_2 is the end of the second phase, $\Delta m_2(t_1) = 0$, and $c_2(t)$ is defined over $t_1 \leq t < t_2$ and is the coverage function over that interval of time.

$$\frac{d\Delta m_3(t)}{dt} = (\tilde{a} - \Delta m_1(t_1) \times r + \Delta m_1(t_1) \times (1 - r) \times \gamma) - \Delta m_2(t_2) \times r + \Delta m_2(t_2) \times (1 - r) \times \gamma)\, K_3(t)\, \frac{dc_3(t)}{dt}$$

for $t_2 \leq t < t_3$ where t_3 is the end of the third phase, $\Delta m_3(t_2) = 0$, and $c_3(t)$ is defined over $t_2 \leq t < t_3$ and is the coverage function over that interval of time.

We rewrite $\frac{d\Delta m_3(t)}{dt}$ as:

$$\frac{d\Delta m_3(t)}{dt} = \left(\tilde{a} - \left(\Delta m_1(t_1) + \Delta m_2(t_2)\right) \times r + \left(\Delta m_1(t_1) + \Delta m_2(t_2)\right) \times (1 - r) \times \gamma\right) K_3(t)\, \frac{dc_3(t)}{dt}$$

So more generally we have:

$$\frac{d\Delta m_i(t)}{dt} = \left(\tilde{a} - r \times \sum_{k=1}^{i-1} \Delta m_k(t_k) + (1 - r) \times \gamma \times \left(\Delta m_k(t_k)\right)\right) K_i(t)\, \frac{dc_i(t)}{dt} \quad (1)$$

or $t_{i-1} \leq t < t_i$ where t_i is the end of the ith phase, $\Delta m_i(t_{i-1}) = 0$, and $c_i(t)$ is defined over $t_{i-1} \leq t < t_i$ and is the coverage function over that interval of time.

If the different K's are constant per phase, we can integrate (1) over each phase and we will obtain after integration:

$$\Delta m_i(t) = \left(\tilde{a} - r \times \sum_{k=1}^{i-1} \Delta m_k(t_k) + (1-r) \times \gamma \times \left(\sum_{k=1}^{i-1} \Delta m_k(t_k)\right)\right) K_i \int_{c_L(i)}^{c_U(i)} \frac{dc_i(t)}{dt} dt$$

which is thus

$$\Delta m_i(t) = \left(\tilde{a} - r \times \sum_{k=1}^{i-1} \Delta m_k(t_k) + (1-r) \times \gamma \times \left(\sum_{k=1}^{i-1} \Delta m_k(t_k)\right)\right) K_i \times \left(c_U(i) - c_L(i)\right) \quad (2)$$

where $c_U(i)$ and $c_L(i)$ are respectively the upper and lower bounds of coverage for phase i.

Example- Let us consider an example software S. S is undergoing three functional test phases. Let us also assume that the upper and lower coverage values for each functional test phase, as well as the number of defects found in each phase is given in Table 1.

Table 1. Multiple Phase Test Profile for Software S

Phases	1	2	3
C_L(i)	0	0	0
C_U(i)	.5	.7	.95
Number of faults found during Phase "i" Functional Test	5	2	0

This profile is representative of safety critical systems which typically will achieve high levels of test coverage at the end of functional testing and are also characterized by no-defects found during the last functional test phase. Let us also assume that r=.9 and γ=.25. Under those conditions the set of equations (2) becomes:

$$\tilde{a}K_1 = .1$$
$$(\tilde{a} - 4.375) \times K_2 = 0.028571$$
$$(\tilde{a} - 6.475) \times K_3 = 0$$

The set of equations contains four unknowns and as such can not be solved without the help of an additional equation. In particular one could use early prediction models to compute a value for ã as suggested in Gokhale [5]. The issue with using early prediction models is of course the large uncertainty in the estimate which can lead us to either overestimate or underestimate the number of faults. Note also that the last equation leads to a situation where one can possibly make two different conclusions. One is that ã=6.475 (which we can interpret conservatively as being ã=7) or K_3=0 (i.e. the tests are not able to trigger failures and correspondingly reveal faults).

In the phase-based functional test expression defined by equation (2), one should also note that:

$$\left(\tilde{a} - r \times \sum_{k=1}^{n} \Delta m_k(t_k) + (1-r) \times \gamma \times \left(\sum_{k=1}^{n} \Delta m_k(t_k)\right)\right) \tag{3}$$

is the total number of faults remaining after all phases of functional testing. For system S this number is given by ã-6.475.

3 Extensions in the Case of a Non-uniform Distribution of Faults

We will now focus on another extension of interest which considers the fact that faults may not be distributed uniformly over the different fault locations. This is of particular importance in safety critical systems because the location of a fault is a determinant factor in the severity of the associated failure. As such it is necessary if possible to locate the position of the remaining faults. We will establish the equations providing the number of failures experienced and the number of faults remaining for multiple test phases.

Our assumptions have now become: *1) Faults are not uniformly distributed over all potential fault sites. The probability that a fault resides in location L at time t during phase "i" is given by $f_i(L,t)$; 2) When a potential fault-site is covered, any fault present at that site is detected with probability $K_i(L,t)$ where "L" is the fault location and "i" is the functional test phase; 3) Repairs take place at the end of each phase. Repair activities are subject to errors. The probability of a perfect repair which eliminates the original fault and does not introduce any new faults is r_i for functional test phase "i". Different repair errors are considered: a) the fault is not corrected and remains in its initial location L, no new fault is introduced; b) a fault moves from its original location L to a new location L'; c) a fault remains in its original location L and a new fault is introduced in a new location L'. To express these different cases we introduce: γ_i the conditional probability that a new fault is introduced during functional test phase "i"; m_i the conditional probability that a fault changes location; $k_i(L,L')$ the conditional probability that given that a fault is introduced or is moved due to a repair at location L, it moves to L'; 4) Coverage is a continuous monotonic non-decreasing function of testing time per phase.*

Let us introduce additional notations for the coverage function. We define by $c_i(L,t)$ the probability that a location is covered by time t in phase "i". $C_i(t)$ is the program coverage at time t during phase "i" and is given by:

$$C_i(t) = \sum_{S} c_i(L,t) \qquad \text{for } t_{i-1} \leq t < t_i .$$

where S is the set of software locations for software system S. From there, one obtains the number of failures experienced since the beginning of phase "i" as:

$$\Delta m_i(t+dt) = \Delta m_i(t) + \sum_{S} \big(c_i(L,t+dt) - c_i(L,t)\big) \times \tilde{a} \times f_i(L,t) \times K_i(L,t) \tag{4}$$

for $t_{i-1} \leq t < t_i$ and where ã as before is the number of faults in the code at time $t_0 = 0$. Dividing by *dt* and taking the limit for *dt* going to zero, we obtain:

$$\frac{d\Delta m_i(t)}{dt} = \sum_{S} \frac{\partial c_i(L,t)}{\partial t} \times \tilde{a} \times f_i(L,t) \times K_i(L,t) \tag{5}$$

for $t_{i-1} \leq t < t_i$. The number of failures experienced during a phase "i" is then given by:

$$\int_{t_{i-1}}^{t_i} \frac{d\Delta m_i(t)}{dt} dt = \int_{t_{i-1}}^{t_i} \sum_{S} \frac{\partial c_i(L,t)}{\partial t} \times \tilde{a} \times f_i(L,t) \times K_i(L,t)\, dt \tag{6}$$

The number of failures experienced due to a particular location over all n phases is:

$$\sum_{i=1}^{n} \int_{t_{i-1}}^{t_i} \frac{d\Delta m_i(L,t)}{dt} dt = \sum_{i=1}^{n} \int_{t_{i-1}}^{t_i} \frac{\partial c_i(L,t)}{\partial t} \times \tilde{a} \times f_i(L,t) \times K_i(L,t)\, dt \tag{7}$$

The number of faults in location L changes as a function of detection and repair. During the phase, the fault count does not change but faults are uncovered. At the end of the phase, faults uncovered due to failures experienced are fixed. Let us denote by t_i+ the time at the end of phase "i" where repair is attempted, the probability that a fault still exists at time t_i+ in location L is given by the following equation:

$$\begin{aligned} f_i(L,t_i+) = {} & f_{i-1}(L,t_{i-1}+) - r_i \times \left[\int_{t_{i-1}}^{t_i} \frac{\delta c_i(L,t)}{\delta t} \times \tilde{a} \times f_{i-1}(L,t_{i-1}+) \times K_i(L,t) dt \right] \\ & -(1-r_i) \times (1-\gamma_i) \times m_i \int_{t_{i-1}}^{t_i} \frac{\delta c_i(L,t)}{\delta t} \times \tilde{a} \times f_{i-1}(L,t_{i-1}+) \times K_i(L,t) dt \\ & +(1-r_i) \times \gamma_i \times \sum_{L' \neq L} \left[\int_{t_{i-1}}^{t_i} \frac{\delta c_i(L',t)}{\delta t} \times \tilde{a} \times f_{i-1}(L',t_{i-1}+) \times K_i(L',t) \times k_i(L',L) dt \right] \\ & +(1-r_i) \times (1-\gamma_i) \times m_i \times \sum_{L' \neq L} \left[\int_{t_{i-1}}^{t_i} \frac{\delta c_i(L',t)}{\delta t} \times \tilde{a} \times f_{i-1}(L',t_{i-1}+) \times K_i(L',t) \times k_i(L',L) dt \right] \end{aligned} \tag{8}$$

The first term corresponds to faults that were in L at the beginning of the phase, the second term corresponds to successful repair of faults detected through failures experienced, the third term corresponds to the attempted repair of a fault in L where the fault will be moved to some unknown location L', the fourth term corresponds to the attempted repair of a fault at location L' resulting in a new fault introduced in location L, and the fifth term to unsuccessful repairs in location L' that resulted in the moving of the fault in L. The number of faults remaining is given by:

$$A(t_i+) = \sum_{S} \tilde{a}\, f_i(L,t_i+) \qquad \text{with } A(t_0+) = \tilde{a}.$$

Example- Let us consider an example software SX. SX is undergoing two functional test phases. Let us also assume that the upper and lower coverage values for each functional test phase are given in Table 2. The case study considers 100,000 different locations. These could be different modules, lines of code, etc dependent upon the level of abstraction selected. Values of the additional parameters are given in Tables 3

Table 2. Multi-Phase Test Profile for Software SX

Phases	1	2
$C_L(i)$	0	0
$C_U(i)$	.67	1

Table 3. Detection probabilities per location for the two phases for Software SX

Case #	(a)	(b)
$K_1(L)$	0 for L= [12000, 21999] U [32000, 41999] U [82000, 94999] .5 for all other values of L	0 for L= [33000, 54999] U [82000, 92999] .5 for all other values of L
$K_2(L)$	.5 for all L in [0, 100000]	.5 for all L in [0,100000]

Table 4. k_i(L',L) for the two phases (i = 1,2)

Case #	For L'=1	For L'=2 to 99,999	For L'=100,000
(a)	k_i(L',L)=1 if L=2 k_i(L',L)=0 otherwise	k_i(L',L)=.5 if L'=L-1 or L'=L+1 k_i(L',L)=0 otherwise	k_i(L',L)=1 if L=99999 k_i(L',L)=0 otherwise
(b)	k_i(L',L)=1 if L=2 k_i(L',L)=0 otherwise	k_i(L',L)=1 if L'=L-1 k_i(L',L)=0 otherwise	k_i(L',L)=1 if L=99999 k_i(L',L)=0 otherwise

Table 5. Remaining Parameters for SX

Case #	(a)				(b)				
	$r_1=r_2$	$\gamma_1=\gamma_2$	$m_1=m_2$	$\tilde{a}$	$r_1=r_2$	γ_1	γ_2	$m_1=m_2$	$\tilde{a}$
	.9	.25	.2	3	.9	.4	.3	.2	3

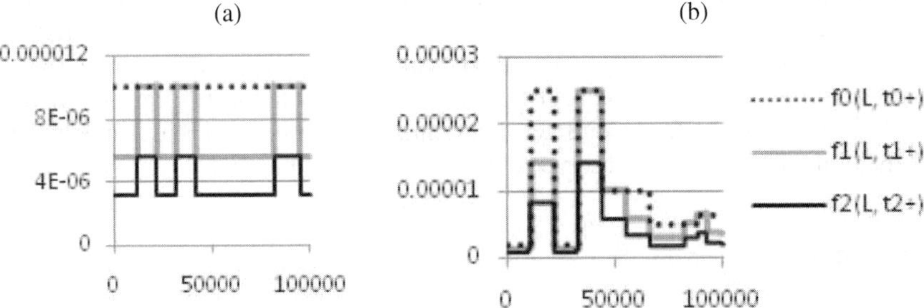

Fig. 2. Fault Location Distributions for SX

to 5. In this example we assume that $K_i(L,t)$ is dependent upon the phase and the location but not upon time. Results are given in Figure 2. The example shows the likely location of remaining defects and their distribution as well as the potential number of faults remaining.

4 Conclusions

This paper has presented a new model which allows: 1) Description of software systems developed through multiple phases of functional testing, 2) Description of software systems where either the initial fault distribution is non-uniform with respect to location, or the repair, test or detection process favor certain locations, 3) Description of software systems which exhibit both characteristics. These extensions are of particular interest for safety critical systems which will typically be developed according to a phase-based process where the last phase of the process is devoid of detectable faults. For safety critical systems fault location information is of importance because the location of a fault determines how frequently it will be executed in operation and whether it will propagate. As such location is primary in determining fault propagation characteristics and whether the fault will have a large impact or not. The fault location distribution could be used in combination with mutation or modeling approaches to determine the fault propagation characteristics (K) of the software in operation before it runs in the field. Such information is important for safety critical systems which cannot be allowed to fail in the field and for which we will not be able to collect field data (failures in operation). Location information can also be used to refine testing and target it towards high impact high likelihood faults if those exist. In this paper the framework was applied to synthetic examples whose characteristics were chosen to be representative of real case studies. Application of the framework to a system with 100,000 locations shows that its computational complexity is limited, that results obtained for diverse sets of parameters display foreseeable trends, and that the tool developed can easily be expanded to handle more complex systems. Through simulations such as those presented in section 3, one can observe the effect of different test strategies, of initial fault distributions, of repair and new fault introduction rates, of the number of functional test phases and determine how these influence the final fault distributions. The knowledge gained can be used to optimize testing and improve reliability. Application of the models developed to an actual case study is not discussed in this paper and will be the object of future extensions. This will in particular entail selection of adequate approaches for parameter estimation. The parameters should be identifiable using a combination of methods and tools such as: code coverage tools for c(L); early prediction methods [11] for $f_0(L)$; limited mutation for transfers of faults k(L',L) [13]; field data for repair rates, fault introduction rates and K(L') updated using information related to faults observed during the different phases.

References

[1] Vouk, M.A.: Using reliability models during testing with non-operational profile. In: Second Bellcore/Purdue Symposium on Issues in software reliability estimation, pp. 103–110 (1993)

[2] Piwowarski, P., Ohba, M., Caruso, J.: Coverage measurement experience during function test. In: Proceeding of The 15th International Conference on Software Engineering, Baltimore, MD, pp. 287–301 (1993)

[3] Malaiya, Y.K., Li, N., Bieman, J.M., Karcich, R., Skibbe, B.: The relationship between test coverage and reliability. In: Proceeding of The 5th International Symposium on Software Reliability Engineering, Los Alamitos, pp. 186–195 (1994)

[4] Malaiya, Y.K., Li, M.N., Bieman, J.M., Karcich, R.: Software reliability growth with test coverage. IEEE Transactions on Reliability 51(4), 420–426 (2002)
[5] Gokhale, S.S., Trivedi, K.S.: A Time/Structure Based Software Reliability Model. Annals of Software Engineering 8, 85–121 (1999)
[6] Gokhale, S.S., Philip, T., Marinos, P.N., Trivedi, K.S.: Unification of finite failure non-homogeneous Poisson process models through test coverage. In: Proceedings of the International Symposium on Software Reliability Engineering, White Plains, NY, pp. 299–307 (1996)
[7] Pham, H., Zhang, X.: NHPP software reliability and cost models with testing coverage. European Journal of Operational Research 145(2), 443–454 (2003)
[8] Cai, X., Lyu, M.R.: Software reliability modeling with test coverage: Experimentation and measurement with A fault-tolerant software project. In: Proceedings of the 18th IEEE International Symposium on Software Reliability Engineering, Trollhättan, Sweden, pp. 17–26 (2007)
[9] USNRC, Guidance on Software Reviews for Digital I &C Systems, NUREG 0800 BTP 7-14 (2007)
[10] IEEE, Systems engineering — Application and management of the systems engineering process, IEEE STD 1220 (2005)
[11] Smidts, C.S., Li, M., Shi, Y., Kong, W., Dai, J.: A Large Scale Validation of A Methodology for Assessing Software Quality (under revision). University of Maryland-College Park (2009)
[12] Koru, A.G., Zhang, D., Eman, K.E., Liu, H.: An Investigation into the Functional Form of the Size-Defect Relationship for Software Modules. IEEE Transactions on Software Engineering 35(2), 293–304 (2009)
[13] Shi, Y., Kong, W., Dai, J., Smidts, C.: A Reliability Prediction Method for Safety Critical Systems Based on Test Coverage. In: The 3rd International Conference on Reliability and Safety Engineering, Kharagpur, India (2007)

A Refined Non-parametric Algorithm for Sequential Software Reliability Estimation

Shintaro Mizoguchi and Tadashi Dohi

Department of Information Engineering, Graduate School of Engineering
Hiroshima University, 1–4–1 Kagamiyama, Higashi-Hiroshima, 739–8527 Japan
dohi@rel.hiroshima-u.ac.jp

Abstract. In this article, we improve a non-parametric order statistics-based software reliability model by Barghout, Littlewood and Abdel-Ghaly (1998), from the standpoints of estimation algorithm and reliability measure. More specifically, we introduce the kernel density estimation method with a truncated Gaussian kernel function and estimate the software fault-detection time distribution with higher accuracy. Also, we use the mean value of the inter-fault detection time instead of its median, and predict the future behavior of it sequentially. In the validation test with real software fault data, it is investigated how the improvement influences the quantitative software reliability assessment.

Keywords: software reliability, non-parametric estimation, kernel density estimation, cross validation, prequential likelihood method, recalibration, u-plot.

1 Introduction

During the last four decades, the software reliability engineering has played a central role to provide several quantitative methods used in real software development processes. Since the assessment of software reliability is one of the main issues in this area, one needs several kinds of mathematical models to assess quantitatively the software reliability, which is the probability that the software system does not fail during a specified time period. In the software reliability research, a huge number of software reliability models (SRMs) have been proposed in the literature [10,12] from the various points of view. In general SRMs can be classified into two categories; parametric SRMs and non-parametric SRMs. Since the parametric SRMs are based on scenarios on the software fault-detection process in software testing phase, it is difficult to validate the physical meaning of scenarios themselves assumed on parametric modeling. Hence, we need to identify the best SRM under several criteria by taking account of parameter estimation, statistical test and model selection.

In past literatures, some authors considered statistically non-parametric estimation methods for software reliability. Sofer and Miller [13] assumed a polygonal line estimator of the software intensity function for the usual non-homogeneous Poisson process (NHPP)-based SRM and proposed a smoothing algorithm based

D. Ślęzak et al. (Eds.): ASEA 2009, CCIS 59, pp. 330–337, 2009.

on the common quadratic programming. The basic idea behind their approach is to interpolate realizations of the software intensity function with polygonal lines. Gandy and Jensen [7] used the well-known Nelson-Aalen multiplicative estimator for the NHPP-based SRM and proved its statistical consistency and asymptotic normality. However, the problem for their approach is to need the multiple time series data on the software fault-detection process, so that it is not feasible in almost software testing processes. Recently, Wang *et al.* [14] applied the kernel intensity estimation method to develop a non-parametric NHPP-based SRM and proposed a quite different approach from the existing ones [7,13]. It is worth noting, however, that the method by Wang *et al.* [14] is based on the local likelihood method with a local weighted log-likelihood function and is regarded as an approximation method. In other words, it cannot guarantee the statistically valid property such as asymptotic optimality, *etc.*

Apart from the NHPP-based modeling, Barghou *et al.* [1] focused on a generalized order-statistics SRM [9] with the software fault-detection time data and proposed a non-parametric method based on the well-known kernel density estimation (KDE). Though an equivalence between the KDE and the kernel intensity estimation is well known [6], Barghou *et al.* [1] developed a series of estimation procedure of design parameters and a prediction method of the inter-fault detection time. First, they used two methods; the likelihood-based cross validation (CV) method and the prequential likelihood (PL) method [5] to tune up the bandwidth in the kernel density function and an unknown parameter which indicates the initial number of software-fault contents. Second, they carried out the so-called *one-stage look-ahead prediction* of the inter-fault detection time, where *the recalibration method* with *the u-plot* [2,3,10] was applied to recalibrate the prediction distribution of the inter-fault detection time. In fact, the series of methodology in [1] is well established, and can be considered as a representative non-parametric estimation method for the generalized order statistics-based SRM.

However, the most serious problems to use the above non-parametric approach are (i) the computation cost is very expensive comparing with the common parametric estimation, and (ii) the goodness-of-fit and the predictive performances do not always outperform the parametric methods, although it does not require to specify the parametric form of the SRM, say, probability distribution function in the generalized order statistics-based SRM. Especially, the accuracy of goodness-of-fit to the past data and the prediction of the future fault-detection time are both important and should be improved for the use in practical situations. Here, we point out two technically weak points for the Barghou *et al.*'s method [1]. Since the KDE method employed in [1] is based on the usual Gaussian kernel density, the resulting kernel estimate of the inter-fault detection time distribution is defined on the real-valued support, instead of its non-negative nature. This may cause to underestimate the fault-detection time in prediction. To improve the prediction accuracy of the inter-fault detection time in the future, in this article we propose to use the truncated Gaussian kernel density at the origin and the MTBSF (mean time between software failures) instead of the median.

In the validation test with real software fault data, it is investigated how the improvement influences the quantitative software reliability assessment.

2 Software Reliability Model

2.1 Parametric Models

We describe a generalized order statistics SRM with the parametric fault-detection time distribution. Suppose that N (> 0) software faults remain before system testing. Let X_i ($i = 1, 2, \ldots$) be the software fault-detection times which are independent and identically distributed non-negative continuous random variables, having the cumulative distribution function (c.d.f.) $G(x) = \Pr\{X_i \leq x\}$ and the probability density function (p.d.f.) $g(x) = dG(x)/dx$. Once a software fault is detected, it is fixed and/or removed immediately. Further, we let $T_i = X_i - X_{i-1}$ ($X_0 = 0$) denote the i-th inter-fault detection time ($= 1, 2, \ldots, N$). Since both T_i and X_i are random variables, we denote their realizations by t_i and $x_i = \sum_{k=1}^{i} t_k$, respectively. Conditioned that the initial number of software faults before testing, N, is known, it is seen that X_i can be regarded as order statistics from a finite population with size N and that the total number of software faults detected by an arbitrary time x is given by the binomial distribution with the success probability $G(x)$ and the failure probability $\overline{G}(x) = 1 - G(x)$. As a special case, if $G(x)$ is the exponential distribution, X_i are reduced to exponential order statistics [11] and the resulting SRM becomes the classical Jelinski and Moranda SRM [8]. From a simple manipulation, the conditional p.d.f. of T_i given $X_{i-1} = x_{i-1}$ can be derived as

$$f(t_i|x_{i-1}) = \frac{(N-i+1)g(t_i + x_{i-1})\overline{G}(t_i + x_{i-1})^{N-i}}{\overline{G}(x_{i-1})^{N-i+1}}. \tag{1}$$

From Eq.(1), the conditional c.d.f is given by

$$F(t_i|x_{i-1}) = 1 - \left(\frac{\overline{G}(t_i + x_{i-1})}{\overline{G}(x_{i-1})} \right)^{N-i+1}. \tag{2}$$

By substituting an arbitrary parametric form into $G(x)$, the conditional p.d.f. of the future inter-fault detection time, $T_i \mid X_1, \ldots, X_{i-1}$, can be represented.

2.2 Non-parametric Models

Instead of the use of parametric form in the c.d.f. $G(x)$, we assume that given $i-1$ fault-detection time data, $(x_1, x_2, \ldots, x_{i-1})$, an estimate of $g(x)$ is given by

$$\hat{g}_{(i-1)}(x) = \frac{1}{i-1} \sum_{k=1}^{i-1} K_h(x - x_k), \tag{3}$$

where

$$K_h(x) = \frac{1}{h}K\left(\frac{x}{h}\right) \tag{4}$$

is called the kernel density function with the kernel function $K(\cdot)$, and h (> 0) is the design parameter called bandwidth. In the standard statistical theory, some representative kernel functions have been proposed. Following Barghou *et al.* [1], we also assume the following Gaussian kernel function:

$$K(x) = \frac{1}{(2\pi)^{1/2}} \exp\{-\frac{x^2}{2}\}. \tag{5}$$

The basic idea in KDE method is to represent bumps at observation points and to approximate the p.d.f. by summing them. Hence, the bandwidth h is more important rather than the selection of the kernel function itself, because larger h is insensitive to the shape of p.d.f. but smaller h is strongly influenced by noises and may result the less prediction performance.

In addition to choice of a suitable bandwidth, it is significant to check the support of the resulting kernel density function. Note that the estimated p.d.f. in Eq. (3) is defined on all real value $x \in (-\infty, \infty)$. More precisely, it is definitely needed to check both the convergence property due to the Gaussian kernel density and the tail behavior in the negative range. However, since the KDE method is rather expensive in computation, such a careful treatment may not be always possible in practice. An alternative idea is to replace the Gaussian kernel function by the truncated Gaussian kernel one at the origin. So, instead of $\hat{g}(x)$ ($-\infty < x < \infty$) in Eq.(3), we apply the following truncated kernel density function $\tilde{g}(x)$ ($0 < x < \infty$):

$$\tilde{g}_{(i)}(x) = \frac{\hat{g}_{(i)}(x)}{\hat{G}_{(i)}(\infty)}, \quad \tilde{G}_{(i)}(x) = \frac{\hat{G}_{(i)}(x)}{\hat{G}_{(i)}(\infty)}, \tag{6}$$

where

$$\hat{G}_{(i)}(x) = \int_{-\infty}^{x} \hat{g}_{(i)}(y)dy. \tag{7}$$

3 Parameter Estimation

Our next concern is the parameter estimation of h and N simultaneously in Eqs.(1) and (2). It is common to apply the least squares-based cross validation (CV) method to do so, because its asymptotic optimality has been proved in [4]. However, our problem is not an optimization problem of a single decision variable h but a bivariate optimization problem of h and N. In dealing with such a somewhat different problem, Barghou *et al.* [1] used the log likelihood-based CV method and the PL method [5].

(1) CV method: By removing an arbitrary j-th data ($j = 1, \ldots, i-2$) from $i-1$ data $(x_1, \ldots, x_{i-1})$, one constructs $i-2$ training data sets. Then an estimate of the p.d.f. $g(x)$ with these sample data is given by

$$\hat{g}_{(-j)}(x) = \frac{1}{(i-2)} \sum_{k \neq j} K_h \left(x - x_k\right). \tag{8}$$

In the refinement with the truncated Gaussian kernel density function $\tilde{g}_{(-j)}(x)$, the estimate of the p.d.f. of T_i given x_{i-1} is obtained by

$$\tilde{f}_{(-j)}(t_i|x_{i-1}) = \frac{(N-i+1)\tilde{g}_{(-j)}(t_i + x_{i-1})\overline{\tilde{G}}_{(-j)}(t_i + x_{i-1})^{N-i}}{\overline{\tilde{G}}_{(-j)}(x_{i-1})^{N-i+1}}, \tag{9}$$

where $\hat{G}_{(-j)}(x)$ is an integral of $\hat{g}_{(-j)}(x)$ and can be calculated by any numerical integration technique, and $\tilde{G}_{(-j)}(x)$ is the c.d.f. of $\tilde{g}_{(-j)}(x)$ in Eq.(6). Then the cross validation log-likelihood function (CVLLF) is formulated as

$$CVLLF = \frac{1}{(i-2)} \sum_{j=1}^{i-2} \log \tilde{f}_{(-j)}(t_i \mid x_{i-1}), \tag{10}$$

so the problem is to derive the optimal (h^*, N^*) satisfying $\mathrm{argmax}_{h,N} CVLLF$.

(2) PL method: Prepare $j-1$ training data sets with only partial data until the j-th one ($j = 1, \ldots, i-2$), *i.e.*, $x_1, (x_1, x_2), \ldots, (x_1, x_2, \ldots, x_{i-2})$, and define the estimate of the p.d.f. $g(x)$:

$$\hat{g}_{(-j)}(x) = \frac{1}{(i-2)} \sum_{k \neq j} K_h \left(x - x_k\right). \tag{11}$$

Similar to the CV method, an estimate of the p.d.f. of T_i given x_{i-1} is obtained by $\tilde{f}_{(-j)}(t_i|x_{i-1})$ in Eq.(9). Instead of CVLLF in Eq.(10), we define the prequential log likelihood function (PLLF):

$$PLLF = \sum_{j=2}^{i-1} \log \tilde{f}_{(-j)}(t_i \mid x_{i-1}). \tag{12}$$

Then the problem is to derive the optimal (h^*, N^*) satisfying $\mathrm{argmax}_{h,N} PLLF$.

Once both parameters (h^*, N^*) are determined, we estimate the one-stage look-ahead prediction of the inter- fault detection time, say, T_i at the observation point x_{i-1}. Barghout *et al.* [1] seek the median of the p.d.f. $\tilde{f}_{(-j)}(t_i|x_{i-1})$ as a prediction. However, when the probability distribution is considered to be biased in many cases, the median and mode may be inappropriate as a prediction of the random variable. The most reasonable prediction devise is the mean value of T_i, so that we calculate the mean value of T_i by $\mathrm{E}[T_i] = \int_0^\infty t\tilde{f}_{(-j)}(t_i|x_{i-1})dt_i$, where the prediction of the p.d.f., $\tilde{f}_{(-j)}(t_i|x_{i-1})$ is normalized so as to satisfy

$\int_0^\infty \tilde{f}_{(-j)}(t_i|x_{i-1})dt_i = 1$ by means of numerical integration. We further apply an improvement technique to the prediction called the recalibration (RB) method [1,2,3]. Suppose that for an arbitrary k=1,. . . ,i-1, an estimated probability model $\hat{F}(t_k)$ is available against the real probability model $F(t_k)$. If there exists a map (function) R_k from $\hat{F}(t_k)$ to $F(t_k)$, an ideal task is to seek the map R_k satisfying $F(t_k) = R_k[\hat{F}(t_k)]$. In the case where the estimate is unbiased, it can be seen that $R_k \approx R$ [1,2,3,10] and that R can be replaced by the *u-plot* which indicates a bias of $\tilde{F}(t_k)$ to the real $F(t_k)$. As well known, the u-plot is defined by a step function $u_k = \hat{F}(t_k)$ $(k = 1, \ldots, i-1)$ with jump size $1/i$. The RB method means the re-prediction of the c.d.f. of T_i with the u-plot.

4 Numerical Illustrations

In this section we investigate the predictive performance of the non-parametric SRM with four fault data sets, which are observed in real software development projects. The respective data sets, DS1, DS2, DS3, DS4, consist of 136, 86, 129 and 54 fault-detection time data. We consider the situation where the one-stage look-ahead prediction is sequentially performed from the 20% point of whole data and the next inter-fault detection time at the observation point is estimated one by one, where the median and mean of the inter-fault detection time p.d.f. in Eq.(9) are used for prediction. As the kernel density, we assume the usual Gaussian kernel with and without truncation and use two parameter

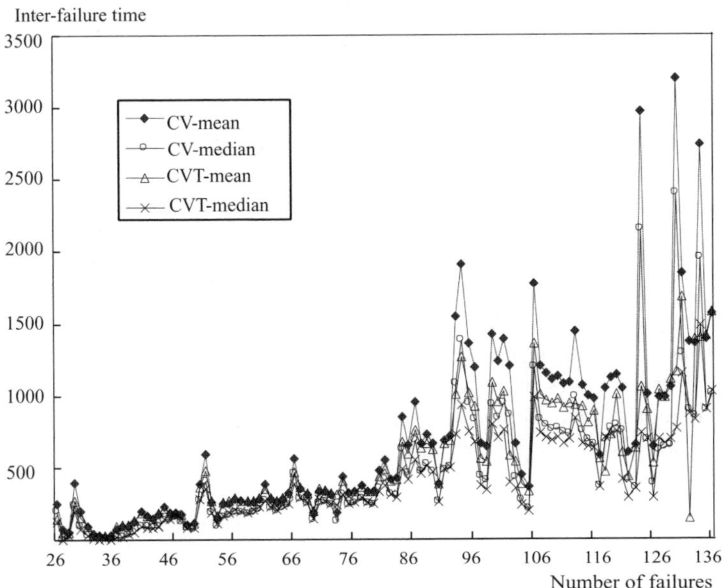

Fig. 1. Sequential estimation of inter-fault detection time with CV/RB method (DS1)

Table 1. PSE with DS1 ($\times\mathbf{10^6}$)

DS1	CV	CVT	PL	PLT
Before recalibration				
mean	1.292	1.3609	2.4729	4.5187
median	1.3351	1.4299	1.5444	2.804
After recalibration				
mean	1.1073	1.1990	1.3985	0.9250
median	1.1835	1.0225	1.1695	1.0235

Table 2. PSE with DS2 ($\times\mathbf{10^6}$)

DS2	CV	CVT	PL	PLT
Before recalibration				
mean	1.8368	1.7548	1.9591	6.9443
median	1.8184	1.9550	1.4733	8.2834
After recalibration				
mean	1.8252	1.4379	1.4648	1.1666
median	1.7225	1.6282	1.4920	1.2148

Table 3. PSE with DS2 ($\times\mathbf{10^6}$)

DS3	CV	CVT	PL	PLT
Before recalibration				
mean	2.7210	2.6674	7.8846	4.1702
median	2.7927	2.8163	8.8748	3.0921
After recalibration				
mean	2.4058	2.3471	2.5388	2.3964
median	2.8397	2.8657	2.7561	2.8592

Table 4. PSE with DS4 ($\times\mathbf{10^7}$)

DS4	CV	CVT	PL	PLT
Before recalibration				
mean	1.0544	1.1418	1.2971	1.2906
median	1.0972	1.0930	0.9033	0.7711
After recalibration				
mean	1.0250	1.3033	1.3019	1.2998
median	1.0930	1.0206	0.9103	0.7761

estimation methods based on the CV and PL methods. In the KDE method, we compare four methods; CV, CVT, PL and PLT, where both the CVT and PLT are based on the truncated kernel density. As a criterion of comparision, we use the predictive mean squares error (PSE).

Figure 1 depicts the sequential estimation of software inter-fault detection time with CV/RB method when DS1 is assumed. By plotting the one-stage look-ahead predictions, it is found that the prediction results with CV method is rather different from another one with PL method, and that RB method strongly influences to PL method but not the CV method. Table 1 $\sim$ Table 4 present the comparison results with four data sets DS1$\sim$DS4. From these results, we can summarize the following observations:

(i) The prediction performance based on the median does not always outperform the mean. In other words, the median-based prediction cannot be always validated as a prediction device.
(ii) In both estimation methods, the Gaussian kernel density with truncation exhibits better results in almost all cases, in terms of minimization of PSE.
(iii) The RB method can function better except in a few cases and is useful to improve the prediction performance.

5 Conclusion

In this article we have improved Barghout *et al.*'s non-parametric algorithm [1] from the view point of predictive performance, by introducing the truncated kernel density function and MTBSF estimator. In the future research we will examine the potential applicability of the refined non-parametric algorithm comprehensively by taking account of the estimation accuracy of the initial fault contents.

References

1. Barghout, M., Littlewood, B., Abdel-Ghaly, A.: A non-parametric order statistics software reliability model. Software Testing, Verification and Reliability 8, 113–132 (1998)
2. Brocklehurst, S., Chan, P.Y., Littlewood, B., Snell, J.: Recalibrating software reliability models. IEEE Transactions on Software Engineering 16(4), 458–470 (1990)
3. Brocklehurst, S., Littlewood, B.: Techniques for prediction analysis and recalibration. In: Lyu, M. (ed.) Handbook of Software Reliability Engineering, pp. 119–166. McGraw-Hill, New York (1996)
4. Brooks, M.M., Marron, S.J.: Asymptotic optimality of the least squares cross-validation bandwidth for kernel estimates of intensity functions. Stochastic Process and Their Applications 38, 157–165 (1991)
5. Dawid, A.P.: Statistical theory: the prequential approach. Journal of the Royal Statistical Society A 147, 278–292 (1984)
6. Diggle, P., Marron, J.S.: Equivalence of smoothing parameter selectors in density and intensity estimation. Journal of the American Statistical Association 91, 793–800 (1988)
7. Gandy, A., Jensen, U.: A non-parametric approach to software reliability. Applied Stochastic Models in Business and Industry 20, 3–15 (2004)
8. Jelinski, Z., Moranda, P.B.: Software reliability research. In: Freiberger, W. (ed.) Statistical Computer Performance Evaluation, pp. 485–502. Academic Press, New York (1972)
9. Joe, H.: Statistical inference for generalized-order-statistics and nonhomogeneous-Poisson-process software reliability models. IEEE Transactions on Software Engineering 15(11), 1485–1490 (1989)
10. Lyu, M.R. (ed.): Handbook of Software Reliability Engineering. McGraw-Hill, New York (1996)
11. Miller, D.R.: Exponential order statistic models of software reliability growth. IEEE Transactions on Software Engineering 12(1), 12–24 (1986)
12. Musa, J.D., Iannino, A., Okumoto, K.: Software Reliability, Measurement, Prediction, Application. McGraw-Hill, New York (1987)
13. Sofer, A., Miller, D.R.: A non-parametric software reliability growth model. IEEE Transactions on Reliability R-40(3), 329–337 (1991)
14. Wang, Z., Wang, J., Liang, X.: Non-parametric estimation for NHPP software reliability models. Journal of Applied Statistics 34(1), 107–119 (2007)

A Tool-Supported Process for Reliable Classification of Web Pages

Domenico Amalfitano, Anna Rita Fasolino, and Porfirio Tramontana

Dipartimento di Informatica e Sistemistica, Università di Napoli Federico II, Via Claudio 21, 80125 Napoli, Italy
{domenico.amalfitano, anna.fasolino, porfirio.tramontana}@unina.it

Abstract. Reliable classification of Web Application User Interfaces for the aim of extracting specific data for each class of interfaces is a fundamental task in migration, testing and reverse engineering processes involving existing Web Applications. A feasible and reliable classification approach is the one that exploits combinations of Web pages structural features for discriminating the page equivalence class. This paper presents a technique based on an iterative process that allows classification rules composed of Web pages structural features to be deduced in dynamically generated web pages. The process is supported by a tool that partially automates the process steps. In order to assess the process feasibility and cost effectiveness, a case study addressing the problem of generating classification rules for a real Web application has been carried out.

1 Introduction

The continuous evolution of Web development paradigms and technologies triggers a scenario where traditional Web applications, implemented with the past generation of Web technologies, become rapidly obsolete and new effort, techniques, and tools are needed for extending their lifetime.

An opportunity for preserving the value of traditional Web applications implemented with Web 1.0 technologies is now being offered by the emergent Web 2.0, whose applications are characterized by a richer user interface, facilitate collaborative content creation and modification, and can be easily created by reusing and combining data and information from different sources [8].

In such a context, Web 1.0 applications may become providers of data and contents to be used in Web 2.0 applications, provided that specific data wrapping techniques are available to make this content accessible. A real issue about this kind of reuse is that the content provided by Web 1.0 applications is usually embedded in different classes of dynamically generated pages, and thus a reliable and automatic classification of these pages is needed for a successful extraction of data from them.

A reliable classification of Web pages is needed to solve several further problems, such as (1) to implement wrappers that encapsulate the original UI of the Web application with the aim of exporting a renewed interface [3]; (2) to support the automatic analysis and interpretation of testing results in several validation activities; (3) to

D. Ślęzak et al. (Eds.): ASEA 2009, CCIS 59, pp. 338–345, 2009.

obtain a model of the UI for the aim of reengineering it according to a different architecture (such as a Model-Driven one) or technology (such as AJAX).

Among the Web page classification techniques proposed in the literature, two main families of approaches can be distinguished: (1) the deductive ones, which are commonly used in the image processing, pattern recognition and text processing fields, and aim at deducing classification rules from a set of training data, and (2) the classification techniques based on pre-defined equivalence criteria, such as similarity-based ones. The former family requires that a set of predefined features related to the content of the HTML page [10], to the hypertext topology of pages [6] or a combination of both [5] are extracted from web pages and used to determine the classification of the page according to given classification criteria. The latter family is based on equivalence criteria defined a-priori: As an example, pages can be considered equivalent if their HTML structure is similar, where the similarity degree is assessed by means of a distance metric (such as the Levenshtein edit distance between vectors describing items contained in the page) [1,2,9]. Experiments showed that clone analysis results are deeply influenced by the choice of the similarity thresholds which must be tuned to work on subject applications [1, 7].

In this paper, we present a Web page classification technique which is based on the deduction of classification rules (composed of key features of Web page classes) that allow the reliable classification of the pages of a Web application. Our technique requires that candidate discriminating features are proposed ad hoc for each subject application, by visually interacting with it. The classification power of these features is assessed and improved by a process based on Formal Concept Analysis which iteratively combines these features until a satisfying combination of them is obtained.

In the paper, the process for generating the classification rules and a tool supporting its execution will be presented, and the results of a case study aiming at showing the process feasibility and effectiveness will be discussed. The remainder of the paper is structured as follows. Section 2 describes the proposed process and the functionality of a tool supporting it. Section 3 presents the case study and Section 4 provides conclusive remarks and future work.

2 The Classification Technique

The technique proposed in this paper can be used for classifying the HTML pages which are returned by the server side of Web 1.0 applications on the basis of user requests and application status. These pages can be either static or dynamically generated and can be partitioned into a finite set of equivalence classes, each one including a well-defined type of output pages.

In particular, given a Web application WA whose output pages are partitioned into a set of n equivalence classes $\{C_1, \ldots, C_n\}$, and given a client page p, the classification task we address in this paper consists of determining the equivalence class C_x which p belongs to. We propose to solve this problem thanks to n *boolean classification rules* $\{CR_1, \ldots, CR_n\}$ where a classification rule is a boolean expression made up by a combination of Web page features. In particular, each CR_i is associated to the corresponding C_i class and it must satisfy the following property:

For each page p belonging to class C_i:

$CR_i(p) =$ true AND $CR_j(p) =$ false for each $j \neq i$

In the following we present a process for discovering a classification rule for each page equivalence class. The process is *Iterative*, i.e. several process iterations are needed in order to obtain reliable classification rules; *Learning based*, i.e. it needs training samples in order to abstract classification rules; *General*, i.e. the process is not biased on a given classification problem; *Produces reliable rules*, i.e. the generated classification rules are able to correctly solve the page classification task.

The process includes six main activities, which are arranged according to the UML activity diagram shown in Figure 1 and are executable with the support of a WPC-CA, a Java-based tool that we have developed and that is available at http://wpage.unina.it/ptramont/download.

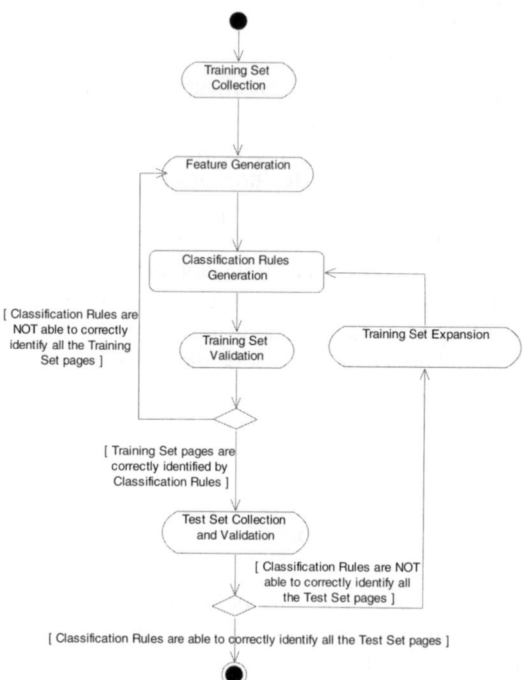

Fig. 1. The Process activity diagram

The Training Set Collection is the activity carried out for collecting several samples of pages of the Web application for each equivalence class. This set of page will provide a Training Set. This activity is accomplished by the software engineer involved in the generation process through navigating the Web application, and recognizing the class of each collected page. The tool supports this task by offering a browser for navigating the application, saving the Web page source code, and storing the declared classification in a tool repository.

The Feature Generation activity of the process aims at collecting a set of candidate features for each class of pages. Candidate features represent properties that are owned by instances of the page classes and are expressed as predicates combining graphical or textual items from the pages and coded using specific technologies, such as XPath. To find features, a semiautomatic technique can be used which is based on a visual exploration of the pages: the user selects the page item that he considers relevant for the classification problem and a set of features owned by this item (such as its position in the page, or further properties of the selected item) is automatically proposed by the tool by applying some feature generation rules.

The goal of the Classification Rules Generation step is of obtaining boolean expressions (composed by the features proposed in the previous step) that solve the classification problem for any page of the Training Set. For generating the Classification Rules we exploit the technique based on Formal Concept Analysis (FCA) that was presented in [3]. This technique uses Concept Analysis for classifying the set of candidate features F of a page class C_i into the following five subsets (cfr. [4]): *Specific features*: i.e. features that are true for all and only the pages of class C_i; *Relevant features*: i.e. features that are true for all the pages of class C_i, but also for other pages belonging to other classes; *Conditionally Specific features*: features that are true for a subset of pages of class C_i and for no other page belonging to other classes; *Shared features*: i.e. features that are true for a subset of pages of the class C_i and for other pages belonging to other classes too; *Irrelevant features*: i.e. features that are not true for any page of the class C_i.

On the basis of this classification, the Classification Rules can be developed using the generation techniques described in [3]. Our tool automatically supports the Classification Rules Generation step. In particular, it is able to build and analyze the involved Concept Lattice by using the Java Tockit package [11] that classifies features in their five categories, and automatically applies the Classification Rules Generation technique.

The goal of the Training Set Validation step is the evaluation of the effectiveness of the classification rules proposed in the previous step with respect to the collected Training Set. The effectiveness of the rules is measured by evaluating Recall and Precision metrics, that are expressed, for any equivalence class C, by the following definitions:

$$Precision(C) = \frac{\#(pagesCorrectlyAttributedToClassC)}{\#(pagesAttributedToClassC)} \qquad Recall(C) = \frac{\#(pagesCorrectlyAttributedToClassC)}{\#(AnalysedPagesBelongingToClassC)} \tag{1}$$

A classification rule is valid if and only if both Recall and Precision values are 1. In this case, the process can continue with the Test Set Collection and Validation step. Elsewhere, if failures are detected (i.e. some pages are not assigned to any class or they are assigned to more than one class or they are assigned to an incorrect class), then the process will return to the Feature Generation step, in order to propose new features that are able to solve the problems related to pages whose identification caused failures.

The goal of the Test Set Collection and Validation step is the evaluation of the effectiveness of the set of proposed classification rules (whose effectiveness has been already proved on the Training Set), with respect to a larger set of pages, called Test Set. The Test Set Validation is performed analogously to the Training Set Validation:

the tool proposes a classification for each collected page according to the proposed classification rules and the expert confirms it or declares the correct classification of the page. If a set of Classification Rules identifies with success all the pages of the Test Set, then the process for generating classification rules ends.

In the Training Set Expansion activity, the Test Set pages that are not correctly identified are added to the Training Set and the process returns to the Classification Rules Generation step for producing a new set of rules for this enlarged Training Set. These classification rules will be re-validated with respect to the Training Set and to the Test Set. The Test Set Validation step can be performed by the tool on the same pages collected in the previous iteration and in a completely automated way.

3 A Case Study

In this section, a case study dealing with the problem of classifying the pages of a real Web application will be presented. The involved Web application is Wikipedia (http://en.wikipedia.org), a free multilingual encyclopaedia project whose English version contains about 2.9 million articles, and we addressed the problem of classifying automatically the pages returned by Wikipedia as a response to a lemma search query. Depending on the queried lemma, these pages can be of five different classes, which an expert of the application named LemmaPage, DisambiguationPage, LemmaPageWithSuggestions, NoResultsPage, and NoResultsWithSuggestions classes, respectively.

The process presented in Section 2 was carried out in order to find classification rules for each class of pages. In a first iteration of the process, one of the paper authors collected a small Training Set composed of 15 Web pages of which he declared the belonging class (3 pages for each class were collected), and the Feature Generator component of the tool automatically proposed 30 features for these pages. The set of collected Training pages was submitted to the classification rules generation step that produced a candidate classification rule for each class. The reliability of these rules was immediately tested on the same training set pages: as the third and fourth columns in Table 1 show, the recall and precision values of the classification rules was 100% for all pages of the Training Set.

Table 1. Classification Rules and validation results after the first iteration of the process

		Training Set		Test Set	
Class	Classification rule	Recall	Precision	Recall	Precision
Disambiguation	/html/body/div/div/div/div/div/div/span/a/text()='Disambiguation pages'	3/3	3/3	14/14	14/14
Lemma	NOT (/html/body/div/div/div/div/div[contains(.,'see')]) AND NOT (//a[contains(.,'disambiguation')])	3/3	3/3	4/6	4/4
LemmaWithSuggestions	//div[contains(.,'For other uses')]	3/3	3/3	20/26	20/20
NoResults	NOT(//div[contains(.,'Did you mean')]) AND (//span/text()='No article title matches')	3/3	3/3	4/4	4/4
NoResultsWithSuggestion	//div[contains(.,'Did you mean')]	3/3	3/3	4/4	4/4

The same classification rules were used for classifying a new Test Set of further 55 pages, and the last two columns of Table 1 report the recall and precision values of the classification rules with respect to this Test Set. As these data show, six pages of the LemmaWithSuggestions class and two pages of the Lemma class were misclassified. These pages were, hence, added to the Training Set and a new iteration of the generation process was performed.

During this new iteration, a new set of classification rules was obtained, and their effectiveness was assessed with respect to the Training Set pages (in particular, new classification rules were proposed for Lemma and LemmaWithSuggestion classes). Since a correct identification of all the pages of the Training Set was obtained, the classification rules were submitted to the Test Set Validation. In this step, the analysis was automatically performed by the tool in about 60 seconds. In this step of the process, just two pages belonging to the Disambiguation class but satisfying the Classification rule of the LemmaWithSuggestions class, too, gave classification problems. Analogously to the previous iteration, these two pages were added to the Training Set and new classification rules were proposed again.

The steps of Classification Rules Generation and Training Set Validation were automatically performed in less than 5 seconds. After the successful validation of the classification rules against the Training Set, they were validated against the Test Set, too (the validation were performed in about 55 seconds). Table 2 reports the obtained expressions and the Recall and Precision values, which were all 100%.

The final classification rules were further tested on a larger set of pages collected and manually classified by some students. In a set of 514 pages, no further exceptions (e.g., misclassified pages) were found.

The case study results showed that the proposed process and the tool supporting it are able to generate reliable classification rules, at least in the considered experimental context. However, we tried to evaluate the overall cost of the process too, in order to deduce some conclusions about the process feasibility. To this aim, the effort spent in the process activities was analysed.

Table 2. Classification Rules and validation results after the third iteration of the process

		Training Set		Test Set	
Class	Classification rule	Recall	Precision	Recall	Precision
Disambiguation	//a/text()='Disambiguation pages'	5/5	5/5	12/12	12/12
Lemma	NOT(//span/text()='No article title matches') AND NOT(//div[@class='dablink']) AND NOT (//a[contains(.,'disambiguation')])	5/5	5/5	4/4	4/4
LemmaWithSuggestions	NOT(//a/text()='Disambiguation pages') AND (//div[@class='dablink']) AND (//div[contains(.,'For other uses')])	9/9	9/9	20/20	20/20
NoResults	NOT(//div[contains(.,'Did you mean')]) AND (//span/text()='No article title matches')	3/3	3/3	4/4	4/4
NoResultsWithSuggestion	//div[contains(.,'Did you mean')]	3/3	3/3	4/4	4/4

The effort devoted to the Training Set Collection activity essentially depends on the number of Training Set pages that must be collected for each class. In the experiment, we initially collected just a few pages for each class and this number was sufficient for discovering an initial set of class candidate features. In general, the expert can decide how many pages to collect, but he should try to minimize this number in order to reduce the collection effort.

Analogously, the effort related to the feature generation step depends on the number of page classes and on the size of considered pages. However, this activity was carried out with the support of the tool, and it lasted about 20 minutes.

The Classification Rules Generation and the Training Set Validation are completely automated steps. The time needed for their executions depends on the size of the Training Set, on the complexity of collected pages to be classified, and on the size of the Feature Set. However, in the case study we experienced that those steps were completed in about one minute in the worst case, so that their effort can be considered unimportant with respect to the one devoted to other steps.

The effort related to the Test Set Collection and Validation step grows with the size of the Test Set. In general, new Test Set pages need to be collected by the software engineer until the validation results confirm the reliability of the classification rules. The Validation activity moreover requires that an expert software engineer judges the correctness of the proposed classification. Both these activities are, hence, human-made and time consuming, however they can be speeded up by using parallel teams of testers. Moreover, the effort needed for the Classification of Incorrectly Identified Pages depends on the number of pages to be re-classified. We experienced that the misclassified pages are usually less than the Training Set pages, so that the effort devoted to this step is negligible with respect to the one devoted to the training set collection one.

The process overall cost depends on the number of performed process iterations too. In the case study, three process iterations were needed. Anyway, the effort devoted to the second and third iterations was less than the one devoted to the first one, because the number of new pages to be taken into account decreased with the iterations. Other case studies that we carried out showed us that the number of needed iterations depends on the ability of the expert to find rapidly an adequate feature set.

Two main conclusions were deduced from this case study. The first conclusion was that, due to the automatic support provided by the tool, the proposed approach can be considered cost-effective. The second conclusion was that the process cost-effectiveness can be improved if a set of right features for each class of pages is rapidly defined in the early process iterations.

4 Conclusions and Future Works

In this paper a process and a tool supporting the semi-automatic generation of Web page reliable classification rules have been presented. This process improves the one that was only sketched in [3] and it is now completely supported by a tool. In the paper a case study was illustrated where the process was successfully used for solving a classification problem regarding the Wikipedia Web application. Experimental results preliminarily showed the feasibility and cost-effectiveness of this approach.

In the future, we plan to carry out a wider experimentation on a larger set of classification problems in order to extend the validity of these experimental results.

References

1. De Lucia, A., Scanniello, G., Tortora, G.: Identifying Clones in Dynamic Web Sites Using Similarity thresholds. In: Proc. of International Conference on Enterprise Information Systems, Porto, Portugal (2004)
2. Di Lucca, G.A., Di Penta, M., Fasolino, A.R.: An Approach to Identify Duplicated Web Pages. In: Proc. of 26th IEEE Annual International Computer Software and Application Conference, Oxford, UK, pp. 481–486. IEEE CS Press, Los Alamitos (2002)
3. Di Lucca, G.A., Fasolino, A.R., Tramontana, P.: Web Pages Classification using Concept Analysis. In: Proc. of the IEEE International Conference on Software Maintenance, ICSM 2007, pp. 385–394. IEEE CS Press, Los Alamitos (2007)
4. Eisenbarth, T., Koschke, R., Simon, D.: Locating features in source code. IEEE Trans. on Software Engineering 29(3), 210–224 (2003)
5. Fernández, V.F., Herranz, S.M., Unanue, R.M., Rubio, A.C.: Naïve Bayes Web Page Classification with HTML Mark-Up Enrichment. In: Proc. of Int. Multi-Conference on Computing in the Global Information Technology (ICCGI 2006). IEEE Comp. Society Press, Los Alamitos (2006)
6. Lindemann, C., Littig, L.: Coarse-grained Classification of Web Sites by their Structural Properties. In: Proc. of WIDM 2006, pp. 35–42. ACM Press, New York (2006)
7. Mesbah, A., Bozdag, E., van Deursen, A.: Crawling Ajax by Inferring User Interface State Changes. In: Proc. of the 8th International Conference on Web Engineering (ICWE 2008), pp. 122–134. IEEE C.S. Press, Los Alamitos (2008)
8. Murugesan, S.: Understanding Web 2.0. IT Professional 9(4), 34–41 (2007)
9. Ricca, F., Tonella, P.: Using Clustering to Support the Migration from Static to Dynamic Web Pages. In: Proc. of 11th IEEE International Workshop on Program Comprehension, Portland, Oregon, pp. 207–216 (2003)
10. Song, M., Kang, D., Lee, S.: Feature Reduction for Web Document Classification, pp. 785–788. IEEE Comp. Society Press, Los Alamitos (2006)
11. Tockit library, `http://tockit.sourceforge.net/tockit/index.html`

Author Index

Printing: Mercedes-Druck, Berlin
Binding: Stein+Lehmann, Berlin